THE
LIFE-EXTENSION
REVOLUTION

The Definitive Guide to Better Health, Longer Life, and Physical Immortality

by Saul Kent

WILLIAM MORROW AND COMPANY, INC.
New York *1980*

To everyone who wants to stay alive, healthy, and youthful

Library of Congress Cataloging in Publication Data

Kent, Saul.
    The life-extension revolution.

    Bibliography: p.
    Includes index.
    1. Longevity. 2. Rejuvenation. I. Title.
QP85.K46   612.6'8   79-19911
ISBN 0-688-03580-9

Book Design by Michael Mauceri

Printed in the United States of America.

First Edition

1 2 3 4 5 6 7 8 9 10

Contents

Chapter Outline

Preservation of Rat Hearts. Preserving the Brain. Freezing Fetal Rat Pancreases. Freezing Rodents, Rabbits, and Monkeys. Survival of Frozen Baby Squirrels. The Frozen Beetle. Suspending Animation in Rodents. Suspending the Animation Process. High-Pressure Freezing. Can We Learn to Hibernate? Trans Time Corporation. Bay Area Cryonics Society (BACS). Alcor Life Extension Foundation. Trans Time Freezes Brain. Cryovita Laboratories. Institute for Cryonics Education (ICE). Cryonics Association. Cryonics Association: New York Chapter. Cryonics Institute. Cryonics Society of South Florida. Cryonics Society of Australia. Institute for Advanced Biological Studies. The Prometheus Society. Are the Russians Freezing People? Is Walt Disney Frozen?

10. Extended Parenthood and Aphrodisiacs
Preserving Embryos for Future Parenthood. Combating the Aging Effects of the "Milk Hormone." Rejuvenating the Female Reproductive System. Inducing Pregnancy in Old Rats. The Seventy-Year-Old Mother. Hypersexual Behavior During L-Dopa Therapy. Studying the Effects of L-Dopa on Human Sexuality. Amphetamine Alters Sexual Behavior. Drug-Induced Hypersexuality in Rats. Reproductive Hormone Boosts Sexuality in Rats. Drug Treatment of Impotence. An Aphrodisiac for Women? . . . And Men Too? Electrical Sex Stimulation. Do Women Possess a Sex Scent?

11. Regeneration, Cloning, and Identity Reconstruction
Can We Regenerate Our Bodies? Facts about Limb Regeneration. Does Regeneration Prevent Cancer? Regeneration in Rat Embryos. Regeneration in Siamese-Twin Cockroaches. Inducing Regeneration in the Newborn Opossum. Electrically Stimulated Limb Regeneration. Boosting Our Healing Ability. Regeneration and Aging. Regenerating Brain Cells. Nerve Growth Factor Spurs Brain Regeneration. Cloning: A Substitute for Immortality. How Cloning Is Accomplished. Variations on Cloning. Is Human Cloning Possible? The Latest Advance in Cloning. Research Benefits of Cloning. 'Identity Reconstruction: The Ultimate Strategy for Survival.

Introduction

The human race is at a critical evolutionary turning point. After millions of years of struggle for survival as a species, we have finally begun to fight for our lives as individuals. Because of recent advances in biology and medicine, we are now in a position to challenge the most basic and formidable of our enemies —aging and death.

In the past two decades, a small group of pioneers has recognized that longer, healthier life may be within our grasp, and has come forth to advocate the pursuit of an extended human life span. Their ultimate goal is physical immortality—a stage of evolution in which individual human beings are free from the constraints on life span imposed by Nature.

Scientists have focused primarily upon biomedical gerontology as the key to life prolongation, and are exploring a variety of approaches aimed at delaying, retarding, or reversing the aging process. They are also pursuing other sciences relevant to life extension including regeneration, resuscitation, transplantation, prosthetics, genetic engineering, identity reconstruction, and suspended animation.

As yet, the life extension sciences have relatively little to offer us in our quest for longer life. While there is much valuable information available on how to avoid diseases and premature aging, there is little hard evidence that we know how to prevent normal aging, or restore youthful function to the elderly.

On the other hand, there is considerable experimental evidence from animal studies that human aging control and rejuvenation can be achieved in the foreseeable future. Techniques such as dietary intervention, immunologic engineering, body temperature manipulation, and drug therapy have already proved capable of extending the life span of a variety of animal species. The possible application of these techniques to humans can be determined only by additional research.

The most radical of the immortalists are unwilling to risk

irretrievable loss of life while awaiting the therapeutic benefits of the life extension sciences. They are prepared to be cryonically suspended (frozen) for future reanimation, if they should die before aging control is possible. They argue that cryonic suspension, though currently unperfected, offers the only available chance of survival for anyone dying today.

The Life-Extension Revolution is written as a guide to better health, longer life, and physical immortality for persons who want the truth about their prospects for an extended life span. Its purposes are threefold.

The first purpose is to provide an objective, comprehensive picture of where we stand today in our efforts to extend the human life span. The book covers the entire field of life extension—every important theory, research effort, and therapeutic approach relevant to the subject.

The book consists of a series of short reports on specialized areas in order to convey the complexity of a field in an early stage of development. Every subject discussed in the book is in a state of profound irresolution. There are multiple theories, practices, and claims based upon a vast jumble of inadequate and often contradictory data.

I've tried to make sense of all this by presenting the material in an order that isolates the critical issues, without losing track of their relation to each other, or to the entire field of life extension. I've made an effort to explain conflicts, controversies, and inconsistencies as clearly as possible, and to offer my own views when I thought them appropriate.

The second purpose is to assist the reader in living a better and healthier life. Every aspect of health care is covered in the book including diet, exercise, lifestyle, and experimental therapies.

My objective is not to tell you what to do, but to provide you with sufficient evidence, both pro and con, to enable you to make up your own mind. The question of whether to take supplemental doses of vitamin C, for example, or how much vitamin C to take, should be based upon individual assessment of the available evidence, rather than the directives of authority figures.

Anyone strongly interested in any subject in the book is encouraged to find out more about it, either by contacting the original sources cited after each report, or by obtaining the scientific papers and books cited in the reference section at the back of the book. This type of follow-up is desirable not only to provide you with additional information, but also to enable you to keep up with the latest developments in fast-breaking fields.

The third purpose is to provide the reader with an effective starting point for action. I think the material in the book makes it clear that all of us have a real chance of living well beyond the limits of our inherited life span. I think it's also clear that there is still a long way to go before we can transform our prospects into reality.

There is no magic timetable for life extension. The more time, money, and effort we put into the project, the greater our chances for success. In Chapters 7 and 12, I've included material on various organizations dedicated to the pursuit of life extension. Anyone interested in becoming a life extension activist should contact the appropriate organization, or write to me at:

SAUL KENT
R.D. 1, Box 418B
Woodstock, N.Y. 12498

Chapter 1

Why Do We Grow Old and Die?

The Evolution of Longevity

We didn't always live to seventy, eighty, ninety, or above. About 3 million years ago, scientists believe, no one lived beyond the age of fifty. And as recently as 300,000 years ago, the maximum life span was only about seventy-seven—at least according to Richard Cutler of the Gerontology Research Center.

Cutler and George Sacher of the Argonne National Laboratory have been independently investigating the roots of life span evolution on this planet. They believe that all life functions have intrinsic, time-dependent limitations, and that life span has increased because of the development of "life-maintenance processes" or "longevity-assurance genes."

For each aging process, contends Cutler, a corresponding process has evolved to counter it. One example of such a process may be the ability to repair deoxyribonucleic acid (DNA)—the genetic material that controls life.

The importance of DNA repair to the evolution of longevity is suggested by the work of Hart and Setlow. They measured the rate of excision repair of ultraviolet-ray injury in the DNA of cultured cells from seven species, ranging in life span from about two years (shrew and mouse) to seventy or more years (elephant and man).

They found an increase in the rate of DNA repair of about tenfold from the shortest-lived animal to the longest-lived animal, which indicates that the increased capacity to repair DNA may be necessary to achieve a longer life span. Hart has recently been collaborating with Sacher in an effort to discover differences in two similar rodent species with different maximum life spans. (See p. 363.)

Another life-maintenance process cited by Cutler is the ability of enzymes, such as superoxide dismutase, to remove or neutralize the damaging by-products of oxygen metabolism. Early in evolution, says Cutler, oxygen was probably harmful to almost all biologic systems. Other scientists contend that oxygen remains a prime factor in human aging (see p. 126) and that supplementary superoxide dismutase produces an anti-aging effect when taken in conjunction with other compounds. (See p. 260.)

Both Cutler and Sacher have concluded that the "rapid" evolution of maximum life span, intelligence, and other key characteristics resulted from relatively few mutations—no more than about 0.6 percent of the total genome. Cutler feels that most or all of these changes involved regulatory gene systems rather than alterations in gene structure. He has developed a research strategy aimed at speeding up the further evolution of human longevity. (See p. 365.)

Richard G. Cutler, Gerontology Research Center, National Institute on Aging, Baltimore City Hospitals, Baltimore, Md. 21224

George A. Sacher, Division of Biological and Medical Research, Argonne National Laboratory, Argonne, Il. 60439

Ronald W. Hart, Department of Radiology, Ohio State University, Columbus, Ohio 43210

Aging: The Number One Cause of Death

Consider the adage "no one ever dies of old age." If you look at any number of death certificates, this piece of conventional "wisdom" seems to hold up. In every instance, one finds a specific disease or event listed as the cause of death.

But if no one ever dies of old age, why is it that everyone

dies when he or she reaches old age? The reason is that old age is characterized by a generalized breakdown in structure and function that has little to do with any disease.

We call this breakdown aging and it is aging that is responsible for our increasing vulnerability to chronic diseases. As our immune system loses its capacity to fight off hostile invaders and our strength and energy ebb away, we are gradually forced to submit to the agents of death. In short, aging is synonymous with dying, and if we hope to live significantly longer, we will have to control the aging process.

The probability of dying doubles about every eight years after physical maturity. This pattern is essentially the same in all species, whether the life span is measured in days or in years. It is also the same in all human civilizations—those with a high death rate during childhood and those in which most persons survive until old age.

In medically advanced countries such as the United States, 75 percent of all deaths are linked to cardiovascular disorders such as heart disease and stroke, malignant neoplasms (cancer), and diabetes. In studying these diseases, scientists have focused upon the diseases themselves or the risk factors implicated in their expression. This approach has been somewhat helpful in improving diagnosis and treatment, but has had little or no effect on life expectancy in adults.

There will probably be no cure for heart disease, cancer, or diabetes until we learn more about how the aging process helps to trigger these diseases. But even if we were to eliminate all three diseases independently of aging, we would add fewer than ten years to the average life span and nothing at all to the maximum life span. Instead of dying of heart disease or cancer in our sixties, seventies, or eighties, we would live a few years longer and then die of pneumonia, the flu, an accident . . . or perhaps even of old age.

Robert R. Kohn, Institute of Pathology, Case Western Reserve University, Cleveland, Ohio 44106

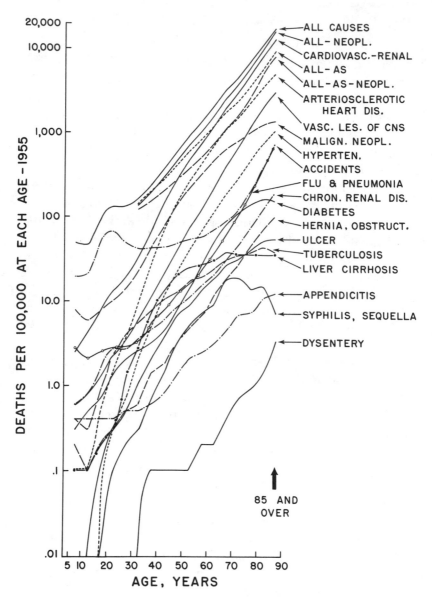

The death rate as a function of age for "all causes" and for sixteen of the most common "causes." After age thirty, the probability of dying doubles about every eight years, which indicates that aging is actually the number one cause of death. If death from cardiovascular diseases and malignant neoplasms (cancer) were eliminated, most of us would die of such "causes" as accidents, influenza, and pneumonia.

Relationships Between Aging and Disease

Nearly all government-sponsored research focuses on individual diseases. In recent years, billions of dollars have been spent on cancer, cardiovascular diseases, and metabolic disorders, with only a tiny fraction of that amount allocated for biomedical aging research.

Yet we are barely closer to understanding these diseases than we have ever been, and they continue to kill us in massive numbers. Neither the health status nor life expectancy of older adults has improved appreciably since the turn of the century.

Let's look at some of the findings that link aging to the diseases that are killing us:

Cardiovascular Diseases

• The chance of dying of a heart attack is about 200 times greater for a fifty-year-old man than for a teen-ager; the odds go up to about 2,600 to 1 for a man of eighty-five.

• Serum cholesterol, tissue cholesterol, and blood pressure all rise progressively with advancing age in healthy human subjects.

• Blood levels of high-density-lipoproteins (HDL), which protect against heart disease (see p. 78), decline significantly with advancing age in healthy human subjects.

• Aging has been estimated to be responsible for a 70 percent decline in cholesterol excretion in old rats. (See p. 76.)

• Alterations in immune function similar to those found during aging have been linked to coronary artery disease, particularly in cigarette smokers.

Cancer

• The incidence of cancer in humans doubles about every nine years between the ages of forty-five and eighty.

• Skin cells from middle-aged mice are more likely to be-

Percent of all Deaths Due to Cardiovascular Diseases by Age United States: 1976

Percent

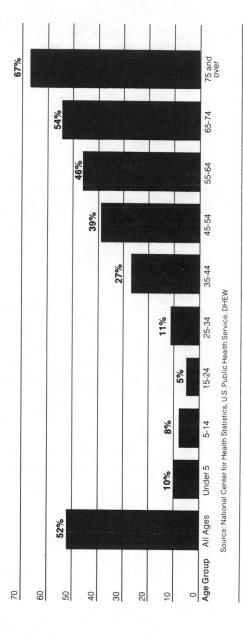

Age Group All Ages Under 5 5-14 15-24 25-34 35-44 45-54 55-64 65-74 75 and over

52% 10% 8% 5% 11% 27% 39% 46% 54% 67%

Source: National Center for Health Statistics, U.S. Public Health Service, DHEW

The progressive increase in deaths caused by cardiovascular diseases with advancing age suggests that aging may be a major cause of these diseases.

come malignant than skin cells from young mice after exposure to chemical carcinogens.

• The incidence of cancer increases markedly in persons suffering from impaired immune function similar to that found in aging.

• Therapies that extend life span in laboratory animals also reduce the incidence and severity of malignant tumors.

Diabetes

• The chance of developing the adult form of diabetes doubles every ten years; in 90 percent of diabetics, the disease is diagnosed between the ages of thirty-five and sixty.

• Diabetes accelerates the onset of other degenerative diseases in a manner almost indistinguishable from aging.

• Blood sugar levels increase significantly with advancing age in healthy human subjects, particularly in response to stress.

• Diabetics exhibit premature degenerative changes in collagen, nerve tissue, and capillary membrane structure similar to those observed during aging.

• Cells from young diabetics show a growth capability in tissue culture comparable to that of cells from old nondiabetics.

• The immune system can produce autoantibodies against insulin from the pancreas to impair carbohydrate metabolism—a process that has been postulated as intrinsic to normal aging. (See p. 40.)

Considered together, these findings argue persuasively that aging and disease processes are inextricably intertwined, and that further study of the biology of aging is imperative if we are to add healthy, productive years to the human life span.

Senility and the Aging Process

When pathologists examine the brains of persons who die while in the throes of senility, they find the same degenerative changes as in the brains of those who die with normal mental function—except that the changes are more extensive. "Although senile dementia differs from normal aging clinically and biochemically," explains Robert Terry of Albert Einstein Medical School, "these differences are quantitative rather than qualitative."

Two of the characteristic lesions of Alzheimer's Disease (the most common form of senility)—neurofibrillary tangles and neuritic plaques—are found in the great majority of persons over sixty and are essentially universal in those over eighty.

This finding suggests that senility may be an accelerated form of aging, perhaps triggered by some environmental factor. Among the factors that have been linked to senility are slow-acting viruses and elevated brain concentrations of aluminum. There is also a decrease in bloodflow within the brain during senility, but this is not believed to be a basic cause of the disease.

Even if senility is not an accelerated form of aging, it is clear that the disease is closely related to the aging process. Though most people do not become senile in old age, it may be that they are spared this indignity only because they don't live long enough. Any therapy that retards the aging process will go a long way toward preventing senility.

Robert D. Terry, Department of Pathology, Albert Einstein School of Medicine, Bronx, N.Y. 10461

How Fast Do Brain Cells Die?

One of the myths of our time is that there is perpetual, large-scale destruction of brain cells (neurons) in humans. This concept of brain cell loss has been accepted by gerontologists, physicians, and laymen alike as one of the fundamental laws of aging and as a prime cause of functional and cognitive decline in the elderly. The most commonly quoted figure is that we lose 10,000 brain cells daily out of the 10 billion or so that we are born with.

Yet there is scant evidence to support such a notion. Although early studies in humans suggested there might be extensive loss of brain cells with age, these studies included individuals with considerable brain pathology. Later studies showed some brain cell loss from birth to age twenty, but little cell loss from adulthood to old age. Most animal studies have found no significant loss of brain cells with age.

Apparently, the brain weights of humans, monkeys, and rodents increase rapidly during development, remain relatively unchanged throughout maturity, and then decline late in senescence. A decrease of about 15 percent in brain volume has been reported in humans between age sixty and eighty, as well as widening and deepening of sulci (grooves) and decrease in the width and mass of gyri (ridges).

But even if the brain decreases in weight and volume during old age, it doesn't necessarily follow that there is a decrease in the number of brain cells. The primary reason for such changes could be a significant decrease in extracellular space—a finding that has been reported in the brains of aging rats.

Kenneth R. Brizzee, Delta Regional Primate Research Center, Covington, La. 70433

How the Brain Disintegrates with Age

A young, healthy brain cell (neuron) stands straight and tall like a beautiful tree. Its branches—the dendrites that receive messages from other neurons—stretch outward with majestic splendor, and its body bursts with high-energy pulses of information. At peak performance, the brain cell is a vital cog in an incredible communications network.

But as it ages, the body of the brain cell swells, thickens, and becomes clogged with debris. Its dendrites become thin and shriveled, finally breaking off entirely. Soon the tree acquires an amputated look, as if its branches had been cut off in guillotine fashion.

Such changes have been described in the brain cells of humans by Madge and Arnold Scheibel of UCLA Medical Center. The Scheibels have focused particular attention on the Betz cell—a distinctive type of neuron that exhibits extensive dendritic branching in youth. By the eighth decade of life, however, the vast majority of persons show severe deficits in 75 to 80 percent of Betz cells in contrast to only 20 to 30 percent of surrounding neurons.

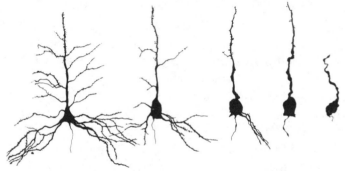

Progression of aging changes in human brain cells. In many respects, these changes retrace the path followed by maturing brain cells during the perinatal stage of development, but in reverse sequence.

Since each cerebral hemisphere contains only about 40,000 Betz cells compared to millions of other types of neurons, these cells appear to be highly specialized units that may play a unique role in aging. The Scheibels have suggested that loss of Betz-cell activity could trigger the loss of neuromuscular function that causes slowness, stiffness, and leg pain in older adults.

They have noted that immature fetal brain cells are similar in appearance to senescent brain cells, which suggests that the degenerative changes of aging may represent a reversal of the developmental pattern that occurs in youth.

Such a pattern could reflect the working of a genetic program that governs both the development and decline of the central nervous system.

Madge E. Scheibel and Arnold B. Scheibel, Departments of Anatomy and Psychiatry, UCLA Medical Center, Los Angeles, Ca. 90024

The Riddle of Age Pigments

The wrinkling of an aging person's skin is usually accompanied by the accumulation of dark spots on the face and hands. Such concentrations of pigment are considered one of the tell-tale signs of old age. Internal aging is also characterized by a gradual buildup of pigment in the cytoplasm (the area surrounding the nucleus) of postmitotic (nondividing) cells.

The most common name for age pigment is lipofuscin ("lipo" from Greek, meaning fat; and "fuscin" from Latin, meaning dusky).

Nobody knows where lipofuscin comes from, though there are several theories about its origin. A prime suspect is the lysosome—the organelle within cells that contains powerful enzymes used to break apart material that needs to be disposed of.

One theory is that lysosomes fail to get rid of by-products from the peroxidation of unsaturated fatty acids caused by free radical activity. It's been suggested that such activity may be involved in aging (see p. 39) and that oxygen may be a critical factor in the process (see p. 126).

Some investigators have noted that lipofuscin tends to accumulate around clumps of mitochondria—the power plants of the cell where oxygen and nutrients are transformed into energy. They suggest that lipofuscin may result from the degeneration of mitochondria leading to the buildup of insoluble fatty acids.

Two Types of Pigment

Several pathologic conditions are characterized by elevated levels of lipofuscin in the brain, including alcoholism, Huntington's Chorea, and senile dementia. In only one such condition, however, is the buildup of pigment associated with brain cell degeneration and death—the Batten-Spielmeyer-Vogt (BSV) syndrome, also known as juvenile amaurotic idiocy.

Analysis of brain cell pigments from deceased BSV patients and aged subjects by A. N. Siakotos has uncovered two similar, but distinct types of pigment—lipofuscin in normal aged subjects and most diseased patients, and ceroid in BSV patients. Wolfgang Zeman has theorized that the rate of formation, rather than the degree of accumulation, determines the type of age pigment. Thus, the normally slow buildup of pigment results in nondestructive lipofuscin, whereas the abnormally fast buildup in BSV patients results in destructive ceroid.

The concentration of lipofuscin in the nerve cells of old animals can be reduced by treatment with the drug centrophenoxine and other compounds (see p. 271). The significance of this achievement is unclear in the absence of an explanation for the origin of this mysterious substance. Solving the riddle of lipofuscin could lead to important clues about the nature of aging, as well as methods of reversing it clinically.

A. N. Siakotos, Indiana University School of Medicine, Indianapolis, Ind. 46202

The Cell Division Controversy

Does the way a cell behaves in a laboratory flask reflect the way it behaves in the human body? Is cell division *in vitro* (in glass) a good model for human aging? Do cells lose their ability to divide as they grow older?

These questions are important because scientists often

study the behavior of cells *in vitro* and interpret their findings in terms of aging. Other scientists contend that the phenomena observed in such experiments have little or nothing to do with aging as it occurs within the body (*in vivo*).

The controversy started in 1961 at the Wistar Institute in Philadelphia, where Leonard Hayflick and Paul S. Moorhead demonstrated that normal human fibroblast cells from four-month-old embryonic lung tissue would divide only about fifty times *in vitro*. Hayflick interpreted this limit on population doublings as an expression of human aging at the cellular level. He proposed that cell division is controlled by a genetic clock mechanism in the cell nucleus, and that the secrets of aging might be unlocked by studying the way cells lose their ability to divide *in vitro*.

This finding, which has come to be known as "the Hayflick limit," was duplicated by many other scientists who set out to study aging in the laboratory. In most cases, they used the same cell line as Hayflick—WI-38 cells—which were grown in the Wistar Institute, freeze-preserved, and then shipped to laboratories around the world.

A Look at the Evidence

The following evidence has been advanced to support the position that loss of proliferative capacity *in vitro* is a manifestation of aging at the cellular level.

• Cells taken from the skin and liver of human donors of different ages—from the fetal state to age ninety—display diminishing capacity to divide *in vitro* with advancing age.

• There is some correlation between the maximum life span of different animal species and the capacity of their cells to divide *in vitro*.

• Normal cells transplanted from old animals into young animals have been able to survive only for limited periods.

Now let's look at the evidence that cell division *in vitro* has little to do with aging in the body.

• Cell division in several types of tissue has been shown to continue at an almost constant rate throughout the life span of mice and rats.

• A study of tongue epithelium cells found an average of 565 population doublings over the life span of mice, and no difference in the rate of cell division among three-, thirteen-, and nineteen-month-old animals.

• There is actually little difference in the *in vitro* proliferative capacity of cells from donors twenty to ninety years of age—the period during which most aging changes take place.

• The doubling capacity of human cells *in vitro* can be increased significantly beyond the proposed limit of fifty by addition of the drug hydrocortisone to the culture medium (see p. 158).

• While it is true that cells transplanted from old to young animals have displayed a limited life span, they have been able to survive as much as three times longer than their donors.

Much of the available evidence appears to support the view that generalized loss of cell division capacity does not occur during normal aging in living systems. Hayflick now believes that functional losses that occur in cells before they stop dividing are the causes of cellular aging *in vivo*.

Edward L. Schneider of the Gerontology Research Center has found significant differences between the behavior of cells from young and old human donors *in vitro*. He has noted that these differences are not nearly as great as those between "young" and "old" WI-38 cells. Schneider suggests that studying cells from donors of different ages may provide a better model for aging than merely following cells throughout their *in vitro* life span.

Leonard Hayflick, Children's Hospital Medical Center of Northern California, Bruce Lyon Memorial Research Laboratory, 31st and Grove Sts., Oakland, Ca. 94609

Edward L. Schneider, *Gerontology Research Center, National Institute on Aging, Baltimore City Hospitals, Baltimore, Md. 21224*

Can Our Cells Become Immortal?

For many years, scientists were convinced that cells could go on dividing forever if placed in the appropriate culture medium. This belief was based upon the experiments of Alexis Carrel, who kept chick fibroblast cells growing and multiplying in glass vessels for more than thirty years—a great deal longer than the life span of a chicken.

Then Leonard Hayflick demonstrated that cultured human fibroblast cells can only divide a maximum of about fifty times before dying out. As a result, the prevailing opinion of the scientific community was completely reversed. Scientists are now convinced that cells have a limited life span, and that Carrel's achievement was the result of the fact that living cells were inadvertently added to his culture medium on a regular basis.

Well, the final work on this issue may not yet be in. At least one scientist—David Harrison of Jackson Laboratory in Bar Harbor, Maine—thinks it may be possible for bone marrow cells to divide forever by moving from one generation to another via tissue grafts.

Cells That Don't Grow Old

Since every organ in the body deteriorates as we grow older, it seems logical that all our cells should deteriorate as well. Many theories of aging are based upon cellular malfunction with time: either from an intrinsic clock mechanism or from accumulating damage caused by radiation, free radicals, or other environmental factors. If such theories are on the right track, then one would expect that cells from old organisms would always be in poorer condition than cells from young organisms.

If, on the other hand, the basic cause of aging involves

disintegration of a delicately balanced system, then it might only be necessary to disrupt the functioning of a few critical cells to produce an environment hostile to all cells. Within such an environment, few cells would be able to function properly, but the majority of them might be intrinsically healthy.

David Harrison has demonstrated that "old" bone marrow cells (the precursors of red blood cells) are healthy enough to survive at least three times longer than the mice they come from. He did this by transplanting marrow cells from old mice into genetically anemic mice incapable of producing red blood cells, or into normal mice whose marrow supply had been destroyed by irradiation.

In most cases, the marrow cells from the old donors were able to cure the anemic mice and save the lives of the irradiated mice as well as marrow cells from young donors. Moreover, the old marrow cells were able to continue their lifesaving act while moving from mouse to mouse during five successive transplants. By the time they lost their ability to function, they had survived for as long as eighty-four months —years longer than the mice they had originally come from.

However, when Harrison transplanted young marrow cells into old mice with defective responses to bleeding, he was unable to improve their condition, even though young anemic mice showed clearcut improvement after such transplants.

Implications for the Future

These experiments suggest that bone marrow cells do not deteriorate within aging mice and that the loss of function reported for these cells may be a consequence of their inhospitable environment—a condition possibly caused by breakdowns in other parts of the system.

Even the loss of function after five transplants was probably not the result of intrinsic aging, says Harrison, because young transplanted cells also lost their ability to function at that time. Further, cells that were transplanted at one-year intervals survived considerably longer than cells transplanted at three-month intervals—a finding that implies imperfections in the transplantation procedure.

Harrison is striving to overcome any such imperfections so he can determine if bone marrow cells, which are also the precursors of immune system cells, are capable of living forever. He believes that other types of cells may also be capable of outliving their donors, and suggests that transplanting many cell types could enable us to discover a few critical types whose intrinsically timed deterioration initiates the aging process.

If such cell types were identified, it might become possible to rejuvenate old mice and, eventually, old persons, by giving them transplants of these cells from young donors. It could also become possible to develop genetic-engineering techniques to eliminate the intrinsic defects that cause aging.

David Harrison, Staff Scientist, The Jackson Laboratory, Bar Harbor, Me. 04609

Breakdowns in the Genetic Machinery

Remember the breakdown of the spaceship computer in the film *2001*. Because of a critical programming error, the machine began to malfunction in ways that were highly detrimental to the crew of the ship. It soon became apparent that the breakdown of the system had reached an "irreversible" threshold that threatened the mission. In an effort to postpone the "inevitable," the human members of the crew proceeded to dismantle the machine, despite considerable resistance on its part.

Ever since it became clear that human life is programmed by genetic machinery in the nucleus of every cell, scientists have looked to this system to explain the aging process. The blueprint of the genetic machinery is contained with nuclear DNA (deoxyribonucleic acid)—a double-stranded molecule in the shape of a helix that bears coded genetic information. This code is passed on to messenger RNA (ribonucleic acid)—a single-stranded molecule that carries it outside the nucleus to cellular factories called ribosomes where structural proteins are synthesized from amino acids, with the help of transfer RNA. Every step in the process is triggered by enzymes, which are also composed of proteins manufactured in the ribosomes.

Some theories of aging suggest that environmental factors such as radiation, food chemicals, oxygen, or viruses attack the genetic machinery in a random manner. According to this view, there is time-dependent accumulation of errors in DNA, RNA, enzymes, or proteins, which leads to the cellular deterioration that characterizes aging.

Arguments Against Random Error Theories

One argument against random error theories is that no one has ever shown that nonrepairable breakdowns of DNA, RNA, or proteins are directly related to the aging process, or that their occurrence is widespread enough to produce the degenerative effects of senescence. There is no evidence for a major loss of genes with advancing age, and no major changes have been observed in the DNA and protein content of cells, or in most enzymes.

Another argument against random error theories is the tremendous variation in life span among species. Why should a man live twice as long as an ape if they are equally subject to the random accumulation of errors? Why the vast differential between the life span of an elephant and a fruit fly? The most plausible explanation for the fixed characteristic life spans of different species appears to be that longevity is an inherited trait that is predetermined genetically.

The final argument against random error theories involves experiments in which the maximum life span of rodents was extended substantially by feeding them low-calorie diets. (See p. 60.) Although it may be that calorie restriction merely postpones the onset of aging and does not alter its expression, the fact remains that underfed animals are just as subject to environmentally induced damage as normally fed animals, and there is no evidence they can repair such damage any better than normally fed animals.

Does Lysosome Deterioration Trigger Aging?

Lysosomes are small, membrane-enclosed sacs that contain powerful enzymes, whose chief purpose is to act as an all-purpose "wrecking crew." They break down nutrients into more basic elements, tear apart portions of the cell prior to regeneration, and pulverize intracellular wastes into excretable fragments.

When lysosomes are functioning properly, there is slow, systematic release of enzymes, according to the needs of the cellular environment. But when the membrane is weakened or broken, there is uncontrolled leakage of lysosomal enzymes into the cells, and sometimes into the extracellular space.

Richard Hochschild of the University of California at Irvine suggests that aging may be triggered by leakage of lysosomal enzymes into the cells and surrounding connective tissue. This leakage occurs, says Hochschild, as a result of membrane damage caused by factors such as male and female sex hormones, bacterial poisons, radiation, and peroxidation of polyunsaturated fatty acids.

According to Hochschild, substances that strengthen or repair lysosomal enzymes are likely to be effective anti-aging compounds. He has been exploring the effects of a variety of "membrane stabilizers" on cell function and longevity since the mid-1960s. Among the compounds he has tested are corticosteroid hormones, analgesic drugs, tranquilizers, antioxidants, antihistamines, antidepressants, and cryoprotective agents. His best results to date have been with two related compounds—centrophenoxine and deanol—both of which have been used to extend the life span of fruit flies and mice. (See pp. 273, 274.)

Though Hochschild's results with centrophenoxine and deanol are encouraging, there is still little hard evidence to support his theory that aging is caused by damage from lysosomal enzymes, or that such damage is a major consequence of aging.

Richard Hochschild, Department of Medicine, University of California at Irvine, Irvine, Ca. 92717

Do Crosslinked Molecules Cause Aging?

If a significant number of workers in a factory were handcuffed together, it would seriously impede productivity. Johan Bjorksten has used this analogy to describe the crosslinkage of molecules in human tissues with advancing age. According to Bjorksten, large molecules become crosslinked through the action of small, motile molecules or free radicals with a reactive hook or other mechanism at both ends.

Among the crosslinking agents cited by Bjorksten are aldehydes, hydroxyl radicals, and polyvalent metals. He estimates that the human body contains about 10^{20} potential cross linkers, most of which are apparently derived from the food we eat, the air we breathe, the water we drink, and such contaminants as cigarette smoke and radiation.

One of the characteristic effects of aging is loss of elasticity in connective tissue, which leads to brittleness and inflexibility of organs and supporting structures. Bjorksten and others have proposed that this effect is caused primarily by crosslinkage of collagen—the most prominent extracellular protein in the body.

However, there is an apparent lack of correlation between the crosslinkage rate of collagen-containing tissues and the aging rate of different mammalian species. Animals with significant variations in maximum life span seem to have the same degree of crosslinkage at the same chronologic age, which suggests that crosslinking is a function of time rather than of biologic aging.

DNA Crosslinks

Richard Cutler of the Gerontology Research Center has collected evidence of age-related changes in chromatin—the nuclear genetic apparatus—which, he believes, may be caused by DNA crosslinks or adducts. Cutler suggests that an age-dependent accumulation of DNA crosslinks may be a primary aging process in mammals, and that the DNA excision repair process recently linked to the rate of aging (see p. 363) may be an intrinsic method of combating crosslinkage.

There is little hard evidence to indicate whether DNA crosslinks are a primary cause or consequence of aging. Bjorksten has suggested antioxidant therapy as a means of preventing crosslinking by free radicals, and enzyme therapy to dissolve or break apart existing aggregates of crosslinked molecules. (See p. 256.)

Johan Bjorksten, Bjorksten Research Foundation, P.O. Box 9444, Madison, Wi. 53715

Richard G. Cutler, Gerontology Research Center, National Institute on Aging, Baltimore City Hospitals, Baltimore, Md. 21224

The Free Radical Theory of Aging

One explanation for the aging process is the free radical theory of Denham Harman of the University of Nebraska. Free radicals are unstable chemical fragments found in all living systems, which readily enter into reactions with other chemical compounds. They can be generated from food, tobacco smoke, air, and water, as well as from the effects of radiation.

According to Harman, the critical factor in aging may be lipid peroxidation, which occurs when free radicals react with unsaturated fatty acids—such as those found in vegetable oils—in the presence of oxygen to form nonfunctional lipid peroxide molecules. Harman contends that various compounds called antioxidants, which inhibit free radical damage caused by lipid peroxidation, may be able to slow the aging process.

The most effective natural antioxidants are vitamins E and C and the trace element selenium. Synthetic antioxidants such as BHT and BHA are added to a host of foods including bread, dry cereals, and salad dressings to preserve their freshness.

Studies by Harman, in which high doses of antioxidants were added to the diets of mice, have produced evidence that these compounds may offer some degree of protection against cancer, amyloidosis, organic brain damage, and other diseases of aging. (See p. 139.) Harman and others have reported extensions of mean life span in mice receiving antioxidants, but in no cases has it proved possible to extend the maximum life span of these animals. (See pp. 131, 137.)

At this time, there is insufficient evidence that free radical damage produces anything resembling the massive, whole-body deterioration of aging. It also is questionable whether cellular damage that occurs with time—whether from free radical reactions or other factors—can legitimately be defined as a cause of aging rather than as a consequence of a more basic process.

Denham Harman, University of Nebraska Medical Center, 42nd and Dewey Ave., Omaha, Ne. 68105

The Immunologic Theory of Aging

When we grow old our defenses fail us. Not only does it become increasingly difficult for us to fight off diseases, but we become victims of our own immune system. To be attacked in this way is called autoimmunity. Roy L. Walford of UCLA Medical Center has suggested that autoimmune mechanisms may be at the root of the aging process.

Walford points out that artificial disruption of the immune system by foreign tissue grafts, removal of the thymus gland (the "master gland" of immunity), genetic breeding, or viral infection produces many of the changes associated with normal aging. Among these changes are degeneration of internal organs, generalized weight loss, wrinkling of the skin, and gradual loss of brain cells.

Moreover, there is evidence that immune system dysfunction plays a role in the genesis of the five principal diseases of aging—amyloidosis, cancer, vascular disease (atherosclerosis and hypertension), maturity-onset diabetes, and senile dementia.

Walford has prolonged the life span of laboratory animals and then measured the immune changes in these animals. When he lengthened the life span of fish by lowering their body temperature (see p. 160), he found that he had also suppressed their immune function. And when he extended the life span of mice by calorie restriction (see p. 189), he found that he had delayed the maturation of the immune system, thereby retarding its age-related decline.

While the decline of the immune system is clearly implicated in the diseases of aging, it's by no means evident that the breakdown of the system is a cause of aging. For one thing, there are mice from long-lived strains that show only marginal immune deficits with advancing age. The same is true in humans, where some individuals of advanced age appear to have almost normal immune function.

Clinical therapies to boost immune function, which should soon be available, will help us to determine the role of the immune system in aging and degenerative disease.

Roy L. Walford, Department of Pathology, UCLA Medical Center, Los Angeles, Ca. 90024

Programmed Aging Theories

The differences in life span among species can be explained as the consequence of a genetic program that unfolds systematically from birth until death. According to this view, we are born with a biologic "clock" etched within our genes that governs such critical stages as puberty, menopause, and senescence.

Some gerontologists hold that aging begins with the cessation of growth, when the genes for youth are turned off or repressed and the genes for senescence turned on. Others point to the differentiation of cells as a key factor in the aging process—the idea being that cells with a special purpose, such as those in the brain, liver, and kidney, have a diminished capacity for renewal or regeneration.

The idea of programmed aging fits in well with the biological scheme of existence. Certainly, every stage of growth and maturation is controlled genetically, as is the process by which we develop individual physical and mental characteristics.

Yet there are several reasons to question the existence of an aging program. First is the lack of evidence for the evolution of a genetic basis for aging. On the contrary, there is considerable evidence that our remote ancestors were quite short-lived, and that a program for longevity has been evolving ever since. (See p. 19.)

Next is the fact that aging differs significantly from development. Except for the menopause, there is no stage of human senescence that resembles the metamorphic processes of growth and sexual maturation. Aging unfolds slowly, almost imperceptibly, over an eighty- to ninety-year period, with little of the drama of the developmental period.

Morphologic and biochemical studies have pinpointed many changes in gene expression during growth and development, but they have yet to reveal similar changes during senescence. While many diseases have been traced to the malfunctioning of specific gene systems, there is no evidence to date that there are specific genes responsible for aging.

Instead of a specific program for aging, it's been argued that we grow old and die simply because we run out of program, or because the program begins to unravel as we approach middle age. Nature's primary interest seems to be the perpetuation of the species, rather than the individual. Once we pass our reproductive years, there is no evolutionary reason for us to continue to live, and so Nature seems content to discard us.

In recent years, gerontologists have begun to focus on the neuroendocrine and immune systems—the physiologic control mechanisms primarily responsible for maintenance of health and well-being. The study of these systems has illuminated some aspects of the aging process, and has served as a springboard for new theories of aging and potential anti-aging therapies.

Regulatory Dysfunction and Aging

A five-year-old child can easily distinguish a twenty-year-old from an eighty-year-old. The weakened physique, wrinkled skin, graying hair, and awkward gait of the old person stands in stark contrast to the strength, flexibility, and vigor of the younger person.

But when scientists compare biochemical profiles of young and old persons, they find it much harder to distinguish between them. And when they measure physiologic parameters, such as blood pressure and heart rate, they may be unable to tell the difference at all.

How is it possible for the body to mask its precipitous decline with advancing age? According to Vladimir V. Frolkis of the U.S.S.R. Institute of Gerontology, the answer lies in a regulatory-adaptive process that makes it possible for us to adjust to the disruption of the subtle, harmonious balance among systems that occurs during aging. The result is a progressive loss of reserve capacity that makes it increasingly difficult to deal with environmental stress.

Thus, there is relatively little functional difference between a twenty-year-old and an eighty-year-old, so long as the body is at rest. But as soon as there is a need to move quickly, lift a heavy object, work long hours, or tolerate extreme weather conditions, the twenty-year-old far outperforms the eighty-year-old. Similarly, if the body is attacked by a harmful virus or physical object, the twenty-year-old can fight off disease or injury much more easily than the eighty-year-old. And if disease or injury should strike, the twenty-year-old recuperates faster and better than the eighty-year-old.

Frolkis believes that the key to the regulatory-adaptive process is the neuroendocrine system. He and his colleagues have demonstrated the influence of the hypothalamus region of the brain on the regulation of hormones, enzymes, and energy metabolism.

Another Soviet scientist who emphasizes the role of the hypothalamus in human aging is V. M. Dilman of the Petrov Institute in Leningrad. Dilman believes that an age-associated elevation of the hypothalamic threshold to feedback control is the timing mechanism that governs growth, sexual maturation, the menopause, and senescence. According to this view, the hypothalamus becomes increasingly sensitive to hormones from the endocrine glands, which inhibit its release of neurotransmitters. The resulting disruption causes hormonal imbalances throughout the body, which leads to abnormal cell and organ function and the onset of aging and the diseases of aging.

Vladimir V. Frolkis, Institute of Gerontology, U.S.S.R. Academy of Medical Sciences, Vyshgorodskaya 67, 252655, Kiev-114, U.S.S.R.

V. M. Dilman, N.N. Petrov Research Institute of Oncology, Leningrad, U.S.S.R.

Breakdowns in Hormonal Regulation

The Pacific salmon is a truly magnificent creature. When the salmon is in peak condition, after years of ocean feeding, it possesses extraordinary physical and adaptive powers. These powers are used to their fullest during the salmon's mysterious, compelling journey toward the stream of its origin.

In the course of this journey, the salmon travels up to 2,000 miles against the current of such major waterways as Alaska's Yukon River, and performs incredible feats of strength, agility, and endurance. It literally leaps up steep waterfalls, battles thundering rapids, surmounts massive logjams, and eludes or fights off ferocious predators.

When the salmon finally reaches its place of birth, it is torn, ragged, thin, and prematurely old. The female lays up to 8,000 eggs in a scooped-out gravel nest, and the male fertilizes them almost immediately. Then they both drift downstream to die.

O. H. Robertson has shown that the accelerated aging of the Pacific salmon is related to an unusually high outpouring of adrenal corticosteroid hormones. Apparently, these hormones, which are mobilized to fuel the salmon's Herculean effort to return to its spawning ground, are also responsible for its rapid physical decline. When the salmon is prevented from reaching sexual maturity by castration, it lives at least twice as long as normal.

Inspired by the saga of the Pacific salmon, Caleb Finch of the Andrus Gerontology Center has been exploring the roles of hormones in aging. Finch has created a model of the aging process in which changes in brain catecholamines (chemicals that transmit messages from one brain cell to another) trigger a "cascade" of detrimental events in hormonally regulated functions throughout the body.

Since Finch believes that neurons involved in catecholamine synthesis may serve as "pacemakers" of aging, he has been studying age-related changes in these substances in the brains of mice. He has found decreases in dopamine and norepinephrine in at least four regions of the aging mouse brain. The greatest catecholamine decrease appears to be in the hypothalamus—the area involved in the regulation of reproduction, temperature, appetite, and sex drive.

Caleb E. Finch, Andrus Gerontology Center, University of Southern California, Los Angeles, Ca. 90007

When Children "Age" Rapidly

In one in 8 million live births, the newborn child seems to age at a highly abnormal rate. In the first year of life, there is a marked slowdown of growth that leads to severe retardation. Soon there is loss of skin elasticity, subcutaneous fat, and hair, giving prominence to the child's superficial veins and an "aged" appearance. By age ten, generalized atherosclerosis sets in, as the child continues to degenerate. Death by heart attack usually occurs between the ages of ten and eighteen.

This rare genetic disorder is known as the Hutchinson-Gilford syndrome, or progeria. A similar disorder is Werner's syndrome, in which accelerated "aging" usually begins between fifteen and twenty years of age, with death occurring in the fourth or fifth decade of life. Other genetic disorders, such as the Cockayne syndrome, Seip syndrome, and Ataxia telangiectasia also feature some of the characteristics of aging—but none so dramatically as progeria.

Scientists have been studying progeria as a model for normal human aging. Tissue culture experiments have revealed similarities in the growth characteristics of fibroblast cells from progeria patients and normally aged subjects. These include shortened *in vitro* life span, decreased DNA metabolism, lack of DNA repair capability, and increased insulin binding.

These findings have raised the hope that insight into the underlying genetic basis for progeria might be helpful in understanding normal aging. However, in many respects progeria is a poor model for aging. There are no degenerative changes of the central nervous system, no increase in the incidence of cancer or diabetes, and no loss of vision or hearing —all of which occur in normal aging. On the other hand, virtually all progeria patients develop atherosclerosis and heart disease, which suggests that it might be a good model for accelerated cardiovascular disease.

A more appropriate model for accelerated aging may be Down's syndrome, or "mongolism," a much more common genetic disorder, in which there is neuropathologic evidence of senile dementia at an early age, as well as other features similar to normal aging.

W. Ted Brown, Division of Human Genetics, New York Hospital-Cornell Medical Center, 1300 York Ave., New York, N.Y. 10021

Hormonal Regulation of Enzyme Activity

The ability to adapt to environmental change can be expressed on a biochemical level by variations in enzyme activity in response to appropriate stimulation. Richard C. Adelman of the Fels Research Institute has demonstrated that the behavior of two rat liver enzymes—glucokinase and tyrosine aminotransferase—is altered as a result of aging. He has shown a progressive, age-dependent increase in the time required for glucokinase to adapt to the administration of glucose, and for tyrosine aminotransferase to adapt to the administration of the pituitary hormone ACTH (adrenocorticotropic hormone).

When Adelman discovered that the adaptive response of both glucokinase and tyrosine aminotransferase requires the presence of at least two hormones—insulin and corticosterone—he gave old rats injections of these hormones. By doing so, he found he could abolish the age-dependent changes in the adaptive response of both liver enzymes.

Adelman believes that most of the evidence to date indicates that the progressive decline in rat liver enzyme adaptation with age is caused by breakdowns in neural or endocrine regulatory factors, and that these factors may also be responsible for the decreased performance and increased vulnerability to disease that afflicts the elderly.

Richard C. Adelman, Fels Research Institute, Temple University School of Medicine, Philadelphia, Pa. 19122

When Aging Cells Fail to Respond to Hormones

When a hormone is released it carries a message earmarked for a specific type of cell. That message can be delivered only if the cell is ready to receive it, a condition determined by the number of active receptors it contains. If there are too few receptors, the message may be lost, garbled, or only partially received.

Receptors are large protein molecules that have the ability to bind, or capture, the molecules of specific hormones. A receptor can be thought of as a lock into which only a certain key can fit, or a magnet that can attract only certain particles.

George S. Roth of the Gerontology Research Center has been exploring the role of hormone receptors in mammalian aging. He has gathered evidence that there are significant losses of hormone-binding capacity in a variety of tissues with advancing age. He recently reported a significant age-dependent decrease in beta adrenergic receptors in the mononuclear blood cells of humans.

In most cases, the loss of hormone-binding capacity appears to be caused by a reduction in the number of active receptors, rather than by a loss of receptor activity. What remains to be determined is whether receptors are lost, blocked, or become inactive in aging cells; or whether there is a decreased rate of receptor synthesis in these cells. Another important question is the extent to which the loss of hormone-binding capacity is an expression of normal aging.

Roth feels that the answers to these questions could

enable us to develop methods of restoring lost responsiveness in aging cells by reconstituting altered hormone receptor systems.

George S. Roth, Gerontology Research Center, National Institute on Aging, Baltimore City Hospitals, Baltimore, Md. 21224

How the Octopus Self-Destructs

When a female octopus is ready to reproduce, she is at her maximum body weight and is healthy and vigorous. But after spawning, she guards her eggs religiously and often neglects to eat. By the time her eggs are hatched—approximately thirty-two days later—she has lost considerable weight and strength. She usually dies about ten days later.

Jerome Wodinsky of Brandeis University has traced the sudden decline and death of the female octopus to the working of the optic glands—two small spherical structures connected to the brain. As the organism's only identifiable endocrine glands, these organs have been compared to the pituitary gland in vertebrates. They apparently control the sexual activity, reproduction, food intake, and longevity of the octopus.

Wodinsky believes that one or more secretions from the optic glands trigger the sequence of events leading to the animal's destruction. When he removes the female's optic glands after she has laid her eggs, she forgets about caring for them, begins to eat more, gains considerable weight, and lives far longer than normal.

The longest a normal female octopus has lived after spawning is fifty-one days. By removing one optic gland, Wodinsky has gotten females to live for as long as ninety-one days, and by removing both glands, for as long as nine months.

These findings suggest that aging and death in the octopus may be programmed by the animal's hormone system as mediated through the optic glands. They lend support to the hypothesis that aging is a function of neuroendocrine factors that act upon cells throughout the body.

Jerome Wodinsky, Department of Psychology, Brandeis University, Waltham, Ma. 02154

When the Pituitary Gland Is Removed?

If the brain is the kingpin of a neuroendocrine system that regulates the rate of aging, then the pituitary gland—a small organ attached to the hypothalamus at the base of the brain —is the instrument through which it operates. The pituitary gland secretes hormones composed of peptides (chains of amino acids) that travel to the other endocrine glands where they stimulate the release of a variety of hormones including thyroxine from the thyroid gland, insulin from the pancreas, and estrogen and testosterone from the ovary or testes.

Arthur V. Everitt of the University of Sydney in Australia has provided evidence that the rate of aging in rats is retarded by surgical removal of the pituitary gland, or hypophysectomy. Among the findings that Everitt has reported in hypophysectomized rats are the following:
- Reduced crosslinking in collagen fibers of tail tendon
- Inhibition of age-associated kidney lesions
- Inhibition of ventricular hypertrophy (enlarged heart)
- Prolonged life span of red blood cells
- Reduced serum cholesterol levels
- Slowing of the loss of oocytes (egg cells) by the ovary
- Elimination of hind leg skeletal muscle degeneration

Everitt has accelerated aging and age-related pathologies in rats by giving them hormones. He believes that environmental influences such as temperature, stress, and food are detected by the nervous system and then relayed to the hypothalamus, which regulates the secretion of pituitary and other hormones. Overstimulation of this system, says Everitt, leads to excessive release of hormones which accelerates the aging process; whereas depression of the system, such as by reducing caloric intake, inhibits the release of hormones which retards the aging process.

Arthur V. Everitt, Department of Physiology, University of Sydney, Australia

How the Aging Clock Works: A New Model

By restricting dietary intake of the essential amino acid tryptophan in rats, Paul Segall of the University of California at Berkeley has delayed reproductive aging (see p. 319), prolonged life span (see p. 68), and achieved temporary rejuvenation of old animals.

Segall has formulated a model of the aging process as a programmed sequence of events. According to this model, the timing mechanism of the clock is the maturation of selected neurons in the brain. These neurons go on to stimulate the development of excitatory and inhibitory neural processes, which regulate the hypothalamo-pituitary-endocrine axis, the spinal cord, and the autonomic nervous system, which in turn control all essential life functions.

In youth, excitation overrides inhibition, as the hormones released by the hypothalamus stimulate the induction of genes that govern the synthesis of enzymes necessary for maturation of the pituitary gland. After puberty, however, the inhibitory neural processes gradually gain ascendancy over the excitatory processes. As a result, the hypothalamic releasing hormones are secreted in a different pattern and the pituitary decreases its rate of enzyme production, which inhibits maturation of pituitary hormones.

These hormones are then released in an incomplete, less biologically active, or "unsculptured" form that prevents them from properly stimulating their target organs. Also, the autonomic nervous system and spinal cord receive less stimulation from the brain. The result is degeneration and decline of the cardiovascular, immunologic, pulmonary, renal, reproductive, urinary, and digestive systems—as well as atrophy of skeletal muscles.

Evidence of "Unsculptured" Hormones

There is some evidence to support Segall's concept that aging may be mediated by the increased secretion of "unsculptured" hormones. For example, proinsulin—which is converted to insulin by enzymes in the pancreas—is immunologically similar, but far less effective than insulin in facilitating the uptake of blood glucose (sugar). It's been shown that the percentage of proinsulin to total insulin secreted after a glucose challenge is 75 percent higher in old persons than in young ones.

Several pituitary hormones have also been shown to exist in different forms, as has the enzyme monoamine oxidase, which is responsible for the breakdown of catecholamines. Whether these variations in form have anything to do with the aging process remains to be determined.

Paul E. Segall, Department of Physiology/Anatomy, University of California at Berkeley, Berkeley, Ca. 94720

The "Juvenile" Hormone

Almost all insects possess a hormone that delays maturity and aging without interfering with growth. The hormone is secreted by a tiny cluster of cells just behind the brain called the corposa allata glands.

When these glands are removed early in development, a dwarfed insect results; when young glands are transplanted into a maturing insect, metamorphosis is postponed and a giant insect results.

The "juvenile" hormone was discovered in 1933 by British biologist V. B. Wigglesworth. It was isolated and has been studied extensively by Carroll M. Williams of Harvard University.

In 1958, Williams suggested that the discovery of a similar

hormone in humans could lead to a "chemotherapy for aging and senescence." As yet, nothing resembling the juvenile hormone has been discovered in humans.

Carroll M. Williams, Harvard University, Cambridge, Ma. 02138

Searching for the Death Hormone

Our organs are brought to life by electrical and chemical messages. The cells divide and the organs perform only if they are told to do so. A muscle cannot function unless it receives directions from a nerve impulse. An egg cell cannot mature unless it is exposed to certain hormones. The conversion of the breast into a milk-producing organ requires at least eight hormones supplied in the proper order and amount. Even the most basic functions, such as the transport of glucose through cell membranes, can be traced to instructions from the central nervous system.

When cells become specialized, they lose virtually all their autonomy. Slavery is the price for joining a community of cells in a highly complex system. Loss of autonomy is essential to the welfare of the organism. Any cell that regains an appreciable degree of autonomy is called a malignant cancer cell. Though cancer cells are potentially immortal "on their own" (in tissue culture), they are detrimental to the welfare of the community.

W. Donner Denckla believes there may be a specific pituitary hormone that directs the cells of the body to grow old and die. He came to this conclusion after years of manipulating the functions of the endocrine system in laboratory rats.

First, he examined the effects of removing each endocrine gland on minimal oxygen consumption (MOC), a physiologic parameter that measures the function of the thyroid gland. Denckla found that MOC, which declines progressively with age, could be restored to juvenile levels in old rats by removing the pituitary gland and giving them thyroid hormones.

He also found that injections of pituitary extract lowered MOC in young hypophysectomized rats, as well as in older rats whose decline in MOC had been delayed by a low-calorie diet. The results of these experiments convinced Denckla that there is a biologically active factor released by the pituitary after puberty that decreases the responsiveness of peripheral tissues to thyroid hormones, and that this triggers the decline of the entire organism with advancing age.

Rejuvenation Effects in Rats

In order to test this hypothesis, Denckla gave hypophysectomized rats injections of all the known pituitary hormones and assessed the effects of this treatment on various parameters of aging. He found that he could rejuvenate old rats in eight of nine age-dependent functions.

In all cases, the rejuvenation effects could be achieved in chronic hypophysectomized animals (six months after the operation), but not in acute hypophysectomized animals (two months after the operation). Since the effects of all the known pituitary hormones are normally dissipated within two months, this finding supported his idea of a new "death" hormone.

The following functions were restored to juvenile levels in old hypophysectomized rats given injections of pituitary hormones:

• Minimal oxygen consumption—a measure of thyroid gland function

• Maximal oxygen consumption—a measure of respiratory function

• Graft rejection and T lymphocyte function—two methods of measuring immune function

• Carbon clearance—a measure of the ability of the reticuloendothelial system to remove foreign bacteria from the body

• Aortic strip relaxation—a measure of the flexibility of blood vessels. Strips from the aorta (a major blood vessel connected to the heart) normally lose the capacity to relax with age after drug stimulation

• RNA polymerase activity—the enzyme that triggers the transcription of RNA from DNA, a function that normally declines with age

• Hair regrowth—young rats normally exhibit faster and thicker regrowth of shaved body hair than old rats

Although Denckla's animals were clearly rejuvenated and looked the part, they failed to live significantly longer than his control animals. In most instances, they died from lung infections, which may have been caused by the loss of B lymphocyte function—the one parameter that was made worse by the treatment.

Denckla's goal is to identify the hormone that he believes responsible for aging, degeneration, and death—and then develop a therapy to neutralize or reverse its effects upon the body. He has narrowed his search to a pituitary extract that contains eighteen proteins, but has not yet been able to isolate the specific hormone he is looking for.

W. Donner Denckla, Institute of Alcohol and Alcoholism, 12501 Washington Ave., Rockville, Md. 20852

A Theory of How Genes Control Aging

Although there appear to be no specific genes for aging, there are indications that all gene activity may be regulated according to a systematic program. M. S. Kanungo of Banaras Hindu University in India suggests that aging may be the result of the sequential activation and repression of gene activity.

Kanungo believes that the synthesis of enzymes is under the control of specific genes, and that enzymes may govern the initiation, duration, and termination of differentiation, development, maturity, and senescence. He has been studying changes in enzymes with age in an attempt to illuminate the workings of the aging program.

He has found that, of two sub-types (A and B) of the enzyme alanine aminotransferase in the liver of rats, only sub-type A is present in immature animals (five weeks of age). As growth proceeds, however, the level of sub-type A gradually decreases and sub-type B appears. By the time the rats are old (100 weeks of age), sub-type A has completely disappeared, and the only form of the enzyme present is sub-type B. Kanungo sees this finding as evidence of the controlled sequential expression of one manifestation of the aging process.

Other enzymes, such as acetylcholinesterase (AChE), which is involved in the transmission of information in the brain, show no structural or biochemical changes with age, but decrease in amount as an animal grows older. In this case, Kanungo proposes the existence of a specific repressor for the gene responsible for the manufacture of this enzyme.

Determination of Life Span

Kanungo envisions an ongoing process by which genes are systematically activated or repressed in sequential order. He suggests that senescence may be caused by the repression or impairment of the genes necessary for the maintenance of health, physical strength, and vigor.

According to this view, the variation in life span among species is related to the duration of each phase of the life cycle. The longer it takes for the early phases of the cycle to unfold, the longer the life span. The relatively long life span of humans, for example, is a consequence of our relatively long periods of gestation and development. And the extension of life span in rats via calorie restriction (see p. 60) is related to the lengthening of the period of maturation in these animals.

Kanungo has recently reported that the activity of histones (chromosomal proteins involved in regulation of gene expression) decreases significantly with age in response to hormonal stimulation. He suggests that similar changes may be at work to modify gene expression in all aging organisms.

M. S. Kanungo, Biochemistry Laboratory, Zoology Department, Banaras Hindu University, Varanasi, India

An Integrated Theory of Aging

Bernard L. Strehler of the University of Southern California has combined many of the recent findings about aging into an integrated theory of its origin and expression—as outlined in his book *Time, Cells, and Aging*.

According to Strehler, the critical factor that leads to the deterioration of aging is the loss of the capacity for cell division in tissue types such as brain, heart, and muscle. The result is a progressive decrease in the functional efficiency of these tissues with the passage of time.

The repression of cell division occurs by virtue of selective inhibition of translation of genetic messages, which leads to various kinds of entropic damage. These include loss of ribosomal DNA, which impairs protein synthesis; loss of receptor sites for hormones, which decreases systemic communication; and the accumulation of lipofuscin age pigments, which signals a breakdown in cellular metabolism.

These changes lead to progressive disruption of homeostatic mechanisms including loss of immunocompetence, declining neuroendocrine system responsiveness, and decreased ability to perform physical work—all of which reduces our ability to respond to environmental and internal challenges and "inevitably" leads to death.

Bernard L. Strehler, Department of Biology, University of Southern California, Los Angeles, Ca. 90007

Chapter 2

Diet and Longevity

Diet Preference and Length of Life

We know little about how the composition of the diet affects life span. How much protein should we eat? How much carbohydrate? To what extent do individual dietary needs differ? How do our needs change as we grow older?

Dietary studies in the laboratory tend to be manipulative. Animals are forced to consume specific diets without consideration for individual taste or appetite. To get away from such artificial conditions, Morris H. Ross has developed a self-selection model for nutritional analysis.

Ross permits individually caged rats to choose among three different diets that contain the same number of calories and amounts of vitamins and minerals. Each diet varies in its ratio of protein to carbohydrate, with casein used as the source of protein and sucrose as the source of carbohydrate.

In a recent study, Ross set the respective protein and carbohydrate components of the diets at 10 percent and 70.5 percent, 22 percent and 58.5 percent, and 51 percent and 29.5 percent—a range wide enough to satisfy almost any preference. He then monitored their dietary behavior throughout life and looked for specific factors associated with longevity.

The life span of the longest-lived rats was more than 1,025 days, exceeding that of the shortest-lived rats by about 700 days.

Here are his findings on the effects of diet on longevity:

• The higher the intake of food—regardless of its composition—the shorter the life span. This association was of maximum significance between fourteen and twenty-one weeks of age (eight to fourteen years in human terms). A rat who consumed 1 gram of food per day more than another rat was likely to die four weeks earlier than the lighter-eating rat. After the animals were mature, however, the amount of food they ate no longer correlated with life span.

• Short-lived rats chose a diet relatively low in protein and high in carbohydrate early in life and relatively high in protein and low in carbohydrate late in life.

• Long-lived rats maintained a moderately high protein, low carbohydrate diet throughout much of their lives and decreased their protein intake late in life.

• The heavier the animal, the shorter its life span. Although heavier rats tended to consume more food than lighter rats, their weight gain was more rapid than could be accounted for by food intake alone. Apparently, ingested food is converted into body mass more efficiently in heavier, faster-growing rats than in lighter, more slowly growing rats.

• Animals who grew slowly between fifty and 150 days of age (4.5 to fourteen years in human terms) were likely to live the longest.

In another dietary preference study conducted by Salvatore Leto, female mice were given the opportunity to choose between diets containing 26 percent or 4 percent protein (in the form of casein). The mice on the low-protein diet lived significantly longer than those on the high-protein diet. By the age of 23.5 months, 50 percent of the high-protein group were dead, whereas 50 percent mortality did not occur in the low-protein group until twenty-eight months of age. The maximum life span attained in the high-protein group was 840 days, compared to 1,167 days in the low-protein group.

Morris H. Ross, The Institute for Cancer Research, The Fox Chase Cancer Center, Philadelphia, Pa. 19111

Salvatore Leto, Gerontology Research Center, National Institute on Aging, Baltimore City Hospitals, Baltimore, Md. 21224

Doubling Maximum Life Span

When rats are maintained on a very low calorie diet throughout their lives, they live far longer than their normally fed contemporaries. Calorie restriction is one of only two experimental models, the other being reduction of body temperature (see p. 160), that has enabled scientists to extend maximum life span. All other life-prolonging regimens have lengthened only the middle period of life.

The calorie restriction effect was discovered more than fifty years ago by Clive M. McCay of Cornell University. McCay first noticed that growth-retarded brook trout consistently outlived normal-sized trout. He then began a series of experiments to investigate chronic underfeeding in rats. Since he was primarily interested in the effects of caloric deprivation, he made sure to give his experimental animals an adequate supply of essential nutrients.

McCay's rats were severely retarded in growth. They re-

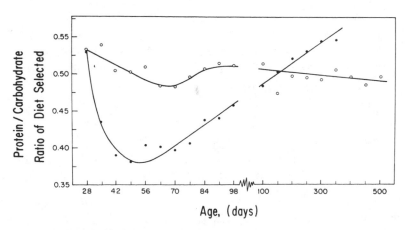

Protein/carbohydrate ratio of diet selected by short-lived rats (●) and long-lived rats (○). The short-lived rats chose a low-protein/high-carbohydrate diet early in life and a high-protein/low-carbohydrate diet late in life; the long-lived rats maintained a moderately high-protein/low-carbohydrate diet throughout most of their lives and decreased their protein intake late in life.

mained small and immature as long as they were kept on the low-calorie diet. They also had periodic convulsions and seizures and were prone to develop lung and middle ear infections. Some animals died from these causes at early ages.

Those who managed to survive, however, outlived controls by a considerable margin. The last member of the control group died at the extreme old age of 965 days, but a good many of the retarded animals lived more than 1,000 days. McCay's longest-lived rat was a female who survived 1,456 days. Morris H. Ross has kept calorically deprived rats alive for more than 1,800 days—about 200 years in human terms.

McCay could induce his rats to grow and mature, even after long periods of retardation, by putting them on a normal diet. The longer the rats were kept retarded, however, the shorter the period of adult life after maturation. Rats whose growth was retarded for 300 days lived an average of 535 days after maturation, whereas those who were retarded for 1,000 days lived an average of only 138 days after maturation.

Effects of the Diet

The low-calorie diet produced profound physiologic changes that postponed aging and other degenerative processes. Chronic diseases progressed more slowly and fewer tumors developed in the growth-retarded animals, yet they all eventually died, whether on the low-calorie diet or not. The aging process seemed to accelerate in the older retarded animals.

There were significant differences in bone structure between retarded and normally fed rats. The bones of rats whose life span had been extended to nearly four years were so fragile that the scalpel crushed them in the process of dissection. In contrast, the rats that grew normally and died within two to three years of life had firm bones that were difficult to crush. Some of the bones of the especially long-lived animals were mere shells that floated in water, while the bones of the younger animals always sank in water.

Some scientists argue that the life-prolonging effect of underfeeding has nothing to do with aging because it extends the period of immaturity rather than the period of adulthood. But other scientists insist that aging is a developmental phenomenon and that any regimen that lengthens maximum life span must have some effect on the aging process.

Certainly McCay's method of prolonging life is inappropriate for humans. We don't want to retard our growth or remain children for decades. Besides, most of us have long since passed puberty, after which the effect of McCay's diet seems to disappear. What we need is a method of dietary manipulation that extends life span in adults as well as children, without harmful side effects.

In his search for such a diet, Benjamin N. Berg of Columbia University restricted the food intake of rats by 33 to 46 percent. By doing so, he prevented accumulation of fat with little retarding effect on skeletal growth. By the age of 800 days, almost twice as many rats on the restricted diet were alive compared to control animals who were allowed to eat as much as they wanted. Further, the restricted animals had fewer tumors and cardiac, renal, and vascular lesions than the unrestricted animals.

Eating Less May Prevent Cancer

Numerous animal studies have documented the tumor-inhibiting power of food restriction. In most of these studies, however, the animals were so deprived of food that they failed to grow to normal size. Such a diet has considerable experimental value, but little to recommend as a model for humans.

Of more immediate relevance is the finding of Mary J. Tucker in England that relatively slight food restriction can markedly reduce the incidence of malignant tumors in mice.

In this experiment, two groups of forty mice each were allowed to eat as much as they wanted of a well-balanced diet, while two other groups of the same size were restricted to 5 and 4 grams of the diet per day respectively.

At the age of eighteen months, the mice in the restricted groups showed only eight tumors compared to fifty-five tumors in the unrestricted groups—a seven-fold reduction in tumor incidence.

The average amount of food consumed by the unrestricted animals was 5.8 grams per day—not much more than the 5 grams per day given to one of the restricted groups. This

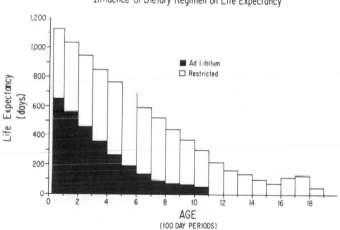

Influence of Dietary Regimen on Life Expectancy

Comparison of the life expectancy of male rats fed an ad libitum diet (as much as they want) and a calorie-restricted diet throughout postweaning life. All the ad libitum rats were dead by 1,100 days, whereas some of the restricted rats lived more than 1,800 days.

implies that we might be able to protect ourselves against cancer by eating 14 percent less food; or perhaps by eating 14 percent less of a particular diet.

On the other hand, it should not be assumed that the differences in caloric intake per se were solely responsible for the differences in tumor incidence. When an animal is given a restricted amount of food, it tends to consume it all quickly and then be wholly without food until the next ration is supplied. But when there is no restriction on food, the animal tends to nibble constantly throughout the day.

This variation in dietary lifestyle leads to differences in daily patterns of hormone balance, enzyme action, and bacterial growth—any of which may be relevant to tumor growth or inhibition. Moreover, the experience of facing an empty food container on a regular basis could conceivably produce a kind of psychologic stress that is unknown in unrestricted animals.

Mary J. Tucker, Imperial Chemical Industries, Ltd., Macclesfield, Cheshire, United Kingdom

Eating Less Improves Fat Metabolism

Food-restricted rats maintain a sleek, smooth appearance and active, alert behavior patterns characteristic of younger animals. One reason for this youthfulness may be that they retain an improved ability to utilize or metabolize fat.

Edward J. Masoro has discovered that restricting food intake in rats substantially delays the age-related declines in the responsiveness of adipocytes (fat cells) to the hormones glucagon and adrenaline. Both these hormones promote fat metabolism by releasing fat from adipocytes and carrying it to the blood for conversion into energy.

According to Masoro, food-restricted animals also maintain fewer and smaller fat cells in the tissues surrounding the kidneys, as well as lower serum lipid levels, than normally fed animals. However, some additional fat cells appear to accumulate in the kidney area of rats with increasing age, regardless of food intake.

These findings provide a partial explanation for the extended life span and delay in the onset of heart disease, diabetes, and cancer in food-restricted animals.

Edward J. Masoro, Department of Physiology, University of Texas Health Science Center, San Antonio, Tx. 78284

Avoiding Fat Prevents Breast Cancer

Everyone knows that eating fat clogs the arteries. Many people know that dietary fat promotes diabetes and other metabolic disorders. But few of us realize that high fat intake increases the likelihood of getting breast cancer.

The key factor associated with populations at-risk for breast cancer is dietary fat intake. The breast cancer rate among American women is almost six times that of Japanese women, yet there is little to distinguish the two groups except for the markedly higher fat intake of women in this country.

No one believes that dietary fat is a direct cause of breast cancer, but scientists theorize that fat can induce hormonal changes that precipitate the carcinogenic process in breast tissue. The critical period for these changes is thought to be the time of puberty when breast development takes place.

In a study of Japanese A-bomb survivors, it was found that irradiation between the ages of ten and nineteen resulted (fifteen years later) in an increased rate of breast cancer of approximately 5½ percent per rad exposure above that of unexposed women of the same age. However, the increased incidence for women exposed to radiation in their twenties was only 1½ percent per rad above that of unexposed women of the same age.

When Japanese women migrate to the United States, they suffer only a slight increase in their breast cancer rate, despite the fact that they soon consume as much fat as long-time residents. But when it comes to their daughters, who are fully exposed to high dietary fat throughout growth and development, the rate of breast cancer is almost identical to that of long-time residents.

Further evidence that dietary fat promotes breast cancer comes from animal studies showing that high fat diets increase the incidence of both spontaneous and chemically induced mammary tumors in rodents. In one study, DMBA-treated rats fed a 20 percent fat diet exhibited a higher mean tumor incidence (56 percent) than rats fed a 0.5 percent fat diet (34 percent).

It appears that chronic high fat intake may promote breast cancer by raising blood levels of the pituitary hormone prolactin, and that mammary tumor cell proliferation is stimulated by a high prolactin/estrogen ratio. (See p. 315.)

J. H. Weisburger, Naylor Dana Institute for Disease Prevention, American Health Foundation, Valhalla, N.Y. 10595

Obesity and Premature Aging

How fat do you think you'd get if you never stopped eating? One organism that eats continuously until it dies—if given enough food—is the protozoan *Tokophrya infusionum*. After a few days of feeding on living prey, this one-cell life form can swell to as much as 120 times its normal size.

Overfed *Tokophrya* giants live two to four days, only one-sixth the life span of organisms kept on an intermittent starvation diet. In a study of this phenomenon, Maria A. Rudzinska of The Rockefeller Institute found "remarkable similarities" between old normally fed and young overfed *Tokophyra*.

Among the signs of premature aging caused by obesity in *Tokophrya* were a sharp decrease in the number, length, and function of tentacles used to trap food; a drastic drop in the reproduction rate; the development of dense lipid-like pigment granules; and breakdowns in nuclear chromatin structure.

How Body Weight Affects Life Expectancy

The heaviest man in history, says the *Guinness Book of World Records*, is alleged to have weighed 1,132 pounds; he died at age thirty-four. The next heaviest man, whose case is fully documented, weighed 1,069 pounds and died at age thirty-two. The average weight of the nine heaviest persons of all time, including one woman, is 927 pounds; their average life expectancy, 39.3 years—about half that of adults in the general population.

There's no doubt that extreme obesity shortens life span dramatically, not to speak of its negative effects on the quality of life. Fat people are at higher-than-normal risk for a variety of disorders including atherosclerosis, hypertension, heart disease, stroke, cirrhosis, diabetes, and most forms of cancer. They are also more likely to die in accidents or commit suicide than persons of normal weight.

Yet, there's no hard evidence that people who are slightly to moderately overweight are any more likely to die than people of normal weight. Reubin Andres, Director of the Baltimore Longitudinal Aging Study (see p. 368), has collected data from six recent studies showing that the highest mortality occurs in the leanest and most obese groups, with little or no difference in groups ranging from "desirable" weight to 30 percent overweight. In his own study, reports Andres, the estimated percent body fat in fifty- to eighty-nine-year-old men who have survived is a mere 1 percent less than in those who have died.

Since moderate obesity is associated with a higher risk of several life-shortening diseases, it may be that the relatively equal mortality figures among groups of varying body weight reflect the existence of counter-balancing survival benefits for those of moderate obesity. Perhaps we have confused aesthetic standards for "ideal" weight with health standards for "optimal" weight, which may vary considerably from one individual to another. One factor that deserves more study is the relationship between body type and weight, and its effects upon health and mortality.

Reubin Andres, Gerontology Research Center, National Institute on Aging, Baltimore City Hospitals, Baltimore, Md. 21224

Dietary Intervention in Adulthood

The classic method of extending life span by dietary means is to prevent young animals from growing old. When dietary intervention is attempted after the animals have matured, nearly all diets shorten life span.

One exception to this rule is a diet devised by Morris H. Ross of the Institute for Cancer Research. When Ross fed middle-aged rats a diet with a protein/calorie ratio of 1:5, under conditions of moderate restriction, he was able to increase their life expectancy significantly. But when he increased or decreased the degree of restriction or modified the protein content of the diet, the life span was shortened rather than lengthened.

This finding suggests that dietary intervention can be used to extend the life span of adults, but that the effect can only be produced under strictly defined conditions. One of the great challenges of nutritional gerontology is to determine the nature of these conditions for individual human beings, and how they change with advancing age.

One method of reducing caloric intake that might be beneficial in adulthood is fasting on alternative days. Animal experiments have shown that such a regimen promotes longevity, and various claims have been made for fasting as a means of cleansing the body of toxic metabolites.

Morris H. Ross, The Institute for Cancer Research, The Fox Chase Cancer Center, Philadelphia, Pa. 19111

Nutritional Manipulation of Aging

Picture yourself at age seventy. Still in reasonably good health, but well past your prime. Suddenly, one day, you make a small change in your diet and you're sent rocketing backwards in time. You feel an explosion of energy that is unlike anything you've ever felt before. Your muscles regain their youthful tone, your posture straightens, your skin

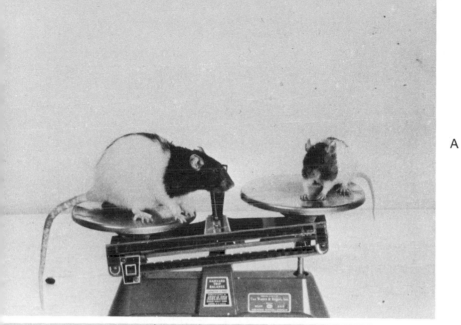

A

B

Effects of tryptophan deficiency on body growth in rats. (a) The small rat on the right was placed upon a tryptophan-deficient diet at twenty-one days of age and maintained on the diet for twenty-two months. The control rat of corresponding age was fed a normal diet (Purina Rat Chow) during this period. (b) After being placed on a normal diet for forty-six days, the same experimental rat *(right)* grew to be almost as large as the control animal.

becomes smoother, dark hair begins to sprout from your head. You find that you can leap and twist with abandon, that your food tastes immeasurably better, and that you have renewed desire for sexual activity.

This scenario closely resembles what happened to experimental rats during a recent study by Paul Segall and Paola Timiras of the University of California at Berkeley. The rats had been kept on a diet deficient in the essential amino acid tryptophan for thirteen months. When they were transferred back to a normal diet at the advanced age of twenty-six months, they displayed clearcut signs of rejuvenation.

They became more energetic, active, and younger in appearance than other rats their age. Of particular note was their remarkable ability to regrow hair that was darker and more abundant than that of young animals. It was a dramatic transformation, says Segall, that was simply astounding.

Unfortunately, the rats' newfound "youth" proved to be short-lived and they soon began to age at a rate reminiscent of Oscar Wilde's *Picture of Dorian Gray*. This pattern of accelerated aging is similar to that reported by Clive McCay in his studies of calorie-restricted animals. (See p. 60.)

The Berkeley scientists have generated many of the same effects caused by underfeeding including growth retardation, postponement of the diseases of aging, and significantly reduced mortality. In an unprecedented achievement, they were able to induce tryptophan-restricted rats to reproduce as late as twenty-eight months of age. (See p. 319.)

Neuroendocrine Effects

Segall and Timiras are particularly interested in the effects of nutritional manipulation on the neuroendocrine system. Since tryptophan is the precursor of the neurotransmitter serotonin, it appears that a reduction in brain serotonin may be a key factor in the aging process. They have also

"Youthful" regrowth of hair in twenty-seven-month-old experimental rats compared to control rats. The experimental rats [*3 and 4 (from left to right)*] were fed a normal diet until thirteen months of age. They were then fed a tryptophan-deficient diet for another thirteen months, and were returned to a normal diet at twenty-six months of age (prior to being shaved). The control rats were fed a normal diet throughout their lives. Note the black stripe of hair on the fourth rat. This animal was entirely black when young, but became lighter with age. The regrowth of youthful black hair on this animal represents a dramatic rejuvenation effect.

been able to produce growth retardation by feeding rats large amounts of PCPA, a drug that inhibits the synthesis of serotonin.

In comparing the neuroendocrine effects of tryptophan deficiency, calorie restriction, and PCPA treatment, Segall and Timiras have concluded that the pituitary gland is inactivated during the period of growth retardation produced by all three regimens. (See p. 50.) Their long-range objective is to discover a safe and effective method of controlling the aging process by altering the balance of neurotransmitter levels in the brain.

Paul E. Segall and Paola S. Timiras, Department of Physiology/Anatomy, University of California at Berkeley, Berkeley, Ca. 94720

Dietary Cholesterol and Heart Disease

When a little man called "Mr. Cholesterol" appears on your TV set, the message is loud and clear. Keep that little fellow out of your kitchen by using margarine instead of butter and you'll protect yourself against heart disease. "Ask your doctor," he suggests, for those skeptical about TV commercials.

If you do ask your doctor, the odds are high he'll back the little fellow by recommending a diet that restricts not only butter, but eggs, whole milk, and meat, while allowing an increase in polyunsaturated fats (margarine and vegetable oils). And if you ask him why he favors such a diet, he'll probably tell you that elevated blood cholesterol is a cause of heart disease, and that low cholesterol diets are supported by the American Heart Association, the American Medical Association, and every other "reputable" medical organization.

With the weight of such authority behind the cholesterol theory of heart disease, you'd think there was incontrovertible evidence of its value. But that is not the case at all. For the cholesterol theory remains an unproved hypothesis, with considerable evidence both for and against it.

There are three lines of evidence that link dietary cholesterol to heart disease:

• The atherosclerotic plaques that lead to heart disease by clogging a person's arteries contain substantial amounts of cholesterol. It's not yet clear why this deposition of cholesterol occurs, but it's reasonable to assume that the process may be related to dietary intake of cholesterol.

• Societies in which people eat low-fat/low-cholesterol diets tend to have a relatively low incidence of heart disease, whereas societies that feature high-fat/high-cholesterol diets tend to have a relatively high incidence of heart disease.

• Laboratory animals fed a high-fat/high-cholesterol diet usually develop more heart disease than animals fed a low-fat/low-cholesterol diet.

There are three lines of evidence that argue against dietary cholesterol as a cause of heart disease:

• In two large-scale studies conducted in Framingham, Massachusetts, and Tecumseh, Michigan, no correlation was found between dietary habits and blood levels of cholesterol and fats. Those who consumed a relatively low-fat/low-cholesterol diet were no more likely to have low blood levels of these substances than those who consumed a relatively high-fat/high-cholesterol diet.

• There have been numerous clinical studies to assess the cardiovascular benefits of low-fat/low-cholesterol diets, both in subjects with a history of heart disease and in subjects with no history of heart disease. None of these studies has yet produced hard evidence that dietary therapy is effective in preventing or treating heart disease.

• In two well-designed clinical trials of drugs that reduce high blood cholesterol, no reduction in the incidence of heart disease was observed over a five-year period among subjects receiving the drugs. During one of these trials (the Coronary Drug Project), the testing of two such drugs—dextrothyroxine and conjugated estrogens—had to be discontinued because of excessive mortality among subjects receiving them.

What Is Cholesterol?

Cholesterol is an alcohol classified as a sterol or lipid (fat-like substance) that is found in all animal fats and oils and egg yolks. The other major category of lipids is triglycerides or fatty acids, which are found in both animal and vegetable oils. Lipids of animal origin are called saturated fats, while most lipids of vegetable origin (except olives, avocados, and nuts) are called polyunsaturated fats.

All lipids are insoluble in water. In order to be transported by the blood, they must first combine with apoproteins and other lipid compounds called phospholipids to form lipoproteins. There are five types of lipoproteins: chylomicrons, very-low-density lipoproteins (VLDL), low-density lipoproteins (LDL), intermediate-density lipoproteins (ILD), and high-density lipoproteins (HDL). The greater the density of a lipoprotein particle, the smaller its size and the higher its protein content.

About 60 percent of the cholesterol in the bloodstream is carried by LDL particles. The average concentration of cholesterol in American adults is from 205 to 225 mg/100 ml. When a person's serum cholesterol level is abnormally high, the condition is called hypercholesterolemia. An elevated serum triglyceride level is called hypertriglyceremia, while the terms hyperlipidemia and hyperlipoproteinemia are used to describe more general high lipid conditions.

Hypercholesterolemia is considered one of the primary risk factors for heart disease. Many people with a high cholesterol level suffer from a genetic disorder called familial hypercholesterolemia. It is more difficult to lower the blood lipid levels of individuals with genetic lipid disorders than individuals with no apparent genetic disorder.

Cholesterol is found to some degree in virtually every tissue in the body. It plays important roles in cellular metabolism, the formation of bile in the liver, and the manufacture of steroid hormones. Only 20 percent of the cholesterol found in the body comes from what we eat; the remaining 80 percent is synthesized within the body, primarily in the liver and intestine.

Cholesterol is essential to our health and well-being. That this vital substance has been implicated in the genesis of atherosclerosis suggests that we are susceptible to breakdowns or malfunctions in one or more of the mechanisms involved in its synthesis, transport, metabolism, and excretion.

When Cholesterol Metabolism Malfunctions

Individuals who inherit one gene for familial hypercholesterolemia have a high serum cholesterol level of 300 to 500 mg/100 ml from birth. They usually begin to develop signs of cardiovascular disease by age thirty. Those who inherit two copies of the defective gene—about one in 500—have an extremely high level of serum cholesterol, often exceeding 800 mg/100 ml. In such individuals, the signs of cardiovascular disease usually develop before age twenty.

The mechanism that malfunctions in familial hypercholesterolemia has been uncovered in a series of tissue culture experiments by Michael S. Brown and Joseph L. Goldstein of the University of Texas. They've found that human cells contain receptors that bind or capture low-density lipoproteins (LDL) to control the amount of cholesterol that flows in and out of cells.

When there is not enough cholesterol in the cells, there is an increase in the synthesis of LDL receptors, which increases the amount of cholesterol entering the cells. When sufficient cholesterol has accumulated, the synthesis of LDL receptors is suppressed, which reduces the amount of cholesterol entering the cells. By this feedback mechanism, the cells obtain sufficient cholesterol for membrane growth and replenishment, but do not accumulate an excessive amount.

In individuals with familial hypercholesterolemia, however, there is a reduction or absence of functional LDL receptors that leads to three metabolic abnormalities: an inappropriately high level of cholesterol production; an overproduction of low-density lipoproteins; and a reduction in the rate of cholesterol degradation. The result is an unusually high level of serum cholesterol, which markedly increases the risk of atherosclerosis and heart disease.

Thus far, functional LDL receptors have been identified in cultured human fibroblasts, lymphocytes, and aortic smooth muscle cells. One possible explanation for the prevalence of atherosclerosis in genetically normal individuals is a breakdown in LDL receptor function. Such a breakdown might be a consequence of excess dietary lipids, nutritional deficiency, environmental toxicity, or aging.

Michael S. Brown and Joseph L. Goldstein, Division of Medical Genetics, University of Texas Health Science Center at Dallas, Dallas, Tx. 75235

Heart Disease: Pathology or Aging Disorder?
Researchers generally agree that heart disease is a pathology rather than a part of normal aging. Their search for the cause of heart disease is confined largely to such factors as

diet, mechanical injury, and metabolic disorder. Rarely do they even consider the role of aging in the genesis of heart disease.

Yet there are age-related changes that make us increasingly vulnerable to heart disease with advancing age. Hruza and Zbuzkova found that the excretion of cholesterol from old rats is as much as 70 percent slower than from young rats. By surgically connecting the bodies of old and young rats (parabiosis), they were able to increase the excretion of cholesterol in the old animals, so that the difference between young and old partners was much smaller than between separate animals.

They also showed that the decreased turnover of cholesterol in old rats may be due, in part, to poorer sensitivity to the hormones thyroxine and insulin. They speculated that excretion of cholesterol may be easier in young animals because cholesterol is bound more loosely to the lipoproteins in their blood.

Evidence in Humans

When it comes to humans, there is convincing evidence that blood lipid levels increase steadily with advancing age in healthy individuals. In a study of 1,492 healthy men, the mean concentration of lipids increased from 160-170 mg/100 ml for subjects in their twenties to 250-260 mg/100 ml for subjects in their fifties.

Postmortem studies have shown that the most prominent lipids in young healthy arteries are phospholipids and the least prominent are cholesterol esters and free cholesterol. By age sixty-five, however, a dramatic reversal occurs, with phospholipids declining to half their previous value and cholesterol esters assuming the predominant position.

In an analysis of the tissues of men and women whose death was unrelated to cardiovascular disease, J. R. Crouse of Rockefeller University found striking age-related differences in cholesterol distribution. The mean concentration of cholesterol in subjects aged sixty to eighty was from 23 to 46 percent higher than in subjects aged twenty to forty, according to the type of tissue studied.

The evidence presented here is not to suggest that heart disease is an inevitable consequence of aging, only that we become increasingly susceptible to heart disease as we grow older, a fact that needs to be taken more seriously to prevent or treat the disease.

Zdenek Hruza, Department of Pathology, New York University School of Medicine, New York, N.Y. 10016

J. R. Crouse, The Rockefeller University, York Ave. and 66th St., New York, N.Y. 10021

How the Body Protects Against Heart Disease
When cholesterol has done its job in your cells, it must be removed efficiently and transported to the liver for excretion. If your body's sanitation system is not up to par, your cells become clogged with used-up cholesterol. When such a buildup occurs in the smooth muscle cells of the arteries, we see the formation of fatty streaks, which may develop into atherosclerotic plaques.

Apparently, the job of removing cholesterol from cells is performed primarily by high-density lipoproteins (HDL)— one of the by-products of the marriage between fat and protein that enables us to make use of essential, but insoluble lipids. Biochemical studies have shown that the amount of cholesterol in the body increases with decreasing serum HDL levels and, conversely, that it decreases as serum HDL is raised.

Proposed Mechanisms of Action
Several mechanisms have been proposed to explain the inverse correlation between HDL and cholesterol. First is that HDL acts as a scavenger for cholesterol by dislodging it from cells and then carrying it to the liver where it can be

excreted. According to this view, the higher the blood level of HDL, the greater the capacity of the body to dispose of cholesterol that would otherwise accumulate in the cells.

Second is the ability of HDL to decrease the uptake of cholesterol-containing LDL particles into the smooth muscle cells of the arteries by interfering with LDL receptor site activity. Thomas A. Carew and associates have found that cultured arterial smooth muscle cells can be inhibited from capturing LDL when HDL is added to the culture medium, with the more HDL added the greater the reduction in LDL.

Third is the fact that HDL activates the enzyme lipoprotein lipase, which induces the breakdown of triglyceride-rich chylomicrons and VLDL particles. As a result of this breakdown, intermediate-size lipoprotein particles (IDL) are formed and either converted into LDL or transported to the liver for excretion. When blood concentration of HDL is high, triglyceride levels are low, which indicates that HDL may also serve as a scavenger for excess fatty acids.

Epidemiologic Studies

Epidemiologic studies have confirmed that high blood levels of HDL are correlated with a low incidence of heart disease. In one study, the relation between HDL levels and coronary heart disease (CHD) was assessed in five groups including: general population samples in Framingham, Massachusetts, and Evans County, Georgia, civil service employees in Albany, New York, and men of Japanese ancestry in Honolulu and San Francisco.

In each of these groups, the mean HDL levels were significantly lower in subjects with coronary heart disease than in subjects free of heart disease. The CHD prevalence was about double for subjects with an HDL level of 30 mg/ 100 ml than for subjects with an HDL level of 60 mg/ 100 ml.

These studies demonstrate that the incidence of heart disease falls with increasing blood levels of HDL, even when such risk factors as obesity, cigarette smoking, and high blood pressure are taken into account. Moreover, HDL levels are also related to such other risk factors as diabetes, physical inactivity, and sex. Both diabetics and inactive persons have relatively low levels of HDL, and women have substantially higher HDL levels than men.

HDL levels are about the same in men and women until age seventeen or eighteen. At that time, there is a sharp, abrupt fall of HDL of 10 to 20 percent in men. HDL in men remains at this lowered level for the next three or four decades; while in women, HDL is stable or rises slowly during this period.

The difference in HDL levels may be one reason men are so much likelier than women to suffer heart attacks, particularly before the onset of menopause. After age fifty, HDL levels go down significantly in both sexes, which helps to explain the increase of heart disease with advancing age.

Thus far, no apparent correlation has been shown between diet and HDL levels. While low-fat/low-cholesterol diets can lower blood levels of LDL, it has yet to be demonstrated that they can raise HDL levels. Exercise, on the other hand, has been shown to be effective in raising HDL levels (see p. 175), which may explain the emerging evidence that it protects against heart disease.

Thomas E. Carew, Division of Metabolic Disease, University of California, San Diego, La Jolla, Ca. 92037

George G. Rhoads, Kuakini Hospital, 347 N. Kuakini, Honolulu, Hi. 96817

Reversing Atherosclerosis

There is a growing body of evidence—in lower animals, nonhuman primates, and humans—that the atherosclerotic process can be reversed, even at highly advanced stages of development. Robert Wissler of the University of Chicago has shown that lowering the blood cholesterol levels of rhe-

POSSIBLE ROLE OF HDL IN CHOLESTEROL TRANSPORT FROM PERIPHERAL TISSUE TO LIVER

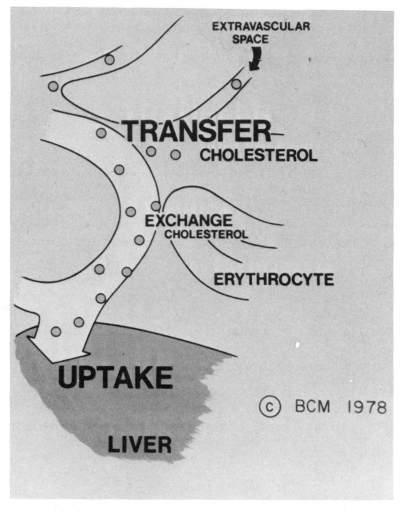

Cholesterol is synthesized by cells (peripheral tissue) in various parts of the body and must be transported to the liver to be degraded and/or excreted. After being deposited in the space between cells (extravascular space), cholesterol is picked up by high-density lipoproteins (HDL), which carry it to the liver. HDL also remove cholesterol from erythrocytes (red cells) in the blood for transport to the liver.

sus monkeys to 140 mg/100 ml can substantially reduce the size of experimentally induced plaques similar to those that develop spontaneously in humans.

David Blankenhorn of the University of Southern California has been working with aerospace engineers to make sequential measurements of atherosclerotic lesions in humans. They have documented regression of the disease as a result of low-fat/low-cholesterol diets, drug therapy, and vigorous exercise in patients who have already suffered heart attacks.

When scientists examine the arteries of animals or humans who have undergone reversal of atherosclerosis, they find that much of the lipid in the plaques has disappeared, and that the remaining fibrous tissue and cells have "condensed" and been "remodeled" in a manner similar to that in fracture- or wound-healing.

The evidence points to the figure of 150 mg/100 ml as the watershed level in conferring protection against atherosclerosis. It seems that by achieving a cholesterol level of 150 mg/100 ml or lower—by whatever means—we can effectively protect ourselves against atherosclerosis.

Robert W. Wissler, Department of Pathology, University of Chicago, Chicago, Il. 60637

David H. Blankenhorn, Department of Medicine, University of Southern California, Los Angeles, Ca. 90033

The Longevity Center

Recent data from the Longevity Center in California suggests that extreme restriction of fat and cholesterol combined with regular exercise can produce dramatic therapeutic benefits in patients recovering from heart attacks.

The Longevity Center program—which is the brainchild of its founder Nathan Pritikin—restructures the typical American diet, which consists of 40-45 percent fat, 12-15 percent protein, 40-45 percent carbohydrate, 600-750 mg/day of cholesterol, and 5-10 gm/day of salt. Instead, patients are placed on a 75 percent carbohydrate diet, which includes a maximum of 10 percent fat, 25 mg/day of cholesterol, and 3 gm/day of salt.

The carbohydrates in the Longevity Center diet are supplied from vegetables, legumes, tubers, whole grains, and raw fruits. Protein is derived almost entirely from vegetable sources; abstinence from smoking, caffeine, and alcohol is encouraged; and regular exercise is an integral part of the program.

In an attempt to document reports of "remarkable improvement" in Longevity Center patients, a study was conducted by the Loma Linda University Survey Research Service on all primary patients attending the center at least twenty-one consecutive days from April, 1976, to October, 1977. Of the 893 patients included in the study, two thirds suffered from atherosclerotic heart disease and one third had a history of myocardial infarction.

The results showed significant reductions in serum cholesterol and triglycerides, blood pressure, cigarette smoking, weight, and blood glucose. In general, the greatest reductions occurred in patients with the highest initial values. By the end of the session, the study subjects were walking an average of six miles per day, and all fifty-five patients who had been taking cholesterol-reducing drugs (clofibrate or cholestyramine) no longer required the drugs.

Longevity Center of California, 1910 Ocean Front Walk, Santa Monica, Ca. 90405

Longevity Center of Florida, Americana, 9701 Collins Ave., Bal Harbour, Fl. 33154

"Milk Factor" Lowers Cholesterol Levels

In their frenzy to lower blood cholesterol levels, many health-conscious consumers have shyed away from whole-milk and milk products because of their relatively high cholesterol and fat content. However, data presented by George Mann of Vanderbilt University suggest that the avoidance of whole-milk products may be a mistake.

When studying the Maasai warriors in Africa, Mann observed that very large daily intakes of fermented cow's milk (yogurt) caused their levels of serum cholesterol—already exceedingly low by western standards—to drop even more.

When he returned to the United States, Mann recruited twenty-six subjects (twenty men and six women), age twenty-four to fifty-five, and began to feed them large amounts of yogurt, as much as four liters daily for twelve consecutive days. The subjects were asked to keep their body weight, activity level, and dietary intake of cholesterol—exclusive of that in the yogurt—at their usual levels. At the beginning of the study, all subjects had normal serum cholesterol levels by U.S. standards (below 275 mg/100 ml).

The yogurt diet, which contained a substantial amount of cholesterol, produced a steady decrease in serum cholesterol levels of up to thirty-seven percent by the sixteenth day after completion of the feeding trial. Afterwards, serum cholesterol rose slowly to near the original levels, even while a second twelve-day trial was begun. But soon the high-yogurt diet once again succeeded in reducing cholesterol levels by 30 percent.

Mann and C. R. Nair then fed large amounts of milk powder to rats receiving a high-cholesterol diet and found a similar cholesterol-lowering effect. They also were able to lower cholesterol levels in rats by including the enzyme hydroxymethyl glutarate (HMG) in the diet.

HMG is known to regulate the synthesis of cholesterol, both in animals and humans, by inhibiting the action of another enzyme (hydroxymethyl glutaryl CoA reductase). Mann believes that HMG may be the "milk factor" that lowers serum cholesterol in humans.

George V. Mann, Departments of Biochemistry and Medicine, Vanderbilt University School of Medicine, Nashville, Tn. 37232

Can Lecithin Lower Plasma Cholesterol?

"Health food" devotees have long advocated dietary lecithin as an "antidote" for elevated plasma cholesterol. It's widely believed, for example, that the lecithin in eggs counteracts their high cholesterol content. Lecithin is also commonly taken in capsule form, often at high doses, because of its alleged anti-cholesterol effect.

The available evidence concerning lecithin's effect on plasma cholesterol is inconclusive. Early clinical trials suggested that soybean lecithin has cholesterol-lowering effects, but later studies failed to confirm this finding.

An open clinical trial was recently conducted at St. Vincent's Hospital in New South Wales to evaluate the cholesterol-lowering potential of high doses (20-30 grams/day) of oral lecithin. Three healthy subjects and seven patients with hypercholesterolemia were studied for periods ranging from eight weeks to eleven months.

In one of the three healthy subjects and in three of the seven patients, there was a significant fall in plasma cholesterol of from 10-18 percent, with little or no effect in the other subjects.

Evidence was presented that oral lecithin may reduce cholesterol by acting as a source of linoleic acid—a polyunsaturated fat contained in safflower oil, which has been shown to lower cholesterol levels.

Two of the patients showed still lower cholesterol levels (21 and 22 percent) when given a combination of lecithin and clofibrate—a commonly used anti-cholesterol drug.

L. A. Simons, Medical Professional Unit, St. Vincent's Hospital, Darlinghurst, New South Wales, 2010

Do Low Cholesterol Diets Promote Cancer?

In 1971, the public was startled to hear that a low-cholesterol diet aimed at preventing heart disease may have inadvertently promoted cancer. It was reported that 9.7 percent, or forty-one of the subjects in a clinical trial at a Los Angeles V.A. hospital, had died from cancer compared with 7.1 percent or thirty of the subjects on the control diet.

Subsequent analysis of similar trials in Oslo, London, Helsinki, and Faribault, Minnesota, failed to substantiate this finding. Only in the Oslo study could an association be shown between low cholesterol and cancer. In the London study, on the other hand, there was only one death from cancer in the experimental group compared with eight deaths from cancer in the control group.

Based upon this evidence, the medical establishment proceeded to reassure the public about the "safety" of low-cholesterol diets. Yet the issue is still not resolved because of evidence that polyunsaturated fats may be more carcinogenic than saturated fats.

Kenneth K. Carroll has shown an increase in mammary tumors induced by the carcinogen DMBA in rats fed a high polyunsaturated fat diet (corn oil) compared with low-fat or high-saturated fat diets. The increase in tumor yield occurred only when the corn oil diet was fed to the rats shortly after treatment with DMBA; if the diet was delayed for a month, there was little or no increase in the number of tumors.

When Hopkins and West fed rats a polyunsaturated (sunflower seed oil) diet, the animals developed significantly more DMBA-inducted mammary and skin tumors than rats fed a saturated fat (tallow) diet. Moreover, rats transferred from saturated to polyunsaturated fats immediately after DMBA administration developed more tumors than rats transferred from polyunsaturated to saturated fats.

These findings suggest that polyunsaturated fats may enhance or stimulate the activity of carcinogens within the body. They further suggest that individuals wishing to protect themselves against both heart disease and cancer might eat a diet low in all types of fat, rather than one in which polyunsaturated fats are substituted for saturated fats.

One explanation for the possible tumor-promoting effect of polyunsaturated fats is that the oxidation of these fats generates damaging free radicals. (See p. 39.) There is experimental evidence that antioxidant therapy can inhibit free radical activity. (See p. 131.)

Kenneth K. Carroll, Department of Biochemistry, University of Western Ontario, London, Ontario, Canada N6A 5C1

Garry J. Hopkins and Clive E. West, Department of Experimental Pathology, John Curtin School of Medical Research, The Australian National University, P.O. Box 334, Canberra City, A.C.T., 2601, Australia

Alcohol May Be Good for Your Heart

A report from the National Heart, Lung, and Blood Institute indicates that alcohol consumption affects lipid metabolism in a positive way that may protect against coronary heart disease (CHD). The report is based upon data collected from an ongoing, long-term project called the Cooperative Lipoprotein Phenotyping Study, which includes groups in Albany, New York; Evans County, Georgia; Framington, Massachusetts; Honolulu; and San Francisco.

Subjects were asked how many bottles of beer, three- to four-ounce glasses of wine or sake, and drinks of liquor they consume in an average week. The reported intake was converted to ounces of alcohol by assuming that a can of beer has 0.44 oz alcohol, a glass of wine, 0.40 oz and a measure of liquor, 0.57 oz. Subjects were then given blood tests to determine their plasma cholesterol and triglyceride levels and how these lipids break down into lipoprotein fractions.

The major finding of the study was a strong positive correlation between alcohol consumption and HDL levels, even at relatively low levels of intake. Subjects who drank five to six ounces of alcohol a week had HDL levels about 10 percent higher than subjects who did not drink alcohol at all. Since elevated HDL has been linked to reduced CHD mortality (see p. 77), it seems that alcohol may protect against heart disease.

Tavia Gordon, National Heart, Lung, and Blood Institute, Landow Bldg., Rm. C841, 7910 Woodmont Ave., Bethesda, Md. 20014

What Do Alcoholics Die of?

High alcohol consumption has detrimental effects on most organs and systems in the body. While alcoholism has traditionally been linked to liver disease, it appears that alcohol toxicity also affects the heart, lungs, pancreas, and brain.

In a study of the pathology of alcoholism, G. E. Corrigan performed or supervised autopsies of 100 alcoholic cadavers and 100 nonalcoholic cadavers and compared the two groups.

He found that alcoholics were afflicted with far more lesions than nonalcoholics. For example, eighty-four alcoholic cadavers had three to five lesions compared with only twenty-eight nonalcoholic cadavers. The majority of the nonalcoholic cadavers had only zero to two lesions, whereas all but one alcoholic cadaver had at least two lesions.

The alcoholic group showed significantly greater damage than the nonalcoholic group in most vital organs. Alcoholics had seventy-five liver lesions compared to nineteen for controls, seventy-one pancreas lesions compared with twenty-four for controls, forty-nine brain lesions compared with thirteen for controls, eighty heart lesions compared with fifty-one for controls, and fifty-seven lung lesions compared with twenty-eight for controls.

These findings suggest that excessive alcohol consumption damages most vital organs and probably contributes to the diseases that afflict these organs. In the case of the kidney, however, Corrigan found that more nonalcoholics (fifty-two) had glomerular disease than alcoholics (thirty-five), and that forty-four alcoholics showed no signs of kidney disease compared with only twenty-nine nonalcoholics.

G. E. Corrigan, Department of Pathology, St. Louis University College of Medicine, St. Louis, Mo. 63104

How Sugar Affects Our Health

In recent years, many health-conscious people have latched onto the idea that sugar (sucrose) is bad for their health. The cover of the book *Sweet and Dangerous* by John Yudkin—the English scientist most responsible for this belief—illustrates it beautifully. A cup of white sugar that is overflowing sits on a black table, with a red skull-and-crossbones painted on its side. The message is clear: "sugar is poison and eating it will kill you."

A look at the evidence, however, suggests that the dangers of sugar may be more myth than reality. According to Yudkin, sugar is at least partially responsible for a long list of maladies, but his most serious charge is that sugar is a major cause of heart disease—a notion that he supports with three arguments:

• The death rate from coronary heart disease in various countries is correlated with sugar consumption in these countries.

• Men afflicted with CHD consume an unusually large amount of sugar.

• Sugar elevates serum lipids when compared with starch and other complex carbohydrates.

The relationship between the death rate from CHD and sugar consumption is based upon calculations by Yudkin from general data collected from fifteen countries. However, Yudkin's conclusion is open to question, argues nutritionist Francisco Grande, because there is also a correlation between the CHD death rate and fat consumption in these countries, which provides an alternative explanation to Yudkin's indictment of sugar.

Grande goes on to list a number of countries where the data contradict Yudkin's hypothesis. These include Cuba, Venezuela, Colombia, Costa Rica, and Honduras, where sugar consumption is high, but CHD is low; Finland and Sweden, where sugar consumption is similar, but the incidence of CHD is higher in Finland; South Africa, where caucasians in the northern part of Johannesburg consume less sugar but have a higher CHD death rate than caucasians in the southern part of the city; and the United States, where the tremendous rise in CHD mortality between 1920 and 1960 did not reflect a proportionate rise in sugar consumption.

With regard to Yudkin's claim of higher sugar consumption in CHD patients, most studies show no significant differences in sugar intake between coronary patients and healthy controls, while several studies show significantly lower sugar intake in coronary patients than in controls. Even Yudkin's own data in this area are open to question because the differences he found in sugar consumption were due to unusually low sugar intake in controls, rather than abnormally high sugar intake in patients.

Effects of Sugar Intake

It's true that sugar can raise serum lipid levels, but primarily in subjects who already have elevated lipid levels, or in normal subjects given unusually large amounts of sugar. Most studies show little or no change in the blood lipid levels of normal subjects given diets containing an amount of sugar comparable to that consumed under real-life conditions.

Another line of evidence that tends to absolve sugar from any significant role in heart disease is the failure of scientists to induce atherosclerosis in animals fed high-sucrose diets.

On the other hand, it's been relatively easy to induce atherosclerosis with high-fat diets, though the validity of these results for humans is open to question. (See p. 72.)

Yudkin also proposes that sugar is a major cause of diabetes—a claim for which there is even less supportive evidence than for heart disease. The origin of sugar's alleged role in diabetes can be traced to the fact that for many years diabetics were placed on low-carbohydrate diets because of the threat of ketoacidosis—the principal cause of death among diabetics a half-century ago.

But today, with insulin available to control ketoacidosis, and most diabetics dying of cardiovascular disease, it's been demonstrated that diabetics need carbohydrates as much as anyone. Studies have shown that diabetics exhibit improved glucose tolerance after eating high-carbohydrate meals, and that sugar intake can "turn on" critical liver enzymes necessary for the metabolism of glucose.

Reasons to Limit Sugar Intake

Nevertheless, there are good reasons to guard against high sugar intake, even if sugar isn't the arch villain that sugarophobes make it out to be.

The best reason to avoid sugar is its high calorie content. Eating a lot of sugar can put on pounds without corresponding nutritional benefits. Sugar does not contain the vitamins and minerals we need, which must be derived from other sources. So if sugar per se is probably not a cause of heart disease or diabetes, it can be a contributing factor to obesity, which is linked to both these diseases.

Furthermore, sugar has also been linked to the occurrence of dental caries. And it can precipitate bouts of hypoglycemia (low blood sugar) in individuals predisposed to this condition.

The main problem concerning sugar's place in the diet is its tremendous appeal as a sweetener. Most people have a "sweet tooth" and many of us suffer from an "addiction" to sweetness. As a result, food companies have been putting increasing amounts of sugar in most processed foods. With such "hidden" sources of sugar in the diet as ketchup, salad dressing, canned vegetables, and even salt (sugar is commonly added to salt to improve the taste), it has become very easy for us to consume more sugar than we should.

One answer to the problem would be safe and palatable, but nonfattening, artificial sweeteners. However, progress in this area has been slowed by the recent "hysteria" over saccharin and cyclamates and the general, though largely undeserved, antagonism toward artificial food additives. (See p. 119.)

John Yudkin, Department of Nutrition, London University, London, England

Francisco Grande, Institute of Biochemistry and Nutrition, Fundacion Cuenca Villoro Gascon de Gotor 4, Zaragoza 6, Spain

Dietary Salt and Blood Pressure

High blood pressure, or hypertension, is virtually unknown in all primitive societies. Edward D. Freis of Georgetown University points out that an absence of hypertension and a failure of blood pressure to rise with age have been observed in New Guinea, the highlands of Malaysia, the Easter Islands, the Amazon Basin, the San Blas Islands of Panama, rural Uganda, and the Kalahari Desert of Africa.

In contrast, there is a high prevalence of hypertension in virtually all civilized societies. The exclusive occurrence of hypertension in civilized societies has been linked to a host of dietary and environmental factors, but the one common denominator among all hypertensive populations appears to be dietary salt. Where salt intake is high, hypertension is common; where salt intake is low, hypertension is rare.

How Salt Raises Blood Pressure

Dietary salt goes primarily to the extracellular space where it combines with water to form extracellular fluid (ECF). This fluid must be excreted through the kidneys via a process that is under neural and hormonal regulation. The more salt a person takes in, the greater the stress on the system.

According to Freis, the increase in urine volume that results from the need to excrete excess fluid can produce a chronic elevation in blood pressure—particularly in individuals who require a higher-than-normal perfusion pressure to maintain ECF homeostasis. Freis also feels that blood pressure tends to rise in older people because of an age-related decrease in their ability to maintain ECF homeostasis in the face of high salt intake—either because of kidney deterioration or declining regulatory capacity.

Apparently, it's necessary to reduce salt intake to 1 gram/day or less in order to control hypertension. In several studies that failed to show a correlation between dietary salt and blood pressure, intake was evaluated primarily on the basis of whether a saltshaker was used. Even the "low-salt" groups in these studies received too much salt from the processed foods they ate. In studies of severe salt restriction, on the other hand, there have been highly significant reductions in blood pressure.

Edward D. Freis, Veterans Administration Hospital, 50 Irving St. N.W., Washington, D.C. 20011

The Health Benefits of Dietary Fiber

In order to inhibit waste elimination in outer space, astronauts are fed a diet that is almost free of fiber. As a result, they develop extreme constipation, with five or six days elapsing between bowel movements. While this approach helps to keep spacesuits clean during extraterrestrial maneuvers, it's not a good idea for those of us who remain earthbound.

Denis P. Burkitt has presented evidence that the lack of fiber in modern western diets may be partly responsible for many of the "diseases of civilization." These include cancer of the colon and rectum, diverticular disease of the colon, and appendicitis. He also suggests that fiber-depleted diets may contribute indirectly to obesity, diabetes, and coronary heart disease.

Burkitt's major selling point is that these disorders—particularly noninfective diseases of the bowel—are rare in countries where the populace consumes a high-fiber diet, and quite common in countries where a low-fiber diet is consumed. For example, in countries such as the United States, where diets are high in refined carbohydrates, the incidence of bowel cancer is about ten times that in African countries, where large amounts of unrefined grains—the major source of dietary fiber—are eaten.

That these differences in disease pattern are environmental rather than genetic in origin is suggested by the fact that American blacks get bowel cancer as often as American whites. Thus, the lower bowel cancer rate among African blacks appears to be the result of their higher fiber intake, or of some other environmental factor.

There have also been reports that dietary fiber lowers blood cholesterol levels. A recent study by Kay and Truswell showed that citrus pectin incorporated into a mixture of sugar, raspberries, and orange juice reduced plasma choles terol levels by a mean of 13 percent and improved fecal fat excretion by 44 percent when added to the diet for three weeks. Pectin is a type of fiber found in fruits and vegetables.

Denis P. Burkitt, 172 Tottenham Court Rd., London W1P 9LG, England

Ruth M. Kay, Department of Family Studies, University of Guelph, Guelph, Ontario, N1G 2W1, Canada

Nutritional Individuality and Health

We all need protein, carbohydrate, fat, vitamins, and minerals to survive, but the amounts of each type of nutrient required for optimal health varies from one individual to another.

Studies have shown that individual animals respond to the same diet in different ways. Underfeeding generally extends the life span of rats, for example, but some animals die before they're one year old, while others live for more than five years. Altering the nutritional content of the diet introduces even more variability in its effects upon health and longevity.

The effect of underfeeding on the incidence of cancer varies according to the type of tumor. Some tumors are so sensitive to low-calorie diets that they occur infrequently or not at all, whereas others are unaffected by such diets. A few tumors occur more frequently in underfed animals.

The risk of developing cancer can be appreciably modified by changing the composition of the diet. A five-fold increase in the proportion of protein leads to a dramatic increase in the incidence of kidney, heart, and prostate tumors in rats. And an increase in dietary fat increases the incidence of mammary tumors in mice.

When you consider the wide variety of foods that we consume, it's likely we display even greater individuality in response to diet than laboratory animals. It's time we spent more time on individual health and longevity and less time in pursuit of "magic" formula diets.

Chapter 3
Environmental Stress and Longevity

What Is Stress?

In 1925, Hans Selye noticed that all sick persons display common symptoms, such as fatigue, aching bones and joints, fever, and loss of appetite and weight. He went on to develop the concept of stress—the common denominator of the body's adaptive reactions to any demand, or "the rate of wear-and-tear caused by life."

Among the agents that commonly cause stress are infection, intoxication, trauma, nervous strain, heat, cold, muscular fatigue, polluted air, and radiation. Though the specific actions of these agents are different, they all share the ability to place the body in a state of stress.

According to Selye, the body reacts to stress by going through a series of changes called the general adaptation syndrome (GAS). First is the alarm reaction, when the body mobilizes its defenses against the stressor agent. At this time, there is a large increase in the release of adrenaline and noradrenaline, which leads to accelerated heartbeat, elevated blood pressure, diversion of bloodflow from the skin and gut to the muscles, and dilation of the lungs to increase respiratory effort.

The second stage of the GAS is resistance to the stressor, in which the body adapts to the challenge. This stage may be characterized by increased immune system activity where stress is induced by infective agents, by neuromuscular changes in response to physically induced stress, by neuroendocrine adaptation to emotionally induced stress—or by a combination of these responses.

95

The third stage is exhaustion, which occurs when the body's defenses can no longer cope with severe or prolonged stress. This stage is characterized by loss of homeostasis, which can lead to death if stress continues unabated. Fortunately, the body is usually able to adapt to stress before stage three is reached.

As Selye defines it, stress is an essential part of life that can lead to great joy and fulfillment if we learn to adjust to its ever-changing presence. If, on the other hand, we fail to adjust to stress appropriately, we become vulnerable to a host of physical and mental disorders.

Hans Selye, Institute of Experimental Medicine and Surgery, University of Montreal, Montreal, Quebec, Canada H3C 3J7

The Need for Sleep

Thomas Edison once said he invented the electric light bulb so people wouldn't have to sleep. Edison himself was apparently able to function on an average of only two hours of sleep a night. However, most people require far more sleep than Edison did, though some of us would like to emulate his sleep habits if we could.

The vast majority of people require five to ten hours of sleep per day, though most of us can function on little or no sleep for a day or two. We require periods of deep, relatively undisturbed sleep, and more active periods of dreaming. Studies have shown that dreaming is essential to health. Anyone deprived of dream sleep for an extended period suffers serious mental and physical consequences.

Ever since Freud proposed that dreams represent the expression of emotions and ideas repressed during the waking state, scientists have sought to explain the mental activity that occurs while we sleep. Current theories suggest that sleep enables us to process and consolidate information that accumulates in the brain during wakefulness. Some scientists liken the sleeping organism to a computer that locks its input after receiving an excess of information and then proceeds to create order out of apparent chaos. Others point to evidence that even during sleep, the brain is able to receive, evaluate, and respond to new information.

Soviet scientist T. N. Oniani proposes that every phase of the sleep-wakefulness cycle serves to decrease anti-homeostatic factors—perhaps shifts in the balance of neuroendocrine hormones—created in the previous phase, while creating new phase-specific anti-homeostatic factors, which have to be removed during the next phase. According to this view, rest is not the function of sleep alone, or any of its phases, but is the product of the entire sleep-wakefulness cycle.

Thus, too much sleep may be as bad as too little sleep, even if the detrimental effects of excess sleep differ from those of inadequate sleep. This conclusion is supported by studies showing that people who average ten or more hours, or less than six hours of sleep per day, have a somewhat shorter life expectancy than people who average six to eight hours of sleep per day.

It has yet to be determined whether the life-shortening effect associated with sleeping fewer or more hours is a consequence of sleep itself, or is attributable to other factors.

T. N. Oniani, Beritashvile Institute of Physiology, Georgian Academy of Science, Tbilisi, U.S.S.R.

What's the Safest Day of the Week?

Recently, a fifteen-year-old girl seized her rifle and started shooting at children and teachers in front of a California elementary school. When she was finally caught after several killings, she was asked why she did it. "Because it was Monday," was her reply.

Actually, the homicide rate is highest on Saturday, but the suicide rate—which best reflects feelings of despair—is, in fact, highest on Monday. And when it comes to deaths from heart attacks, strokes, respiratory diseases, and diabetes, "blue" Monday heads the list.

When it comes to the safest day of the week, there's a three-way tie among Tuesday, Wednesday, and Thursday—the days when so many of us are absorbed in tranquilizing routines.

Interestingly, the death rate from heart attacks is exceptionally high on three national holidays—Independence Day, Christmas Day, and New Year's Day—and is exceptionally low on Memorial Day and Labor Day.

Eugene Rogot, Epidemiology Branch, Division of Heart and Vascular Diseases, National Heart and Lung Institute, Landow Bldg., Room C-825, Bethesda, Md. 20014

Emotional Stress and Heart Disease

In recent years, heart disease has been linked to a stress-producing personality pattern called "type A behavior." Individuals who follow this pattern—as described by Meyer Friedman and Ray H. Rosenman in their book *Type A Behavior and Your Heart*—display excessive competitive drive, impatience, and a harrying sense of time urgency. They also frequently exhibit free-floating hostility and deep-seated insecurity. In contrast, individuals who display type B behavior are calm, relaxed, confident, and harbor no free-floating hostility.

According to Friedman and Rosenman, type A individuals suffer three to seven times more coronary heart disease than type B individuals—even when their diets and exercise habits are almost identical—because they are in a perpetual state of emotional stress. As a result, they generate excessive hormone secretion, which produces elevated blood cholesterol and lipid levels, a decrease in cholesterol excretion capacity, a prediabetic state, and an increased tendency to form blood clots.

A fundamental problem in evaluating the stress and personality theory of coronary heart disease is the difficulty of differentiating between personality types. Although Friedman and Rosenman claim that ninety percent of Americans have either type A or type B personalities, the opposite seems true—that the vast majority of persons are a combination of both personality types.

Meyer Friedman and Ray H. Rosenman, Mt. Zion Hospital and Medical Center, San Francisco, Ca. 94120

Thyroid Deficiency and Heart Disease

Broda O. Barnes, a Colorado physician, who has been treating thyroid disorders for forty-two years, believes that stress-prone individuals suffer from thyroid deficiency, which is the underlying cause of their susceptibility to heart attacks. Barnes points to evidence that removal of the thyroid gland often leads to atherosclerosis in both animals and humans.

He contends that currently used thyroid function tests are inadequate because they measure the amount of thyroid hormones in the bloodstream rather than in the cells. The result, he says, is that "thyroid deficiency is the most common illness entering the physician's office and is the diagnosis most often missed."

Barnes prefers to use the measurement of body temperature as an indicator of thyroid deficiency, since patients with hypothyroidism tend to have below-normal temperatures. Although low temperature can be caused by other factors as well, he feels that any person with a chronically low temperature is a good bet to be suffering from thyroid deficiency.

Reduced body temperature has been linked to increased life span in several "cold-blooded" species (see p. 160), but it's possible that low body temperature could have a life-shortening effect in individuals suffering from thyroid deficiency and a life-prolonging effect in individuals with normal thyroid function. It's also possible that the Barnes model for heart disease is related to the mysterious "pituitary factor" that Donner Denckla suggests as a cause of aging. (See p. 53.)

Broda O. Barnes, 2838 Elizabeth, Ft. Collins, Co. 80521

Sex Hormones and Heart Disease

Women have fewer heart attacks than men. Scientists have long suspected that the higher ratio of estrogen to testosterone (E/T) in women exerts a protective effect against heart disease. Presumably, such an advantage would be lost after menopause when there is a marked decline of estrogen production in women.

A recent study showed twice the number of cardiovascular events among postmenopausal women than among premenopausal women of approximately the same age—a finding that tends to support this theory. However, when men with previous heart attacks have been treated with estrogen, they've exhibited a subsequent rise in heart attacks.

Now there is evidence supporting the opposite theory— that a higher than normal estrogen to testosterone ratio may be a cause of heart attacks in men. This evidence comes from a study of fifteen myocardial infarction (heart attack) victims and thirteen age-matched controls by Gerald B. Phillips of Columbia University. Phillips found that men who had suffered heart attacks prior to age forty-three had higher levels of estradiol (the most active form of estrogen) in their blood than men who had not had heart attacks.

Phillips also found an elevated E/T ratio linked to several other risk factors for heart disease including abnormal glucose (sugar) tolerance, abnormal insulin response, and elevated serum cholesterol and triglycerides. As he sees it, these symptoms comprise a glucose-insulin-lipid defect that accompanies myocardial infarction as a consequence of an altered sex hormone balance in men.

Gerald B. Phillips, Columbia University College of Physicians and Surgeons, Roosevelt Hospital, New York, N.Y. 10019

Water Hardness and Heart Attacks

Investigators in several parts of the world have shown that residents of areas with soft-water supplies have a higher death rate from ischemic heart disease (IHD) than residents of hard-water areas. In one study, the death rate from IHD declined from 416 per 100,000 in an area with water hardness of less than 100 parts per million (ppm) to 365 deaths per 100,000 in an area with water hardness of more than 200 ppm. The higher death rate in the soft-water areas was found to be entirely the result of an excess of sudden deaths.

Water hardness refers to the mineral content of the water; the more minerals the water contains, the harder it is said to be.

Terence W. Anderson of the University of Toronto has compared the water composition of 575 Canadian communities and the mineral composition of the tissues of postmortem subjects who had resided in these communities.

He found that the amount of magnesium in myocardial (heart) tissue was 22 percent lower in subjects who died of IHD than in subjects who died in accidents. IHD victims also had relatively low magnesium concentrations in their diaphragm and pectoral muscles. This finding suggests that the higher heart attack rate in soft-water areas may be caused by a lack of magnesium in the water. One of the manifestations of magnesium deficiency in experimental animals, points out Anderson, is an increased tendency to develop cardiac arrhythmias (irregular heartbeats).

Anderson speculates that the amount of magnesium in the

water supply may be critical because of a reduction in the amount of this mineral in the highly refined foods that dominate western diets. On the other hand, it's possible that the relatively low concentrations of magnesium in IHD victims is a consequence of an already diseased heart.

Terence W. Anderson, School of Hygiene, University of Toronto, Toronto, Canada M5S IAI

The Zinc/Copper Theory of Heart Disease

When laboratory rats are denied copper, their cholesterol levels zoom upward and their hearts become enlarged and pale. A closer look reveals degenerating muscle fibers, hemorrhaging, inflammation, and excessive fibrous tissue.

Leslie M. Klevay of the University of North Dakota believes that a high zinc/copper (Z/C) ratio within the body leads to hypercholesterolemia and increased mortality from coronary heart disease (CHD). He supports this theory with the following evidence from human studies:

• High-fiber diets, which are associated with a low incidence of CHD (see p. 92), decrease the ratio of zinc to copper in the body. Such high-fiber foods as cereals, nuts, and legumes contain relatively high amounts of phytic acid, a naturally occurring chelating agent that decreases the absorption of zinc from the intestinal tract.

• Heart tissue from victims of heart attacks contains less copper than heart tissue from accident victims.

• Deaths from CHD are fewer than normal among patients with cirrhosis, a disease that lowers the Z/C ratio in the liver.

• Exercise, which lowers the risk of CHD, produces increased sweating which leads to a greater loss of zinc than copper and the incorporation of zinc into bone and muscle, both of which decrease the Z/C ratio.

• Chronic kidney disease, which produces an increase in

the Z/C ratio in the liver, leads to an increase in the risk of CHD.

• Calcium and magnesium, which are associated with reduced risk of CHD in communities with hard-water supplies, also increases the amount of copper available for metabolism when added to the diet of rats.

• Agents that tend to decrease blood cholesterol generally decrease the Z/C ratio, whereas agents that tend to increase blood cholesterol levels generally increase the Z/C ratio.

Klevay's zinc-copper theory of coronary heart disease has never been tested in a controlled study of the effect of dietary manipulation of these minerals on the incidence of heart disease.

Leslie M. Klevay, Human Nutrition Laboratory, P.O. Box 7166, U. Station, Grand Forks, N.D. 58201

What Causes Atherosclerosis?

When one considers that diet, cigarette smoking, aging, genetic makeup, physical inactivity, blood coagulation, diabetes, water composition, sex hormones, and hypertension all seem to be related to atherosclerosis, one wonders whether there is an underlying mechanism, related to all these factors, that is responsible for the disease.

One explanation for atherosclerosis is that perpetual stress produces lesions in the arterial walls, and that these lesions serve as focal points for lipids, connective tissue proteins, clotted blood, calcium, and other plaque-building substances. According to this view, the innermost layer of the artery, which is comprised of endothelial cells, is especially vulnerable to certain food chemicals; noxious agents in cigarette smoke, water, and air; hormones and other substances carried by the blood; and high blood pressure.

By using injury-provoking techniques, scientists have induced the formation of arterial plaques in animals that resemble, but are not identical to the plaques that form spontaneously in humans. Apparently, an important step in the process is the rapid growth of smooth muscle cells in the middle layers of the artery, and the subsequent migration of these cells to the innermost layer where they secrete connective tissue proteins and other macromolecules

According to Laurence Harker and Russell Ross of the University of Washington, the critical event that stimulates the smooth muscle cells to divide may be the release of a mitogen (an agent that induces cell division) from blood platelets at the site of injury. When platelet activity is inhibited by the drug dypiridamole in baboons with arterial lesions, there is a striking reduction in these lesions.

Another factor that may stimulate the growth of smooth muscle cells is exposure to low-density lipoproteins (LDL), which have been found in great quantities in diseased artery walls. Robert Wissler of the University of Chicago has demonstrated that LDL carries most of the lipid into the arterial wall, and that it causes smooth muscle cells to proliferate in tissue culture.

Despite the evidence that atherosclerotic-like plaques develop in response to repeated injury, many scientists doubt that the same process occurs under normal conditions in humans. They point out that virtually all the response-to-injury evidence has been obtained from animal studies where plaque-formation has been induced by artificial means.

Laurence Harker and Russell Ross, Department of Pathology, University of Washington School of Medicine, Seattle, Wa. 98195

Robert W. Wissler, Department of Pathology, University of Chicago, Chicago, Il. 60637

Is Atherosclerosis a Form of Cancer?
Could it be that atherosclerotic plaques are actually tumors that are triggered by the same agents that cause cancer? Earl

and John Benditt of the University of Washington have presented evidence that the proliferating smooth muscle cells in human atherosclerotic plaques may be of monoclonal origin (derived from the same cell), and that these cells are fundamentally different from cells found in normal arteries. One striking difference is the collagen that surrounds plaque cells in contrast to the elastin that normally surrounds smooth muscle cells in the artery.

The Benditts have found that twenty-four of thirty atherosclerotic plaque specimens appeared to be of monoclonal origin, whereas all but two of fifty-nine specimens from normal tissue appeared to be of mixed-cell origin. A similar study of cells from sixteen subjects, ranging in age from twenty-four to ninety-four, by researchers at Johns Hopkins University showed 89.7 percent of plaque specimens to be of monoclonal origin compared to only 2 percent of specimens from normal tissue.

These findings suggest two possibilities: the cells in atherosclerotic cells are derived from a cell population that is different from cells normally found in the arterial wall; or that normal cells are transformed into abnormal cells during the early stages of atherogenesis. In either case, it's possible that carcinogenic agents may play a role in the process.

The possibility that atherosclerosis may develop in a manner similar to cancer suggests that we should pay more attention to the effects of carcinogens on the incidence of cardiovascular disease, and to the mechanisms by which factors such as cigarette smoking and dietary fat increase the risk of both types of disease.

Earl P. Benditt and John M. Benditt, Department of Pathology, University of Washington School of Medicine, Seattle, Wa. 98195

Smoking As a Cause of Atherosclerosis
One theory of atherosclerosis holds that cigarette smoke

may be a direct cause of the disease by inflicting damage to the arterial wall. Immunologists have found that more than 50 percent of patients with coronary artery disease who smoke display an allergic reaction to tobacco leaf protein, whereas only 14 percent of smokers without coronary artery disease display such a reaction. So it may be that smoking is especially dangerous for a specific segment of the population that is at-risk for atherosclerosis.

In a study of 104 heart disease patients at Rancho Los Amigos Hospital, coronary angiograms were used to document the degree of atherosclerotic blockage in the coronary arteries of each patient. Sixty of the subjects had never smoked or had become nonsmokers after they began to suffer from atherosclerosis; the remaining forty-four subjects continued to smoke throughout the study. After an eighteen-month rehabilitation period, which included exercise, diet, and antihypertension therapy, the patients were retested. (See p. 178.)

The results showed a significant worsening of coronary artery disease in 60 percent of the vessels of smokers, compared to only 32 percent of the vessels of nonsmokers. No difference was observed between light and heavy smokers.

The investigators concluded that cigarette smoking is the most important risk factor for patients with coronary atherosclerosis, and that cessation of smoking decreases the risk of increased coronary artery blockage by a factor of two.

Ronald H. Selvester, Rancho Los Amigos Hospital, 7601 East Imperial Highway, Downey, Ca. 90242

A New Approach to Heart Disease

What accounts for the explosive twentieth-century epidemic of coronary heart disease in the western world? In searching for the answer to this question, scientists have identified various risk factors for CHD, but attempts to lower the incidence of heart disease by modifying these factors have met with only limited success.

According to Terence Anderson, the problem may lie in our reliance on an inappropriate model for heart disease. He notes that there has been a major rise in the heart disease rate in men, but not in women, even though the sex ratio for other cardiovascular diseases has not changed appreciably.

As recently as 1921, the age-specific death rates for both men and women were essentially the same for both coronary heart disease and cerebrovascular disease (stroke); however, by 1971, men in the forty-five to fifty-four age bracket had become five times more likely to die of heart disease than women of the same age, but were no more vulnerable to stroke than they had been in 1921.

Why the tremendous rise in heart disease but not stroke, asks Anderson, if both these syndromes are caused, as is generally believed, by the same underlying disorders—atherosclerosis, intravascular thrombosis (blocking of the arteries by blood clots), and hypertension? His answer is that the rise in heart disease during this century may have been caused by increased vulnerability of the heart muscle to impaired blood supply. It's not that our arteries are in worse shape than our grandfathers' arteries, but that our hearts can't stand the strain as well.

Anderson points out that scattered foci of degenerating tissue—the characteristic sign of heart disease—are plentiful in men who die of heart attacks, but rare in accident victims of the same age. He suggests that factors which cause focal degeneration of heart muscle may be relevant to heart disease.

First in line are the catecholamines, a group of neurotransmitters that are involved in the regulation of all critical life functions, and have been implicated in the aging process. (See p. 45.) Next are free radical agents such as polyunsaturated fats, oxygen, radiation, and environmental pollutants—all of which have been implicated in both aging and cancer.

Terence W. Anderson, School of Hygiene, University of Toronto, Toronto, Canada M5S IAI

What Is a Carcinogen?

Cancer is the generic name for diseases characterized by uncontrolled cellular growth. Approximately 17 percent of deaths in the U.S. occur as a result of cancer. Scientists estimate that 80 to 90 percent of human cancers are caused, at least in part, by environmental agents called carcinogens.

A carcinogen is a chemical compound or other agent that induces abnormal or neoplastic changes in living cells that eventually lead to their uncontrolled growth. Carcinogens are found in food, water, air, and radiation. About twenty chemicals have been identified as human carcinogens.

Although some chemical carcinogens can induce neoplastic changes by direct action, the majority of them must first be activated by some factor within the host. Other chemicals that are not carcinogenic in themselves are able to activate or accelerate the effects of carcinogens.

Thus, it appears as if most human cancers are the product of interaction between environmental carcinogens and biochemical changes within the body. Such changes may be related to hormonal or enzymatic action, immune function, growth and development, or aging.

Where Are Carcinogens Found?

Many people have the impression that the majority of human cancers are the result of modern technology. They believe that carcinogens are mainly found in food additives, pesticides and insecticides, synthetic contaminants in drinking water, industrial chemicals, and drugs.

Actually, it appears that only 5-15 percent of human cancers are caused by such agents; the majority of cancers result from a variety of factors including diet, cigarette smoking, hormonal imbalances, viruses, immune dysfunction, genetic abnormalities, and the aging process.

John H. Weisburger of the American Health Foundation points out that the introduction of manufactured cigarettes in the U.S. after World War I was the first time a society had been systematically exposed to a carcinogen on a large scale. The result was a dramatic rise in the incidence of lung cancer—first among men and then, after World War II, among women. The lung cancer rate for men rose from about two per 100,000 in 1930 to fifty per 100,000 in 1973, while the lung cancer rate for women rose from about one per 100,000 in 1930 to eleven per 100,000 in 1973.

On the other hand, the introduction of insecticides, pesticides, and food additives appears to have had no detectable effect on the incidence of the main human cancers in the United States. There is some evidence, in fact, that food additives may have contributed to the reduction in the incidence of stomach cancer during this period. (See p. 146.)

When it comes to cancer of the large bowel, breast, prostate, ovary, pancreas, and kidneys, there is persuasive evidence that these malignancies are caused in large part by western dietary habits. For one thing, the incidence of such cancers is much lower in Japan—a highly industrialized country with pollution problems similar to those in the U.S.—but with a greatly different dietary pattern. This conclusion is reinforced by the finding that Japanese immigrants are afflicted with the same cancers as native Americans soon after they conform to U.S. eating habits.

John H. Weisburger, American Health Foundation, Valhalla, N.Y. 10595

How Much of a Carcinogen Is Dangerous?
When the artificial sweetener saccharin was banned because of suspicion that it may be a carcinogen, many people

were unconvinced by the evidence that led to the ban. Researchers had induced an "abnormal" number of malignancies by feeding rats enormous amounts of saccharin, and this was interpreted as an indication that saccharin may be dangerous for humans.

What people found hard to understand was the idea that such an experiment was analogous to real life. A much-quoted remark that reflected this skepticism was that "a person would have to drink 800 cans of diet soda a day" to match the amount of saccharin fed to the rats in this study. Not only was the public dubious about the rat study, it was also aware that hundreds of millions of people had used saccharin for decades without apparent problems.

The saccharin issue brought forth a critical assumption that scientists have been making for years—that even the smallest dose of a carcinogen is damaging, so that repeated exposure, even at considerable intervals, produces an additive effect that can eventually lead to cancer. This assumption challenges the commonsense idea that a very small amount of any substance, even a poison, is not dangerous and, conversely, that a very large amount of even the most benign substance can be highly toxic.

When scientists give laboratory animals huge doses of an alleged carcinogen, they assume that each animal is a stand-in for millions of people. If a huge dose of the substance can induce one cancer in ten animals over a short period of time, then a very small dose of the substance can presumably induce perhaps ten cancers in 10 million people over a long period of time.

This assumption is based upon the observation that carcinogens transform normal cells into abnormal cells by triggering changes in nuclear DNA. Once a cell carrying abnormal DNA begins to divide, it is believed, it is no longer possible for the cell's repair system to fix the abnormality. Thus, the cell becomes permanently abnormal and has moved one step closer to becoming cancerous.

The only thing wrong with this is that no one has yet come up with hard evidence that it is valid. We don't really know how a carcinogen triggers abnormal changes in nuclear DNA, or if these changes are truly irreversible once cell division has begun. Furthermore, there are a number of carcinogens, such as cigarette smoke, which apparently do not produce irreversible damage to cells. Even lifelong heavy smokers can eliminate much of the risk of lung cancer as soon as they stop smoking and, after ten years of abstinence, it's almost as if they had never smoked at all.

Thus, it may be that some substances banned as carcinogenic may be safe for human consumption, just as other substances now in use may be carcinogenic or otherwise dangerous to our health.

The Risk of Death from Smoking

We all know that smoking is dangerous, but how much of a risk is involved? How much more likely are we to die if we smoke? How does smoking affect our chances of dying from specific diseases? What are the chances of ex-smokers? How about pipe and cigar smokers? And finally, is there any condition for which smoking is beneficial?

One of the largest and best studies to tackle these questions has been continuing since 1951 in Great Britain. At that time, the British Medical Association forwarded to all British doctors a questionnaire about their smoking habits. All but a few of the 34,440 who replied have been followed since then, with records kept of the causes of all deaths, and of changes in smoking habits.

After twenty years of data collection, Doll and Peto reported 10,072 deaths and a substantial reduction in cigarette consumption, far greater than among members of the general population. They found smoking to be linked, in varying degree, with twenty-three causes of death, which were divided into three categories.

Ischemic Heart Disease

First was ischemic heart disease, which was placed in a category by itself because so many subjects (3,191) died of it and because the correlation with smoking was so high. The risk of dying of ischemic heart disease before age forty-five was fifteen times greater for heavy smokers than for non-smokers. Among older men, however, the relative risk was much less pronounced, dropping to two to one in the fifty-five to sixty-four age group and less than 50 percent in men over sixty-five.

One reason for the fall in the relative risk of heart disease with age—a pattern that was followed for other diseases as well—may be the progressive elimination of smokers susceptible to heart disease. Another reason might be that individuals often stop smoking when they are seriously threatened by a disease, so that their subsequent death is recorded in the nonsmoker category. A third might be that, with advancing age, there is increasing competition among many causes of death.

Other Diseases

The second category included eight diseases closely associated with smoking: cancer of the lung, cancer of the esophagus, cancer of other respiratory sites, respiratory tuberculosis, chronic bronchitis and emphysema, pulmonary heart disease, nonsyphilitic aortic aneurysm, and hernia. For each of these conditions, the risk of death was at least three times as high in smokers as in nonsmokers.

Third were conditions with a positive, but relatively small correlation with smoking, including cancers of the rectum and pancreas, cancer of the bladder, pneumonia, myocardial degeneration, hypertension, arteriosclerosis, cerebral thrombosis, cirrhosis of the liver and alcoholism, peptic ulcer, suicide, and poisoning.

Types of Smokers

The risk of death was significantly higher in cigarette smokers than in subjects who smoked pipes or cigars or both. Pipe or cigar smokers showed mortality rates which, with few exceptions, were similar to, or only slightly above, subjects who did not smoke at all.

In general, the risk of death from cigarette smoking increased progressively from light, to moderate, to heavy smokers. There was notably higher mortality for most diseases among men who said they inhaled cigarette smoke than among men who said they did not. However, the death rate for lung cancer was lower among inhalers than noninhalers, but only for those who smoked lightly or moderately. Interestingly, men who couldn't decide whether they were inhalers or not showed the highest mortality rates, regardless of how much they smoked.

Most subjects who gave up smoking during the study, except those who quit in the late stages of their disease, showed a progressive decrease in the risk of dying. Fifteen years after they stopped, the mortality pattern for ex-smokers was similar to, but not quite as good as lifelong nonsmokers. For chronic bronchitis and emphysema, however, the mortality rate continued to rise in ex-smokers for five to nine years, after which there was a rapid decline in mortality to about a quarter of that for continuing smokers.

The reduction in total mortality over the twenty-year period was about three times greater for those in the study group, than for the general population. This finding reflects the fact that far more doctors stopped smoking during this period than did members of the general population.

The One Benefit of Smoking

The only condition for which there was a negative correlation with smoking was Parkinson's Disease. More deaths

Annual death rate per 100,000 men, standardized for age

Cause of death	No. of deaths (excluding ex-smokers)	Non-smokers	Cigarettes only	Current Smokers				
				Pipe and/or cigars only	Mixed (cigarettes and others)	Cigarettes only, No./day: 1-14	15-24	≥25
Closely associated causes								
Cancer of lung	362	10	140	58	82	78	127	251
Cancer of oesophagus	56	3	14	11	27	11	12	21
Cancer of other respiratory sites	38	1	13	9	10	5	7	33
Respiratory tuberculosis	38	3	15	3	8	9	10	30
Chronic bronchitis and emphysema	167	3	74	28	34	51	78	114
Pulmonary heart disease	35	0	10	9	14	6	9	25
Aortic aneurysm (non-syphilitic)	91	5	33	18	23	17	38	52
Hernia	12	0	5	4	0	3	4	11
Ischaemic heart disease								
Ischaemic heart disease	2205	413	669	425	528	608	652	792
Other associated causes								
Cancer of rectum	51	6	16	10	17	11	11	33
Cancer of pancreas	70	14	22	12	16	19	20	29
Cancer of bladder	58	9	19	14	13	20	20	13
Pneumonia	218	54	73	38	59	56	84	105
Myocardial degeneration	408	67	189	101	103	136	116	202
Hypertension	162	37	50	34	30	33	59	65
Arteriosclerosis	82	21	29	17	17	21	25	68
Cerebral thrombosis	402	86	115	99	104	94	134	137
Cirrhosis of liver, alcoholism	63	7	21	9	13	11	14	44
Peptic ulcer	57	8	20	10	13	9	30	27
Suicide	135	21	33	32	28	22	30	53
Poisoning	66	9	19	11	11	14	17	28
Parkinsonism								
Unrelated causes								
Parkinsonism	25	14	6	4	4	9	2	6
All other causes	2157	518	616	473	434	615	573	697
All causes	6958	1317	2154	1434	1591	1857	2066	2843
(No. of deaths)		(940)	(3343)	(1527)	(1148)	(1209)	(1137)	(997)

Death rate by cause of death, method of smoking, and number of cigarettes smoked per day when last asked. Subjects were male British doctors who answered questionnaires.

from Parkinsonism occurred in nonsmokers than in smokers, with heavy smokers showing the lowest death rate. Other studies have confirmed this finding, but no one has yet come up with an explanation for it.

Since nicotine potentiates the secretion of catecholamines and Parkinson's Disease is characterized by a deficiency of dopamine, it may be that the nicotine in cigarette smoke increases the amount of dopamine available to the brain.

Richard Doll and Richard Peto, Radcliffe Infirmary, Oxford OX2 6HE, England

Occupational Cancer Hazards

Every major industry studied to date has shown some risk of cancer for workers. In the rubber industry, for example, stomach cancer is high for workers who handle raw materials. In the steel industry, workers exposed to coke ovens are at-risk for lung cancer. Uranium and other miners have excess lung cancer and luminous dial painters are at-risk for bone cancer.

Approximately 100 materials used or appearing in industrial processes have been identified as carcinogens. Most of these materials are in limited use with few workers exposed, but several of them pose serious problems.

Perhaps the most serious risk of cancer comes from exposure to asbestos. Numerous studies have documented that asbestos workers are at-risk for cancers of the lung, stomach, colon and rectum, and esophagus. There are several diseases, in fact, that virtually never occur, except in persons exposed to asbestos fibers. These include asbestosis, pleural mesothelioma, and peritoneal mesothelioma.

Because of the slowness of the carcinogenic process, the possibility of getting cancer is like a time bomb that ticks away for decades. In the case of asbestos workers, this is apparently true for their families and friends, as well as for themselves. A study of 326 family contacts of former asbestos workers showed that 35 percent of these individuals had X-rays with abnormalities characteristic of asbestos exposure.

The risk of lung cancer is particularly devastating for asbestos workers who smoke. In one study, the risk of death from lung cancer among smoking asbestos workers was shown to be ninety-two times greater than for individuals who neither smoke nor work with asbestos.

Vinyl Chloride

Several studies have documented the carcinogenic effects of vinyl chloride—a commonly used plastic. Vinyl chloride workers have been shown to be at-risk for hemangiosarcoma —a type of liver cancer, as well as tumors of the brain, lung, and lymphatic system.

Since vinyl chloride is used in many consumer and industrial products, concern has been raised about its threat to the general public. However, it appears that once vinyl chloride is polymerized and formed into products, it poses no risk to users of the products.

William J. Nicholson, Department of Community Medicine, Mt. Sinai School of Medicine, New York, N.Y. 10029

Drugs That May Cause Cancer

When drugs are taken via conventional dosage forms— by pill, injection, etc.—they produce undesirable side effects. Some drugs have been shown to be potential carcinogens. The choice of whether to take a drug depends upon its risk/benefit ratio. If the disease for which we take the drug is likely to kill us without it, we can readily accept a high degree of risk. But if the drug provides only minor benefits, even a small risk may be unacceptable.

Here are the major findings about potentially carcinogenic drugs:

• The synthetic estrogen diethylstilbestrol (DES) has induced a rare form of cancer of the vagina (clear cell adenocarcinoma) in a small number of daughters of women who took the drug to prevent miscarriage. Thus far, 250 cases of the disease have surfaced out of an estimated 600,000 to 2,000,000 young women believed to be at-risk.

• Numerous reports indicate that women receiving synthetic estrogens in birth control pills are at increased risk for benign liver tumors, which can sometimes lead to fatal internal hemorrhaging.

• The use of conjugated estrogens by women seeking to avert the aging changes of the menopause (see p. 247) has been associated with an increased risk of endometrial cancer of the uterus. In a recent study, the risk of endometrial cancer was 4.5 to 7.6 times greater among estrogen users than among controls.

• Several reports suggest that patients receiving androgens (male steroid hormones) may be at increased risk for liver cancer.

• Some drugs used to treat cancer may themselves increase the risk of cancer. In particular, alkylating agents, such as 2-naphthylamine mustard and cyclophosphamide, which are used to treat leukemia and Hodgkins disease, have been reported to increase the incidence of bladder cancer in both animals and humans.

• Transplant patients receiving immunosuppressive drugs to prevent graft rejection are more likely to get lymphomas (reticulum cell sarcoma) than controls. It's not yet clear whether immunosuppression itself or the effect of the drugs is responsible for the increased risk of cancer.

• The use of rauwolfia alkaloids such as reserpine for the management of hypertension has been linked to an increased risk of breast cancer in women in some studies; other studies have failed to confirm this finding.

• There have been reports that phenylbutazone (an antiinflammatory drug) and chloramphenicol (an antibiotic) may be associated with an increased risk of leukemia.

Once again, it's important to understand that most drugs

that are potential carcinogens provide important therapeutic benefits that may outweigh any risk of cancer. The solution to the problem is to minimize or eliminate the risks and improve the effectiveness of drugs by controlling their delivery into the body. (See p. 382.)

Philippe Shubik, Eppley Institute, 42nd and Dewey Aves., Omaha, Ne. 68105

Caffeine: The World's Favorite Stimulant

The most-consumed drug in the world is caffeine—a natural compound found in coffee, tea, cola drinks, cocoa, pain killers, and stay-awake pills. Caffeine is a central nervous system stimulant that is commonly taken to inhibit sleep, but can also induce nervousness, anxiety, irritability, and agitation. About 25 percent of individuals who stop taking caffeine suffer from severe withdrawal headaches.

Because of the disagreeable symptoms sometimes associated with caffeine, it has long been suspected that high intake of the drug has detrimental effects on health. At various times, caffeine has been accused of being a cause of heart disease, hypertension, diabetes, hyperlipidemia, and peptic ulcer.

However, most studies have failed to confirm a link between caffeine consumption and any of these diseases. For example, the Framingham study of heart disease did not show an increase in any of the common risk factors for heart disease among heavy coffee drinkers, except for cigarette smoking. Subjects who drank coffee but did not smoke cigarettes did not have a higher-than-normal incidence of heart disease.

A more recent study examined the coffee-drinking habits of the residents of Evans County, Georgia. Subjects who said they drank five or more cups of coffee daily were classified as high coffee consumers; others were classified as low or no coffee consumers.

Between July 31, 1969, and January 1, 1974, there were

339 deaths in the Evans County group, of which 130 (38 percent) were attributed to cardio- and cerebrovascular causes. The results showed no significant differences in total mortality or in the incidence of cardio- or cerebrovascular disease between high coffee drinkers and low or no coffee drinkers, even without controlling for cigarette smoking. If anything, the high coffee consumers had a slightly lower mortality rate than those with low or no coffee consumption.

S. Heyden, Department of Community Health Sciences, Duke University Medical Center, Durham, N.C. 27705

How Dangerous Are Food Additives?

The most popular word on Madison Avenue these days is "natural." Everything from bread to ice cream to shampoo is being sold with slogans such as "100 percent natural" or "no artificial anything." One brand of cigarettes is even advertised as being "natural," presumably to convince the public that it's safer than other brands.

The reason for this embrace of Mother Nature is that people seem to think that whatever is "natural" is healthy and whatever is "artificial" or "synthetic" is unhealthy.

Yet, natural substances like tobacco, sugar, and fat can be detrimental to health, whereas most artificial food additives are probably safe.

What's scared people most is the idea of getting cancer from artificial chemicals in processed foods. The banning of cyclamates, red dye #2, saccharin, and other compounds as alleged carcinogens has magnified that fear.

There is no definitive evidence that any of these substances cause cancer in humans. But even if you believe they may be carcinogenic, the threat to your health is not very imposing. The sum total of all the evidence against food additives accounts for only a very small fraction of the cancers found in the United States and other industrialized countries of the world.

Non-Toxic Food Additives

Whatever the real danger of food additives, a solution to the problem is on the horizon—the "leashing" of food additives to polymer molecules too large to pass through the gastrointestinal tract into the bloodstream. The resulting chemical compounds can be added to foods to provide coloring, flavoring, sweetening, texture, or protection against spoilage, but are separated from these foods during the digestive process. Instead of going into the liver, kidneys, or bladder where they can potentially cause damage, leashed food additives are excreted in the feces.

The leading purveyor of this new food additive technology is the Dynapol Corporation, which is developing polymer-leashed colors, antioxidants, and sweeteners. The most advanced of these projects—the food colors—should yield several products in the next few years.

Dynapol Corporation, 1454 Page Mill Road, Palo Alto, Ca. 94304

Probing the "Aging" Effects of Radiation

The life-shortening effect of high doses of radiation was demonstrated in humans when atom bombs were dropped on Hiroshima and Nagasaki. Studies of the survivors showed significantly high mortality rates.

Because of the extensive development of nuclear power since World War II, there has been considerable investigation of the effects of radiation on biologic systems. Here are some findings on the relationship between radiation and aging:

• When rodents are given large doses of whole-body radiation early in life, they die sooner than nonirradiated rodents. In the process, they display many features of accelerated aging including loss of hair, decreased activity, and general debilitation.

• The life-shortening effect of radiation is dose-dependent —the more radiation the animals are exposed to, the sooner they die.

Though radiation poisoning mimics aging, there is significant evidence that its life-shortening effect may be related to other factors.

• Radiation increases the incidence of cancer to a greater extent than would be expected as a result of accelerated aging.

• The life-shortening effect of radiation varies enormously between the sexes and among different strains of inbred mice.

• There is considerable variation in the effects of radiation on different types of tissues.

• There is poor correlation between chromosome abnormalities and aging in irradiated animals.

• The amount of radiation given to experimental animals far surpasses anything normally encountered in real life.

In addition to natural sunlight, we are exposed to "insignificant" amounts of low-level radiation from color TV sets, X-ray machines, microwave ovens, radar systems, nuclear generating plants, high voltage electrostatic air filters, and tests of thermonuclear weapons.

Though it's generally agreed that long-term exposure to low-level radiation may be detrimental to our health, there have been no definitive studies on the subject.

John B. Storer, Biology Division, Oak Ridge National Laboratory, Oak Ridge, Tn. 37830

Radiation-Induced Cancer

It's common knowledge that chronic exposure to ultraviolet (UV) radiation from the sun increases the risk of skin cancer, but recent work suggests that it may also increase vulnerability to other types of cancer. Scientists at the University of Utah have discovered that mice exposed to 1/10 the UV radiation needed to cause skin cancer were rendered susceptible to tumors that untreated mice were capable of rejecting.

They theorize that the sun's radiation may inhibit "effector" cells that normally challenge invading tumors, and that the process involves stimulation of "suppressor" cells that normally hold the effector cells in check. The resulting imbalance in the mouse's immune system, say the Utah scientists, resembles the loss of immune function that occurs during aging.

Other studies indicate that radiation used in treating cancer may itself be a cancer threat. In one study, the incidence of adenomas and carcinomas of the thyroid gland increased significantly as a result of exposure to radiation, while in another study the incidence of leukemia in exposed subjects increased about tenfold compared with unexposed subjects.

Certain radioisotopes present a cancer threat when used therapeutically because they are retained in the body for long periods of time. The most thoroughly investigated example is colloidal thorium dioxide (Thorotrast), which is used as a radiologic contrast medium to help outline hollow vessels. A Portuguese study of patients exposed to Thorotrast from 1930 to 1955 revealed a high level of risk of leukemia and primary liver cancer in the Thorotrast group compared to controls treated with a nonradioactive contrast medium.

There are two ways of dealing with radiation-induced stress: avoiding exposure to radiation, or attempting to protect against its damaging effects. The Utah scientists are developing techniques to restore normality to the immune system by treating UV-exposed animals with an anti-serum capable of reacting against suppressor cells.

Raymond A. Daynes, Department of Pathology, University of Utah Medical Center, 50 N. Medical Drive, Salt Lake City, Ut. 84112

The Beneficial Effects of Sunlight

Fresh air and sunshine have long been associated with good health and physical fitness. Health-conscious individuals make frequent trips to beaches, mountains, lakes, and other recreational areas to bask in the natural splendor of the great outdoors.

In recent years, however, the idea of going outdoors has come under fire from the medical profession. Most doctors now warn of the dangers of solar radiation and point to evidence that chronic exposure to sunlight can lead to skin cancer and accelerated aging of the skin.

In contrast to the prevailing trend has been the work of John N. Ott—the inventor of time-lapse photography—who has spent the past half-century investigating the effects of light on health. Ott has gathered evidence that regular exposure to natural, full-spectrum light may be essential for good health, and that living in artificial light can precipitate or worsen eye diseases, hypertension, arthritis, and cancer.

Ott contends that light waves absorbed through the eye stimulate the pituitary gland which, in turn, affects the entire neuroendocrine system. According to Ott, those of us who perpetually wear sunglasses are being deprived of essential ultraviolet energy.

The Hazards of Color TV

Ott was the one who blew the whistle on the potential health hazards of color TV. In 1964, he showed that radiation from color TV sets could distort the growth of plants and alter the behavior of animals. In one study, rats exposed to regular TV "viewing" became increasingly hyperactive and aggressive within three to ten days and then became progressively lethargic. After thirty days, they were so lethargic that it was necessary to push them around their cages to get them to move.

This work was instrumental in persuading manufacturers

to reduce the amount of radiation emitted by TV sets. Despite these changes, Ott still questions the safety of watching color television for extended periods.

The concept that natural, full-spectrum light may be an essential "nutrient" does not contradict the findings that excessive exposure to sunlight can lead to cancer and accelerated aging. It only warns us that we should be equally wary of excessive exposure to artificial light. It also suggests that we should pay more attention to the effects of light in animal experiments.

Full-spectrum, fluorescent light bulbs that simulate natural sunlight and sunglasses that permit access to full-spectrum light are now available from several companies.

Assessing Urban Life

The best "large city" to live in is Portland, Oregon—according to a study of the quality of life in U.S. metropolitan areas. The study, which was conducted by the Midwest Research Institute, compared groups of large, medium, and small areas with regard to 123 factors.

Five categories were considered: economic development; political or government activity; environmental safety and climate; health and education; and social, recreational, and cultural activities.

The best medium-sized city to live in was Eugene, Oregon, and the best small city, La Crosse, Wisconsin. Among the large cities—with populations of at least 500,000 (as of 1970) —the worst was Jersey City, New Jersey. New York ranked thirtieth (out of sixty-five), Chicago was thirty-seventh, Los Angeles, twenty-first, and San Francisco, ninth.

Midwest Research Institute, 425 Volker Blvd., Kansas City, Mo. 64110

Air Pollution and Human Health

On Thanksgiving weekend 1966, New York City experienced one of the worst periods of air pollution in its history. A study published the following year showed a significant rise in the death rate during this period compared with periods of normal air pollution. On the average, there were twenty-four more deaths per day than during control periods, with a rise in deaths from all causes except influenza, pneumonia, and hypertension.

Though such periods offer dramatic testimony to the health hazards of polluted air, scientists are more concerned with the average level of air quality than with occasional episodes of acute pollution. They have documented a multitude of damaging effects on human health from such pollutants as sulfur dioxides, particulate matters, oxidants, carbon monoxide, nitrogen oxides, and other substances.

It's been estimated that the death rate from bronchitis would be reduced 25 to 50 percent in urban areas by reducing air pollution to the lowest prevailing level in the area under consideration. And that the death rate from lung cancer would fall by 11 to 44 percent from such an improvement in air quality.

In a study of 187,783 white Americans, aged fifty to sixty-nine, Hammond and Horn found that the age-standardized death rate from lung cancer was thirty-nine (per 100,000) in rural areas of low air pollution compared with fifty-two in cities of population over 50,000. Similar results have been found when comparing areas of high and low air pollution within large cities, and when comparing members of the same profession in areas of high and low pollution.

An association has been found between air pollution and cardiovascular diseases and nonrespiratory forms of cancer, but the evidence is weaker for these diseases.

The effects of air pollution are significant for both smokers and nonsmokers. The mortality and morbidity rates are considerably higher for smokers living in cities than for those living in rural areas, with the effect becoming more marked with increasing age.

There is also evidence that home heating is a significant

source of air pollution. In general, the mortality rate increases as the rate and amount of home heating increases. However, the increase in mortality is associated with the use of heating fuels, not with heating itself.

Lester B. Lave, Graduate School of Industrial Administration, Carnegie-Mellon University, Pittsburgh, Pa. 15213

The Dangers of Oxygen

About 2 billion years ago, there was a dramatic change on Earth that had a profound effect on evolution. Plant life came into existence and began to release oxygen into the atmosphere through the photosynthetic breakdown of water.

At first, exposure to free oxygen was lethal to virtually all living systems. However, a few organisms managed to survive and began to adapt to the continuous presence of oxygen in their systems. Gradually, these organisms evolved protective mechanisms against oxygen toxicity and developed methods of using it to create energy.

Today, oxygen is the driving force behind most metabolic processes that power all complex forms of animal life. Yet it remains highly toxic to many vital processes and can combine with other substances to inflict damage upon delicate cell structures.

The toxicity of oxygen is revealed when we are subjected to levels of exposure beyond the one fifth of an atmosphere to which we have become accustomed. A few hours of breathing pure oxygen at one atmosphere of pressure causes tracheitis (inflammation of the trachea). A few days of such exposure produces lung damage that can lead to death, ironically from anoxia (lack of oxygen). Rats exposed to 2.5 atmospheres of oxygen convulse and die within a few hours, while cultured mammalian cells are damaged by exposure to high levels of oxygen.

When oxygen enters living cells it is reduced to intermediate forms that are highly reactive. These intermediaries are often called "free radicals" because of their ability to combine with organic compounds to produce damaging chain reactions, which generate even more highly reactive radicals.

The body has various lines of defense against free radical reactions. There is a battery of enzymes—including catalases, peroxidases, and superoxide dismutases—that protects cells against oxygen toxicity by serving as free radical scavengers. Additional protection against oxidative attack can be obtained from natural antioxidant compounds such as vitamins C and E, or synthetic antioxidants such as BHT and BHA, which are used to prevent foods from spoiling.

Oxygen and Aging

Irwin Fridovich of Duke University, who has been studying the action of superoxide dismutases, has proposed that the root cause of aging may be chronic damage from oxygen toxicity. In his view, neither inborn defense mechanisms nor dietary antioxidants can prevent low-level oxidative "wear and tear" from accumulating with time.

In support of Fridovich's theory is the fact that large amounts of supplementary antioxidants have increased the mean life span and reduced the incidence of malignancies in laboratory mice. (See p. 131.) And at least one physician has been using superoxide dismutase in conjunction with other compounds to treat aging and degenerative disease. (See p. 360.)

However, antioxidants have repeatedly failed to prolong maximum life span—the "acid test" for any regimen proposed as an anti-aging therapy. Further evidence that oxygen is not a cause of aging is the finding that long-lived calorie-restricted animals consume more oxygen than shorter-lived normally fed animals.

Irwin Fridovich, Department of Biochemistry, Duke University Medical Center, Durham, N.C. 27710

Water Quality and Health

Water is not a major health hazard in technologically advanced countries. Though there is considerable pollution from sewage effluents and industrial wastes—particularly in large rivers and lakes—most public water supplies are relatively safe from contamination.

In addition, health-conscious consumers who are wary of local water treatment or distribution, have the option of further purifying water at the tap with commercially available filters, or purchasing bottled water from private sources. In Florida, bottled water is even available from vending machines in shopping centers.

In many of the developing countries, however, there is still considerable morbidity and mortality from waterborne infectious diseases. Such countries as India, Iran, and The Philippines must deal with cholera, typhoid fever, viral and protozoal diseases, and parasitic worm diseases—all of which can be transmitted by water.

Weather and Death

A recent study suggests that our desire for warm weather may be a strategy for survival. Rogot and Padgett have demonstrated an inverse relationship between temperature and mortality from heart disease and stroke.

The temperature at which lowest mortality occurs is 60°–79° F. Any temperature above or below that range increases the likelihood of death. Evidently, any departure from an "ideal day" constitutes a threat—sufficient in some cases to kill.

For individuals living in particularly hot climates such as Southern Florida or Arizona, the "ideal" temperature is somewhat higher (80°-89° F) than in other climates, with the same pattern of increased mortality at higher or lower temperatures.

Excessive mortality is also associated with snowfall, for

the day of the fall and for five to six days afterwards. As there is little correlation between the amount of snowfall and mortality, it may be that factors associated with snow rather than snow itself are responsible for the increase in mortality during the snow period.

Birmingham, Alabama

The relationship between weather and death was examined for 21,000 deaths occurring between December, 1968, and November, 1972, by Stanley J. States of the University of Pittsburgh. He found that weather exerts a strong influence on death from respiratory and circulatory causes, but has a relatively minor influence on cancer mortality and deaths caused by accidents and violence. Also, that the effects of weather increase with age, and are more pronounced among whites than nonwhites.

According to States, mortality in Birmingham is inversely correlated with temperature and dewpoint, and directly correlated with wind velocity and barometric pressure. Unstable barometric pressure has a particularly important influence on the death rate in old people.

The highest mortality in Birmingham occurs in autumn, when the long hot summer breaks and sudden influxes of colder air begin to arrive.

Eugene Rogot and Stephen J. Padgett, Epidemiology Branch, Division of Health and Vascular Diseases, National Heart and Lung Institute, Landow Bldg., Room C-825, Bethesda, Md. 20014

Stress, Health and Longevity

Stress has become one of the foremost villains of our time. It has been blamed for the entire spectrum of human ills— from bad breath to death. When something goes wrong, we say that we are "under stress." We are told that modern life is stressful. That stress can cause schizophrenia, cancer, and heart disease. Even that it is the cause of aging.

In truth, stress is an essential factor in health and longevity. It is the process by which biologic systems adapt to the environment . . . to such agents as air, water, temperature, and gravity. As such, it is instrumental in building strength, flexibility, and immunity to disease.

We need the stress of exercise to keep us physically fit, the stress of immunization to protect us against disease, the stress of problem-solving to improve our thinking ability, and the stress of intimate relationships to satisfy our emotional needs.

Stress can only hurt us if we react inappropriately to the environment. If we are unable to deal effectively with others, with responsibility, or with our feelings. In short, the harmful effects of stress, or "distress," are consequences of our own making.

Hans Selye contends that aging is determined by the amount of stress the body is exposed to. That we are born with a fixed amount of adaptation energy, which we use by making "withdrawals," but cannot replace by making "deposits." As he sees it, stress is the process by which we live *and* die.

However, the evidence suggests otherwise. That stress—when experienced on an appropriate level—is an anti-aging process by which we seek to stave off death. It's true that we gradually lose our ability to adapt to the environment as we grow older, but this loss appears to be caused by basic aging changes, rather than by stress itself.

Chapter 4

Anti-Aging Therapies

Antioxidants Extend the Life Span of Laboratory Animals

Over the past twenty years, Denham Harman of the University of Nebraska has been trying to retard aging in mice by feeding them large doses of antioxidants "to inhibit free radical damage caused by lipid peroxidation." (See p. 39.) In testing a dozen or more dietary supplements, Harman has reported significant success with the following compounds:

• 2-MEA (2-mercaptocthylamine)—a drug that protects against radiation—extended the mean life span of mice by 12.8 percent, 26 percent, 29.2 percent, and 45 percent in different experiments.

• BHT (Butylated hydroxytoluene)—a commercial food additive—extended the mean life span of mice by 45 percent and 61 percent in different experiments.

• Ethoxyquin—a commercial food additive for livestock—extended the mean life span of mice by 74.6 percent.

Here are some other findings about the effects of dietary antioxidants on life span in animals.

• In experiments at University College in London, gerontologist/sexologist Alex Comfort improved the survival time of mice by feeding them ethoxyquin. The experimental group showed a 20 percent increase in maximum life span compared with the control group.

• Eight of twelve rats given NDHGA (nordihydroguaiaretic acid) lived longer than 796 days, while only two of twelve controls lived that long.

• There have been modest life span extensions in male

mice and female guinea pigs, but not in female rats, from the effects of sulfhydril (SH-group) compounds, including the amino acid cysteine and a combination of thiazoledine-carboxylic acid and folic acid.

• Richard A. Passwater has experimented with various antioxidants. He claims increases in median life span ranging from 30 percent to 167 percent in laboratory mice, but has supplied few details about his protocol or findings. One of several "nutritional supplements" he has developed (Agerex 1) contains alpha tocopherol (vitamin E), cysteine, and selenocystine; another supplement (Agerex 2) contains BHT in addition to the ingredients in Agerex 1.

Denham Harman, University of Nebraska Medical Center, 42nd and Dewey Aves., Omaha, Ne. 68105

Richard A. Passwater, 529 Southview Ave., Silver Spring, Md. 20901

The "Anti-Aging" Advertisement

In the summer of 1976, a two-page ad by the Monsanto Company appeared in the magazine *Scientific American.* As the manufacturer of the antioxidant ethoxyquin (under the trade name Santoquin), Monsanto posed the question: "Can it actually slow the process of aging?"

Within the ad—which they called Monsanto Report No. 6 on Current Technology—they spelled out their message clearly:

"Is it possible that the well-established and long commercialized Santoquin feed antioxidant has this unexplored effect? The ability to slow the aging process in living bodies would include poultry, and that could perhaps be a way to prolong the producing life of chick breeders and laying hens. The same age-delaying mechanism might extend the siring virility of top-of-breed horses, bulls, and boars and stretch out the milk-giving period of dairy cows. It might give pet dogs and cats a longer lease on life."

There was not a mention of the possibility of ethoxyquin slowing the aging process in humans, though the implications for humans was obvious. The ad went on to quote the ideas and findings of Denham Harman, Johan Bjorksten, and Bernard L. Strehler—all of whom are interested in developing anti-aging therapies for humans.

Thus, it may be that the Monsanto Company wanted to explore public interest in the possibility of using ethoxyquin to retard aging in humans. Their choice of *Scientific American*—a national publication aimed at the general public—reinforces this premise. If their sole interest was the livestock industry, they would have confined the ad to chicken and bull breeders journals.

The Monsanto people did not discuss the use of ethoxyquin in humans because the compound has never been tested clinically and the evidence that it retards aging is far from conclusive. Certainly, the U.S. Food and Drug Administration (FDA) would not have appreciated such remarks. In fact, it's been reported that the FDA wasn't too happy about the idea of ethoxyquin extending the life span of cats and dogs.

Yet the interest shown by a major corporation like Monsanto in the effect of ethoxyquin on aging indicates that the time may soon come for clinical trials in humans on the anti-aging and anti-disease effects of anti-oxidants and other compounds.

The Monsanto Company, 800 N. Lindbergh St., St. Louis, Mo. 63166

Failure of Antioxidants to Retard Aging

Although proponents of the anti-aging effects of antioxidants rarely mention them, there have been negative findings on the subject as well.

In 1943, Clive M. McCay of Cornell University fed rats a diet enriched with wheat germ, which is high in the

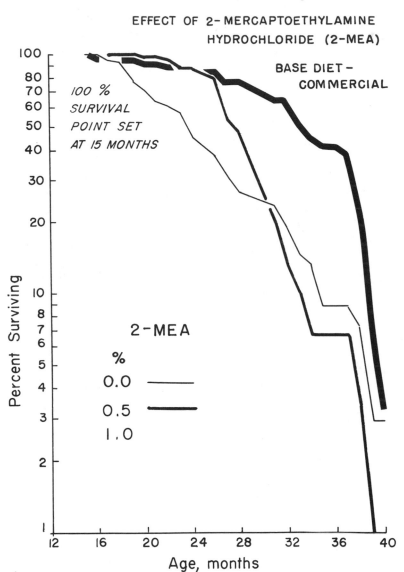

MORTALITY RATE OF MALE LAF$_1$ MICE

EFFECT OF 2-MERCAPTOETHYLAMINE
HYDROCHLORIDE (2-MEA)

*100 %
SURVIVAL
POINT SET
AT 15 MONTHS*

BASE DIET –
COMMERCIAL

2-MEA

%
0.0 ——
0.5 ——
1.0

Percent Surviving

Age, months

High doses of the synthetic antioxidants 2-MEA *(left)* and BHT significantly increased the mean but not the maximum life span of male LAF$_1$ mice. Use of a semi-synthetic diet *(right)* shortened the life span of both experimental and control animals.

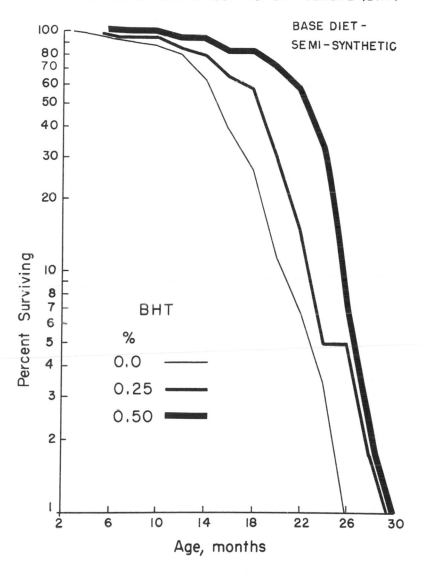

MORTALITY RATE OF MALE LAF₁ MICE

EFFECT OF BUTYLATED HYDROXYTOLUENE (BHT)

BASE DIET –
SEMI–SYNTHETIC

Percent Surviving

BHT
%
0.0
0.25
0.50

Age, months

natural antioxidant vitamin E. He found a 20 percent increase in mean life span for female rats and a lesser increase for males when compared to controls. However, this result was clouded because his control diet was probably deficient in vitamin E, which is an essential nutrient.

A more recent study of the effects of three combinations of dietary antioxidants—including vitamin E, vitamin C, BHT, selenium, and methionine—on age-related factors in mice produced largely negative results.

The only factor influenced positively by the antioxidant regimen was the accumulation of lipofuscin age pigment (see p. 29) in various tissues, which was inhibited in animals receiving diet three, which contained the highest concentration of antioxidants. Diet three also produced a slight shortening of maximum life span. The other diets had no effect on life span.

The results of this study should be given special attention because it was conducted by Al Tappel, a researcher whose work on antioxidants has been generally supportive of the idea of using these compounds therapeutically.

Al Tappel, Department of Biochemistry, University of California, Davis, Davis, Ca. 95616

Vitamin E and Nerve Cell Degeneration

Studies have shown that the vitamin E content of human tissues is quite low at birth, reaches maximum values during late childhood and early adulthood, diminishes during the third and fourth decades, and approaches the initially low birth levels at more advanced ages. It has also been observed that the nerve cells of mice degenerate with advancing age and that vitamin E deficiency accelerates this process.

Based on these findings, scientists at Ames Research Center, NASA, supplemented the diet of mice with vitamin E and then looked for degenerative changes in the dorsal column nuclei of the animals at different ages. They found that "vitamin E, added to the diet in the amount of 3 percent, did not protect the nuclei from age-associated degeneration," and concluded that the experiment argues against the effectiveness of dietary vitamin E in preventing age-associated degeneration of the central nervous system.

Jaime Miquel, Ames Research Center, NASA, Neurosciences Branch, Moffett Field, Ca. 94035

Assessing the Effect of Antioxidants on Life Span in Animals

The proposed anti-aging effect of dietary antioxidants in animals is open to question because of failures to extend life span in some studies, relatively modest life span extension in others, and the fact that the most successful results have come in strains of mice specially bred to develop cancer and die before reaching old age. The life-prolongation effects observed in these animals may have been caused by anti-cancer activity or protection against environmental damage.

In an effort to assess the value of dietary antioxidants as an anti-aging therapy, Robert R. Kohn of Case Western Reserve University studied the effects of these compounds on long-lived mice and came to the following conclusion:

"When survival of control mice is optimal, these antioxidants are without effect on life span. When survival of controls is suboptimal, as manifested by shortening of either 50 percent survival time or maximum life span, BHT and MEA cause lengthening of these life spans. In no case, however, do the antioxidants increase the 50 percent survival time or maximum life span significantly beyond values obtained from control mice surviving under optimal conditions. It is concluded that the antioxidants evaluated in this study . . . inhibit some harmful environmental or nutritional factors which cause control mice to show suboptimal survival in some experiments."

Robert R. Kohn, Institute of Pathology, Case Western Reserve University, Cleveland, Oh. 44106

Effect of Vitamin E on Human Life Span

The only study in which there has been an attempt to measure the effect of vitamin E on human life span was conducted by Romanian physician Ana Aslan in the process of testing her controversial "youth" drug—Gerovital-H$_3$. (See p. 29.) Aslan reported that, over a fifteen-year period, 10 percent of elderly patients receiving vitamin E died, compared to 15 percent of controls.

This finding cannot be given serious consideration because of the lack of details about the protocol of the study.

Ana Aslan, Institutul National de Gerontologie Si Geriatrie, Str. Mînăstirea Căldărusani, 9-Sector 8, Bucharest, Romania

Can Vitamin E Prolong the Life Span of Cells in Tissue Culture?

In 1961, Leonard Hayflick reported that embryonic human fibroblast lung cells (WI-38s) would divide a maximum of about fifty times when grown in tissue culture. (See p. 31.) In 1974, Lester Packer and James R. Smith reported that they had more than doubled the *in vitro* life span of WI-38 cells by adding vitamin E to the culture medium. They claimed that the "senescence" of the cells had been delayed because vitamin E acted "to stabilize the membrane and inhibit free radical reactions," and suggested that human fibroblasts may be capable of a very large, perhaps indefinite number of divisions.

This finding has been widely interpreted as support for the free radical theory of aging and for use of dietary vitamin E to retard the aging process. It has been mentioned repeatedly in articles, books, and documentaries and been accepted as gospel by many proponents of the health benefits of vitamin E.

However, no scientific finding can be presumed authentic until it has been duplicated by others. In the case of vitamin

E's ability to boost cell division in tissue culture, several investigators, including Packer and Smith, have been unable to duplicate this effect, despite extensive efforts to do so. Packer and Smith finally reported their failure to reproduce past results in April, 1977—only this time there was little of the publicity that surrounded their initial positive report.

Sometimes important discoveries sit for years before anyone moves to exploit their potential. Other times, people act on the basis of poorly substantiated or unverified findings. The increased use of vitamin E as an anti-aging therapy based upon media reports of the Packer-Smith finding appears to be an example of the latter type of inappropriate response.

Lester Packer, Department of Physiology/Anatomy, University of California, Berkeley, Berkeley, Ca. 94720

Antioxidants Postpone Diseases of Aging

In the course of his experiments on the effects of antioxidants on aging, Denham Harman noticed that these compounds delayed the onset of spontaneous tumors in mice predisposed to develop cancer. He interpreted this phenomenon as a consequence of retarded aging, but it may have been caused by an anti-cancer effect.

More recently, Harman has found that the addition of vitamin E or ethoxyquin to the diet of mice helps to offset the normal decline of immune response with advancing age. Perhaps the delay in the occurrence of cancer in animals fed antioxidants is the result of their ability to boost immune function in these animals.

In further work by Harman, vitamin E, BHT, and particularly ethoxyquin were able to inhibit amyloidosis—a common disease of aging that has been linked to immune system dysfunction.

Harman's explanation for the depressing effect of antioxidants on amyloid formation is their inhibition of free radical reactions involved in the disease process. An alternative explanation is that antioxidants boost thymus gland function. There is evidence that T cell (the immune cells developed by the thymus gland) impairment is related to the pathogenesis of experimentally induced amyloidosis, and that administration of thymosin—a hormone produced by the thymus gland—reduces the incidence and severity of this disease. (See p. 203.)

Harman has also reported that rats make fewer mistakes in running a maze if their diet has been supplemented with vitamin E—a finding that suggests the possible value of vitamin E therapy in treating age-related mental impairment.

Denham Harman, University of Nebraska Medical Center, 42nd and Dewey Aves., Omaha, Ne. 68105

Vitamin E Therapy for Heart Disease

There have been many reports of benefits from vitamin E therapy in heart disease patients, but these reports have largely been anecdotal case histories rather than controlled studies. At the Shute Institute, for example, where Evan and Wilfred Shute have pioneered in the clinical use of vitamin E, there have been numerous claims about the value of vitamin E in treating angina pectoris (heart pain).

In 1974, a double-blind, controlled study of vitamin E therapy for angina was conducted by Anderson and Reid of the University of Toronto. After consulting with the Shute brothers, they decided on a daily dose of 3,200 International Units (IU) of vitamin E for a nine-week period in patients suffering from angina. Forty-eight patients treated by eighteen physicians were initially enrolled in the study, but twelve dropped out before its completion. The remaining thirty-six were equally divided between those receiving vitamin E or placebo. Each group contained eleven males and seven females.

The majority of patients in both groups experienced no change in their condition as a result of treatment. One patient receiving vitamin E was "much improved" and one patient receiving placebo was "slightly worse." The distribution of the results was slightly more favorable to the vitamin E group, but the difference was not statistically significant.

Anderson and Reid concluded that the results of the study do not support the claim that patients with angina pectoris benefit from large doses of vitamin E. They suggested two possible explanations for the failure of their double-blind trial to confirm the dramatic effects reported by others. Either vitamin E is of no value in treating angina and the favorable reports are the result of spontaneous remissions and placebo effects, or vitamin E has a small effect and spontaneous remissions and placebo effects make up the balance.

Evan V. Shute and Wilfred D. Shute, The Shute Institute, 10 Grand Ave., London, Ontario, Canada

Terence W. Anderson, School of Hygiene, University of Toronto, Toronto, Canada M5S 1A1

Vitamin E Helps Arteriosclerosis Patients

Several controlled studies have demonstrated that vitamin E therapy is of substantial benefit to patients suffering from intermittent claudication (arteriosclerosis of the legs)— a condition in which decreased blood flow makes it difficult to walk.

In a Swedish study, Knut Haeger compared vitamin E therapy with vasodilating agents, anticoagulant therapy, and plain vitamin tablets without vitamin E. He found that patients receiving vitamin E were able to walk significantly longer distances than patients on the other regimens. Also, that the vitamin E group displayed considerably better arterial blood flow than the other groups. However, this improvement did not become apparent until twelve to eighteen months after the treatment was started.

Knut Haeger, Department of Surgery, Mälmo Hospital, Mälmo, Sweden

The Vitamin E Mystique

A serious obstacle to the development of new therapies—particularly for life-threatening diseases—is the conflict between those who tend to believe "miraculous" claims from almost any source and those who automatically reject such claims. Once a nutrient or drug becomes embroiled in such controversy, an aura of emotionalism that impedes scientific inquiries into its true value soon surrounds its use.

The saga of vitamin E typifies this sort of irrational behavior. As one of the superstars of a nationwide movement, in which "natural" foods have become status symbols for health-conscious Americans, a mystique has grown around its use. Vitamin E has been touted as a cure for heart disease, circulatory problems, muscular dystrophy, atherosclerosis, sterility, respiratory disorders, sexual dysfunction, and aging. On the other hand, the vast majority of scientists and physicians believe there is little or no need for vitamin E supplementation, and that there are no diseases for which vitamin E therapy is indicated.

In truth, there is little evidence of any kind that vitamin E can retard normal aging, but a fair amount of evidence that it may be beneficial for some conditions of aging. Clearly, more research and less emotionalism is needed.

Effect of Vitamin C on Life Span

"If you take 10 grams of vitamin C every day as I do," declared Linus Pauling at the 1978 Palm Springs conference to celebrate the fiftieth anniversary of its discovery, "you'll live sixteen years longer than people who take the minimum required amount of vitamin C." Pauling then mentioned something about "calculations" in an apparent attempt to justify his claim.

What he failed to do was provide evidence to back it up. Not that he could be entirely blamed for this oversight because, until recently, no one had any evidence on the effect of vitamin C on life span.

One reason for this neglect is that most life span studies have been performed in mice or rats—two species that synthesize their own vitamin C, a feat that we are not capable of. So when researchers tested the effects of antioxidants on life span in mice (see p. 131), they invariably left vitamin C out of their formulations, despite the fact that vitamin C is a natural antioxidant.

But now there are two reports on the subject. In one study, Harold R. Massie fed fruit flies (who, like us, do not make their own vitamin C) large amounts of the substance throughout their lives. He found that high dietary intake of vitamin C shortened the life span of these insects by 5.4 percent to 12.8 percent, with the higher the concentration of vitamin C, the greater the life-shortening effect. There was no appreciable effect on life span of small amounts of vitamin C.

In the second study, J.E.W. Davies and R. E. Hughes fed guinea pigs (the only rodents who do not produce their own vitamin C) either 0.5 milligrams per 100 grams of body weight or 1 milligram per 100 grams of body weight of vitamin C, starting at five weeks of age.

Once again, there was a shortening of life span in animals receiving the higher dosage of vitamin C. In particular, there were a significant number of early deaths associated with a high level of ascorbic acid consumption. There was no evidence that the animals in the lower dosage group lived longer than normal.

The results of these studies will require confirmation from

other sources. They suggest that vitamin C is of no value as an anti-aging therapy, and that it may be harmful at high doses.

Harold R. Massie, Masonic Medical Research Laboratory, Utica, New York 13503

J. E. W. Davies and R. E. Hughes, University of Wales Institute of Science and Technology, Cardiff, Wales

Vitamin C as a Treatment for Cancer

There is a growing body of evidence that vitamin C may be beneficial in treating cancer. The most remarkable news of this possibility comes from Ewan Cameron of the Vale of Leven District General Hospital in Scotland.

Cameron and Linus Pauling have reported a threefold increase in the survival time of 90 percent of terminal cancer patients treated with vitamin C compared to untreated control patients. In late 1976, the survival time of the remaining 10 percent of the ascorbate-treated group was estimated to be at least twenty times that of controls.

The original group consisted of 100 patients with advanced cancer of all types who were given 10 grams of vitamin C per day by intravenous (IV) infusion for the first ten days of treatment, and then maintained on the same dose

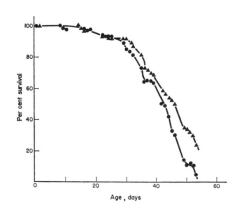

Drosophila (fruit flies) fed vitamin C (●) had a shorter life span than controls (▲).

orally. Prior to the initiation of treatment, every patient in the experimental group was examined independently by at least two physicians, who agreed that their situation was "totally hopeless" and their condition "quite untreatable." All patients had previously been treated by conventional methods such as surgery, radiotherapy, and chemotherapy.

The control group was obtained by a random search of the case record index of cancer patients treated at Vale of Leven Hospital over the previous ten years. For each ascorbate-treated patient, ten age- and sex-matched controls, who had suffered from cancer of the same primary organ and tumor type, were chosen. Two hundred of the 1,000 patients in the control group were contemporaries of the ascorbate-treated group.

Daily ascorbic acid intake	Mean life span (days)		
	Total	First six deaths*	Last six deaths
0·5 mg/100 g body weight	864 ± 56	564 ± 39	1251 ± 54
1% in drinking water	783 ± 69	315 ± 71	1179 ± 33

*Difference between means significant, $p < 0.05$.

Guinea pigs fed a higher dose of vitamin C (1 percent) had a shorter mean life span than guinea pigs fed a lower dose (0.5 percent) of vitamin C.

The case records of all control patients were analyzed independently by Francis Meuli of Otago, New Zealand, to establish the date they were declared "untreatable." This date was matched with the date vitamin C therapy was started in the experimental patients in order to compare the survival time of both groups.

Updating the Study

In an updated version of the study, a revised set of 100 ascorbate-treated patients, including most of those from the original group, was compared with a new set of 1,000 matched controls. This time the precise date of first hospital attendance was used as a reference point (along with date of death) in addition to the date of "untreatability" in comparing the two groups. Of the 1,000 control patients, 370 were concurrent with the ascorbate-treated patients.

The ascorbate-treated group was found to have a mean survival time about 300 days longer than controls. Only four of the 1,000 controls survived more than one year after the date of untreatability compared with twenty-two of the 100 ascorbate-treated patients. As of May 15, 1978, the mean survival time for these twenty-two patients was reported to be 2.4 years. Eight of the patients were still alive, with a mean survival time of 3.5 years beyond the date they were declared untreatable. None of the control patients were still alive.

According to Cameron and Pauling, the dramatic life-extending effect of vitamin C therapy in advanced cancer patients is probably the result of the bolstering of host resistance to malignant disease processes. Treatment with higher doses of vitamin C than 10 grams daily, they suggest, might improve patient survival even more. Even greater success might be expected if vitamin C therapy was begun at an earlier stage of cancer development. Life expectancy in such patients, predict Cameron and Pauling, might be increased "from five years to twenty years," or they might be "cured" of the disease entirely.

The remarkable Cameron-Pauling findings await confirmation from other investigators.

Ewan Cameron and Linus Pauling, The Linus Pauling Institute of Science and Medicine, 2700 Sand Hill Road, Menlo Park, Ca. 94025

Vitamin C May Prevent Stomach Cancer

In the past forty years, there has been a threefold decrease in the U.S. death rate from stomach cancer. One explanation for this decrease is the widespread use of antioxidants to preserve such foods as bread, cereal, and salad oil. Many studies have shown that antioxidants inhibit the carcinogenic process and reduce the number of malignant tumors in laboratory animals.

Other studies suggest that ascorbic acid (vitamin C), which has antioxidant properties, can inhibit a class of compounds called nitrosamines, which are believed to be involved in the genesis of stomach cancer. Nitrosamines are formed when nitrites, which are found in smoked meats and fish, combine in the stomach with amines released from the proteins in these foods.

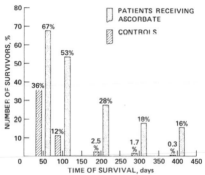

Patients receiving ascorbate (vitamin C) therapy showed a much higher survival rate than matched controls.

A recent study showed that a type of raw fish commonly eaten in Japan—which has the highest death rate from stomach cancer in the world—exhibits high mutagenic activity when treated with nitrite. This activity was prevented by the addition of vitamin C. The same study showed no mutagenic activity when meats commonly eaten in the U.S., such as hot dogs, were treated with sizable amounts of nitrite.

The ability of vitamin C to inhibit formation of nitrosamines has also been demonstrated in a type of beef stew similar to that eaten in Eastern European countries with a high rate of stomach cancer. In general, an ascorbate-nitrite ratio of at least 2:1 appears to be necessary for significant prevention of carcinogenic activity.

Hildegard Marquardt, American Health Foundation, Valhalla, N.Y. 10595

Vitamin C for Colon Cancer

Scientists at the Vince Lombardi Colon Clinic have shown that 3 grams of vitamin C taken daily over a twenty-two- to thirty-month period can reduce and, in some cases, eliminate rectal polyps in seventeen- to fifty-nine-year-old patients. Since the risk of developing rectal or colon cancer is linked to the presence of such polyps, it appears that long-term administration of ascorbic acid may help to prevent such cancers. Preliminary results of a study at Memorial Sloan-Kettering Cancer Center to assess the effects of ascorbic acid treatment for colon cancer show "little in the way of difference" between treatment and placebo groups.

Jerome J. DeCosse, Memorial Sloan-Kettering Cancer Center, 1275 York Ave., New York, N.Y. 10021

Vitamin C and Atherosclerosis

If you suffer from vitamin C deficiency, you may be at-risk for atherosclerosis. Studies have shown that animals deprived of vitamin C have higher blood and tissue levels of cholesterol and a greater incidence of atherosclerosis than animals on a vitamin-C-enriched diet. This association holds for species such as guinea pigs and monkeys, who are not capable of manufacturing their own vitamin C, and rats and rabbits, who have the capacity to produce their own vitamin C.

Emil Ginter has presented evidence that the excretion of cholesterol may be controlled by vitamin C. Ginter has demonstrated that a decrease in the concentration of vitamin C in the liver of guinea pigs causes a corresponding decrease in the conversion of cholesterol to bile acids, which leads to an accumulation of cholesterol in the serum and liver of these animals. Also, that an increase in liver vitamin C content stimulates the conversion of cholesterol to bile acids, which are then excreted from the body.

When it comes to humans, we see a direct correlation between vitamin C levels and several key cardiovascular risk factors. Smokers have lower vitamin C levels than non-smokers, men have lower vitamin C levels than women, and old persons have lower levels than young ones. Moreover, a strong negative correlation has been found in England and Wales between vitamin C intake and death from ischemic heart disease and stroke.

Clinical Trials

A look at the clinical trials conducted to assess the effect of vitamin C on cholesterol levels reveals a somewhat confused picture. It has generally been found that vitamin C lowers plasma cholesterol in subjects with higher-than-normal levels, but has no effect on subjects with normal levels. However, some studies have shown that vitamin C raises plasma cholesterol in subjects with elevated cholesterol levels.

In one such study, vitamin C therapy raised plasma cholesterol levels significantly in subjects with atherosclerosis, but reduced it in most healthy subjects. It was suggested that vitamin C might have dislodged previously immobilized cholesterol from arterial plaques—a finding supported by the animal experiments showing that vitamin C facilitates transport of cholesterol from the arteries to the liver and adrenal glands.

Emil Ginter, Institute of Human Nutrition Research, Bratislava, Czechoslovakia

S. D. Turley, Department of Experimental Pathology, John Curtin School of Medical Research, The Australian National University, P.O. Box 334, Canberra City, A.C.T., 2600, Australia

How Much Vitamin C?

In 1970, Linus Pauling stated that a daily intake of 1 to 3 grams of ascorbic acid would reduce the incidence and severity of upper respiratory infections. In a letter to the Canadian Medical Association journal, he claimed that regular intake of 1 gram of vitamin C daily would lead to 45 percent fewer colds and 60 percent fewer days of sickness.

When subsequent studies at these doses failed to confirm these claims, Pauling insisted that the doses weren't high enough. Every time evidence was presented against the therapeutic value of vitamin C, Pauling would raise his proposed dosage level. Today, he recommends a regular dosage of 10 grams a day, with considerably higher intake during illness—a regimen that has been generally embraced by vitamin C advocates.

The most radical of these advocates is Robert Cathcart, an orthopedic surgeon now practicing at Incline Village, Nevada, near Lake Tahoe. Cathcart claims we can tolerate considerably more ascorbic acid when we are sick than when we are well. His approach to the treatment of respiratory illness is to push his patients to the limits of their ability to tolerate ascorbic acid.

Thus, he recommends 10 to 15 grams of vitamin C per day for a person in good health; but prescribes 30 to 60 grams (by mouth or intravenously) for a moderate cold, 100 to 150 grams for a bad cold or the flu, and more than 200 grams a day for viral pneumonia or mononucleosis. When his patients begin to recover, Cathcart gradually reduces the dosage of vitamin C until the normal maintenance level is reached.

According to Cathcart, this type of therapy rapidly knocks out most of the symptoms of the disease, although it has little effect on the duration of serious illnesses. He insists that his patients can then weather the infection without complications and boasts that they almost never miss any work time.

The problem with this approach is the potential dangers of such high doses. Vitamin C is one of the least toxic substances around, but there have been reports of harmful side effects from doses far lower than those prescribed by Cathcart, Pauling, and others. Among these effects are vitamin B_{12} deficiency, excessive clearance of uric acid, increased destruction of red blood cells, and possible contribution to the death of a man from kidney failure. Added to these data are the two animal studies showing reductions in life span as a result of vitamin C intake. (See p. 143.)

Although it is certainly permissible to give megadoses of vitamin C to advanced cancer patients with "no hope of recovery," there is good reason to question such doses for patients with a good prognosis for recovery, or for normally healthy individuals.

Robert F. Cathcart, III, Incline Village, Nevada 89450

Victor Herbert, 130 West Kingsbridge Rd., Bronx, N.Y. 10468

Exploring the Powers of Selenium

One of the most potent substances on Earth is selenium—a rare element that is essential in trace amounts for good health, but is highly toxic in larger amounts. For many years, selenium was thought to be a poison and carcinogen, but recent studies suggest that it may protect us against heart disease, cancer, and premature aging.

Scientists at the Cleveland Clinic have reported that Americans living in selenium-deficient areas are three times more likely to die of heart disease than those living in selenium-rich areas. In Colorado Springs, for example, which is rich in selenium, the death rate from heart disease was 67 percent below the national average; whereas in the selenium-deficient

District of Columbia, the death rate from heart disease was 22 percent above the national average.

Other studies have demonstrated a high incidence of sudden death associated with degeneration of the heart and skeletal muscles in pigs and lambs deprived of selenium. When rats were fed a selenium-deficient diet, they developed atherosclerotic plaques, abnormal vascularization, and weakened arterial walls.

The incidence of cancer has also been found to be higher than normal in selenium-deficient areas and lower than normal in selenium-rich areas. (Most densely populated areas in the U.S. have low to marginal amounts of selenium in the soil.)

Selenium compounds have been used to inhibit the formation of certain types of cancer in animals exposed to carcinogens. In one study, rats fed a high-selenium diet lived 13 percent to 16 percent longer than control animals.

Various mechanisms have been proposed for the action of selenium, but the best documented rationale is that it acts as an antioxidant. The powers of selenium are just beginning to be understood. Its potential value as a therapeutic agent may depend upon its interaction with other nutrients.

Raymond J. Shamberger, The Cleveland Clinic, Cleveland, Oh. 44106

What Is the Value of Pangamic Acid (Vitamin B₁₅)?

Before Muhammad Ali defeated England's Richard Dunn in May, 1976, he waved a bottle of pangamic acid at the worldwide TV audience as if to say he had discovered a new secret weapon. Ali had been taking supplementary doses of pangamic acid as part of a nutrition program suggested to him by researcher and author Richard Passwater.

Pangamic acid is a water soluble factor found in virtually all seeds that is often designated as vitamin B_{15}. It is consumed as a nutritional supplement in the form of its salt —calcium pangamate.

The principal supplier and consumer of pangamic acid is the Soviet Union where it was first approved for use in 1965 by the U.S.S.R. Ministry of Health. It has been used extensively in that country for the treatment of cardiovascular disease. Daily oral doses of 50-300 mg of calcium pangamate have been reported to diminish the frequency, intensity, and duration of ischemic heart attacks and increase exercise tolerance in patients recovering from heart attacks.

In a study of eighty patients with atherosclerotic heart disease, A. A. Apanasenko found that daily doses of calcium pangamate given for twenty to thirty days significantly improved the contractile function of the heart, while enhancing the circulating blood volume, lowering blood pressure, and suppressing cardiac pain.

Other Soviet studies suggest that pangamic acid may reduce serum cholesterol levels, conserve oxygen in the bloodstream, potentiate muscular activity, and normalize blood sugar levels in diabetics. It also has been suggested that pangamate is useful in treating alcoholism, liver disease, asthma, and emphysema.

It's difficult to evaluate the extensive claims for pangamic acid because most of the Soviet studies lack suitably matched controls and present inadequate data. Since no controlled studies on pangamic acid have apparently been conducted in the U.S. or Western Europe, the jury is still out on the value of this substance.

A. A. Apanasenko, Medical Institute of Blagoveshchensk-on-Amur, U.S.S.R.

Peter W. Stacpoole, Vanderbilt University School of Medicine, Nashville, Tn. 37203

The Vitamin That May Retard Aging

If a female bee is fed in routine fashion, she becomes an infertile worker bee and lives about a month. But if the same bee is fed with royal jelly, she grows up to be a fertile queen bee and lives six to eight years. The enormous disparity between the life span of worker and queen bees suggests that pantothenic acid—the primary nutritional constituent of royal jelly—might be able to prolong life span in other species.

In 1948, T. H. Gardner reported that pantothenic acid could extend the life span of another type of insect—the fruit fly. But the only experiment to test the life-extending potential of pantothenic acid in mammals has been a 1958 study by Richard B. Pelton and Roger J. Williams.

In this study, they used thirty-four male and forty female C-57 black mice, which were divided into two groups at four to five weeks of age. One group of thirty-three mice (thirteen males and twenty females) was given 0.3 mg of extra pantothenic acid per day (in the form of calcium pantothenate). The other group of forty-one mice (twenty-one males and twenty females) served as controls.

The mice who received extra pantothenate had a mean life span about 19 percent longer than the control mice (18 percent in males, 20 percent in females). The forty-one control animals lived an average of 550 days, while the thirty-three pantothenate-treated animals lived an average of 653 days.

Pantothenic acid is a member of the B complex vitamin group. It functions as a component of coenzyme A—an essential compound that plays an important role in energy metabolism, detoxification of harmful substances, steroid hormone production, and maintenance of membrane integrity. Another component of coenzyme A is 2-mercaptoethylamine (2-MEA), which has also been shown to prolong the life span of mice. (See p. 131.)

When M. E. Dunn and E. P. Ralli gave rats large doses of pantothenic acid, the animals were able to swim for sixty minutes in cold water (18° C) compared with only thirty minutes for untreated animals. Large doses of pantothenic acid had a similar effect on the swimming endurance of humans in cold water.

Despite all the ballyhoo over vitamins C and E, pantothenic acid is the only vitamin that has been shown to prolong life span in mammals. Its apparent ability to protect the body against stress suggests that it may influence normal rather than pathologic processes.

Why pantothenic acid has been ignored for so long is hard to understand when every other vitamin under the sun seems to have its own fan club. It's time to take another look at pantothenic acid in order to assess its possible value as an anti-aging therapy.

Roger J. Williams, Clayton Foundation, Biochemical Institute, University of Texas, Austin, Tx. 78712

L-Dopa Prolongs the Life Span of Mice

L-Dopa, or levodopa, is a drug developed to treat patients with Parkinson's Disease (see p. 250), who suffer from a deficiency of dopamine—a chemical neurotransmitter (message sender) produced in the brain, which has been linked to aging. (See p. 45.) As the amino acid precursor to dopamine, L-Dopa is converted into dopamine in the body, which relieves the symptoms of the disease.

In order to determine the long-term effects of L-Dopa, George C. Cotzias fed Swiss albino mice the maximum concentration of the drug they could tolerate in their food supply, which proved to be 40 milligrams per gram (mg/g) for males and 80 mg/g for females. This regimen was started at four to five weeks of age and was continued thereafter.

At maturity, the mice were consuming an enormous daily dose of L-Dopa—about 5,000 mg per kilogram (mg/kg) in males and 10,000 mg/kg in females. In comparison, the maximal daily dose of L-Dopa usually taken by humans is 150 mg/kg.

Effects of L-Dopa

At early ages, the L-Dopa-treated mice showed thinning of body hair, which gave them an unhealthy appearance compared with controls. During the third and fourth months, a significant number of them died and, by the sixth month, it was noted that the surviving animals refused to fight among themselves, as normally occurs with Swiss albino mice.

At about one year of age, there was a marked, striking change in the appearance of the L-Dopa-treated mice. They looked leaner and more youthful than the control animals, as their fur became dense and smooth. Despite the continued absence of fighting, the experimental mice gave the impression of being "more vivacious" than controls. On the negative side, the L-Dopa mice suffered a higher incidence of corneal opacities than did controls.

L-Dopa treatment prolonged the mean life span of the experimental animals up to 50 percent. At nineteen months of age, 39 percent of the control animals were still alive compared with 73 percent of the L-Dopa group. No significant extension of maximum life span was reported for the experimental group.

It was suggested that an alteration in immune response may have produced the life-prolongation effect. An alternative explanation is that L-Dopa may have lowered the body temperature of the experimental animals to protect them against some of the ravages of aging and disease. (See p. 165.)

Samuel T. Miller, Memorial Sloan-Kettering Cancer Center, 444 E. 68th St., New York, N.Y. 10021

Iodine Compound Increases Life Span of Fruit Flies

When Harold R. Massie raised fruit flies on a medium containing the iodine compound methylene iodide (diiodomethane)—which has been used to accelerate the growth of plants—he observed an increase in median and maximum survival of up to 29.3 percent compared with controls. The only apparent side effect was a perpetual state of lethargy characterized by diminished flight activity. By stopping the treatment when the flies reached adulthood, Massie was able to prevent them from becoming lethargic, but was able to extend their lives by only 13.6 percent.

Similar compounds were unsuccessful in prolonging the life span of fruit flies. Iodine produced little or no change in life span over a wide range of concentrations; iodoform decreased life span by up to 23.8 percent; and hydrogen iodide was toxic at virtually all concentrations tested. None of these compounds produced the lethargy associated with the life-producing effect of diiodomethane.

Harold R. Massie, Masonic Medical Research Laboratory, Utica, N.Y. 13503

Rats Live Longer on Sulfa Drug

Sulfa drugs are used to combat bacterial infections. One such drug—sulfamerazine—has been used to extend the life span of both male and female rats by Gladys A. Sperling of Cornell University.

The drug was given to rats at a concentration of 250 mg/kg of the diet. Male rats fed sulfamerazine lived an average of 707 days compared with 621 days for controls, while female rats on sulfamerazine lived an average of 914 days compared with 671 days for controls.

The animals receiving sulfamerazine reached an average maximum weight of 32 grams more than controls. There was no consistent difference in the bone density of treated and control animals.

An additional finding was that rats given an opportunity to exercise lived an average of eighty-one days longer (809 vs. 728) than controls. (See p. 184.)

Gladys A. Sperling, 113 Cobb St., Ithaca, N.Y. 14850

Prolonging Life Span of Human Cells in Culture

When human diploid cells are grown in tissue culture, they divide about fifty times and then die out. (See p. 30.) There have been many attempts to increase the *in vitro* life span of cells by adding substances to the culture medium. The best success to date has been with the adrenal gland hormone hydrocortisone (and to a lesser extent with cortisone and other corticosteroid hormones)—a finding first reported by Vincent J. Cristafalo.

Cristafalo achieved a 30-40 percent increase in population doublings of cultured human diploid cells treated with hydrocortisone. The effect was most pronounced when the hormone was added just as the cells were about to divide. There was no rejuvenation effect when the hormone was added after the cells stopped dividing.

When Cristafalo added hydrocortisone to cells from birds, reptiles, amphibians, and fish, he found that cell division was inhibited. But when he added the hormone to seven types of human fibroblast cells—including fetal, infant, and adult skin cells—he found a stimulatory effect.

He suggests that hydrocortisone prolongs the life span of human cells in culture by stabilizing the membranes of lysosomes—the cellular components containing enzymes that break down materials. An age-related leakage of lysosomal enzymes has been linked to the aging process (see p. 37) and "membrane stabilizers" have been used to extend the life span of fruit flies and mice. (See p. 273.)

Vincent J. Cristafalo, Wistar Institute of Anatomy and Biology, 36th St. at Spruce, Philadelphia, Pa. 19104

Can Aspirin Prevent Heart Attacks?

The results of several clinical trials suggest that aspirin therapy may be beneficial for individuals with a history of myocardial infarction or stroke.

For example, participants in the Coronary Drug Project Aspirin Study, who took 1 gram of aspirin (the equivalent of about three standard tablets) every day for ten to twenty-eight months, had a lower mortality rate than controls. Overall mortality was 5.8 percent in the aspirin group compared with 8.3 percent in the placebo group—a difference of 30 percent.

While this finding suggests that aspirin may protect against mortality from heart disease, it is far from conclusive. Other trials have produced less positive results, and still others have produced negative results.

One explanation for the variability of these results is that aspirin appears to act by inhibiting both TXA_2 (the factor that promotes bloodclotting) and PGI_2 (the factor that inhibits bloodclotting). Scientists believe that the balance between TXA_2 and PGI_2 determines whether or not clotting will occur.

Blood clots are a major cause of both heart attacks and strokes. Studies by L. O. Pilgram have shown a progressive increase in clotting abnormalities with advancing age, which may be a contributing factor to the age-related increase in heart attacks and strokes.

The National Heart, Lung, and Blood Institute is currently sponsoring a large clinical trial of aspirin therapy, which includes 4,524 patients who have already suffered at least one heart attack. The trial is called AMIS (the Aspirin Myocardial Infarction Study). It is hoped that AMIS will produce conclusive results about the therapeutic value of aspirin for heart disease.

William Friedewald, The National Heart, Lung, and Blood Institute, NIH, Bethesda, Md. 20014

L. O. Pilgeram, P.O. Box 132, Palo Alto, Ca. 94301

Extension of Maximum Life Span by Lowering Body Temperature

Is your body temperature lower than normal? If so, you may have higher life expectancy than others your age. "There are no exceptions that I know of to the rule that animals live longer at lower temperatures," says Bernard Strehler of the University of Southern California. "It's possible that turning down the human thermostat a few degrees could add fifteen to twenty-five years to our lives."

Reduction of body temperature is the only experimental regimen to date—other than calorie restriction (see p. 60)— that has enabled scientists to extend the maximum life span of animals.

In 1917, researchers at The Rockefeller Institute extended the life span of fruit flies by keeping them at 19° C instead of the usual 25° C. A similar life-extending effect was later produced in rotifers.

The most extensive experiments in lowering body temperature have been performed at UCLA Medical Center by Robert K. Liu and Roy L. Walford. They were able to extend the maximum life span of poikilothermic (cold-blooded) annual fish of the genus *Cynolebias* by lowering the temperature of the water in which the fish were kept.

Fish that were maintained at the temperature of 15° C lived considerably longer than fish maintained at 20° C, but the longest life span was obtained in fish transferred from 20° C to 15° C at mid-life. The maximum life span attained in fish kept at 20° C throughout their lives was twenty-one months, whereas fish transferred from 20° C to 15° C at eight months of age were able to survive for as long as thirty-eight months—a 76 percent increase in maximum life span.

Biochemical tests showed that fish maintained at 15° C were physiologically younger at any given chronologic age than fish maintained at 20° C. And that the metabolic rate of the fish was actually faster at 15° C than at 20° C. This finding suggests that the positive effect of lowered body temperature on life span cannot be explained by a slowing of metabolic function.

Effect on Immune Function

Walford suggests that reduced body temperature extends life span by depressing the autoimmune reactions that normally contribute to bodily deterioration. He points out that all experiments to date indicate that temperature reduction can extend longevity most effectively during the latter part of an animal's life span, the time at which autoantibodies become prevalent. He has proposed that autoantibodies, which attack the body itself, play a key role in the expression of aging and the diseases of aging. (See p. 40.)

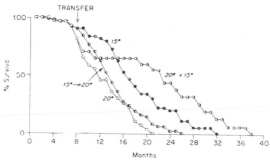

Survival of South American annual fish *Cynolebias bellotti* at different temperatures. The longest life span was obtained in fish transferred from 20°C to 15°C at mid-life.

Liu and Walford tried to lower the body temperature of mice with injections of the drug chlorpromazine (CPZ) and extracts of marijuana. They found that CPZ had an "all-or-nothing" effect that was unsatisfactory in both cases. At high doses, it produced a state of deep hypothermia (reduced temperature) that markedly depressed physical activity and led to toxic side effects. At lower doses, its hypothermia effect was short-lived, as the animals developed rapid tolerance to the drug.

Marijuana, on the other hand, produced a milder degree

of hypothermia with less inhibition of activity, but only on a temporary basis.

Biofeedback has been suggested as a possible means of lowering body temperature. By using this technique, individuals have learned to control such autonomic functions as blood pressure, heartbeat, and brain wave patterns. In his travels to the far east, Walford found yogis who could apparently lower their body temperature through biofeedback.

Roy L. Walford, Department of Pathology, UCLA Medical Center, Los Angeles, Ca. 90024

Lowering the Body's Thermostat

Our normal body temperature of 37° C (98.6° F) is a heritage of our evolution as warm-blooded mammals. No matter what external conditions we are exposed to—whether Arctic cold or tropical heat—there is little change within us. Because of our temperature-control system, we are able to maintain consistent physiologic activity in the face of environmental adversity.

With 37° C as the set point of our thermostat, it is generally assumed that this is the optimum temperature for good health and long life. Certainly, it is true that elevated body temperature (fever) is a sign of illness or distress that can become life-threatening. But what of the reverse? Could a chronic reduction in body temperature be life-enhancing? Experiments on cold-blooded animals (who have a less precise thermostat) suggest that this may be the case, but the only way to find out would be to lower the temperature of a warm-blooded animal.

Efforts to do so have been largely unsuccessful because of the difficulty of counteracting the thermostat in a warm-blooded animal. Various drugs have been shown to be capable of reducing body temperature, but usually on a temporary basis only. As soon as the thermostat has time to "evaluate" the situation, it orders the body to step up its rate of heat production in order to re-establish its normal temperature level.

Resetting the Thermostat

But what if we were able simply to reset the thermostat at a lower level? Such a possibility has been explored by R. D. Myers of Purdue University. Myers has found that the set point of the thermostat in mammals may involve the balance between sodium (Na^+) and calcium (Ca^{2+}) ions in the posterior hypothalamus region of the brain. Once that set point has been determined, the body's efforts to maintain it are apparently controlled by alterations in the levels of neurotransmitters such as serotonin and norepinephrine in the anterior hypothalamus.

Myers has demonstrated that if you perfuse the posterior hypothalamus of a monkey with artificial cerebrospinal fluid (CSF) containing excess calcium, the monkey's temperature is reduced in a way that enables him to thermoregulate around a new set point. The monkey's set point can be raised in similar fashion with a solution containing excess sodium.

Myers is convinced that altering temperature by this method actually resets the body's thermostat because the temperature of his experimental animals always returns to the new set point, rather than to the normal level of 37° C, after he raises or lowers the temperature with infusions of hot or cold water.

In one experiment, he maintained a new set point of between 34° C and 35° C for thirteen hours. Only when the calcium level in the posterior hypothalamus was reduced to its normal level did the animal's temperature return to 37° C. During the animal's journey into hypothermia, its other brain functions—as measured by electrical brain wave readings and responsiveness to drugs—appeared to be entirely normal.

Further evidence that the set point of the body's thermostat is determined by the sodium/calcium balance in the brain is the fact that repeated infusions of excess calcium can drive a monkey's temperature downward until the animal is threatened with death.

Myers has shown that fevers of bacterial origin are caused by disturbances in the brain's sodium/calcium balance, and that the rise in temperature associated with vigorous exercise is similarly altered by a change in the sodium/calcium balance. By giving an exercising monkey a low concentration of calcium ions, he found that he could block the expected rise in body temperature without significantly altering the animal's work output. At higher concentrations, the monkey's exercise rate was reduced.

These findings suggest that a slight elevation of calcium ion concentration in the posterior hypothalamus of a warm-blooded animal might permanently lower its body temperature without harmful side effects. One way of accomplishing this might be through use of the Alzet Osmotic Minipump—a self-powered device for the continuous infusion of agents into experimental animals. (See p. 385.)

If we find that lower body temperature does contribute to good health and long life, we could then develop an appropriate therapeutic system to accomplish the same end in humans.

Robert D. Myers, Department of Pharmacology, FLOB Building, University of North Carolina, Chapel Hill, N.C. 27514

Drugs to Lower Body Temperature

There is evidence that regulation of body temperature in warm-blooded mammals depends upon the balance of two neurotransmitters—serotonin and norepinephrine. When injected into the anterior hypothalamus of the brain, serotonin raises and norepinephrine lowers, the body temperature of rats, cats, dogs, and monkeys.

Andrew Janoff and Barnett Rosenberg have been searching for drugs to lower the temperature of mammals by altering neurotransmitter levels in the brain. Among the drugs they've been working with in laboratory mice are chlorpromazine (CPZ), L-Dopa, p-chlorophenylalanine (PCPA), and reserpine.

They've found that CPZ and PCPA are poor candidates for long-term inducement of hypothermia because animals soon adapt to their temperature-lowering action, but that L-Dopa and reserpine can lower body temperature for as long as thirty-two days without an adaptive response. In the case of reserpine, the hypothermic effect of a single injection lasts for more than twenty-four hours, regardless of dose.

Of interest is the fact that L-Dopa—which can reduce serotonin levels by 30 percent and raise dopamine (another neurotransmitter) levels by 300 percent—has also been used to extend the life span of mice (see p. 155), and to re-establish youthful estrous patterns in aging rats. (See p. 317.) In addition, some patients taking the drug as a treatment for Parkinson's Disease, have exhibited signs of an accelerated sex drive. (See p. 321.)

Janoff and Rosenberg speculate that the extension in life span produced by L-Dopa may have been caused by the drug's ability to lower body temperature. They suggest that a neurotransmitter "cocktail" consisting of L-Dopa and reserpine plus two enzyme inhibitors (RO4-4602 and Nilamide) might be "an extremely effective nonadapting hypothermic agent."

Other Hypothermic Agents

In a separate study, Sharkawi and Cianflone demonstrated that intraperitoneal injections of disulfiram and methimazole—which increase dopamine activity in the brain—can produce a dose-dependent lowering of body temperature in normal rats. They also found that the hypothermic effect of these agents could be reduced significantly by subsequent administration of pimozide—an agent that selectively blocks dopamine receptors in the brain.

Several naturally occurring peptides including neurotensin and bombesin have been shown to lower body temperature in mice and rats when injected into the cerebrospinal fluid. However, these compounds produced little or no hypothermic effect unless the animals were placed into a cold environment during treatment, and were ineffective when administered intravenously.

Barnett Rosenberg, Department of Biophysics, Michigan State University, East Lansing, Mi. 48824

M. Sharkawi, Department of Pharmacology, Faculty of Medicine, University of Montreal, P.Q., Canada

Marvin Brown, Laboratory for Neuroendocrinology, Salk Institute, San Diego, Ca. 92112

Chapter 5

How Exercise Extends Life Span

Only Vigorous Exercise Protects Against Heart Disease

Since 1956, more than a dozen studies have failed to confirm that a physically active lifestyle reduces the risk of heart disease. But there also have been at least as many studies indicating that an active lifestyle does reduce the risk of heart disease.

Evidence is accumulating that the reason for the conflict among these studies is that only vigorous exercise protects against heart disease and few people get enough exercise to make a difference. As a result, studies that fail to differentiate between light or moderate and vigorous exercise are unlikely to uncover any health benefits for exercise.

One study that has been instrumental in bringing this issue to light was started in 1968 by J. N. Morris in England. Morris has followed the leisure-time physical activities of 16,882 male executive-grade civil service office workers, age forty to sixty-four, based upon their own written accounts of their activities on selected days.

In 1973, he reported that 232 of these men had suffered coronary heart attacks, and that each of them had been matched with two control subjects who had not suffered a heart attack. Both groups were similar in age and cigarette-smoking habits.

An attempt was made to measure how much exercise the subjects in both groups had been engaging in. "Vigorous" exercise was defined as any activity likely to require peaks of energy output of at least 7.5 kilocalories (Kcals) and an oxygen intake of more than 1.5 liters per minute. In order to be classified as vigorous, such exercise had to continue uninterrupted for more than fifteen minutes. Among the activities in the vigorous category were running, swimming, and bicycling.

According to these criteria, Morris found that the risk of developing coronary heart disease in men reporting regular, vigorous exercise was about a third of that in comparable men not reporting vigorous exercise. Those engaging in light or moderate exercise showed no advantage over nonexercisers in the risk of heart disease. The apparent protective effect of vigorous exercise against heart disease continued throughout middle age.

J. N. Morris, Department of Community Health, London School of Hygiene and Tropical Medicine, London WC1E 7HT, England

Exercise Improves Heart Performance

The most common method of assessing the performance of the heart under normal conditions is to measure its electrical activity at rest with a machine called an electrocardiograph. Heart activity is recorded as a series of squiggly lines on paper. The resulting electrocardiogram (ECG) is then analyzed for evidence of such danger signs as ectopic (premature) beats, sinus tachycardia (more than 100 beats per minute), and irregularities that indicate possible myocardial ischemia (reduced blood flow to the heart).

In 1971, 509 middle-aged male executive-grade civil service officers were selected from among the 16,882 subjects taking part in Morris' ongoing study of the effect of leisure-time physical activity on the incidence of heart disease. Two electrocardiograms were recorded for each subject (at different paper speeds), as well as other tests—with interpretation of the results by independent scientists who had no information about the study subjects.

Significantly fewer cardiac irregularities were found

among the 125 subjects who said they engaged in vigorous exercise than among the 384 subjects who said they did not. For example, prominent Q waves, which are considered definite signs of myocardial ischemia, did not occur in the vigorous exercise group, but were found in 3 percent of the men not reporting vigorous exercise. In all, 11 percent of those reporting vigorous exercise had one or more note-worthy ECG abnormality compared to 22 percent of those not reporting vigorous exercise.

As there were no significant differences in age, height, weight, skinfold thickness, plasma cholesterol, and blood pressure between the two groups, it seems that the differences in ECG abnormalities were caused primarily by the variation in physical activity. There was no trend toward increasing ECG abnormalities with increasing plasma cholesterol or cigarette smoking, regardless of exercise category.

The number of ECG abnormalities did rise with increasing blood pressure in both exercise groups, but remained lower among those reporting vigorous exercise than those not reporting vigorous exercise, even at hypertensive levels.

One explanation for these data could be that the men with ECG abnormalities avoided physical activity for health reasons, rather than that physical activity promoted good health. However, there was no excess of subjects with a history of heart disease among those not reporting vigorous exercise, and the findings remained essentially unchanged when those with previous evidence of heart disease were excluded from the analysis.

J. N. Morris, Department of Community Health, London School of Hygiene and Tropical Medicine, London WC1E 7HT, England

Physical Fitness Improves Heart Disease Risk Factors

If vigorous exercise protects against coronary heart disease, then it should have a beneficial effect on CHD risk factors.

To test this hypothesis, Kenneth H. Cooper—who developed the "aerobics" system for physical fitness—examined CHD risk factors in nearly 3,000 men with an average age of 44.6 years, and compared the results with their level of physical fitness. Among the risk factors measured were resting heart rate, percent body fat, serum cholesterol and triglycerides, glucose, and systolic blood pressure.

Physical fitness was evaluated by a maximal performance treadmill stress test with multilead ECG monitoring. The stress test measures cardiorespiratory endurance by forcing subjects to run until they reach voluntary exhaustion, ECG abnormality or other signs of physical distress, or a minimum of 85 percent of their predicted maximal heart rate.

The results of the study show an inverse relationship between physical fitness and CHD risk, with the higher the level of fitness, the lower the CHD values. Five levels of fitness were designated—very poor, poor, fair, good, and excellent. The differences in CHD risk were minimal for adjacent fitness levels, but became marked when comparing disparate levels such as very poor and excellent. This finding supports the concept that only vigorous exercise confers protection against heart disease.

Kenneth H. Cooper, Institute for Aerobics Research, 11811 Preston Rd., Dallas, Tx. 75230

Work Activity and Fatal Heart Attacks

The twentieth century has witnessed an epidemic of coronary heart disease among middle-aged men. In 1970, a fifty-year-old man was five times more likely to die of a heart attack than a fifty-year-old man at the turn of the century.

One of the major changes in lifestyle among adult men during this period has been a progressive decline in physical activity at work. In 1900, the majority of men worked on farms, in factories, or at other types of hard labor. Today, in our highly mechanized and automated society, most men work in offices, where their brains and mouths are far more active than their bodies.

Could this decline in physical activity be partly responsible for the modern scourge of heart disease? The results of a long-term study of 6,351 San Francisco Bay longshoremen shed some light on the relationship between work activity and fatal heart attacks.

From 1951 to 1973, Ralph S. Paffenbarger, Jr., followed these workers, who were thirty-five to seventy-four years of age when the study began, until they died or turned seventy-five. Each subject was placed into categories of high, intermediate, or light energy output, according to his job assignment. On the average, those in the high energy output category were required to expend 1,876 kilocalories (Kcals) beyond their base level per eight-hour day; those in the intermediate category required 1,473 Kcals; and those in the light category, 865 Kcals.

Whenever subjects were transferred from one job to another, their status was re-evaluated and, when appropriate, they were moved into a different work category. According to union rules, men always entered the industry in jobs demanding high energy output, where they were required to remain for at least five years. Transfer to lighter jobs occurred after an average of thirteen years of heavy work. Because of union policy, most men who suffered heart attacks and subsequently returned to work, resumed their original jobs. As a result, there was no disproportionate shift of heart attack victims to the lighter work categories.

Other Cardiovascular Risk Factors

All subjects underwent multiphasic screening for other cardiovascular risk factors including heavy cigarette smoking, high blood pressure, history of previous heart attack, obesity, abnormal glucose metabolism, and elevated blood cholesterol. Since the first three of these factors were shown to increase the risk of fatal heart attacks in the study population, they were taken into account when calculating the effect of work activity on cardiac mortality.

The major finding of the study was that high energy output on the job substantially reduced the risk of fatal heart attack, especially among subjects between the ages of thirty-five and fifty-four. Less active workers were three times more likely to die of a heart attack than heavy workers, with the odds moving to four to one when it came to the risk of sudden death.

The Threshold Effect

Of interest is the fact that intermediate work activity conferred no protection at all for subjects in that category, who were just as much at-risk for fatal heart attacks as those performing light work. Apparently, there was a threshold level of physical activity that had to be passed before exercise could be of benefit to the workers.

The most active longshoremen worked in repeated bursts of peak effort rather than at a steady slower pace of energy output. Their work habits may have simulated the intensive exercise pattern now recommended to achieve cardiovascular conditioning. According to this view, twenty to thirty minutes of stressful physical activity is better than a full day of light or moderate activity.

When the effects of the three most significant risk factors—low energy output, heavy cigarette smoking, and high blood pressure—were combined, it was found that subjects with all three factors had a twenty times greater chance of suffering a fatal heart attack than subjects with none of these factors. It was estimated that elimination of these risk factors in all San Francisco longshoremen might have reduced the rate of fatal heart attack by 88 percent during the twenty-two-year study period.

Ralph S. Paffenbarger, Jr., Department of Epidemiology, Stanford University School of Medicine, Stanford, Ca. 94305

What Is the Threshold Level of Benefit from Exercise?

Recent studies indicate that vigorous exercise is necessary for protection against heart attacks, but the threshold level for such protection has not yet been defined. In Ralph Paffenbarger's study of San Francisco longshoremen, he found that workers who expended 8,500-10,750 kilocalories per week (Kcal/wk) had considerably fewer heart attacks than workers who expended less than 8,250 Kcal/wk.

In another study, Paffenbarger reported a similar finding for 16,936 male alumni of Harvard University, aged thirty-five to seventy-four, who were studied between 1962 and 1972—except that the threshold level for this group was only 2,000 Kcal/wk. In this study, men whose energy expenditure was below 2,000 Kcal/wk were at a sixty-four percent higher risk for heart attacks than classmates who expended 2,000-4,000 Kcal/wk—an effect that was shown to be independent of other cardiovascular risk factors.

A meaningful comparison of these findings is difficult because of the differences in the two study populations and in the methods of data collection. The longshoremen were more active than the Harvard alumni primarily because their work was more physically demanding than the work of most of the alumni. Moreover, the assessment of the longshoremen's energy output was based upon oxygen-consumption measurements on the job, whereas the assessment of the energy output of the Harvard alumni was based upon self-determined reports of activity.

The fact that such dissimilar populations showed a significantly lowered risk of heart attack for subjects at higher exercise levels suggests that the protective effect of exercise may apply to all populations, and perhaps to all individuals.

From the available data, it's not possible to determine whether the more active Harvard alumni could lower their risk of heart attack further by approaching the level of energy output of the more active longshoremen. Only future studies will reveal whether there are two or more threshold levels of benefit from exercise.

Ralph S. Paffenbarger, Jr., Department of Epidemiology, Stanford University School of Medicine, Stanford, Ca. 94305

How Exercise Protects Against Heart Disease

It seems that our blood carries a "good" form of cholesterol as well as a "bad" form. The good form—alpha cholesterol—is found within small particles called high-density lipoproteins (HDL), while the bad form—beta cholesterol—is found within larger particles called low-density lipoproteins (LDL). It seems that HDL particles act as garbage disposal agents by plucking gobs of imbedded cholesterol from the walls of our arteries and then transporting it to the liver where it can be excreted. (See p. 77.)

For years there has been confusion about the effects of exercise on the fat content of the blood. Although exercise has been shown to lower plasma triglyceride levels, it has had little or no apparent effect on plasma cholesterol. In some studies, in fact, exercise has produced a rise in plasma cholesterol. Many scientists have therefore come to the conclusion that exercise is not likely to improve an individual's blood-lipid profile.

But now it looks as if these scientists may have been deceived by their reliance upon *total* plasma cholesterol as an indicator of cardiovascular risk. Apparently, the total amount of cholesterol in the bloodstream is less important than the ratio of HDL to LDL. And the good news is that exercise not only lowers LDL levels, it also raises HDL levels dramatically.

The best demonstration of this effect to date comes from a study of male and female runners by Peter D. Wood of the Stanford Heart Disease Prevention Program. In this study, plasma lipoprotein levels were measured in forty-one men, aged thirty-five to fifty-nine, and forty-three women, aged thirty to fifty-nine, who had averaged at least fifteen miles of running per week during the previous year; and 145 men and 101 women of similar age who had not exercised during the previous year.

Wood found that plasma triglyceride levels were strikingly lower in runners of both sexes than in sedentary controls; that total cholesterol was somewhat lower in runners—modestly so for men and more substantially for women; and that LDL cholesterol levels were lower and HDL cholesterol levels considerably higher in runners of both sexes than in controls. The average HDL level was 33 percent higher in men runners than in sedentary men, while the average HDL level was 25 percent higher in women runners than in sedentary women.

The HDL/LDL Ratio

A look at the HDL/LDL ratios showed an even greater advantage for runners over controls. The average HDL/LDL ratio in men runners was 0.51 (64/125) compared to 0.31 (43/139) in sedentary men, while the average HDL/LDL ratio in women runners was 0.66 (75/113) compared to 0.45 (56/124) in sedentary women.

In the United States and other industrialized countries, where cardiovascular disease has become a modern plague, the principal carrier of plasma cholesterol is LDL. But in young children, certain primitive cultures, and animals such as the rat where atherosclerosis almost never occurs, it is common to find more cholesterol carried by HDL than LDL.

In the Stanford study, the HDL levels of a number of the women and a few of the men runners were, in fact, higher than their LDL levels—a finding that suggests an extraordinary degree of protection against cardiovascular disease. Moreover, there were higher HDL levels with advancing age

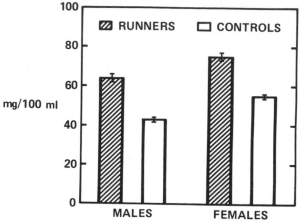

Plasma HDL-cholesterol concentrations (mean ± standard error) for male and female runners and controls.

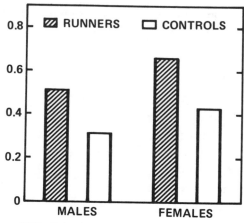

Ratio of plasma HDL-cholesterol concentration to LDL-cholesterol concentration for male and female runners and controls.

in runners of both sexes compared to a slight decrease or no change with age in controls.

Peter D. Wood, Stanford Heart Disease Prevention Program, Stanford University School of Medicine, Stanford, Ca. 94305

Can Exercise Help Sedentary Individuals?
Although both runners and controls ate similar diets in Peter Wood's Stanford study, the runners were clearly leaner

than their sedentary counterparts. This finding raises several questions about self-selection in study subjects. Were those who chose an active lifestyle leaner, healthier, and in better condition than those who did not? Did they have higher HDL levels than controls even before they started exercising? To what extent can exercise improve cardiovascular risk factors in heavier, less athletic individuals?

In an attempt to answer the latter question, Arthur S. Leon of the University of Minnesota placed six obese, sedentary college men on a program of brisk walking for 1½ hours a day, five days a week for sixteen weeks, without any dietary restrictions. They found a significant rise in HDL/LDL ratios, an average loss of 4 percent body fat (about ten pounds), and significant reductions in blood insulin and glucose levels. So it looks as if regular exercise can protect us against cardiovascular disease even if we have never exercised before.

Arthur S. Leon, Laboratory of Physiological Hygiene, School of Public Health, University of Minnesota, Minneapolis, Mn. 55455

HDL Goes Up with Exercise

The best way of raising high-density lipoproteins (HDL) —the "good" form of cholesterol that protects against heart disease—is by exercising. What you eat or drink matters little. And you don't have to exercise a whole lot, though it has to be vigorous activity that "raises a sweat."

These are the findings of a recent study by G. Harley Hartung of the Baylor College of Medicine, who looked into the effects of diet and exercise on HDL levels. He compared three groups of volunteer professionals and businessmen in the Houston area during a five-month period in 1977.

One active group—the marathon runners—included fifty-nine subjects with a mean age of 44.5, who ran forty or more miles a week; another active group—the joggers—included eighty-five subjects with a mean age of 46.8, who exercised regularly, jogging or running at least three times a week for a total of less than twenty miles; and the third group—the sedentary men—included seventy-four subjects with a mean age of 46.1, who either did not exercise at all, or engaged only in relatively nonvigorous activities such as golf.

The active groups ate considerably less red meat (beef, pork, lamb) than the sedentary group, and the marathoners ate more cottage cheese and drank more beer than the other two groups; but none of these dietary factors were significantly correlated with HDL.

On the other hand, the differences in HDL among the three groups were directly related to their level of physical activity. The average HDL level of the sedentary men was 44.3 milligrams/100 ml of blood, whereas the average HDL level of the joggers was 58 mg/100 ml and the average level of the marathoners was 64.8 mg/100 ml.

The study showed substantial benefit for men who engaged in a moderate amount of regular vigorous exercise over nonexercisers. Even men who jogged only eleven miles a week had significantly higher HDL levels than sedentary men.

G. Harley Hartung, Baylor University College of Medicine, Houston, Tx. 77025

Exercise Reverses Atherosclerosis

Doctors can now "look into" the heart to determine how much it is damaged and to what degree the coronary arteries are blocked. High-speed X-ray motion picture photography is used to record the passage of an injected X-ray opaque fluid through the heart. At Rancho Los Amigos Hospital in Downey, California, two such techniques—coronary angiograms and biplane ventriculograms—are used to evaluate the effects of exercise on the progression of atherosclerosis and myocardial infarction in heart disease patients.

In a study of 104 test subjects, fifty-six had suffered a previous myocardial infarct and forty-eight had experienced angina pectoris (heart pain) without previous infarction. All subjects were offered a program of progressive exercise in addition to a low-fat diet and strategies aimed at eliminating cigarette smoking and controlling blood pressure.

In the initial phase of the exercise program, a relatively mild level of physical conditioning was pursued through walking, calisthenics, and group games. Later on, the activity level was gradually intensified until the subjects were achieving at least 70 percent of their predicted maximum capacity.

Fitness Categories

As the subjects chose their own level of fitness, they were classified into four categories:

• Inactive— No regular recreational or planned exercise

• Low Level— Some exercise each week, usually below fifty percent of predicted maximum

• Moderate— Exercised an average of one to two times per week for twenty to thirty minutes to 60-70 percent of predicted maximum

• Trained— Exercised at least three times per week for at least thirty minutes to 70 percent or more of predicted maximum

By the end of the study, nine subjects (8 percent) had reached Group 4 or trained status, twenty subjects (19 percent) were in the moderate activity group, thirty-nine subjects (37 percent) were in the low-level activity group, and thirty-six subjects (35 percent) were in the physically inactive group.

The results of the study showed that increased exercise—especially to fitness levels—was associated with decreased progression of atherosclerosis in the coronary arteries of

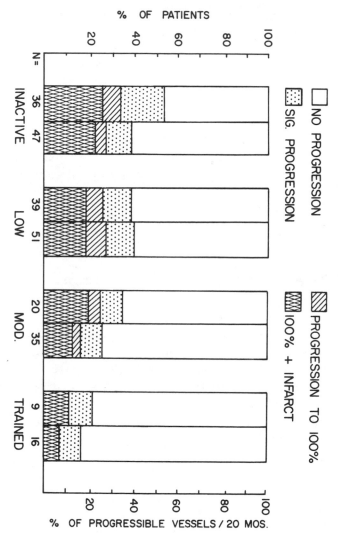

Increased exercise, especially to fitness levels, is associated with decreased progression of atherosclerosis in coronary arteries. The left-hand bars show the coronary progression rate related to average activity levels in 104 patients. The right-hand bars show the percentage of progressible vessels after a mean follow-up period of twenty months.

heart disease patients. In the inactive group, there was increased blockage in twenty-one of forty-seven arteries (45 percent) compared with only three of sixteen arteries (19 percent) in the trained group.

Elimination of cigarette smoking was also effective in slowing the progress of coronary artery disease. Some degree of benefit was attributed to lowering of serum lipids and blood pressure. Analysis of all these factors, however, showed that the risk of increased coronary artery blockage was independently decreased by a factor of 1.7 in patients who attained a high level of physical fitness.

Ronald H. Selvester, Rancho Los Amigos Hospital, 7601 East Imperial Highway, Downey, Ca. 90242

Are Marathon Runners Immune to Heart Disease?

The image of the heart attack victim is that of an overweight, middle-aged man, who eats rich foods, smokes cigarettes, and is physically inactive. The image of the marathon runner, on the other hand, is that of an extremely thin, highly active man, who abstains from smoking and eats a sparing, low-fat diet.

If anyone is likely to have protection against heart disease, it is the marathon runner. His entire lifestyle is geared to maintaining a low cardiovascular-risk profile. But does he have actual immunity to heart disease? Is there a threshold level of conditioning beyond which it is impossible to get a heart attack? According to Thomas J. Bassler, there is indeed such a threshold, which he defines as the ability to complete a marathon.

Bassler's immunity theory, which he has discussed extensively in various medical journals, is based upon his ongoing, worldwide analysis of the deaths of marathon runners, which he started about 1967. At last count, Bassler said he had received in excess of 200 reports, with not one histologically proven death from heart disease among marathoners.

A Controversial Theory

Bassler's contention that marathoners are immune to heart disease has sparked controversy among physicians, exercise physiologists, and runners. Hardly anyone agrees with Bassler's extreme position, which has been called "misleading," "unscientific," and "just plain wrong." Yet Bassler has been fairly successful in challenging a succession of reports from physicians around the world aimed at disproving his theory.

In doing so, he has defined and redefined his criteria for proof of heart disease in marathoners. By 1977, he had made it clear that "immunity" could only be granted from deaths caused by atherosclerosis in runners who have successfully completed a marathon, with autopsy records to document the cause of death. He also made it clear that immunity from heart disease stays in effect only while the runner remains in training, and that the effect results from the marathoner's entire lifestyle, not just exercise.

According to these criteria, it's rather difficult to come up with a case that completely disproves Bassler's immunity theory. But the question of whether marathon runners are immune from heart disease is less important than the evidence that the marathoner's lifestyle offers significant protection against the disease. Completing a marathon may not guarantee immunity from heart disease, but regular vigorous exercise, good diet, and abstinence from cigarette smoking is the next best thing to a guarantee.

Thomas J. Bassler, Department of Pathology, Centinela Hospital, Inglewood, Ca. 90307

Exercise Therapy for Lung Disease

Athletes almost never smoke. They know that sucking poison into their lungs impedes their ability to perform. They also know that exercise makes their lungs strong, healthy, and efficient—not only during competition, but in everyday life as well. They can breathe better and provide their body with more oxygen than their sedentary fellow beings.

The changes in lung structure and function produced by exercise can be therapeutic for patients suffering from chronic obstructive lung disease (COLD). Many investigators have noted striking improvement in such patients following exercise therapy.

In one study, thirteen mild or moderate COLD patients were placed on a long-term exercise program at the Toronto Rehabilitation Center in Canada. Seven of the patients had chronic bronchitis, two had emphysema, and four had a combination of emphysema and chronic bronchitis. All led extremely sedentary lives and were limited in their ability to move about.

Following clinical, cardiopulmonary, and fitness testing, each patient was given an individualized prescription for graded walking or jogging. Once a week the patients attended the rehabilitation center for a supervised exercise session, while they continued a diary-monitored home program on the remaining days of the week. Testing was repeated on all thirteen patients at six months and one year, and on six of the patients at eighteen months and two years.

Improved Lung Function

At the end of the study, eight of the thirteen patients said they felt much better as a result of their participation in the program. They spoke of improved exercise tolerance, increased sex drive, improved sleep, less frequent respiratory infections, and greater general well-being. In contrast, five patients reported no improvement or deterioration during the course of the study, but only one of the five followed the exercise protocol diligently.

Among the gains achieved by the regular exercisers were increased muscular endurance, reduction of oxygen debt, and cessation in deterioration of lung volume. The most striking laboratory gain was increased strength and endurance of the patients' leg muscles, which markedly increased their mobility.

The benefits of exercise therapy were greater for the chronic bronchitis patients than for the emphysema patients, where the progressive destruction of lung tissue is believed to be "irreversible." Yet even the emphysema patients showed significant improvement in lung function if they stuck to their exercise program.

T. Kavanagh, Department of Preventive Medicine and Biostatistics, University of Toronto, Toronto, Canada

How Exercise Affects Aging Mice

When Charles L. Goodrick allowed twenty-three-month-old mice to engage in wheel exercise, he found that they lived about 10 percent longer than male control mice. No such benefit was apparent for female mice, whose lives were not extended by the opportunity to exercise. However, both males and females given voluntary exercise were more exploratory and less emotional than control animals.

Charles L. Goodrick, Gerontology Research Center, National Institute on Aging, Baltimore City Hospital, Baltimore, Md. 21224

Daily Exercise Prolongs Life Span of Rats

A study of albino Sprague-Dawley rats by Ernest Retzlaff of Ohio State University found that animals forced to exercise vigorously on a regular basis lived considerably longer than controls.

At the age of thirty days, fifty male rats and sixty-two females were divided into two equal groups of both sexes. One group was permitted normal cage activity, while the other was exercised every day for ten minutes in a motor-driven drum.

Lifelong controlled exercise led to a significant increase in the life span of both male and female rats. The mean life span of males in the exercise group was 605 days compared with 474 days for males in the nonexercise group and the mean life span of females in the exercise group was 665 days compared with 476 days for females in the nonexercise group. The longest-lived male in the exercise group survived 773 days compared with 717 days for the longest-lived male in the nonexercise group, and the longest-lived female in the exercise group survived 1,002 days compared with 736 days for the longest-lived female in the nonexercise group.

These data should be interpreted with caution because the control animals lived four to six months less than the normal mean life span of albino Sprague-Dawley rats, whereas the mean life span of the experimental animals was about equal to the normal mean life span of these animals. None of the experimental animals surpassed the known maximum life span for rats of the Sprague-Dawley strain.

Ernest Retzlaff, Department of Psychiatry, College of Medicine, Ohio State University, Columbus, Ohio 43210

Can Exercise Shorten Life Span?

Support for a threshold age beyond which it may be disadvantageous to begin exercising comes from animal experiments by D. W. Edington of the University of Massachusetts. In this study, sedentary rats of 120, 300, 450, and 600 days of age were subjected to a training routine for 360 to 600 days. The rats were forced to run every day on a motor-drive treadmill on an eight-degree incline. As the animals aged, their running speed was reduced to 7.5 meters per minute.

A 74 percent survival rate was reported for animals who started training prior to 400 days of age compared with a 41 percent survival rate for untrained controls. However, there was only a 54 percent survival rate for animals who started training after 400 days of age compared with an 83 percent survival rate for untrained controls—with a significant decrease in survival for only those rats who started exercising after 600 days of age.

One explanation for this finding is that forced exercise may have imposed greater stress upon the old animals than the young ones, which may have had an adverse effect on their survival.

Studies in humans have shown significant benefits for sedentary middle- and old-aged subjects placed on controlled exercise programs, though there are no longevity statistics yet available for such a group.

Herbert A. DeVries, who has conducted several studies of the effects of exercise on persons of advanced age, points out that vigorous exercise is potentially hazardous for older individuals, especially in the presence of undiagnosed coronary heart disease, and should be supervised closely by trained personnel.

Recent work at the Longevity Center in Santa Monica, California (see p. 81), indicates that properly supervised exercise can be of value for older individuals—even in patients with advanced heart disease.

D. W. Edington, University of Massachusetts, Amherst, Ma. 01002

Herbert A. DeVries, Andrus Gerontology Research Center, University of Southern California, Los Angeles, Ca. 90007

Increased Longevity of Endurance Skiers

Cross-country skiers usually enjoy an active career of about twenty years, and a large proportion of former skiers continue to engage in the sport after retirement from competition. A study by M. J. Karvonen of Helsinki, Finland, compared the longevity of 396 Finnish skiing champions born from 1845 to 1910 with that of the general population.

By 1967, when data collection was terminated, fifty-seven

skiers were still alive, 325 had died, and fourteen had disappeared in wars or emigrated. The deaths occurred between 1893 and 1967; the median year of death was 1947.

The median age at death in the general population was 68.9 years during 1931-35, 68.7 years during 1946-50, and 70.2 years during 1956-60, whereas the median age at death of the skiers throughout the entire period was 73.0 years. Thus, the skiers survived an average of 4.3 to 2.8 years longer than the corresponding male population in Finland.

When Karvonen conducted a parallel cross-sectional study of former Finnish long distance skiers and runners, aged forty to seventy-nine, it showed that 69 percent of them were still physically active compared to 37 percent of age-matched nonathletes. The study also showed that the skiers had lower blood pressure and smoked less than the nonathletes.

M. J. Karvonen, Institute of Occupational Health, Helsinki, Finland

Exercise Does Not Retard Normal Aging

Habitual, lifelong exercise increases strength, flexibility, and endurance. It improves the quality of a person's life, and seems to protect against diseases of the cardiovascular system. As such, it is probably instrumental in preventing premature aging and death in the middle years of life. However, there is no significant evidence that exercise retards the rate of normal aging or extends maximum life span.

In a recent cross-sectional study of the effects of lifelong endurance training on biologic aging, researchers at the Finland Department of Health measured various structural and functional parameters in twenty-nine trained and twenty-nine sedentary men, aged thirty-one to seventy-two years.

The trained subjects scored significantly higher than controls in tests related to physical training, such as maximal oxygen uptake, aerobic muscle metabolism, and collagen biosynthesis. They also had lower body weight, blood pressure, and serum triglyceride levels than controls.

But when it came to tests not directly related to physical conditioning, such as the concentration and solubility of skin and muscle collagen, the trained subjects fared no better than controls. And when it came to the degree of functional change with age, the decline of the trained group paralleled or slightly exceeded that of the control group—even in those functions influenced by exercise.

This study indicates that there is no significant correlation between exercise and the rate of physiologic aging. Apparently, exercise helps to keep us alive, healthy, and vigorous during the middle years of life, but has little effect on health and longevity in the later years, even if the exercise has been lifelong.

H. Suominen, Department of Public Health, University of Jyväskylä, Jyväskylä, Finland

Chapter 6

Can We Become Immune to Aging?

Immunoengineering: An Approach to Aging Control

If aging is caused by attacking viruses, bacteria, chemicals, gases, or radiation, we need to alter our immune system to fight off these invaders. If, on the other hand, it is a normal biologic process unleashed by a genetic program, then we need to maintain our immune system in a youthful, vigorous state, or restore it to such a state.

Whether a youthful immune system would keep us from growing old depends upon whether immune dysfunction is a primary cause of aging. (See p. 10.) However, even if immune dysfunction is a consequence rather than a cause of aging, there's little doubt that a youthful immune system would add to our health and life expectancy. Any therapy capable of keeping us immunologically young would also have beneficial effects on other age-related factors.

Roy L. Walford has been exploring the relationship between immune function and longevity by investigating immunologic changes caused by the only two regimens known to extend maximum life span—calorie restriction (see p. 60) and reduced body temperature. (See p. 160.) Walford's goal is to develop methods of prolonging health, youth, and vigor in humans by manipulating the immune system or, as he calls it, "immunoengineering."

By markedly restricting the food intake of mice, he was able to induce significant immunologic changes in these animals. When the mice were young, their immune response was weaker than that of mice fed a normal diet. But later in life, when aging began to take its toll on both groups, the situation reversed in favor of the restricted mice. After one year of age, the immune response in the restricted mice was significantly stronger than in the unrestricted mice.

Apparently, the calorie-restricted diet delayed the maturation of the immune system in the experimental animals, which slowed the age-related decline of the system. The stronger immunity of the old restricted mice was one reason they outlived their normally fed contemporaries. When the study was completed, 23 percent of the animals on the low-calorie diet were still alive, while all the animals on the unrestricted diet were already dead.

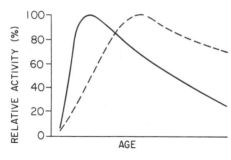

Restricting the food intake of mice delays the early maturation of immune response and retards the age-related decline in that capacity (dotted line). Solid line represents the immune response of control mice.

If underfeeding seems to postpone the aging of the immune system, decreasing body temperature appears to inhibit the harmful autoimmune processes that occur in adulthood—at least in poikilothermic (cold-blooded) fish. When Walford and R. K. Liu prolonged the life span of these fish up to 76 percent by transferring them at mid-life from water at 20° C to water at 15° C, they found that the change in temperature acted as a potent immunosuppressive agent.

Walford suggests that further research into the life-prolonging effects of nutritional manipulation early in life and temperature reduction late in life might yield a combined therapeutic approach that could add years of good health to our lives.

Roy L. Walford, Department of Pathology, UCLA Medical Center, Los Angeles, Ca. 90024

Genetic Control of Immune Function

The forty-six chromosomes in the nucleus of every cell contain thousands of genes—the units of heredity that determine who we are, how we look, and what our talents are. Though each gene codes for a specific purpose, such as eye color, height, or brain size, there is increasing evidence that complex functions are controlled by clusters or families of genes on the same chromosome.

Such "super gene" systems include hundreds of genes that apparently work together to build tissues, synthesize hormones, and regulate metabolic activities. As part of larger systems, the individual units of multigene families are thought to be interdependent, interlocking and, perhaps, even interchangeable to a significant degree. Consequently, it is believed that evolution cannot act upon single genes, but only upon entire systems, or parts thereof.

All vertebrate species investigated to date possess a major histocompatibility complex (MHC), which appears to serve as a master gene system for the control or influence of immune response. Examples of such complexes are the H-2 system on the seventeenth chromosome of mice and the HLA system on the sixth chromosome of humans.

The H-2 System

The most-studied MHC is the mouse H-2 system. Among the functions believed to be under the influence of this system are susceptibility or resistance to leukemia viruses and spontaneously occurring tumors; susceptibility to various autoimmune diseases; the development of specific suppressor cells for immunorecognition of "self"; and the age-specific mutation rates, peaks, and rates of decline of immune response.

Walford has compared life span and spontaneous cancer incidence in fourteen strains of congenic mice, which were derived from three standard strains of mice of varying life span. Each strain was genetically "identical" to one of the standard strains, except for the chromosome region carrying the H-2 system. The purpose of such selective inbreeding was to isolate the effect of the histocompatibility system on aging and disease.

He found substantial differences in life span and cancer incidence among congenic mice derived from the same strain, which suggests that the genes controlling immune function may also influence aging and carcinogenesis.

When Walford studied immune function in nine of these strains—in mice ranging from two to more than thirty months of age—he found that the longest-lived strains exhibited the best immune response, and the shortest-lived strains the worst response. This finding suggests that the life span differences among these species may reflect complex, age-related effects of histocompatibility genes on immune mechanisms.

Correlations in Humans

Walford points out that there is some correlation in humans between the HLA histocompatibility system and nasopharyngeal carcinoma, Hodgkin's disease, acute lymphatic leukemia, lymphosarcoma, and other cancers, as well as a wide variety of autoimmune and immunodeficiency diseases.

One gene of immunity—HLA-B8—has been singled out because of its association with autoimmune and other diseases. HLA-B8 has been linked to diabetes, a disease that displays many features of accelerated aging. (See p. 25.)

Walford is fascinated by the fact that transformed malignant cells are immortal in tissue culture, although they have pretty much the same structure and biochemistry of normal cells. As he puts it: "The cancer cell has learned something the normal cell doesn't know, or has forgotten something the normal cell might well forget."

Recent evidence indicates that the transformation of a normal cell into a cancer cell does not require extensive genetic modification, but can be induced by the insertion of only one or a few oncogenic genes into the cell. The transformation process seems to occur as a result of minor regulatory changes rather than changes in genetic structure, which may be related to the idea that the evolution of longevity has been the product of relatively few changes in regulatory gene activity. (See p. 20.)

Walford speculates that the HLA system may be one of the select regulatory gene systems involved in control of aging.

Roy L. Walford, Department of Pathology, UCLA Medical Center, Los Angeles, Ca. 90024

Influence of MHC Genes on DNA Excision Repair

In his most recent work, Walford has linked the major histocompatibility complex (MHC) gene system that controls immune function to the DNA excision repair rate in spleen cells of congenic mice. He has found that several strains of mice congenic for the H-2 chromosome region (the MHC system in mice) show a direct correlation between DNA excision repair capacity and maximum life span, with longer-lived strains showing better DNA repair than shorter-lived strains.

Other studies have demonstrated a correlation between the maximum life span of a number of mammalian species and DNA excision repair in these species. (See p. 363.) Also, that DNA repair capacity varies according to mean life span in three unrelated strains of mice, and that humans suffering from systemic lupus erythematosus and xeroderma pigmentosum display lower-than-normal DNA excision repair ability.

These findings suggest that DNA excision repair capacity may be a factor in determining the rate of biologic aging in mammals, as reflected by maximum life span. Walford's study suggests that the MHC gene system may influence the rate or level of DNA excision repair which, in turn, may influence the rate of biologic aging.

Mechanism of Action

Walford speculates that the effect of MHC genes on DNA repair has little to do with immune mechanisms, but may represent a "linkage phenomenon," in which a large number of biologic processes are controlled by a few gene clusters, one of which may be the MHC system. On the other hand, he also proposes that the relationship between the MHC and DNA repair could involve an "unorthodox" immune response to the recognition of DNA defects.

Thus far, Walford has assessed DNA excision repair capacity in congenic mice by measuring unscheduled DNA synthesis in spleen cells following damage by ultraviolet (UV) radiation, and by measuring cell division in spleen cells in the presence of bleomycin, an agent that damages DNA by causing strand breaks, which are then repaired by the cell. He is currently exploring the effects of other types of DNA injury to further elucidate the extent of the influence of MHC genes on DNA excision repair mechanisms.

Roy L. Walford, Department of Pathology, UCLA Medical Center, Los Angeles, Ca. 90024

Preventing Premature Aging

The life of a hypopituitary Snell-Bagg dwarf mouse is short and unpleasant. Because of severe endocrine and immunologic deficiencies, it undergoes highly accelerated aging leading to early death. The average dwarf mouse lives only 1 to 5.5 months in contrast to normal mice who live two to three years. At three months of age, the hair of the dwarf

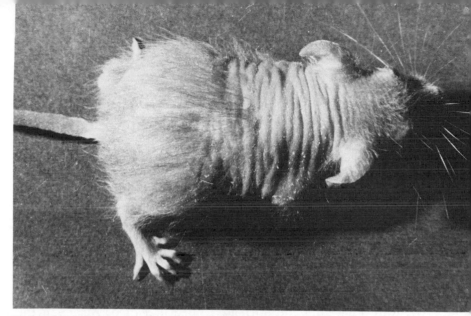

The Snell-Bagg dwarf mouse undergoes severe premature aging in the first few months of life. Note the atrophied body, graying, and loss of hair in an untreated five-month-old mouse *(top)*. However, when the Snell-Bagg dwarf receives lymph node lymphocytes from a forty-day-old normal Snell-Bagg mouse at twenty days of age, all signs of aging are prevented, as in the seven-month-old mouse below.

mouse becomes discolored and begins to fall out, its skin and tissues begin to atrophy, and it usually develops bilateral cataracts.

This rapid deterioration can be prevented, however, if the immune system of the dwarf mouse is bolstered by an infusion of young lymphocytes from normal Snell-Bagg mice. N. Fabris has almost tripled the maximum life span of dwarf mice by giving them an injection of 150 million peripheral lymph node cells at thirty days of age.

The treated dwarf mice survived for more than twelve months. They did not develop the accelerated aging pattern of untreated mice, and displayed a youthful cell turnover rate long after the untreated mice had died. Although they failed to grow, they were able to maintain their weight and youthful appearance well into the first year of life.

Similar life-prolongation effects were achieved by injections of growth hormone and thyroxine (thyroid hormone), except when the thymus gland had been removed prior to therapy. Injections of other types of immune system cells—thymocytes or bone marrow cells—failed to delay aging and prolong life span in these mice.

N. Fabris, Research Department, Experimental Gerontology Center, I.N.R.C.A., Via Birarelli 8 60100, Anconia, Italy

Rejuvenating the Immune System

A popular method of "rejuvenation" is the injection of young cells into an old body. Every year, thousands of persons visit cell-therapy clinics in Europe to receive injections of fetal lamb cells. (See p. 243.) Although claims of great success have been made for this type of therapy, there is little evidence to back them up.

There is evidence, however, that a special type of cell therapy—the injection or grafting of young immunocompetent mouse cells into old mice—may be able to rejuvenate the immune system of these mice. Scientists have focused on the two basic consequences of immunologic aging: the decline of the immune system's ability to fight off disease, and the increasing propensity of the immune system to attack the body itself (autoimmunity).

Reversing Autoimmunity

Attempts to reverse autoimmunity have been made in mice bred to develop autoimmune diseases. These animals have a shorter life span than normal mice, and exhibit some of the characteristics of accelerated aging.

The best results to date have been achieved with a strain of New Zealand black mice (NZB/W) that serves as a model for the human autoimmune disease systemic lupus erythematosus. By injecting young spleen cells into old NZB/W mice, Gelfand and Steinberg were able to restore normal allograft (tissue from a genetically different donor of the same species as the recipient) rejection capacity in these animals.

In another study, a small, but significant increase in survival was observed in NZB/W mice receiving multiple thymic grafts from two-week-old donors. The average life span of treated animals was 387 days compared with 350 days in untreated animals.

The prolonged survival of aging mice treated with young thymus cells was attributed to the bolstering of suppressor or regulatory thymic function. It was further suggested that a greater increase in survival might be achieved by combining cell therapy with the repeated administration of a thymic hormone.

Long-Lived Mice

Attempts to restore impaired immune function in aging mice of long-lived strains have generally met with only limited success. Investigators have found that grafting of young thymus or bone marrow cells into old mice produces somewhat positive effects on immune function, but does not extend life span significantly. However, a recent study by Takashi Makinodan indicates that combined immune cell therapy may be more effective than therapy with single cell types.

When old mice were given combined grafts of newborn thymus and young adult bone marrow cells, their immune system responses reverted to levels of activity approaching or even exceeding those of young adult mice. The rejuvenation effects were observed for at least six months, suggesting that such grafts may produce long-lasting effects.

Makinodan expects to conduct studies to determine the effects of marrow-thymus grafts on age-related diseases and life span in mice.

Alfred D. Steinberg, Arthritis and Rheumatism Branch, National Institute of Arthritis and Metabolic Disorders, NIH, Bethesda, Md. 20014

Takashi Makinodan, GRECC, V.A. Wadsworth Hospital Center, Los Angeles, Ca. 90073

Preserving the Cells of Youth

The idea that the secrets of youth are contained within the cells of the young has been with us for centuries. Among the practices engaged in by old people pursuing the fountain of youth have been sexual intercourse with young women, drinking the blood of the young, and testicle transplants from young monkeys.

Now that there is evidence that it may be possible to rejuvenate the immune system by transplanting young cells into an old, aging body, it's time to consider the establishment of banks of frozen cells from young persons for use in their own bodies later in life. Such cells might be used to help the aging person fight off diseases; to reconstitute an immune system weakened by radiation, toxic chemicals, or environmental mutagens; or to combat the aging process.

The ability to freeze-preserve immune system cells was

demonstrated as far back as 1963 at Oak Ridge National Laboratory in Tennessee. A later study demonstrated that old mice can survive lethal doses of virulent *Salmonella typhimurium* for ten to twelve weeks if treated with previously frozen spleen cells from young mice immunized with a vaccine against the organism. The potency of cells stored in liquid nitrogen at —196° C for two weeks was as good as fresh spleen cells.

Since then, scientists in the U.S., England, and Denmark have successfully frozen human lymphocytes, and the techniques for preserving such cells have improved considerably. It would be relatively easy to develop rejuvenation banks of frozen cells and tissues. Immunologic cell therapy would work best with cells from the individual's own body, but could also be achieved with closely matched cells from others.

J. Farrant, Division of Cyrobiology, Clinical Research Centre, Watford Road, Harrow, Middlesex, HA1 3UJ, United Kingdom

Why Immunologic Transplants May Not Work

Transplanting young cells to rejuvenate the aging immune system is a great idea if there are intrinsic defects in old cells. But if there's nothing wrong with them except that they are within a disintegrating system, then an infusion of young cells may not help very much.

David Harrison has presented evidence that immune system dysfunction is caused primarily by defects in the cellular environment, rather than in the cells themselves. Harrison transplanted mouse stem cells (the forerunners of the lymphocytes that populate the immune system) from the bone marrow and spleen of aged mice into young recipient mice. All recipient mice were lethally irradiated and a chromosome marker was used to distinguish between the recipient's native cells and the donor cells.

He found that both marrow and spleen grafts from old animals generally produced antibody-forming cells as effectively as grafts from younger animals. The only conditions under which the old cells proved to be deficient were during the first few weeks after transplantation, or when the recipients had their thymus gland removed prior to irradiation.

According to Harrison, the failure of other researchers to demonstrate normal immune responses in recipients of old donor cells may have been the result of "life-shortening factors" in the strains of mice used, or of premature testing of the animals. He suggests that the delay in the responsiveness of old transplanted cells may occur because of the presence of age-related suppressor cells among the donor cells, which are gradually removed or inactivated by "youth factors" within the recipient mice.

David E. Harrison, The Jackson Laboratory, Bar Harbor, Me. 04609

Effects of Drugs on Autoimmunity

If aging is an autoimmune process, or if autoimmunity plays an important role in the aging process, than immunosuppressive drugs, which are used to facilitate organ transplantation, might also be able to retard aging. On this premise, Roy Walford examined the effect of azathioprine on the life span of a short-lived autoimmune-susceptible strain of mice.

He found that a dietary dose of 100 mg/kg of the drug extended the 50 percent survival of these animals by about ten weeks over controls, but had no appreciable effect on maximum life span. Treatment with imuran and cyclophosphamide—two other immunosuppressive agents—followed a similar pattern.

Roy L. Walford, Department of Pathology, UCLA Medical Center, Los Angeles, Ca. 90024

Mercaptoethanol Boosts Immunity in Aging Mice

In his efforts to boost the immunologic capabilities of aging mice, Takashi Makinodan has screened a variety of immunostimulatory agents. He's found that the drug mercaptoethanol (2-ME) can restore the T-cell dependent humoral immune response of old mice to almost that of young adult mice.

Denham Harman has shown that 2-ME can prolong the mean life span of mice. (See p. 131.)

Takashi Makinodan, GRECC, V. A. Wadsworth Hospital Center, Los Angeles, Ca. 90073

Transferring Immunity to Cancer

RNA therapy has been used experimentally to bolster the immune response against cancer. Animal studies have shown that both natural and synthetic RNAs can enhance several types of immune response against various tumors.

In one study, previously immunized mice were given injections of 2 mg of yeast RNA daily after being challenged by a live syngeneic (from the same mouse strain) tumor. Animals who were immunized but did not receive RNA had a mean survival time of 21.9 days, whereas animals who received RNA had a mean survival time of 36.1 days, and four of them survived for more than ten months.

In a variation of this approach, immune RNA (I-RNA) is now being tested as a form of clinical immunotherapy for human malignancies at several hospitals in Southern California. I-RNA is an RNA-rich nucleic acid preparation extracted from lymphoid cells or tissues following exposure to specific tumors. The I-RNA being used to treat cancer patients is extracted from the lymphoid organs of sheep with tumor cells of the same type as the patient. Apparently, injections of I-RNA can transfer some degree of immunity from one organism to another.

Preliminary results suggest increased survival in some patients with advanced cancer, and a possible decrease in the cancer recurrence rate in patients treated with I-RNA in conjunction with drug therapy after surgery. More definitive results should soon be available from a clinical trial now being conducted in patients with colon and rectal cancer.

Nucleic acid therapy is also used by New York physician Benjamin S. Frank to treat aging and degenerative diseases. (See p. 258.)

Yosef H. Pilch, Department of Surgical Oncology, University Hospital, San Diego, Ca. 92103

The "Master Gland" of Immunity

The thymus gland, a small organ located behind the breastbone and below the neck, is considered the "master gland" of immunity. The thymus "instructs" cells from the lymph nodes and spleen to reject foreign tissue and combat attacking organisms.

When we're young and healthy, these "T-cells" are vigorous in defending the body, but as we grow older they gradually lose their powers. At about age fourteen, the thymus gland begins to involute, eventually shrinking to a fraction of its former size. How this loss of mass relates to the decrease in immune function that accompanies aging is unknown.

It is now clear that the thymus functions as an endocrine gland. There have been more than two dozen reports of thymic extracts that influence the immune system. None of these extracts have been fully characterized biochemically, and it may be that many of them are variations of a few basic hormones. The best-known factors to date are thymosin, thymic humoral factor (THF), thymopoietin I and II, and serum thymic factor (STF).

Thymosin Boosts Immunity in Animals

Animal studies have shown that injections of thymosin can prevent or modify many of the immunologic consequences of aging or of thymectomy (surgical removal of the thymus gland). Here are some of the findings:

• Thymosin stimulates the regeneration of lymphoid tissue and prolongs the life span of irradiated mice.

• Thymosin improves immune function, increases body weight, and prolongs the life span of neonatal (newborn) thymectomized mice.

• Thymosin boosts deficient T-cell suppressor function in autoimmune susceptible mice.

• Thymosin reduces the incidence and severity of amyloidosis in casein-treated mice.

• Thymosin accelerates the rejection of foreign tissue grafts in normal mice.

These findings suggest that thymosin may be useful in treating patients with congenital immunodeficiencies, as well as patients suffering from age-related diseases linked to impairment of the immune system. Such clinical trials are underway.

One of the two scientists who isolated thymosin in 1965—Allan L. Goldstein—plans to study the effects of thymosin on aging and life span in mice.

Allan L. Goldstein, Department of Biochemistry, George Washington University Medical School, 1335 H St. N.W., Washington, D.C. 20005

Thymosin Boosts Immunity in Cancer Patients

As we grow older, we suffer a progressive decline in blood thymosin levels that parallels our declining immune function. This decline is accelerated in cancer patients, in whom impairment of immune function is often exacerbated by the side effects of anti-cancer drugs.

The first randomized trial of thymosin's value in cancer therapy was recently conducted by the National Cancer Institute. In this study, the drug was given to patients with nonresectable small cell lung carcinoma during the early intensive phase of cancer chemotherapy.

A total of fifty-five patients was divided into three groups and given either 60 mg/m² of thymosin (twenty-one patients), 20 mg/m² of thymosin (fifteen patients), or a buffer placebo (nineteen patients) twice weekly for the first six weeks of therapy. During this period, the patients received a battery of powerful anti-cancer drugs. Thereafter, the patients were maintained on less intensive anti-cancer drugs, without the addition of thymosin.

In the final analysis, the high-dose thymosin group lived far longer than either the low-dose thymosin or placebo groups. The median survival was 243 days for placebo patients, 255 days for patients receiving 20 mg of thymosin, and 425 days for patients receiving 60 mg of thymosin.

The increase in survival among the high-dose thymosin group was related to their immune status prior to treatment, as assessed by *in vitro* measurement of T-cell levels. Patients with low initial T-cell levels responded to thymosin therapy better than patients with high initial T-cell levels.

This study suggests that thymosin acts to restore lost immune function in cancer patients, rather than to combat the disease itself. Apparently, thymosin's ability to boost immune function potentiates the action of anti-cancer drugs, particularly in patients with markedly depressed T-cell levels.

It will be interesting to see if thymosin can prevent or postpone the onset of cancer, and whether it has any effect on the aging process.

Paul B. Chretien, Tumor Immunology Section, Surgery Branch, National Cancer Institute, Bldg. 10, Room 10B18, NIH, Bethesda, Md. 20014

Chapter 7
Transplants and Artificial Organs

How Good Are Heart Transplants?

When Christiaan Barnard announced the first human heart transplant, many people were shocked. Not by the operation itself, but by the idea of replacing the organ that symbolized life itself. If hearts could be interchanged, then perhaps the entire body could be replaced. The concept of identity would never be the same again.

In the swell of enthusiasm over the apparent success of the operation, it was widely assumed that transplantation would become a cure-all for heart disease. Transplants were being performed in patients suffering from the entire gamut of disorders including angina, coronary atherosclerosis, congenital heart disease, valvular heart disease, acute carditis, and cardiomyopathies.

When many of these transplants ended in failure, there was a strong counterreaction that brought with it the notion that heart transplants should not be used under any circumstances. As a result, the majority of surgeons who had "dabbled" in the field quickly got out of the heart transplant business.

One of the surgeons who stuck with it was Norman Shumway of Stanford University Medical Center, which soon became the leading heart transplant center in the world. Recently, Shumway and Eugene Dong, Jr., reported on the fate of 109 patients who had received 114 heart transplants at Stanford since 1968.

Survival Rate at Stanford

As of August, 1976, the post-transplantation survival rate of the entire group was 52 percent at one year, 43 percent at two years, 33 percent at three years, 31 percent at four years, 28 percent at five years, and 17 percent at six years. The longest-surviving patient had lived for 6.5 years. (A year later this patient was still alive.)

As with kidney transplantation, the highest risk was during the first three months after the operation. The one- and two-year survival rates for patients still alive after three months was 80 percent and 60 percent, respectively.

In contrast, the average survival of thirty-four patients who were accepted for heart transplants, but did not go through with the operation, was fifty days. Only five of these patients survived longer than three months after selection.

A follow-up study of fifty-one Stanford patients who survived at least six months after receiving a new heart showed that forty-six of them had returned to active employment or housekeeping functions.

Since the inception of the program at Stanford, the survival rate has improved significantly. In the first year of the program (1968), ten hearts were transplanted into nine patients, with only two of them (22 percent) surviving the first anniversary of their operation. By the 1974-76 period, the one-year survival rate had risen to 66 percent, with the two- and three-year rates at 63 percent and 58 percent, respectively.

Reasons for Progress

According to Dong and Shumway, the progress in heart transplantation at Stanford has been due to better selection of patients for surgery, improvements in surgical technique, development of methods to diagnose rejection, improved immunosuppression of rejection, and better diagnosis and treatment of infections.

One reason for the success of the Stanford heart transplant program has been the restriction of the operation to patients with a high probability of success. The vast majority of transplant recipients suffer from severe damage to the heart itself, often from coronary artery disease.

One contraindication for heart transplantation is advanced age. Because of the sharp decline in survival among patients older than fifty, the Stanford program has been restricted to patients younger than fifty-five, with most being under forty-five. Apparently, older patients have difficulty in tolerating the rigors of surgery and post-operative treatment.

Eugene Dong, Jr., Department of Cardiovascular Surgery, Stanford University Medical Center, Stanford, Ca. 94305

Preventing Coronary Artery Disease in Transplant Recipients

When surgeons take out a diseased heart with plaque-clogged arteries and replace it with a disease-free organ, they often find that the arteries of the patient's new heart soon become clogged with the same life-threatening plaques.

Researchers at Stanford Medical Center believe that the atherogenic process in graft recipients may be initiated by immune injury to the walls of the coronary arteries when the body tries to reject the newly acquired heart.

Next, they suggest, comes the formation of small blood clots at the sites of injury and the rapid growth of new cells to repair the wounds. And finally, infiltration of fat particles from the bloodstream, which further stimulates cell proliferation.

Prophylactic Therapy

In an attempt to prevent the secondary stages of the process, the Stanford researchers have been giving transplant recipients the anti-thrombotic drugs warfarin and dipyridamole and putting them on a low-cholesterol, low-saturated fat diet.

Recently, they compared the incidence of coronary artery disease in forty-four heart transplant survivors who had been given this prophylactic therapy between 1970 and 1975 to that in nine survivors who had not been placed on the regimen in 1968 and 1969.

They found that the incidence of coronary artery disease in the nontreated group reached 100 percent three years after transplantation. In contrast, only 17 percent of the treated group had coronary artery disease two years after transplantation.

Since the two groups were neither concurrent nor closely matched, the reduction in coronary artery disease among treated patients could have been due to other factors. For example, the nontreated group was significantly older and smoked more than the treated group—factors that are both linked to coronary artery disease.

However, the Stanford researchers believe that their use of postoperative therapy has been the primary reason for the reduction in coronary artery disease. Since they've failed to find any differences in serum lipid levels between treated and nontreated patients, they've concluded that the antithrombotic drugs, rather than the low lipid diet, have been responsible for the reduction in coronary artery disease.

Administration of oral anticoagulants, such as warfarin, has been shown to improve survival in heart attack patients, and dipyridamole is believed to protect against atherosclerosis by breaking up aggregations of platelets that form at arterial lesion sites.

The combination of warfarin and dipyridamole has also been shown to prevent progressive arterial disease in kidney transplant recipients. It's possible that chronic administration of these drugs, or similar compounds, could help to prevent coronary artery disease in persons at-risk for the disease.

Randall B. Griepp, Division of Cardiothoracic Surgery, Downstate Medical Center, 450 Clarkson Ave., Brooklyn, N.Y. 11203

Here Comes the Artificial Heart

In the 1980s, a man rushed to a hospital after a massive heart attack will become one of the great stories of the century. Instead of winding up on a cold slab in the morgue, he will emerge from the hospital with an artificial heart in his chest.

As the first recipient of a total artificial heart, he will be followed by the media as no one has ever been followed before. As the hopes of millions of heart disease victims ride on his every move, the event will spark heated debates about medical, moral, and theologic issues.

The groundwork for the artificial heart is being laid by scores of researchers in several countries. Most groups are working on left-heart devices designed to assist the damaged natural heart on a temporary basis. As of mid-1978, there were fifty to sixty patients who had such devices implanted. In most cases, the patients died within several months, usually because of right-heart failure.

There also has been a tremendous effort—fueled by $50 million of government and corporate funds—to develop a nuclear-powered artificial heart. That effort is largely coming to an end because of the difficulty of developing a unit small enough to be practical.

The Electric-Powered Heart

A more likely prospect is an electric-powered heart with a rechargeable battery. At the University of Utah, a team headed by Donald B. Olsen is developing such a unit. The power source in their system is a small electric motor (about the size of a D-cell battery) that pumps hydraulic fluid into a flexible plastic heart.

The blood-pumping action of the plastic heart is generated by rapid reversal of the motor, which changes direction every fifteen milliseconds at a speed of 10,000 revolutions per minute. The motor was put together by Robert K. Jarvik, who also designed the polyurethane heart into which the motor is placed.

In the current Utah program, Jarvik-type hearts powered by a compressed-air drive system are surgically implanted into calves. Once the heart is in place, the calf must remain connected to the drive system via plastic tubing, which markedly limits its mobility. The calves are cared for around the clock by two full-time attendants, who exercise the animals regularly on a treadmill.

The longest-lived survivor to date was a calf named Curley Joe who died in November, 1978, after 210 days with an artificial heart in place. Nine other calves have been sustained at least three months by artificial hearts at the University of Utah, the Cleveland Clinic, the Klinikum Westend in West Berlin, and Tokyo University in Japan.

Causes of Death

The primary causes of death in these animals were infection around the heart valves, inflow obstruction due to pannus (connective tissue) formation, mechanical failure of the heart, and multiple thromboembolism (vessels blocked by blood clots).

Another potential problem is the growth of the calf. Calves are used in artificial heart research because they are similar in size to adult humans. At some point, however, the calf may become too large to be sustained by the artificial heart.

Although survival times with compressed-air hearts have been impressive, it's unlikely that this approach will be used extensively in humans. The practical difficulties of using a heart that must be permanently attached to an external machine, as well as the psychological problems associated

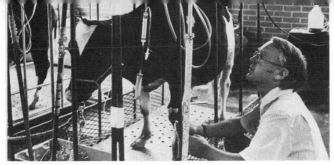

Dr. John Lawson of the University of Utah checks calf with total artificial heart.

with such a set-up, will probably restrict the use of compressed-air hearts.

Temporary Replacement

However, such an artificial heart might be of considerable value for a patient waiting for a heart transplant. In such a case, the patient's heart could be replaced by a compressed-air unit, with the understanding that he will receive a natural heart in the near future. The Utah team has already tested this procedure in identical twin calves, one of whom received the heart of the other after first receiving an artificial heart.

Electrically powered artificial hearts should soon be implanted in experimental calves. Since the plastic heart itself is almost identical to the models that have already enjoyed success in previous experiments, the crucial factor will be the performance of the power source. If Jarvik's electric motor does the job, we may soon see impressive survival times in calves leading to artificial heart implants in humans.

The Utah artificial heart program is under the overall di-

University of Utah artificial hearts: pneumatically powered model *(left)* and electrically powered model.

rection of Willem Kolff, the inventor of the artificial kidney, who is head of the Center's Division of Artificial Organs. Because of his desire to make the artificial heart available for clinical use as soon as possible, Kolff and his fellow researchers have formed a company called Kolff Associates.

Willem J. Kolff, Division of Artificial Organs, Department of Surgery, University of Utah Medical Center, Salt Lake City, Ut. 84112

Improving Kidney Transplantation

Kidney transplants were first performed in the 1950s, but the "modern" era of transplantation began in 1962 with the first successful use of immunosuppressive drugs.

Use of the artificial kidney, or renal dialysis, became widespread in the 1960s and is now the most popular method of treating end-stage kidney disease. About 37,000 persons are currently sustained by dialysis in the United States, and the number is expected to increase by 50 percent within the next six years.

Until recently, the mortality rate from transplantation was higher among transplant patients than among dialysis patients.

Data from the national Dialysis Registry indicate that 5-10 percent of dialysis patients die each year, primarily from complications of atherosclerosis.

The latest report of the Human Renal Transplant Registry showed that in 1974, 14 percent of patients who received kidneys from living relatives died within the first year, as did 28 percent of patients who received kidneys from cadavers.

But now there is a 1978 report from one of the leading kidney transplant centers in the U.S.—Peter Bent Brigham Hospital in Boston—of substantial improvement in the kidney transplant mortality rate. Of 186 patients receiving transplants since 1974, only seven (4 percent) died within one year of the operation.

The survival rate at Peter Bent Brigham Hospital is now 98 percent among recipients of kidneys from living relatives and 95 percent among recipients of cadaver kidneys.

Among the reasons for the improvement in kidney transplant survival are the following:

• The incidence of wound infections has been reduced from about 25 percent in 1972 to 2 percent since 1976 by the use of a single high dose of broad-spectrum antibiotics at the time of anesthesia.

• The risks and limitations of immunosuppressive drugs are better understood, with less emphasis placed on salvaging failing grafts.

• Ultrasound is used with increasing frequency to evaluate patients post-operatively.

• Needle biopsy of the transplanted kidney has replaced the more dangerous open biopsy technique.

The improved survival rate for cadaver transplants is particularly encouraging because of the difficulty of obtaining donor kidneys from living relatives. There have been more than twice as many kidney transplants from cadavers as from living relatives, despite the greater safety of the latter procedure.

When it becomes possible to freeze kidneys successfully (see p. 286), the creation of organ preservation banks could make cadaver kidneys available to anyone in the world dying of kidney disease.

Nicholas L. Tilney, Peter Bent Brigham Hospital, 721 Huntington Ave., Boston, Ma. 02115

The Wearable Artificial Kidney

The traditional artificial kidney is about the size of a washing machine. In order to receive proper treatment, patients must travel to a renal dialysis center three times a week. At each session, they must sit connected to the machine for several hours, while an array of pumps, dialyzers, bubble traps, and other devices filters the wastes from their blood.

Since the invention of the artificial kidney in the 1940s, researchers have been trying to compress its components into increasingly smaller spaces. They have developed various types of portable artificial kidneys that promise to free patients from some of the drudgery of conventional dialysis.

One such unit is the wearable artificial kidney (WAK), which was designed and built by mechanical engineer Stephen C. Jacobsen, in conjunction with the Division of Artificial Organs, at the University of Utah Medical Center. Not only does WAK remove urea and other wastes from the body, it also makes minor adjustments in the electrolyte content of the blood.

WAK enables the patient to function more normally outside the clinical environment while dialyzing. It consists of an eight-pound pack that is strapped with belts to the front of the body. Blood flows from and is returned to the patient through a single needle in the arm. The pack must be connected intermittently to a twenty-quart tank that serves as a regeneration reservoir.

The artificial kidney does a pretty good job of filtering out wastes, but is deficient in the endocrine functions normally performed by the kidneys, such as regulation of blood pressure. One solution to the problem might be to grow healthy kidney cells within the artificial kidney. Such cells might be able to boost the endocrine capabilities of the unit.

Willem J. Kolff, Division of Artificial Organs, Department of Surgery, University of Utah Medical Center, Salt Lake City, Ut. 84112

Current Status of Liver Transplantation

A team of surgeons recently removed the liver from a freshly dead body in Los Angeles, perfused it with cold

Collins' solution (see p. 283), flew it to Denver on a commercial jetliner, and successfully transplanted it into a patient with liver disease at the University of Colorado Medical Center. The team was headed by Thomas E. Starzl, who performed the world's first liver transplant in 1963, and has performed more than a hundred such procedures since.

Starzl and his colleagues have demonstrated that long-term survival is achievable in liver transplant recipients, despite a high percentage of failures during the first post-operative year. Of the group's first 100 patients, twenty-eight lived at least one post-operative year, fifteen were still alive as of April, 1977, and one had lived for 6.6 years. Long-term survival also has been achieved by teams at Cambridge-Kings College in England, the University of Montreal, and New York's Memorial Hospital.

The major reason for the high one-year mortality rate among liver transplant recipients is the technical difficulties of the operation. One complication that can arise in patients with end-stage liver disease, for example, is severe hemorrhaging caused by inadequate clotting and hypertension. Another is irreversible brain damage, which is believed to be caused by tiny air bubbles released from the transplanted liver during the operation.

Liver transplantation differs from kidney and heart transplantation in that immunologic rejection of the transplanted organ is only a relatively minor problem. Thus, there should be a dramatic rise in the success of the procedure as the technical problems are solved. Though liver transplantation is still an experimental procedure, it promises to become increasingly common in the near future.

Thomas E. Starzl, Department of Surgery, University of Colorado Medical Center, 4200 E. Ninth Ave., Denver, Colo. 80262

Artificial Replacement of the Liver

The liver is a highly complex organ. As a result, it's proved difficult to create an artificial system to simulate its action. However, systems have been devised to help the liver remove toxins and wastes in times of crisis. One of these systems is the "artificial liver" developed at McGill University in Montreal under the direction of T. M. S. Chang.

Chang is the inventor of microencapsulated "artificial cells," which have been used to substitute for red blood cells, for enzyme replacement in inborn errors of metabolism, removal of urea, and suppression of tumors—as well as in patients suffering from kidney or liver disease.

In treating liver failure, the patient's blood is redirected through an albumin-coilodion microencapsulated activated charcoal (ACAC) hemoperfusion chamber, where it is cleansed of the toxins and metabolites normally removed by the liver.

In the past several years, ACAC hemoperfusion has been used to treat more than 100 comatose patients suffering from liver failure. Because of considerable variation in the survival rate of these patients, it has been difficult to evaluate the technique.

Animal Studies

Chang has been studying its use in rats given an injection of galactosamine to induce liver damage similar to that found in humans. He's found that 71 percent of rats with induced liver failure survived after exposure to ACAC hemoperfusion compared to only 30.4 percent of rats with induced liver failure who were not given the treatment. In both groups, animals who did not survive lived only about three days after the injection of galactosamine.

This finding indicates that the ACAC hemoperfusion chamber can substitute for the liver in removing toxic amounts of galactosamine. It encourages further use of the system in humans, as well as additional research to develop a better artificial liver.

Thomas M. S. Chang, Artificial Organs Research Unit, McIntyre Medical Sciences Bldg., McGill University, Montreal, Quebec, Canada

Preventing "Rejection" of Transplanted Organs

The most critical problem in organ transplantation is the body's immunologic "rejection" of foreign tissue. To counter this effect, doctors give patients immunosuppressive drugs, which also weaken their resistance to disease. Most transplant failures occur because the body's weakened immune system is overwhelmed by a disease process.

The best way of solving the rejection problem is by matching transplant donor and recipient as closely as possible, according to HLA tissue type. With identical twins, for example, there is no rejection problem because they both have the same tissue type. Close relatives are often used to provide organs for patients requiring transplants because of the similarity in their tissue types.

The largest tissue typing laboratory in the world is directed by Paul I. Terasaki of UCLA's Department of Surgery. During the past twenty years, Terasaki has refined tissue-typing techniques on more than 160,000 persons. In "a striking testimonial to the power of HLA typing," he recently reported the matching of fraternal twins with two different fathers.

Paul I. Terasaki, Department of Surgery, UCLA Medical Center, 1000 Veteran Ave., Los Angeles, Ca. 90024

Reversing Diabetes in Rats

Josiah Brown of UCLA Medical Center has been able to reverse diabetes in rats by transplanting fetal pancreases into adult animals. First, he induced diabetes of moderate severity by intravenous injection of the drug streptozotocin.

Then fetal pancreases were grafted beneath the animal's kidney capsule. The rat's own pancreas was retained.

To accomplish complete reversal of diabetes, it was necessary to transplant four or six fetal pancreases into a suitable adult animal. The ideal age for transplantation was between 16½-17½ days of gestation. At this age, total success was achieved in 73 percent of rats receiving four pancreases and in 93 percent of rats receiving six pancreases.

Immediately after transplantation, both recipient and control animals with diabetes were given insulin for about eight days. During this period, plasma glucose levels fell from 400-500 mg/100 ml to 160 mg/100 ml in transplant recipients, but only to 290 mg/100 ml in controls. Shortly after the insulin treatment was stopped, plasma glucose shot back up to diabetic levels in controls, while remaining within the normal range in transplant recipients.

Once established, reversal of diabetes was apparently permanent so long as the pancreas transplants were retained. But if they were removed five or six months after placement, the diabetic state soon returned. This finding indicates that the reversal of diabetes observed in this experiment was due solely to the activity of the transplanted pancreases.

The ability to transplant fetal pancreases to reverse diabetes in adult rats suggests that a similar procedure might be effective in humans. Recent success in the freeze-preservation of fetal rat pancreases (see p. 292) suggests the possibility of setting up an organ bank to provide pancreases of all tissue types for transplantation.

Josiah Brown, Department of Medicine, UCLA Medical Center, Los Angeles, Ca. 90024

Regulating Blood Sugar with an Artificial Pancreas
Injections of insulin do not provide the diabetic with an appropriate amount of insulin at the moment of need. Instead, they produce widely fluctuating blood insulin levels

that subject the patient to alternating states of hyper- and hypoglycemia. This perpetual metabolic stress may contribute to the high incidence of cardiovascular disease among diabetics.

Scientists at the University of Toronto have created an artificial pancreas capable of responding to short-term variations in blood sugar. The unit operates at the patient's bedside. It is composed of a glucose sensor, computer, and delivery mechanism.

An indwelling catheter is used to draw blood into the sensor for glucose measurement. The computer receives and interprets electrical signals generated by the sensor and then instructs the delivery mechanism to pump insulin into the body at the rate needed to maintain the correct blood sugar level.

The artificial pancreas has been able to maintain normal blood sugar levels in diabetics during meal-eating, glucose challenge, and illness. Only after vigorous exercise has the device failed to achieve a fully normal metabolic response. But even here, the response was far better than in diabetics who received an injection of insulin prior to exercise.

The long-term goal of researchers in the field is to develop an implantable artificial beta cell capable of duplicating the biologic activity of the pancreas. Such an achievement would herald the coming of a new era in life extension —artificial organs comparable to human organs. Such devices might be used for "fine tuning" of endocrine imbalances associated with aging.

A. Michael Albisser, Biomedical Research, Hospital for Sick Children, 555 University Ave., Toronto M5G 1X8, Canada

Electric-Powered Drug Delivery

A device the size of a pocket calculator that uses electric current to deliver drugs through the skin—without pain, puncture, or risk of infection—has been developed at the

University of Utah. Thus far, the device, called the Phoresor, has been used successfully for local anesthesia in drainage of abscesses, removal of warts, minor finger surgery, and anesthetizing the forearm of kidney patients before insertion of the large needle used in dialysis.

The Phoresor consists of a portable power unit attached by cable to a band holding two electrodes, which can be strapped over the skin. A small pouch under the positive electrode holds the active drug, while the negative electrode is saturated with conductive jelly.

The Phoresor uses a technique called iontophoresis, whereby substances of like electric charge repel each other and substances of unlike charge attract. Since the ions of local anesthetic drugs are electropositive, they are driven through the skin at a controlled rate when subjected to electric current.

It takes about six or seven minutes for the Phoresor to administer enough drug to produce ten to fifteen minutes of anesthesia. The device reduces tissue trauma and distortion by delivering active drug alone. In contrast, injected anesthetic solutions contain only 2 percent of active drug.

The principle of iontophoresis can potentially be used to deliver any electropositive compound into the body. Alza Corporation is currently developing the technique for its transdermal drug delivery system. (See p. 384.) In theory, it could be used to improve the therapeutic process by providing feedback control of drug delivery via an attached minicomputer. (See p. 389.)

Stephen C. Jacobsen, Projects and Design Laboratory, Department of Mechanical Engineering, University of Utah Medical Center, Salt Lake City, Ut. 84112

Developing Artificial Skin
Burn patients may soon be treated with artificial skin, rather than with grafts from human cadavers or animals.

One type of artificial skin being developed at the U.S. Army's Institute of Surgical Research is a derivative of Teflon that adheres to the wound via electrostatically induced negative charges.

Aside from its use as a temporary dressing in burn patients, artificial skin could provide a model system to evaluate the biologic effects of such environmental agents as light, heat, oxygen, and chemical pollutants.

Paul Silverstein, U.S. Army Institute of Surgical Research, Brooke General Hospital, Fort Sam Houston, Texas

Potential Uses of Artificial Blood

"Bloodless" rats have survived without any apparent ill effects, after an artificial blood substitute prepared with liquid fluorocarbons had replaced their natural blood supply. Afterwards, the rats were able to carry out their normal functions, regenerate blood cells and plasma protein, and continue to grow and develop.

Here are some of the potential clinical uses of artificial blood:

• Temporary replacement of natural blood during surgery or in accident victims suffering blood loss.

• Treatment of diseases such as sickle-cell anemia and anerobic infections by providing higher oxygen pressure.

• Improvement of cancer chemotherapy by removing the enzymes in natural blood that normally attack anti-cancer drugs.

• Removal of "aging and disease factors" normally carried by the blood. (See p. 254.)

In addition to its therapeutic potential, artificial blood could have considerable value as a research tool. Scientists could manipulate the amount and proportion of substances in the substitute blood supply including hormones, enzymes, oxygen, or lymphocytes (immune system cells). By so doing, they might learn a great deal about the changes that accom-

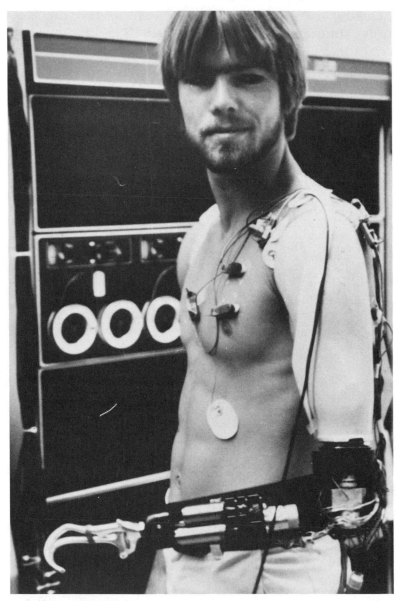

Patient wearing University of Utah artificial arm.

pany aging and degenerative disease, and be able to devise successful therapies based upon that knowledge.

Robert P. Geyer, Department of Nutrition, Harvard University School of Public Health, Boston, Ma. 02115

Automatic Control of an Artificial Arm

You don't have to be taught to move your arm—all you do is move it. Even the most complicated sequence of moves is performed automatically. For an artificial arm to imitate the human arm, it must have an electronic control system that interacts with the brain and spinal cord. Such a system has been incorporated into an artificial arm developed by Stephen C. Jacobsen at the University of Utah.

The arm is attached by inserting the amputee's limb remnant into a socket containing electrodes, which detect electrical signals coming from the muscles. These electromyographic signals—which are transmitted by the brain—are relayed to the control system which interprets them and then "tells" the arm how to move.

The amputee simply moves the arm automatically, without conscious deliberation or effort. Four types of movement are possible: elbow flexion, shoulder rotation, wrist rotation, and hand closure. The arm is designed to look like a human arm as much as possible.

Prototype models of the Utah arm are currently undergoing field testing to evaluate its effectiveness under real-life conditions.

Stephen C. Jacobsen, Projects and Design Laboratory, Department of Mechanical Engineering, University of Utah Medical Center, Salt Lake City, Ut. 84112

"Eyes" for the Blind

There are 300,000 legally blind persons in the United States, but only one—a man in his mid-thirties who was blinded at age twenty-three by a gunshot wound—who can "see" with the aid of an artificial eye. The man has electrodes on the occipital cortex of his brain that connect to a pedestal or plug screwed to his skull above the ear.

During experiments, the plug is connected to a computer-directed stimulator that sends electrical impulses into his brain to produce "phosphenes," which are experienced as points of light. These impulses are transmitted through a TV camera, enabling the patient to visualize shapes and patterns—even in the absence of optic nerves or visual tracts within the brain.

He can scan a blackboard and tell the difference between a horizontal line and a vertical line. He can read braille without touching a printed page.

The artificial eye was developed at the University of Utah under the direction of William H. Dobelle. It is now a joint project of the Utah Center's Advanced Microcircuit Laboratory and Columbia University in New York, where Dobelle is now stationed.

The primary objective of the project is to develop a "mobility prosthesis" to enable blind persons to move about without bumping into people or objects.

William H. Dobelle, Columbia University Medical Center, 168th St. and Broadway, New York, N.Y. 10032

And "Ears" for the Deaf

There are probably three times as many deaf persons in the world as blind ones. In an effort to help them to hear, scientists at the Utah Medical Center and Columbia University are working on an artificial ear.

The model now being developed stimulates the branches of the eighth nerve in the cochlea of the inner ear. Platinum wires threaded up into the cochlea and connected to a pedestal screwed to the bone behind the ear are used to deliver electrical impulses from a computer-directed stimulator.

With the aid of this system, totally deaf persons can distinguish rhythm, loudness, and some degree of pitch, but as yet are unable to understand human speech.

William H. Dobelle, Columbia University Medical Center, 168th St. and Broadway, New York, N.Y. 10032

The Value of the Artificial Placenta

Research on the artificial placenta has been impeded by widespread fears about "test-tube babies." (See p. 390.) When the Italian scientist Daniele Petrucci announced (in 1960) that he had maintained a human embryo in an artificial womb for fifty-nine days, the Pope reportedly ordered him to terminate the experiment. Though Petrucci never documented his claims, there have been at least a dozen scientific teams that have used animal models to experiment with artificial life-support systems for prenatal care.

Warren Zapol and Theodor Kolobow of the National Institute of Child Health and Development used a blood-circulation system, coiled spiral lung, and nutrient infusion bottle to maintain a prematurely born lamb fetus "in a metabolically stable state" for several days.

Robert Goodlin of Stanford University constructed a thick steel womb with a window, which he filled with a highly oxygenated saline solution compressed to 200 pounds per square inch—the same pressure an underwater diver encounters 450 feet below the surface. The idea was to force oxygen through the skin of the fetus, but Goodlin's chamber never became practical because he was unable to eliminate wastes.

The failure of these projects underscores the complexity and extraordinary performance of the natural placenta, which serves as the interface between mother and child. Through its rich, permeable tissues, the mother supplies her child with oxygen and nutrients, disposes of wastes, and protects it against infection and injury.

Though we are still far from a workable artificial placenta, progress is being made at both ends of the reproductive spectrum. Incubators at perinatal centers can support the life functions of prematurely born babies as young as twenty-five weeks of age.

And at Johns Hopkins University, Yu-Chih Hsu has maintained mouse embryos in Petri dishes for up to 8½ days—almost halfway to term. At this point in life, the mouse has a visible pumping heart, a developing spinal cord, and rapidly differentiating organ systems.

The artificial placenta could enable us to cure fetal abnormalities, prevent the diseases of childhood and adulthood, and counter many of the factors responsible for limiting life span.

Theodor Kolobow, National Institute of Child Health and Development, NIH, Bethesda, Md. 20014

Yu-Chih Hsu, School of Hygiene and Public Health, Johns Hopkins University, Baltimore, Md. 21205

Transplanting Brain Tissue

Everyone loses brain cells and brain cell function with advancing age. Those afflicted with neurologic disorders often show degeneration of discrete populations of brain cells. For example, Parkinson's Disease patients suffer losses of dopamine-containing neurons in the substantia nigra region of the brain.

Recent studies have demonstrated that transplanted embryonic rat brain tissue can reinnervate previously damaged portions of the adult rat. Scientists at the University of Lund in Sweden have used implants to repopulate brain regions that produce four neurotransmitters—acetylcholine, dopamine, norepinephrine, and serotonin—that play key roles in maintaining critical life functions.

The Swedish scientists measured the growth cells after implantation, the activity of enzymes associated with normal brain cell function, and the survival of the implanted cells. In their latest study, they report electron microscopic evidence of the formation of new synaptic contacts by ingrowing axons from brain stem implants. Synapses are interconnecting links that are essential for communication among brain cells.

Altering Behavior

A team of scientists at St. Elizabeth's Hospital in Washington, D.C., has produced further evidence of the effectiveness of brain tissue transplants—a positive change in behavior among transplant recipients. They grafted fetal rat dopamine-containing neurons to an area of the brain (adjacent to the caudate nucleus) in adult rats where endogenous dopamine capacity had been destroyed.

The grafts showed good survival and axonal outgrowth, and they significantly reduced motor abnormalities that had been caused by cell destruction. The alteration in the behavior of the recipient animals was consistent with the normal function of the grafted tissue—a finding that indicates that brain tissue transplantation may be a viable means of restoring lost function in injured, diseased, or aging animals.

These studies have tremendous implications for humans. They suggest the possibility of therapeutic benefits for patients suffering from organic neurologic disorders such as Parkinson's Disease and senile dementia, as well as rejuvenation effects in normally aging persons.

Anders Björklund, Department of Histology, University of Lund, 5-223 62, Lund, Sweden

Mark J. Perlow, Unit on Geriatric Psychiatry, Laboratory of Clinical Psychopharmacology, National Institute of Mental Health, St. Elizabeth's Hospital, Washington, D.C. 20032

Transplanting Brains, Heads, and Bodies

Suppose your body was crippled, wracked with cancer, or ravaged by old age, but your brain was intact and functioning well. One solution to your problem might be to receive an entire body transplant from an otherwise healthy person dying of brain damage. Instead of suffering or dying yourself, you might live for many years within a new body.

A series of experiments by Robert J. White of Case Western Reserve University School of Medicine in Cleveland suggests that whole body transplants may someday be a viable means of extending life span. In experiments with dogs and monkeys, White has maintained isolated brains, heads, and headless bodies for three to eight hours, and has successfully transplanted brains and heads onto new bodies for up to seven days.

White's isolated brains were maintained by a mechanical extracorporeal perfusion system employing chemically diluted blood, and his transplants were connected via bilateral carotid-jugular loops to provide blood circulatory exchange.

Monkey heads attached to new bodies in this fashion displayed "excellent" neurologic, behavioral, and electroencephalographic function. They were able to see, hear, taste, eat, drink, bite, and feel sensations around the face. If threatened, they would blink their eyes and grimace just like intact animals.

The major problem that remains to be solved in perfecting the brain/head-body transplant is to reattach the brain to the spinal cord of the new body. Although surgeons have successfully reconnected bone, blood vessels, and nerve tissue in severed limbs, they have yet to perform this feat with a severed spinal cord.

Robert J. White, Department of Neurosurgery, Case Western Reserve University School of Medicine, Cleveland, Oh. 44106

Chapter 8

Rejuvenation Therapies

Gerovital-H₃—the "Youth" Drug

The most famous rejuvenation therapy is Gerovital-H₃, which has been the center of controversy for almost three decades. Gerovital is the brainchild of Romanian physician Ana Aslan, who began using it to treat the elderly in 1951 at the Geriatric Institute in Bucharest.

Over the years, hundreds of thousands of people have flocked to Romania and other countries where Gerovital is available to receive injections of the drug. Among the celebrities linked to Gerovital have been John F. Kennedy, Marlene Dietrich, Charles de Gaulle, W. Somerset Maugham, Kirk Douglas, and Konrad Adenauer.

Aslan has repeatedly claimed that Gerovital therapy can reverse many of the symptoms of aging, and that it is beneficial in treating cardiovascular disease, arthritis, Parkinson's Disease, depression, loss of energy, decline in memory, sexual dysfunction, wrinkled skin, graying of hair, and baldness.

Early Studies

In the early 1960s, controlled studies in the United States and England failed to support Aslan's claims. A few scientists pointed out that these studies were poorly designed and that the drug they used was similar, but not identical, to the preparation used by Aslan. But the vast majority of physicians were convinced that Gerovital was worthless and that it would soon be abandoned by all but a few hardcore believers.

But this was not to be the case. Gerovital continued to grow in popularity, as one country after another approved its use in treating the elderly. Even in England—where several of the most negative studies had been published—it was finally decided to give people access to the drug.

And now there is public pressure to make the drug available in the United States. Since 1972, the Rom-Amer Company has been seeking U.S. Food and Drug Administration approval to market Gerovital as an antidepressant for adults over age fifty.

Nevada recently became the first state to approve clinical use of Gerovital, and the drug also is available in several other states as well as spas such as Touch of Eden in Montego Bay, Jamaica, in the Caribbean.

Rom-Amer Pharmaceuticals, 300 S. Fourth, Las Vegas, Ne. 89101

Touch of Eden, 2401 E. Washington Blvd., Pasadena, Ca. 91104

What Is Gerovital-H₃?

Gerovital-H_3 is a 2 percent procaine hydrochloride solution that contains trace amounts of benzoic acid, potassium metabisulfate, and disodium phosphate. The biologically active agent in the drug is procaine, which was synthesized by Einhorn in 1905 in his search for less toxic substitutes for cocaine. Procaine hydrochloride is used extensively in the United States as a local anesthetic under the name novocaine.

When procaine is absorbed into the body, it is broken down into two metabolites: para-aminobenzoic acid (PABA) and diethylaminoethanol (DEAE). PABA is a member of the B group of vitamins that is used by green-leafed vegetables to synthesize folic acid. It is commonly used in lotions that protect against sunburn. DEAE is a close relative of deanol

(DMAE), which has been used to extend the life span of fruit flies and mice (see p. 274) and is a component of chlorpromazine, which is used to treat the elderly. (See p. 276.) It also participates in the synthesis of choline, which has been linked to memory and other cognitive functions. (See p. 263.)

Both metabolites are organic compounds that are rapidly excreted from the body. As a result, Gerovital is a relatively nontoxic drug that produces few side effects.

Many imitations of Gerovital-H₃ have been marketed in Europe. The most popular is KH-3, a West German drug that contains procaine plus hematoporphyrin, a somewhat toxic antidepressant.

Taking the "Geriatric Cure" in Romania

Every year, thousands of persons go to Romania to receive Gerovital therapy. They can choose among a variety of geriatric clinics and hotels in the Bucharest area and in other parts of the country. If they wish, they can be treated at the Geriatric Institute, where Ana Aslan is director.

In addition to Gerovital-H₃, the Romanian geriatric centers offer Aslavital, a new product that contains procaine plus "an activating factor and an anti-arteriosclerosis factor efficient in the prophylaxis and cure of . . . the process of aging of the central nervous system and the cardiovascular apparatus."

Patients are advised to stay in Romania for at least two weeks. During this period, the clinical laboratory tests are performed prior to initiation of treatment. At the end of the treatment period, patients receive a medical bulletin with test results and recommendations for continuing the treatment at home. When the patients leave, they are given a one-year supply of Gerovital and Aslavital.

Romanian National Tourist Office, 573 Third Ave., New York, N.Y. 10016

Can Gerovital-H₃ Prolong Life Span?

In 1957, Ana Aslan reported that 5,251 persons had received Gerovital treatment—4,251 as therapy for aging or specific disorders, and 1,000 to retard the aging process. She gave the impression that most of these patients improved substantially as a result of the treatment, but no overall figures were supplied. Case histories described dramatic improvements in physical and mental functions.

Aslan recently reported the results of an open fifteen-year study (1951-1966) to test three compounds in groups of thirty to forty elderly patients from sixty to ninety-two years of age. One group received Gerovital, another group vitamin E, and the third a pineal gland extract. Aslan said there was 15 percent mortality in the control group during the fifteen-year period, ten percent mortality in the vitamin E group, and 5 percent mortality in the Gerovital group.

When Aslan gave Gerovital-H₃ to 920 white rats, she found that the treatment increased the life span of males by 21.2 percent and of females by 6.7 percent. Also that Gerovital-treated animals of both sexes were more efficient in maze-running and showed less impairment of cardiac function than control animals.

In a similar but much smaller study, the Austrian gerontologist Frederick Verzar found neither prolongation of life span nor protection against loss of function in his experimental animals. However, Verzar gave his animals very high doses of Gerovital, which may have produced toxic side effects.

A recent study by T. Samorajski showed that mice receiving Gerovital had a 33 percent higher survival rate at twenty-five months of age (when they were sacrificed) than control animals. The study also showed that Gerovital tended to stabilize cell membrane function, in contrast to the characteristic deterioration of membranes noted in untreated animals.

Ana Aslan, Institutul National de Gerontologie Si Geriatrie, Str. Mînăstirea Căldărusani, 9-Sector 8, Bucharest, Romania

T. Samorajski, Texas Research Institute of Mental Sciences, 1300 Moursund Ave., Texas Medical Center, Houston, Tx. 77025

Is Gerovital-H₃ an Effective Antidepressant?

The only therapeutic claim for Gerovital-H$_3$ for which there is clinical evidence in the U.S. is as an antidepressant in geriatric patients. There have been several controlled, double-blind studies indicating that Gerovital can improve the mood and behavior of depressed patients over fifty, as well as experiments suggesting its mechanism of action.

In one such study by Kurland and Hayman, thirty-three patients received injections of Gerovital and thirty received injections of saline solution. The investigators reported significant improvement in patients receiving Gerovital compared to patients receiving placebo, with minimal side effects reported for both groups.

Another study by William W. K. Zung of Duke University compared both Gerovital and imipramine (a commonly used antidepressant) with placebo. He found that both Gerovital- and imipramine-treated patients improved significantly, but that Gerovital was superior to imipramine.

Leonard Cammer of New York Medical College examined forty patients—twenty receiving Gerovital and twenty receiving placebo. He concluded that Gerovital was significantly better than placebo in the treatment of depression, and cited the results of laboratory tests as evidence of the drug's safety.

In describing the therapeutic benefits of Gerovital, Cohen and Ditman reported that most patients who took the drug "felt a greater sense of well-being and relaxation, slept better at night, and many obtained some relief from depression and the discomforts of chronic inflammation or degenerative disease."

On the other hand, Israel Zwerling, who conducted a study at Bronx Hospital in New York, concluded that Gerovital was not effective in treating depression. And Olsen, Bank, and Jarvik concluded that Gerovital was no better than placebo in treating depressed patients at the Brentwood V.A. Hospital in Los Angeles.

Proposed Mechanism of Action

The proposed mechanism for Gerovital's action as an antidepressant is that it inhibits the activity of monoamine oxidase (MAO), the enzyme that normally holds levels of monoamines (neurotransmitters) in check. High levels of MAO have been linked to several psychiatric disorders, and the increasing incidence of depression with advancing age is associated with elevated brain levels of the enzyme.

Several MAO inhibitors are now marketed in the United States as antidepressants. These drugs produce feelings of psychic well-being and physical vigor in patients suffering from depression, but can also produce side effects such as liver damage and hypertensive crises characterized by chest pain, headache, and intracranial hemorrhage.

According to several investigators, Gerovital's antidepressant action produces no such side effects because the drug is a weak, reversible inhibitor of MAO that gently and selectively modifies levels of brain monoamines.

Recent data collected by James Clemens of the Eli Lilly Company in Indianapolis showed only "slight and transitory" inhibition of MAO by Gerovital in rats, at doses much higher than those used in humans. Clemens concluded that if Gerovital produces an antidepressant effect clinically, it is probably not as an MAO inhibitor.

William W. K. Zung, Duke University Medical Center, Durham, N.C. 27705

Lissy F. Jarvik, Department of Psychiatry, UCLA Medical Center, Los Angeles, Ca. 90024

Gerovital-H₃: Where Do We Stand Today?

After many years of controversy, it seems that the Gerovital-H_3 story is still far from over. At this point, there is some evidence from animal studies that Gerovital may be able to retard aging or rejuvenate the aged, but no solid clinical evidence to support this notion. At the same time, there are several clinical studies indicating that the drug may be an effective antidepressant, and several studies suggesting it has no antidepressant effect.

To further complicate matters, there are biochemical studies suggesting that Gerovital's antidepressant effect may be the result of its action as an MAO inhibitor, and at least one study indicating that it probably doesn't function as an MAO inhibitor.

One reason for the confusion about Gerovital is the aura of emotionalism that has surrounded the drug since its "anti-aging" effects were trumpeted to the world by Ana Aslan. Many older persons are less critical than they should be about such "miracle" drugs—in part because conventional medicine has so little to offer them. And there are always hucksters around to exploit this susceptibility. On the other hand, members of the medical establishment can be "blind" to the value of a controversial drug simply because they're afraid of being labeled hucksters.

What's needed is more and better research on Gerovital-H_3 and other such therapies before any further claims are made.

The Laetrile Controversy: What Are the Facts?

In the past two decades, an estimated 70,000 Americans have used laetrile for the prevention or cure of cancer. During this period, thousands of case histories and testimonials in support of laetrile therapy have been collected by groups such as the Committee for Freedom of Choice in Cancer Therapy.

The laetrile "movement" has led to legalization of the product in thirteen states including Nevada, Florida, Oregon, and New Hampshire—despite opposition by the U.S. Food and Drug Administration and leading experts in cancer treatment and research.

Examining the Evidence

Laetrile has consistently failed to show an anti-cancer effect in every *in vitro* and *in vivo* animal test-system used to evaluate the compound. In most studies, the control animals have outlived the laetrile-treated animals, which suggests that laetrile may have toxic side effects.

A controversial laetrile study was conducted by Kanematsu Sugiura at Sloan-Kettering Cancer Center in New York. In 1973, preliminary results of this study, which indicated that control mice had a 78 percent incidence of lung cancer compared to only 13 percent in laetrile-treated mice, were "leaked" in *Science* magazine and the *St. Louis Globe Democrat*. By the end of the study, however, Sugiura reportedly found "no significant differences between the two groups." A subsequent study using the identical protocol at the Catholic Medical Center in Queens, New York, was reported to have "reaffirmed laetrile's ineffectiveness."

Both studies were sponsored by the National Cancer Institute (NCI). Because of the apparent "turnabout" from the early "success" of the Sugiura study, there have been persistent rumors of a government "cover-up" of all positive laetrile findings.

Two subsequent animals studies, also sponsored by NCI, provide additional published evidence of the ineffectiveness and potential toxicity of laetrile.

Clinical Studies

There have been no good clinical studies of laetrile in humans. In the late 1950s, Manuel D. Navarro of Santo Tomas University in The Philippines produced anecdotal evidence of laetrile's effectiveness in combating cancer, but failed to provide control subjects or effective follow-up of patients. Other studies, both positive and negative, have suffered from similar flaws.

In response to widespread public interest, NCI recently conducted a retrospective analysis of laetrile therapy. Through an intensive national publicity campaign, accounts were sought of patients who thought they had benefited from laetrile. There was a press conference, articles in the medical and lay press, contact with pro-laetrile groups, and distribution of 455,000 letters to physicians and other health professionals.

Although only positive case histories were solicited, NCI received replies from 220 physicians who claimed knowledge of more than 1,000 patients showing no beneficial response to laetrile. There were only sixty-seven satisfactory case histories received showing a beneficial effect from laetrile treatment.

Summaries of sixty-eight courses of laetrile treatment were evaluated by a panel of twelve cancer specialists not on the staff of NCI. The panel concluded that there were was clear-cut evidence of a beneficial response in six (two complete and four partial) of the sixty-eight courses of laetrile treatment. In the fall of 1978, NCI announced it would spend $250,000 for additional clinical testing of laetrile.

Is Laetrile a Vitamin?

One point of controversy is whether laetrile should be considered a drug or a vitamin. Laetrile proponents contend that it is a B vitamin, the lack of which leads to cancer. Critics point to studies indicating there are no disease states associated with dietary lack of laetrile, and that there is no unique physiologic function for laetrile—as there is for all accepted vitamins.

Actually, the term "laetrile" denotes a class of compounds called cyanogenic glucosides, but it has generally come to represent amygdalin—a naturally occurring cyanoglucoside that is found in various plant sources including apricot, peach, and plum pits. Most of the laetrile used today is produced from ground apricot pits in Mexico.

Laetrile therapy is available in injectable or oral form at various Mexican clinics, most notably the Del Mar Medical Center in Tijuana under the direction of Ernesto Contraras. It is also available from some American physicians, particularly in states where it has been legalized, and it has been sold in health food stores as vitamin B_{17}, under the names "Aprikern" and "Bee-17." Interestingly, the Mexican government has recently moved to terminate production of laetrile in that country because of its apparent lack of value in cancer therapy.

One of the breakdown products of laetrile is hydrogen cyanide, which is similar to the poison cyanide. Laetrile proponents insist that hydrogen cyanide—as contained within the "vitamin" structure of laetrile—is harmless, and point to the rarity of reports of toxicity from laetrile therapy.

Unfortunately, reports of toxicity have been coming in with increasing frequency in the last couple of years. On July 12, 1977, Joseph F. Ross of UCLA Medical Center reported thirty-seven documented cases of poisoning and seventeen deaths from either laetrile or cyanide-containing fruit kernels based upon data from the U.S. and six other countries.

Committee for Freedom of Choice in Cancer Therapy, 146 Main St., Suite 408, Los Altos, Ca. 94022

Neil M. Ellison, National Cancer Institute, Bldg. 31, Room 11A52, Bethesda, Md. 20014

Placental Tissue Therapy in the Soviet Union

"RUSSIANS STOP THE AGING PROCESS," blared the front-page headline of a recent issue of the *National Inquirer*. In an era when sensational headlines about alleged anti-aging therapies have become commonplace, this particular story demanded special attention for several reasons.

First, because it was about a unique therapy developed in the Soviet Union—a country with a long history of efforts to extend human life and a government policy that strongly supports life-extension research.

Next, because the story emanated from an institute in the Ukrainian Black Sea port of Odessa, a city renowned for its many revitalization and rehabilitation clinics.

Finally, because the treatment described in the story—injections of human placenta extracts—is a reasonable approach to rejuvenation. The idea of giving old people some type of "youth" factor has long been pursued clinically (see p. 243) as well as in the laboratory. (See p. 196.)

As it turned out upon my visiting the Soviet Union, the *Inquirer* story—in which it was claimed that patients had not aged for more than ten years—was an exaggeration of claims made by doctors at the Filatov Institute, where the treatment has been practiced since 1965. According to Sergei N. Goncharenko, head of the Institute's gerontology department, and Institute director Nadezda A. Puchkovskaya, placental tissue therapy is useful in preventing and treating the symptoms of premature aging, but is not an elixir of youth capable of turning back the clock.

Description of Treatment

Geriatric patients at the Filatov Institute receive injections of very small pieces of human placental tissue suspended in a physiologic saline solution. Each course of treatment includes three injections of 2 ml of placenta given every ten days. Then there is a three- to six-month interval before the next series of injections.

Patients of both sexes are divided into two groups before receiving placental therapy; one consists of individuals aged forty-five to fifty-nine, suffering from premature aging; the other consists of elderly patients, aged sixty to seventy-four,

Institute of Filatova, Odessa, U.S.S.R.

beset by the normal deficits of aging. In some cases, patients over age seventy-five are also given placental therapy.

Results of a Ten-Year Study

A ten-year study of 130 geriatric patients given placental therapy at the Filatov Institute showed fewer post-treatment complaints about general weakness, fatigue under physical and psychic stress, limited mobility, memory weakness, vision weakness, reduction or loss of sexual potency, heart pain, and joint pains.

Among the symptoms for which placental therapy showed little or no apparent benefit were hearing weakness, hair graying, hair loss, face-skin wrinkling, and sensitivity to cold.

In the premature aging group, the average blood pressure reading was about 140/87 before treatment compared to about 137/78 after treatment. Among the elderly patients, the average blood pressure reading was about 159/87 before treatment compared to about 153/79 after treatment.

As can be seen, there was small apparent benefit to patients suffering from high blood pressure.

Most other parameters measured showed similarly minor or marginal benefits from placental therapy. The greatest improvements in function were observed early in the therapeutic program among patients in relatively poor condition, with the efficacy of treatment declining somewhat as the patients grew older.

It would be interesting to know more about the effects of the other therapeutic approaches used at the Filatov Institute. These include aloe (plant extract) therapy, peloidodistillate therapy (biologically active estuary mud), FIBS therapy ("medicinal" mud plus cinnamic acid and cumarin), and torfot (peat extract) therapy.

S. N. Goncharenko, Institute of Filatova, Proletarsky Blvd., 49/51, Odessa—61, U.S.S.R.

Ginseng: The Oriental "Rejuvenator"

Ginseng is an aromatic root that has been used in medicine by the Chinese and Koreans for thousands of years. It has long enjoyed a reputation as an aphrodisiac and rejuvenator with little or no evidence of potency from western sources. In the last few years, however, there have been reports suggesting that ginseng—or a drug in which ginseng is the major component—may have value in treating the elderly.

In a German study, the preliminary results of which were presented at the XI International Congress of Gerontology in Tokyo in 1978, it was claimed that two products—Ginsana (an extract of the Korean ginseng root) and Geriatric Pharmaton (a multi-agent compound that includes ginseng) —had lowered blood pressure in hypertensive patients, normalized pancreatic function in diabetic patients, and improved mental functions in most of the 540 patients treated.

In an Austrian study, Geriatric Pharmaton was given to

fifteen of thirty patients, fifty-three to ninety years of age, for 100 days, in a controlled, double-blind trial. "Marked improvement" was reported in the drug-treated group for a variety of mental and intellectual functions including the capacity to perceive abstract relationships, accuracy of picture interpretation, and emotional outlook on life.

Protection Against Stress

According to Consultox Laboratories in London, ginseng may protect against environmental stress. This finding is based upon a study in which mice were given ginseng at low (3 mg/kg/day) and high (30 mg/kg/day) doses, or placebo, for fourteen, twenty-one, and twenty-eight days, and then placed into a water bath at about 18°C and forced to swim until exhaustion.

The swimming performance of the ginseng-treated mice was reported to be significantly better than controls at high doses after fourteen days, with the degree of improvement increasing as the period of administration was extended. By the end of twenty-eight days, both high- and low-dose ginseng-treated animals outperformed control animals by 38.4 to 51.8 percent.

While the findings of these studies are interesting, one should be especially cautious about accepting them because they were supplied by the manufacturer of the products. A search of the scientific literature revealed no similar studies (in English) to support or refute them.

Ginseng Products Ltd., P.O. Box 57736, CH-6903, Lugano, Switzerland

Pharmaton, Ltd., P.O. Box 145, CH-6903, Lugano, Switzerland

Ginseng Does Not Extend the Life Span of Mice

A recently published English study concluded that long-term administration of ginseng had no significant effect on the life span of LACa mice.

The mice were divided into three groups of ninety animals, each group containing equal numbers of males and females. One group was given ginseng extract from eight weeks of age until the end of their life span; the second group was given ginseng from fifty-two weeks of age until the end of their life span; and the third group (the controls) was not treated.

The ginseng extract was dissolved in the drinking water given to the mice. The average dose consumed was about 8 mg extract/kg body weight/day, which is roughly comparable to the recommended dose for humans.

At various stages in their lives, ten male and ten female mice from each group were tested for their behavioral response to mild stress. Individual mice were placed upon a circular open field under bright illumination for five minutes—a situation that normally induces measurable fear responses in the mice.

The results of the study showed no significant differences in the mean, median, or maximum life spans of the three groups. An earlier Russian study had demonstrated an increase in the life span of white rats given ginseng at higher doses, but too few animals were used to permit statistical analysis.

The animals receiving ginseng crouched more often and displayed less movement in response to stress than the control animals. It was suggested that this behavior pattern could be interpreted as evidence that ginseng protects against stress—perhaps by stimulating hormone production along the hypothalamic-pituitary-adrenal axis.

A. H. Bittles, Department of Human Biology, Chelsea College, University of London, London, England

Can Fetal Lamb Cells Rejuvenate People?
Every week, a new group of patients enters Clinique La Prairie in Clarens-Montreux, Switzerland, to receive injec-

tions of "fresh cells" from the fetus of a newly slaughtered lamb. The treatment is called cellular therapy and its objective is to rejuvenate or "revitalize" the body.

Cellular therapy was started in 1931 by Paul Niehans, who believed that living cells from the organs of a young donor animal could migrate to the corresponding organs of a human recipient to stimulate regeneration of tissue. Niehans practiced cellular therapy at Clinique La Prairie until his death in 1969. His work was continued by Walter Michel until Michel died in 1976, when Niehan's last disciple, Bernard Bovet, took over.

Among the more than 50,000 patients who have visited Clinique La Prairie have been Konrad Adenauer, Gloria Swanson, Christian Dior, Lillian Gish, Bernard Baruch, and Groucho Marx. The technique became world renowned in the mid-1950s when Pope Pius XII was reportedly "raised from his death bed" by cell injections administered by Niehans.

Protocol for Cellular Therapy

Patients enter Clinique La Prairie, a large elegant chalet facing Lake Geneva at the foot of the Alps, early on Monday morning to be interviewed and undergo a medical examination. On Wednesday afternoon between 2 and 3 P.M., they return for their room assignments. Early Thursday morning, they receive a series of cell injections in the buttocks. Afterwards, they must remain in bed under medical supervision for five days, until the following Monday morning. At that time, they receive counseling from Bovet before being discharged from the clinic before noon on Tuesday.

The fetal cells used at Clinique La Prairie are obtained from a herd of black mountain sheep maintained at a nearby farm. A lamb fetus is removed from a healthy pregnant ewe via cesarean section. The fetus is then rushed to the clinic

Clinique La Prairie, Clarens-Montreux, Switzerland.

laboratory where tissue specimens are extracted and cell suspensions prepared.

According to Bovet, patients suffer no adverse effects from fresh cell therapy, except for occasional mild allergic reactions. He points out that fetal cells are not rejected by the body's immune system—as adult foreign cells are—and that "rigorous sterile procedures" virtually preclude the risk of infection.

The therapeutic claims for cellular therapy have never been recognized in the United States where it is illegal to practice it. Despite scores of European studies extolling its virtues, no hard data have yet been presented to substantiate its value as a rejuvenation treatment.

Clinique La Prairie is now selling cosmetics based upon a "unique method for topical application of fresh cells." These include an anti-wrinkle cream, day cream, night cream, and beauty milk. The cosmetic line is available at department stores in the United States.

Bernard Bovet, Clinique La Prairie, 1815 Clarens-Montreux, Switzerland

Other Methods of Cellular Therapy

"To explain the indications for 'cellvital' therapy," says Swiss physician Alfred Pfister, "I use the metaphor of an electric battery which runs down and thus needs a new charge or a 'revitalization.'" Pfister's Clinique Lemana in Clarens-Montreux, where he administers cellvital therapy, is a beautiful retreat that sits on the mountainside overlooking Lake Geneva—just a mile or so above the Niehans clinic.

Pfister was once an associate of Niehans. He claims he parted company with Niehans because of the unacceptably high rate of infection he found in patients receiving cells from freshly slaughtered animals. Another drawback of the Niehans method, says Pfister, is "loss of therapeutic efficacy" if the suspension is not injected within twenty to thirty minutes after the slaughter.

Two other methods of preparing cells for therapy are cryopreservation, in which cells are frozen to −40° C and subsequently thawed for treatment; and lypholisation, in which cells are freeze-dried for long-term storage. Most of the clinics at which cellular therapy is practiced use one of these two methods.

Cellvital Therapy

Pfister says his method was developed to permit patients to enjoy "the therapeutic efficacy of fresh cells with all the necessary safeguards against infection." The key factor, he says, is a "preserving fluid" within which the cells are placed immediately after extraction from the fetus. According to Pfister, this fluid—the composition of which he refuses to reveal—enables the cells to keep "breathing" for "many weeks."

The bottom line on cellular therapy is that it remains

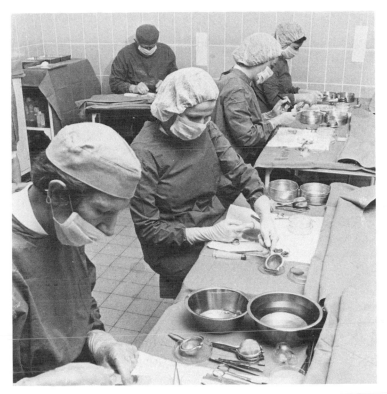

Preparing live cells for cellular therapy injections at Clinique La Prairie in Switzerland.

an unproven technique, despite decades of practice. There is no adequate scientific basis to evaluate its effects upon aging or any diseases, nor are there sufficient data to effectively differentiate among the various methods by which it is practiced.

Alfred Pfister, Clinique Lemana, Au Bosquets-de-Julie 21, CH-1815, Clarens-Montreux, Switzerland

Evaluating Estrogen Replacement Therapy

Menopause is a dramatic manifestation of aging. It involves a sharp reduction in the production of sex hormones resulting in loss of reproductive capacity. For most women, it is a discomforting period characterized by menstrual irregularities, hot flushes, and accelerated aging.

The most serious sign of aging related to the menopause is osteoporosis, a skeletal disorder in which there is a decrease in bone mass and density leading to increased bone fragility. Osteoporosis occurs to some extent in all aging men and women, but it generally occurs earlier and more severely in women—a phenomenon that has been linked to loss of estrogen.

The most effective treatment for menopausal symptoms is estrogen replacement therapy. By taking estrogen (and in some cases progesterone), women are relieved of the distressful symptoms of hormonal deprivation. They usually feel better, look better, and behave better.

There is persuasive evidence that estrogen therapy can prevent or retard osteoporosis. For example, a recent British study of estrogen therapy in seventy-two postmenopausal women showed considerable bone loss over a two-year period in untreated women, but no bone loss at all in women receiving estrogen.

Risk of Uterine Cancer

But if the benefits of estrogen therapy are documented, so is the fact that women taking estrogen—either in natural or synthetic form—are at increased risk for endometrial (uterine) cancer. A half-dozen recent studies have shown that women who take estrogen have a three to fifteen times greater chance of getting endometrial cancer than women who do not take estrogen.

However, these figures sound more threatening than they actually are. Endometrial cancer is relatively rare, and it is highly unlikely that estrogen users will get it—even if their risk is significantly higher than nonusers. Moreover, by monitoring for signs of the disease, a woman can usually detect it at an early stage when it is treatable.

And there are health benefits from estrogen therapy beyond the relief of symptoms. For example, spinal compression fractures are about four times as common in women as in men, and hip fractures are about 2.4 times as common. The risk of hip fracture is at least 20 percent by age ninety, and one-sixth of all hip fracture patients die within three months of injury. Estrogen therapy can help to prevent such fractures.

It's unfortunate that the benefits of estrogen replacement therapy are offset to some degree by the risk of uterine cancer. However, there's good reason to believe that controlled delivery of estrogen (see p. 382) may soon minimize the risks and potentiate the benefits of this anti-aging therapy.

A. Horsman, MRC Mineral Metabolism Unit, General Infirmary, Leeds LS1 3EX, England

Paul D. Stolley, Department of Research Medicine, University of Pennsylvania, Philadelphia, Pa. 19104

The Controversy over Chelation Therapy

In advanced atherosclerosis, calcium is bound to the plaques that clog a person's arteries. One treatment for the disease is chelation therapy, in which a synthetic amino acid called EDTA (ethylenediaminetetraacetic acid) is slowly introduced into the bloodstream.

As EDTA circulates throughout the body, it binds to, or chelates, calcium in the blood, which is then excreted. According to chelation practitioners, the body then scavenges calcium from the arteries in order to replenish it in the bloodstream, a process that reduces the size and severity of plaque buildup.

Another disease for which there is evidence of benefit from chelation therapy is rheumatoid arthritis. There have been reports showing reduced pain, swelling, and stiffness in rheumatoid arthritis patients given chelation therapy, with "dramatic improvement" in some cases.

The controversy over chelation therapy revolves around

its potentially toxic side effects. Studies in the 1950s and 60s indicated that it could produce hypocalcemia, trace metal depletion, mucocutaneous lesions, and kidney damage. In several cases, patients on chelation therapy died of kidney failure.

As a result, the medical establishment largely abandoned this form of therapy, despite its promise for certain age-related disorders. However, the minority of physicians who have continued to use chelation therapy contend that advances in its method of administration have eliminated or minimized the risks associated with its use.

Harry Foreman, School of Public Health, University of Minnesota, Minneapolis, Mn. 55455

American Academy of Medical Preventics, 2811 "L" St., Sacramento, Ca. 95816

Use of L-Dopa in Humans

Clinical use of L-Dopa has largely been confined to patients with Parkinson's Disease. When given L-Dopa, the majority of such patients experience "a true rejuvenation of body and mind" that enables them to become independent for the first time in years.

Before L-Dopa became available, almost 90 percent of patients with Parkinson's Disease were either dead or seriously disabled after sixteen years. The chance of such a patient dying was nearly three times greater than that of a nonafflicted person. The use of L-Dopa has reduced the sixteen-year mortality rate to about 35 percent, which is close to the life expectancy of healthy aging adults.

Yet the results of several five-year studies of L-Dopa-treated patients show a gradual worsening of their condition with time, particularly after the first two years of treatment.

One problem with L-Dopa is that 95 percent of the drug is metabolized before it reaches its intended site of action in the brain. The "wasting" of drug occurs because the enzyme

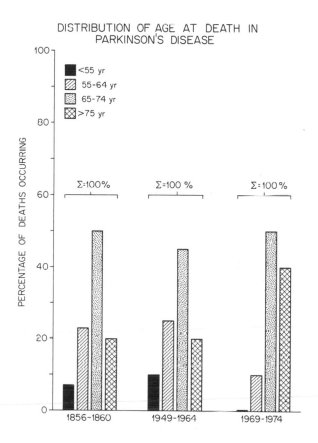

DISTRIBUTION OF AGE AT DEATH IN
PARKINSON'S DISEASE

Before L-Dopa therapy was available, 30 to 35 percent of patients died before
the age of sixty-five. With the use of L-Dopa (1969–1974), only 10 percent of
patients died before age sixty-five.

that transforms L-Dopa into dopamine—dopa decarboxylase
—is found in most tissues of the body and dopamine produced outside the brain is prevented from entering that
organ by the blood-brain barrier.

In order to potentiate the therapeutic effect of L-Dopa,
doctors have been giving patients dopa decarboxylase inhibitors—either RO 4-4602 or carbidopa—in addition to
L-Dopa. These agents inhibit the transformation of L-Dopa
to dopamine outside the brain, permitting a five-fold reduc-

tion in L-Dopa dosage and a concomitant reduction of side effects.

Charles H. Markham, Department of Neurology, UCLA Medical Center, Los Angeles, Ca. 90024

Searching for a Fungal Rejuvenator

Sometimes drugs are found in unexpected places. Penicillin was discovered by accident in a plant fungus. LSD is structurally related to ergot, another fungus that grows on rye plants. Hydergine—a drug used to treat senile dementia—is one of many derivatives of this fungus.

Scientists are studying the five bioactive derivatives of ergot—the ergot alkaloids—in their quest for new drugs to treat the mental disabilities of aging. In 1977, James Clemens of the Eli Lilly Company announced he was testing an ergot derivative called lergotrile as a possible treatment for Parkinson's disease.

Clemens presented evidence that lergotrile, which acts to boost dopamine levels, can extend the life span of rats. He noted that the drug was especially effective in females where there was a "highly significant prolongation of life span."

Clemens also noted that blood levels of the hormone prolactin were elevated in old rats, and that lergotrile was able to restore them to normal. Since prolactin has been implicated in the genesis of breast cancer (see p. 315), it seems that ergot drugs may have potential as anti-cancer agents.

Shortly after Clemens announced his preliminary findings with lergotrile, his company discovered that it was producing unacceptable side effects in humans, which led them to discontinue further testing of the drug. Clemens is now screening other ergot derivatives in the hope of finding a potent but safe anti-aging drug.

It's possible that lergotrile, or a similar compound, could be used as an anti-aging drug without the risk of side effects if incorporated into a controlled delivery therapeutic system. (See p. 382.)

James A. Clemens, Lilly Research Labs, Eli Lilly & Company, Indianapolis, In. 46206

Can Young Blood Rejuvenate an Old Body?

Whatever causes us to grow old and die, we can be sure that our blood is involved in some way. One possibility is that blood carries a "youth factor" that is reduced or changed in old age. Accordingly, the blood of a young organism might protect an older organism against the consequences of aging.

To test this hypothesis, Frederic C. Ludwig fused the bodies of young and adult rats of the same sex at the abdominal and thoracic walls (parabiosis), so that both animals shared the same blood circulation. The young rats were sixty to eighty-five days of age and their partners approximately 280 days older.

Ludwig compared the mortality of these animals to that of parabiont controls of the same age (sixty to eighty-five days), as well as single control animals. He found that single males lived longer than the younger partners of both male parabiont groups, but that the life span of the older partners of the male heterochronic parabionts was nearly the same as that of the single animals. Also, that the life span of the older partners of the female heterochronic parabionts was significantly longer (about 20 percent) than that of single female animals.

Ludwig hasn't figured out how this life-prolonging effect is conveyed, or if it reflects deceleration or reversal of the aging process. The idea that infusion of a younger blood supply can reverse certain parameters of aging is supported by another parabiosis experiment in which the older partners showed significant improvement in cholesterol metabolism. (See p. 75.)

Frederic C. Ludwig, Department of Pathology and Radiological Sciences, University of California, Irvine, Irvine, Ca. 92664

Can "Old" Blood Be Rejuvenated?

Bloodletting was practiced for centuries as a means of ridding the body of disease. In a modern version of the practice, Norman Orentreich removes a subject's blood, separates the plasma from the blood by centrifugation, and then returns the red blood cells in a physiologic solution. The procedure is called plasmapheresis, and its objective is to remove extracellular, plasma-carried "aging factors" and rejuvenate the subject through the formation of fresh plasma proteins.

Orentreich has been experimenting with plasmapheresis in rats, dogs, and humans for the past eleven years at the Orentreich Foundation for the Advancement of Science. (See p. 373.) One subject has had more than 1,000 pints of blood removed and processed with no apparent detrimental effects. Orentreich has yet to present evidence that plasmapheresis can improve the health or increase the longevity of any species tested.

Norman Orentreich, Orentreich Foundation for the Advancement of Science, 910 Fifth Ave., New York, N.Y. 10021

New Treatments for Baldness

Products that promise to restore lost hair by "nourishing," "stimulating," or "revitalizing" bald areas are worthless because hair loss is not caused by lack of nutrition or blood supply to the scalp.

Three factors are known to contribute to baldness. The first is a genetic predisposition to the condition; men with this trait usually start getting bald in their early twenties. The second is the age of the individual. A gradual loss of hair with advancing age is almost universal in both men and women. The third is the action of the male sex hormones. Eunuchs do not develop common male baldness, regardless of age or hereditary disposition, and if a man is castrated after he has begun to lose his hair, the hair loss will stop.

At this time, the only safe method of treating baldness is hair transplantation—a procedure originated by Norman Orentreich and now practiced throughout the world. It involves the transfer of small pieces of scalp containing twelve to fifteen hair follicles from a hairy area (usually the back of the scalp) to a bald area.

Scientists at the Orentreich Foundation are testing drugs that stimulate hair growth in patients with common male baldness. According to Orentreich, these drugs can produce some degree of hair growth, but only at doses that have undesirable side effects.

A key to the process of hair growth, says Orentreich, may be receptor proteins in the cells of the skin that interact with androgens in triggering the process. Apparently, some men—such as American Indians—have very little beard or body hair because they lack receptor proteins. No matter how much male hormone they're given, they'll never have much of a beard. It may be that baldness is caused by deactivation or repression of such receptor proteins, and that hair growth would resume if they could be "turned on" again.

Another area being explored by Orentreich's group, in conjunction with Bijan Safai of Memorial/Sloan-Kettering Cancer Center, involves the effects of immunologic abnormalities on a type of hair loss known as alopecia areata, in which there are circumscribed patches of baldness on the scalp and face.

In clinical trials with Levamisole, a drug that boosts immune response, they've observed hair regrowth in a small number of alopecia areata patients. They've also used the chemical dinitrochlorobenzene in attempts to neutralize the inhibition of hair follicle growth in this disease.

Although none of these therapies are available today, they

offer promise of an eventual cure for premature baldness. When it comes to the reversal of hair loss because of aging, however, a more generalized rejuvenation therapy may be required.

Norman Orentreich, Orentreich Foundation for the Advancement of Science, 910 Fifth Ave., New York, N.Y. 10021

Searching for the Rejuvenation Enzyme

Imagine a powerful enzyme that fights its way through an aging body by dissolving the dense crosslinked aggregates responsible for the disabilities of old age. In its wake, we grow young and vigorous again, as new and healthy cells arise to revitalize failing tissues and organs.

Such a vision has motivated Johan Bjorksten, the originator of the crosslinkage theory of aging (see p. 38), in his quest for a practical method of rejuvenation.

In 1971, Bjorksten inoculated insoluble "gerogenic" aggregates suspended in agar from old cadaver brains with various microbe-rich infusions. He found that a few cultures dissolved the gray suspended matter to form "halos" in the Petri dishes.

After four years, he separated and purified an enzyme from a mutant strain of Bacillus cereus that is "highly effective" in solubilizing crosslinked protein aggregates. He later discovered at least seven other enzymes with similar properties from other organisms.

When he gave ten-month-old mice intraperitoneal injections of the Bacillus cereus enzyme, there were no apparent toxic reactions. By continuing the injections in two of these animals, he observed that they were "leaner and more youthful-looking" than two control animals. Bjorksten was unable to follow up this preliminary work because of lack of funds.

Johan Bjorksten, Bjorksten Research Foundation, P.O. Box 9444, Madison, Wi. 53715

Effects of Inhibiting Crosslinkage on Longevity

The drug B-aminopropionitrile (BAPN) has a lathyrogenic effect that is believed to inhibit crosslinkage of collagen and elastin. Several researchers have given it to rodents in the hope that it might delay damaging connective tissue crosslinking after maturation.

Kohn and Leash found no beneficial effect of BAPN in pathogen-free rats at different dosage levels for varying periods of time. However, the treatment did appear to reduce the incidence of benign tumors in male mice.

When BAPN was given to two-month-old mice throughout their lives by La Bella and Vivian, they found no significant differences from controls in either mean or maximum life span. But when they administered the compound for three, six, nine, or twelve months only, there was an increase in survival and maximum life span in all experimental

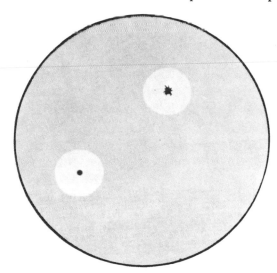

Insoluble "gerogenic" aggregates from old cadaver brains were suspended in agar in Petri dishes. In two cases, the development of clear halos after injections of soil microorganisms suggested that these organisms had secreted enzymes capable of dissolving the aggregates.

groups. The greatest increase occurred in the group treated for twelve months, in which the median life span was about 20 percent longer and the maximum life span one to three months longer than controls.

These findings suggest that BAPN's effect on crosslinkage is probably limited to early life when it may act to promote survival. It doesn't appear to affect the crosslinkage of proteins with age and may be toxic for older animals.

Frank S. La Bella, Department of Pharmacology, University of Manitoba, Canada RE3 OW3

Effect of Prednisolone on Life Span

In 1968, there was a report from England that mice receiving prednisolone phosphate in their drinking water lived significantly longer than control animals.

Prednisolone is a glucocorticoid hormone put out by the adrenal glands that has anti-inflammatory and anti-autoimmune effects on tissues.

Since the English study involved a short-lived autoimmune-susceptible mouse strain, it's possible that the experimental animals outlived the controls because of prednisolone's immunosuppressive effect.

When La Bella and Vivian gave prednisolone phosphate to longer-lived male LAF/J mice—starting at two months of age—they found no significant differences in life span from controls. And when W. F. Forbes gave DBA/2J mice a high concentration of the drug—starting late in life (232 days of age)—there was also no significant effect on life span.

W. F. Forbes, Department of Statistics, University of Waterloo, Waterloo, Ontario, Canada N2L 3G1

Can Nucleic Acid Therapy Rejuvenate Humans?

For more than seventeen years, New York physician Benjamin S. Frank has been independently investigating the use of nucleic acids in the treatment of aging and degenerative disease. During this period, he has treated thousands of patients, performed animal experiments, and written several books on the subject.

Frank contends that dietary RNA, combined with metabolically associated B vitamins, minerals, amino acids, and sugars, enters the cell to aid in its repair and regeneration. The result, he says, is a vast increase in energy that reduces stress, helps to fight off diseases, and reverse some of the symptoms of aging.

Frank's work became controversial after his book, *Dr. Frank's No Aging Diet*, became a best seller in 1977. His claims were attacked by scientists as being untested and unsubstantiated. In some circles, he was ridiculed for his emphasis on sardines as a primary source of nucleic acids, and his publisher was accused of being opportunistic for not checking the "validity" of his claims.

In truth, Frank is a serious investigator with interesting and provocative ideas, but he has never fully documented his claims and his data are open to criticism. Since his findings are based upon his own data collection and evaluations, they are clearly subject to bias and placebo effects. Moreover, he has never published in an established scientific journal, which seriously limits his credibility with most other scientists.

There are numerous published studies of the use of exogenous RNAs that lend some support to Frank's basic thesis—that dietary nucleic acids are valuable in treating aging and degenerative disease. (See p. 201.) However, none of these studies were designed to test any of his therapeutic claims.

New Findings

Frank's most recent work involves the combination of nucleic acids and antioxidants. He is particularly interested in the enzyme superoxide dismutase, which has been shown to counteract the potentially toxic effects of oxygen metabolism. (See p. 127.)

Frank describes an initial study with eighteen human subjects of both sexes, aged forty to eighty-seven, who took 600-2,000 mcg (in two separate doses) of superoxide dismutase in addition to 800-2,000 mg of nucleic acids, 50 mg of B complex vitamins, 800 units of vitamin E, and 1 gm of vitamin C, while eating a diet rich in nucleic acids and vegetable juices.

According to Frank, these subjects showed increased energy levels and vitality, increased strength, tightened skin and reduced wrinkling, diminution of gray hair, and improved vision. Six other subjects, aged fifty-two to sixty-six, who took superoxide dismutase, but no nucleic acids, showed no visible anti-aging effects, but did experience reduction of arthritic pain.

Frank has twelve elderly rats—about three years of age—which he plans to treat with nucleic acids, BHT (an antioxidant), and daily injections of superoxide dismutase and catalase (another antioxidant enzyme). The effects of this regimen on aging and life span will be compared with control animals on a normal diet.

Benjamin S. Frank, 301 E. 78th St., New York, N.Y. 10021

Nucleic Acids Prolong Life Span in Rats

The longest extension of life span ever reported in a scientific journal was by London physician Max Odens. In a study to test the effects of nucleic acids on aging, Odens gave weekly injections of DNA and RNA to five rats, starting at the age of 750 days, and compared them to five untreated controls.

According to Odens, all five untreated rats died before the expected maximum age of 900 days, whereas four of the treated rats lived 1,600 to 1,900 days, and the fifth lived 2,250 days.

Thus, the maximum life span of these animals was allegedly doubled in four of the experimental rats and tripled in the fifth.

The Odens study, which was published in 1973, has been ignored by gerontologists because of its small size, limited data, and remarkable findings—which virtually nobody believes. As a result, no one, including Odens, has apparently done any sort of follow-up study.

Max Odens, 2 Devonshire Place, W1, London, England

Improving Memory with RNA

People who eat fish because they think it's good "brain food" may be on the right track. It turns out that most kinds of fish are rich in nucleic acids, which may be capable of improving learning and memory.

The administration of RNA has produced clinical improvement and increased memory scores in patients with senile memory impairment—a finding that suggests that RNA may have a stimulatory effect on the synthesis or transmission of acetylcholine in the brain.

The ability of RNA to improve cognitive function was demonstrated in rats by Leslie Solyom. Both young and old rats were given "chronic" injections of 160 mg per kilogram of yeast RNA, while two control groups were given saline injections.

The animals were taught to press a bar for water, first on a continuous reinforcement schedule and then at various intervals. During continuous reinforcement, the rate of bar-pressing increased only in the older group receiving RNA, but during interval training it increased in both old and young animals. In all cases, the RNA-treated rats learned faster and remembered better than the saline-treated rats.

Leslie Solyom, Allan Memorial Institute, McGill University, Montreal, Quebec, Canada

Manipulating Memory Function in Rats

Learning requires the transfer of energy between neurons in the brain. The area across which the energy is transmitted in the form of electrical or chemical impulses is called the synapse. According to current theory, the process of learning is mediated by the action of acetylcholine, a chemical messenger that is released at synapses.

During normal transmission of information, acetylcholine is rapidly destroyed by the enzyme cholinesterase. J. Anthony Deutsch has shown that the ability of rats to remember learned behavior can be manipulated by injections of drugs such as physostigmine and diisopropyl fluorophosphate (DFP), which prevent destruction of acetylcholine by inactivating cholinesterase.

Deutsch has shown that brain injections of DFP can either block *or* restore a memory—according to when the drug is administered. When rats trained to run a simple maze were retested fourteen days later, they displayed almost perfect retention of the learned behavior. But if they were given DFP prior to the retest, they displayed almost total amnesia. On the other hand, if they were retested twenty-eight days after they learned to run the maze, they were unable to remember how to do so, unless they were first given DFP.

Thus, DFP could block an otherwise well-remembered habit at fourteen days, or restore an otherwise forgotten habit at twenty-eight days. This dual capacity of DFP to block or to facilitate the retention of learned behavior suggests that the physiologic changes that cause us to remember, or to forget, are reversible.

If so, then it seems likely that the age-related decline in memory, and perhaps even the severe memory deficits in senile dementia, can be reversed clinically by appropriate drug-induced manipulation of the cholinergic system.

J. Anthony Deutsch, Department of Psychology, University of California, San Diego, La Jolla, Ca. 92097

Mimicking the Effects of Aging on Memory

If the age-related decline in memory is caused by a decline in the effectiveness of acetylcholine, then drugs that inhibit the action of this neurotransmitter should be able to induce similar effects in young persons. To explore this hypothesis, David A. Drachman injected volunteer students, aged nineteen to twenty-five, with the anticholinergic drug scopolamine an hour before giving them tests to measure immediate memory, memory storage, retrieval from memory store, and dichotic listening (the ability to comprehend different messages simultaneously).

He found that scopolamine produced no impairment in immediate memory, but did produce significant impairment of other cognitive functions—a pattern "strikingly similar" to that found in normal aged persons. Drachman also demonstrated that physostigmine, which increases the availability of acetylcholine, could reverse the cognitive impairment caused by scopolamine.

Both Drachman and Raymond T. Bartus, who has demonstrated similar effects in the rhesus monkey, have presented persuasive evidence that scopolamine-induced memory impairment is caused by direct dysfunction in central cholinergic mechanisms.

David A. Drachman, Department of Neurology, University of Massachusetts, Amherst, Ma. 01003

Raymond T. Bartus, CNS Biology, Medical Research Division, American Cyanamid Company, Pearl River, N.Y. 10965

Boosting Cognitive Performance in Humans

Until recently, there was little evidence that human learning and memory could be improved by drugs that stimulate cholinergic activity. Now there are at least two reports indicating that such drugs can boost cognitive performance in normal adults.

In one study by scientists at the National Institute of Mental Health, the drug arecholine, a cholingeric agonist, enhanced the ability of young adults, mean age 22.4, to learn a fixed sequence of ten words belonging to a familiar category, such as "vegetables," "cities," or "trees." The sequence was repeated until the subject could recite all ten words in correct order on two consecutive trials. Arecholine also was able to reverse the impairment of learning produced by scopolamine.

In a second study by this group, ten subjects, mean age 24.3, who received choline chloride, a precursor of acetylcholine, were able to learn ten-word sequences significantly faster than controls.

In a study at the Veterans Administration Hospital in Palo Alto, California, long-term memory was enhanced significantly in nineteen normal male subjects, age eighteen to thirty-five, by 1 mg doses of physostigmine given by slow, intravenous infusion over a period of one hour. Most subjects displayed far better recall of memorized word sequences than control subjects when tested eighty minutes after treatment. Physostigmine had no apparent effect on short-term memory.

Two problems must be overcome before physostigmine can be used clinically as a memory booster. First is the fact that the drug is only effective within a narrow dosage range that varies, to some extent, from person to person. Then there is the matter of its undesirable cardiopulmonary and muscular side effects.

The answer to both these problems—which physostigmine shares with many other pharmacologic agents—may be the incorporation of the drug, or one of its analogs, into a therapeutic system that permits its controlled release at a safe and effective dosage level. (See p. 382.)

N. Sitaram, Unit on Sleep Studies, Biological Psychiatry Branch, National Institute of Mental Health, Bethesda, Md. 20014

Kenneth L. Davis, Veterans Administration Hospital, 3801 Miranda Ave., Palo Alto, Ca. 94304

Lecithin Increases Neurotransmitter Levels

The major dietary source of choline—the compound that combines with acetic acid to form the neurotransmitter acetylcholine—is lecithin, which is found in many foods including egg yolks, liver, and soybeans. Lecithin also is commonly taken in capsule form as a dietary supplement in the U.S., and is used as a drug in Europe.

Recent work by Hirsch and Wurtman indicates that direct intake of lecithin can significantly increase the concentrations of both choline and acetylcholine in the brain and adrenal glands of rats. They showed that the consumption of a single meal containing lecithin granules produced a 62 percent increase in serum choline within three hours.

These findings suggest that lecithin therapy might prevent or reverse the loss of memory and cognitive function associated with old age, which has been linked to the progressive breakdown of the cholinergic system.

Richard J. Wurtman, Laboratory of Neuroendocrine Regulation, Department of Nutrition and Food Science, Massachusetts Institute of Technology, Cambridge, Ma. 02139

ACTH Enhances Memory

Two research teams have discovered that adrenocorticotrophic hormone (ACTH) may be able to enhance memory in both animals and humans. ACTH is the pituitary hormone that stimulates the adrenal glands to secrete their full spectrum of hormones.

James L. McGaugh of the University of California at Irvine found that retention of learning could be enhanced in rats by post-training injections of ACTH, with the response varying according to the dosage. Animals receiving a dose of 0.3 I.U. (International Units) of ACTH scored significantly better than controls, whereas animals receiving a dose of 3.0 I.U. of ACTH scored significantly poorer than controls.

At New York University (NYU), Stephen H. Ferris found a possible enhancement of visual memory retrieval in twenty-four impaired elderly patients who received ACTH. The NYU scientist is currently evaluating the results of a double-blind study of a new oral analog of ACTH in fifty mildly impaired elderly patients.

James L. McGaugh, Department of Psychobiology, University of California, Irvine, Irvine, Ca. 92664

Stephen H. Ferris, Department of Psychiatry, NYU Medical Center, New York, N.Y. 10016

Vasopressin: "The Memory Hormone"

Who doesn't recall what he or she was doing on the day John F. Kennedy was assassinated? On such occasions, our sensibilities are so jarred that photographic slices of life are indelibly imprinted within our brains.

Recent work suggests that vasopressin—a hormone synthesized in the anterior hypothalamus of the brain and released from the posterior region of the pituitary gland—may be one of the factors responsible for the process by which memories are imprinted or consolidated. Apparently, vasopressin induces changes within the brain and central nervous system that transform the electrical impulses of learning into chemically encoded "long-term" memories. The final step in the process seems to involve the synthesis of new proteins, which are deposited in cells located in selected areas of the brain, such as the thalamus or hippocampus.

The role of vasopressin in learning and memory was discovered by David de Wied of the University of Utrecht in

The Netherlands. For years, the hormone has been called antidiuretic hormone (ADH) because of its ability to concentrate urine by conserving body water.

The idea that vasopressin also acts to consolidate memory arose from de Wied's observation that removal of the posterior lobe of the pituitary in rats interferes with the maintenance of a conditioned avoidance response. Further experiments showed that injections of vasopressin could prevent this loss of memory.

David de Wied, Rudolf Magnus Institute for Pharmacology, Medical Faculty, University of Utrecht, Utrecht, The Netherlands

Vasopressin Boosts Memory in Aging Humans

A recent study by J. J. Legros of the University of Liège in Belgium indicates that vasopressin may be able to restore lost memory and learning in normally aging people.

The drug was given by nasal spray for three days to twelve subjects, age fifty to sixty-five, and eleven matched controls. A battery of psychometric tests was performed on all subjects before and after treatment.

Legros found that subjects given vasopressin performed significantly better than controls on tests involving attention, concentration, motor rapidity, visual and verbal memory, and learning and recognition.

Jean-Jacques Legros, Neuroendocrinology Section, Department of Clinical and Medical Pathology, Université de Liège —Sart Tilman, 4000 Liège, Belgium

Vasopressin Cures Amnesia

A dramatic return of long-term memory was recently reported in four patients treated with vasopressin by J. C. Oliveros at San Carlos Hospital in Madrid. Three of the patients were victims of accidents and the fourth was a chronic alcoholic.

In one case, a twenty-one-year-old man could remember nothing that had happened to him in the three months prior to and after a severe car accident. After one day of vasopressin therapy, however, the patient could recall several features of the accident; by the fourth day of treatment, his memory had improved greatly; and by the seventh day, he had completely recovered.

In another case, a fifty-five-year-old man, who had suffered from severe memory impairment for six years, began to recover rapidly after the initiation of vasopressin therapy. After five days of treatment, he became happier and more alert, in addition to regaining long-term memories that had eluded him for years.

J. C. Oliveros, Central Department for Clinical Electro-neurophysiology, Hospital Clinico de San Carlos, Madrid, Spain

Clinical Trials for Vasopressin

In response to reports from Europe of vasopressin's ability to restore memory in amnesiacs and boost it in normally aging persons, two American teams have started clinical trials with the drug. Earl A. Zimmerman of Columbia University is testing vasopressin on outpatients with memory deficits, and Philip W. Gold of the National Institute of Mental Health is testing a less toxic analog of vasopressin—1-desa-mino-D-arginine vasopressin (DDAVP)—on patients with major mental disorders.

All subjects in these studies suffer from diseases that produce memory impairment including senile dementia, schizophrenia, and stroke. Evidence that the drug can help such patients would be exciting, but even more so would be evidence that vasopressin can rejuvenate memory in all old people—diseased or not.

Earl A. Zimmerman, Department of Neurology, Columbia University Medical Center, New York, N.Y. 10032

Philip W. Gold, Psychobiology Branch, National Institute of Mental Health, Bethesda, Md. 20014

Force-Feeding the Brain with Oxygen

When a group of elderly Jewish patients was led to a large steel chamber for "treatment," some of them became quite agitated and refused to enter. Recalling the Nazi atrocities of World War II, they feared they were being led to a gas chamber for liquidation and pointed accusatory fingers at their doctor, who was named Goldfarb.

In fact, the patients were suffering from senile dementia and the chamber was a facility where they could receive hyperbaric (high pressure) oxygen therapy. In theory, their thinking ability would improve as their brains were force-fed with oxygen.

The results of the experiment were disappointing, but some scientists attributed the failure to the extreme mental deterioration of the patients—a state of mind that could lead to feelings of paranoia about the treatment itself.

Earlier there had been reports of "highly significant" improvement in cognitive function in elderly patients treated in this fashion. The first such report came in 1969 from the V.A. Hospital in Buffalo, New York, where Eleanor A. Jacobs exposed thirteen elderly men with cognitive deficits to 100 percent oxygen at 2.5 atmospheres of pressure. Each subject was treated for ninety minutes twice a day for fifteen consecutive days. Five control subjects were exposed to a low-oxygen mixture that maintained normal oxygen tension despite increased pressure.

The group receiving 100 percent oxygen showed uniform, major increases in post-exposure cognitive test scores, whereas the group on the low-oxygen mixture showed no significant improvement. When the controls were switched to the 100 percent oxygen treatment, they too showed considerable improvement in cognitive function.

From 1969 to 1975, there were five studies confirming

these observations, but only one of them included a control group. On the other hand, two controlled studies failed to note any significant differences between experimental subjects and controls. However, the subjects in these studies were more impaired than those in the Jacobs study.

The Latest Study

In an attempt to clear up the confusion over the value of hyperbaric oxygen therapy, a joint team from the National Institute of Mental Health and New York University randomly assigned eighty-two elderly subjects with moderate mental impairment into four treatment groups: hyperbaric oxygen, hyperbaric air, normobaric oxygen, and normobaric air. As in the Jacobs study, treatment consisted of two ninety-minute sessions a day for fifteen consecutive days. All subjects were evaluated for memory and intellectual capacity and psychiatric symptoms before and immediately after treatment and at one, two, three, and eight weeks after treatment.

The results showed that the experimental subjects who received hyperbaric or normobaric oxygen did not perform significantly better than controls on either the cognitive or psychiatric tests. Efforts were made to isolate patients with cerebrovascular disease and cardiopulmonary insufficiency, where oxygen delivery to the brain is clearly impaired, and for whom hyperbaric oxygen might be especially beneficial, but no improvement was noted in these patients.

This time around, the experimental subjects were not beset with Nazi war fantasies. On the contrary, they felt less anxious than controls because of the "mystique" surrounding the hyperbaric chamber, the interior of which resembled a spaceship or submarine.

Allen Raskin, Psychopharmacology Research Branch, National Institute of Mental Health, 5600 Fisher's Lane, Rockville, Md. 20852

Centrophenoxine Reduces Age Pigment

For the past fourteen years, Kalidas Nandy has been studying the effects of the drug centrophenoxine on lipofuscin age pigment (see p. 29) in the neurons of laboratory rodents. In early studies, he found that daily injections of centrophenoxine could reduce the amount of lipofuscin in the neurons of senile guinea pigs.

Nandy noted a marked reduction in the activity of oxidative enzymes around the areas of pigment deposition in the cells of drug-treated animals. The enzymes showing diminished activity were succinic and lactic dehydrogenase, cytochrome and monoamine oxidase, acid phosphatase, and simple esterase. On the other hand, the activity of glucose-6-phosphatase dehydrogenase was markedly increased as a result of treatment.

Nandy interpreted this altered pattern of enzyme activity to mean that centrophenoxine had induced a shift in glucose from its normal metabolic route (the Krebs pathway) to an alternative route (the pentose phosphate pathway). Since Nandy had observed similar enzyme alterations in regenerating nerve tissue, he concluded that this mechanism might play a role in the repair and restoration of nerve cells. He also suggested that reduction of two of these enzymes—acid phosphatase and simple esterase—might be caused by the effect of centrophenoxine on subcellular lysosomes.

Other investigators have shown that centrophenoxine can reduce the lipofuscin content of neurons in rats—both *in vivo* and *in vitro*. And recently, Nandy showed that the drug can inhibit formation of lipofuscin in the brain cells of mice if given to them after one month of age.

Kalidas Nandy, Geriatric Research, Education and Clinical Center, Veterans Administration Hospital, Bedford, Ma. 01730

Centrophenoxine Improves Learning in Mice

Centrophenoxine has been used clinically in Europe for the past twenty years. Physicians have reported marked improvement in geriatric patients suffering from a variety of mental disorders.

In light of these reports, Kalidas Nandy looked into the effects of centrophenoxine on learning and memory in "old" mice, and correlated the results with changes in lipofuscin pigment in the brains of the treated animals.

Twenty female mice, aged eleven to twelve months, were treated daily with centrophenoxine for three months at a dosage of 80 mg/kg of body weight. A similar number of untreated mice of the same age and younger (three to four months of age) were used as controls. Both groups were trained to choose the side of a T maze containing a bottle of water and given sixty seconds to make the correct response.

According to Nandy, the young mice learned to run the maze faster than either treated or untreated older animals. In the initial trials, the treated older mice performed only slightly better than their untreated counterparts, but the difference became significant in later trials when the water bottle was moved to the opposite side of the maze. At this point, the older treated mice did almost as well as the young mice.

A significant reduction in lipofuscin was observed in the brain cells of all treated animals compared to controls—both in the cerebral cortex and hippocampus—an area that has been linked to memory storage.

Kalidas Nandy, Geriatric Research, Education and Clinical Center, Veterans Administration Hospital, Bedford, Ma. 01730

Centrophenoxine Extends the Life Span of Mice

In 1968, Richard Hochschild came across a report by Kalidas Nandy that centrophenoxine could shrink concentrations of lipofuscin age pigment. Among the enzymes Nandy said had declined in activity as a result of the treatment was acid phosphatase, an enzyme used as an index of lysosomal membrane breakdown. Nandy's observation suggested to Hochschild that centrophenoxine was slowing the flow of enzymes out of damaged lysosomes, perhaps by preventing or repairing membrane damage.

Hochschild had just formulated the theory that aging may be caused by the leakage of destructive enzymes from damaged lysosomes (see p. 37), and was preparing to screen compounds for their potential membrane-stabilizing ability. He soon discovered that centrophenoxine could significantly extend the life span of fruit flies.

And when he added the drug to the drinking water of male Swiss Webster Albino mice starting at 8.6 months of age, he found that the treated animals had a mean survival time (from the start of the trial) that was 27.3 percent longer than controls; a maximum survival time that was 39.7 per-

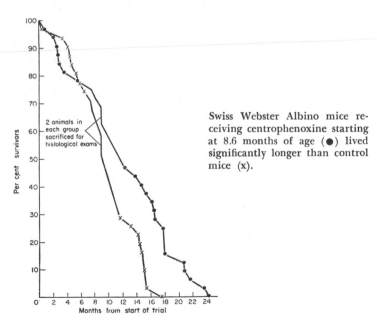

Swiss Webster Albino mice receiving centrophenoxine starting at 8.6 months of age (●) lived significantly longer than control mice (x).

2 animals in each group sacrificed for histological exams

Per cent survivors

Months from start of trial

cent longer than controls; and a maximum life span that was 26.5 percent longer than controls.

The life-extending effect of centrophenoxine was later corroborated in a study by Nandy, who obtained results similar to those of Hochschild.

Richard Hochschild, Department of Medicine, University of California, Irvine, Irvine, Ca. 92717

Deanol Extends the Life Span of Mice

When Richard Hochschild was studying the action of centrophenoxine, he concluded that the life-extending effect of the drug was caused by one of its two components—dimethylaminoethanol (DMAE), or deanol—a natural compound manufactured in the body. Deanol has been used clinically in the U.S. for more than thirteen years as a treatment for learning and behavioral disabilities. The other component of centrophenoxine is p-chlorophenoxyacetic acid—a synthetic compound related to the plant growth hormone auxin.

Hochschild then gave deanol dissolved in drinking water to fifty-seven old male A/J mice, aged 604-674 days, for the duration of their lives. These animals were considerably older at the onset of the experiment than the mean life span of the strain, which is about 490 days for males.

He found that deanol-treated mice had a mean survival time (from the start of the trial) that was 49.5 percent longer than controls; a maximum survival time that was 36.3 percent longer than controls; and a maximum life span that was 10.9 percent longer than controls. None of his experimental animals survived longer than the maximum recorded life span for the strain.

Since deanol is a precursor of choline, which is believed to play a role in membrane biosynthesis, Hochschild suggests that deanol may retard or reverse age-related degeneration caused by breakdowns in membrane structure, particularly lysosomal membranes. Another function of choline is to combine with acetic acid to form acetylcholine, the neurotransmitter that has been linked to learning, memory, and other cognitive functions. (See p. 262.)

Richard Hochschild, Department of Medicine, University of California, Irvine, Irvine, Ca. 92717

Deanol Shortens the Life Span of Japanese Quail

The availability of twenty-nine very old male Japanese quail (3.7 years of age) led Arthur Cherkin to test the effect of deanol on the life span of this species. Deanol was given to the birds in their drinking water via individual tubes starting at 195 weeks of age and continuing until termination of the experiment at 264 weeks of age. Controls were given water brought to the same pH 4.0 as the deanol solution by adding tartaric acid.

The major finding of the study was a significantly higher

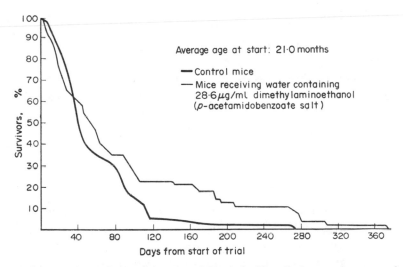

Senile male A/J mice receiving deanol lived significantly longer than control mice.

mortality rate among the birds receiving deanol. After sixty-nine weeks, the drug-treated group showed a mortality rate of 80 percent compared to 42.8 percent for controls, and a mean survival time of about forty-nine weeks compared to about sixty weeks for controls.

This finding suggests that the life-extending effect of deanol reported in fruit flies and mice may not be applicable to all species. Further work is needed in various animal models to determine if chronic administration of deanol is beneficial or detrimental.

Arthur Cherkin, Psychobiology Research Laboratory, Veterans Administration Hospital, Sepulveda, Ca. 91343

How Deanol Affects Senile Dementia Patients

Several years ago, researchers at NYU Medical Center conducted a four-week clinical trial of deanol in fourteen senile outpatients. The study group consisted of eight men and six women, aged sixty-two to eighty. The starting dose of the drug was either 100 or 200 mg three times daily (300-600 mg/day), which was gradually increased to 1800 mg/day. Various cognitive and behavioral tests were carried out before, during, and after treatment.

No changes in cognitive performance were observed as a result of deanol treatment, but there were several positive behavioral changes including reduced anxiety, depression, and irritability, and increased motivation and initiative.

Stephen H. Ferris, Department of Psychiatry, NYU Medical Center, New York, N.Y. 10016

Chlorpromazine and Aging in the Brain

The most popular antipsychotic drugs are the phenothiazines, particularly chlorpromazine (CPZ), which is used as a tranquilizer in emotionally disturbed patients.

After hearing of Hochschild's findings with deanol, which is one of the components of CPZ, Samorajski and Rolsten decided to study the effects of chronic CPZ treatment on the aging mouse brain. They separated forty-five female C57BL/10 mice into three groups. Mice in the two experimental groups received oral doses of 5 mg/kg and 10 mg/kg of CPZ three times a week, while the third group received corresponding doses of oral placebo.

The animals were treated with CPZ from thirteen to twenty months of age unless death occurred sooner. At this point, they were decapitated and their brains removed for analysis. There were five deaths in the 10 mg/kg group, two deaths in the control group, and no deaths in the 5 mg/kg group.

One finding of the study was a marked reduction in the size and concentration of lipofuscin pigment in the brain stem reticular formation of animals in both CPZ groups. The reduction in lipofuscin was greatest in mice treated with 10 mg/kg of CPZ, which also was the group with the highest death rate. Survival may have been lowest in this group because of toxic side effects, which often occur at high doses in humans. On the other hand, the 100 percent survival in the 5 mg/kg group suggests that chronic moderate administration of chlorpromazine might have a life-prolonging effect.

T. Samorajski, Texas Research Institute of Mental Sciences, 1300 Moursund Ave., Houston, Tx. 77030

Chapter 9

Cryonics and Suspended Animation

What Is Cryonics?

"When everything else fails, there's always cryonics," reads the caption of a cartoon showing a man frozen in a block of ice.

"Cryonics is for those who would pay anything to avoid death," said an observer at the funeral of Howard Hughes, the eccentric billionaire who didn't get the message in time.

"Give me immortality or give me death!" is another way of expressing the philosophy that has spawned the cryonics movement.

Cryonics is the freezing of the human body after "death" in the hope of future reanimation. It is an act of defiance against the forces of Nature that dictate the terms of our extinction.

Those who have made preparations to be frozen have done so for the following reasons:

• They prefer life—as they know it—to physical death, whether they believe that such death is final or not.

• They know that freezing is the best available method of preserving the body.

• They recognize that all of us are at risk of dying at all times.

• They think it is possible that medical scientists of the future may be able to bring frozen people back to life and good health—even those frozen by imperfect methods.

Cryonics has come under heavy criticism because it is not yet possible to preserve humans, or any other mammals, without inflicting damage during the freeze-thaw process. Thus, anyone frozen today must depend upon future advances to determine whether he or she can be revived.

Many scientists have concluded that it will be "impossible" for future scientists to revive persons frozen by today's methods, or that the chance of revival is "negligible." They have done so, however, by intuition or guesswork rather than by calculation, with their conclusions based primarily on the known difficulties of repairing freezing damage, and little on the unknown capabilities of future medical science.

Predicting the Future

There is no precise way of predicting the nature or timetable for future advances, but history is replete with examples of advances that most "authorities" were certain couldn't be done. Nearly every facet of modern life—from high-speed computers to television to space travel—was once considered impossible. But now we take such marvels for granted, just as the inhabitants of the twenty-first century may take the reanimation of frozen bodies for granted.

Coming Back from the "Dead"

"How can you bring people back to life after they're dead?" asked a woman at a cryonics meeting in San Francisco.

"When you're dead, you're dead!" proclaimed a silver-haired man on a TV show in Houston, when asked about cryonics.

"The brain dies after four minutes without oxygen and there's no way you're going to see a functioning human being after that!" declared a New York physician to a patient who had inquired about cryonics.

Such skepticism is common when people are confronted with the idea of freezing people *after death* for revival in the future. To some, it is preposterous to even entertain the notion of bringing the dead back to life. To others with medical training, the idea smacks of fraud or naiveté. Yet there are good reasons to believe it may be possible to bring the dead back to life.

The first is that it's done all the time during the early stages of the dying process. Drowning victims are regularly brought back to life with artificial respiration and cardiac massage. The techniques of cardio-pulmonary resuscitation (CPR) are now taught to persons in all walks of life—even schoolchildren—because it's been shown that anyone can learn how to revive an apparently lifeless body.

In hospitals, there are fancy heart-lung machines that can substitute for a person's heart and lungs for long periods of time. These devices are used to keep "dead" persons alive until they regain the capacity to live on their own. They are also used to replace the heart and lungs during serious operations.

Defining Death

"But are such people *really* dead? Isn't it true that a person dies only after the brain stops functioning?" The answer is yes, but it's only recently that cessation of brain function has been considered the *sine qua non* for death. In the past, the primary criteria for death were lack of heartbeat and breathing.

You see, death is defined according to arbitrary standards based upon existing medical capabilities. In the past fifty years or so, the definition of death has evolved rapidly in response to advances in medical science. Today, people are revived and cured routinely from conditions that were considered hopeless in the past. Think of the millions of people who used to die of such diseases as tuberculosis, influenza, and diphtheria.

It's likely that future medical progress will continue to upgrade the standards by which we define death. Just as we can now revive patients who would have died in the past, we should soon be able to revive patients we must now give up for dead.

It's true that few persons can be revived after more than four minutes without oxygen, but recent animal experiments suggest that advanced techniques may soon enable us to revive those who have been deprived of oxygen for an hour or more. In fact, there is evidence that the brain is our most durable organ, and that there is enormous untapped potential for its repair and reconstitution—even to the extent of reconstructing a person's identity. (See p. 356.)

Moreover, the brain's suceptibility to injury from oxygen deprivation declines dramatically with declining body temperature. Thus, it is possible to prevent all or most of the damage to the brain of a dying person by lowering that person's temperature—the first stage in the cryonic suspension process.

Finally, it must be understood that in the majority of cases a person is pronounced "dead" at a time when most of his or her body is still in good working order. Death is pronounced because the attending physician is unable to bring the patient back to life, not because the patient has reached an absolute state of non-being from which revival is impossible. We grow old, suffer, and die only because we don't yet know how to prevent or reverse the dying process—not because that process is either irreversible or inevitable.

Reversing Brain "Death"

One of the great myths of our time is that the brain "dies" after four to six minutes without oxygen. Everyone seems to believe this notion—doctors, researchers, science writers, and lay people—as if it was a universal law of Nature.

Yet there have been numerous instances of accident victims surviving considerably longer than four minutes without oxygen. In many of these cases, such as in drowning victims, the body was chilled during the period of ischemia (absence of blood flow), which protected the brain against damage.

Robert J. White of Case Western Reserve University School of Medicine in Cleveland has cooled monkey brains to 5-8° C for one hour with normal recovery in the animals. In humans, the temperature of patients is commonly lowered to protect the brain against damage during surgery.

But even in cases where there was no reduction in body temperature, patients have been known to recover after long periods of ischemia. Several years ago, a fireman trapped in a burning building was reported to have been without oxygen for twenty minutes before being brought back to life.

The Work of Hossmann

The most impressive body of evidence that contradicts the notion of irreversible brain damage after four minutes of ischemia is the work of K. A. Hossmann of the Max Planck Institute for Brain Research in West Germany. Hossmann has demonstrated that the brains of cats, dogs, and monkeys can recover—as assessed by measurement of neuronal function, electrical activity (EEG readings), and energy metabolism—after as long as one hour of ischemia at normal body temperature.

His work suggests that the difficulty in resuscitating patients after four minutes of ischemia results from the inability to restore full blood circulation to the brain. That the brain fails to recover—and eventually dies—primarily because the blood is prevented from reaching the brain cells.

According to Hossmann, the inability to restore normal blood circulation to the brain is caused by swelling of the tissues, aggregation of blood particles in the capillaries, changes in blood viscosity, and shrinkage of the brain cells.

Hossmann was able to restore circulation to the brain by inducing the blood to flow at a higher-than-normal pressure. Thus, the blood forced its way through the brain's complex system of narrow, winding vessels to replenish the cells with oxygen and nutrients.

More research is needed before the techniques developed by Hossmann can be applied in clinical practice, but his findings suggest that it's time to abandon the notion of four-minute brain death.

Robert J. White, Department of Neurosurgery, Case Western Reserve University School of Medicine, Cleveland, Oh. 44106.

Konstantin-Alexander Hossmann, Max-Planck-Institut fur Hirnforschung, Abteilung fur Allgemeins Neurologie, 5 Cologne/Merheim, Federal Republic of Germany

Helping the Body Survive Without Oxygen

There is now evidence that the human body can survive at normal temperature with little or no oxygen for as long as eighty minutes if it is protected by mannitol, a sugar alcohol found in many plants. Japanese neurosurgeon Jiro Suzuki finds he can safely cut off blood flow to a patient's brain while repairing a burst blood vessel (cerebral aneurysm) if he gives the patient an infusion of mannitol prior to the operation. He's used the technique in hundreds of patients, the vast majority of whom have left the hospital in "good" to "excellent" condition.

Mannitol has also been used as part of a perfusate solution—in conjunction with hypothermia—to preserve isolated dog kidneys up to seventy-two hours by surgeons at the UCLA School of Medicine. The kidneys functioned normally when reimplanted into donor dogs, even if they had undergone thirty minutes of warm ischemia (diminution of blood supply) prior to being cooled to 2° C.

Apparently, mannitol surrounds the cells to prevent excessive water from entering them. When it is combined with a high potassium solution that discourages changes in elec-

TABLE 1—*Effect of 1 h complete cerebral ischemia on various circulatory and blood parameters*

Measurements were performed prior to ischemia, at the end of 1 h ischemia, and after 30–45 min of recirculation (means ± S.E.M., number of animals in parentheses).

	Control	Ischemia	Recirculation	
			Recovery	No recovery
Cerebral blood flow (ml/100 g/min)	32.31 ± 6.65 (13)	—	46.1 ± 12.1 (7)**	8.4 ± 4.1 (4)**§§
Mean arterial blood pressure (mm Hg)	116.9 ± 10.3 (30)	57.5 ± 12.0 (22)**	135.9 ± 20.1 (11)**	129.4 ± 31.7 (8)
Arterial pH	7.37 ± 0.04 (30)	7.44 ± 0.09 (23)**	7.35 ± 0.09 (11)	7.32 ± 0.11 (8)*
Arterial P_{CO_2} (mm Hg)	39.1 ± 5.3 (30)	30.5 ± 5.0 (23)**	40.3 ± 6.2 (11)	44.0 ± 10.1 (8)
Arterial P_{O_2} (mm Hg)	101.2 ± 11.3 (30)	123.7 ± 22.0 (23)**	148.6 ± 31.0 (11)**	118.1 ± 22.1 (8)**§
Standard bicarbonate (mEq./l)	22.9 ± 1.8 (28)	23.3 ± 2.8 (20)	21.8 ± 2.9 (11)	20.4 ± 2.9 (7)**
Arterial glucose (mg%)	76.3 ± 21.1 (26)	124.0 ± 31.8 (20)**	94.3 ± 31.0 (7)	110.0 ± 55.5 (4)**
Hematocrit (%)	38.8 ± 6.2 (30)	36.0 ± 6.6 (22)	33.7 ± 5.7 (11)*	37.9 ± 6.8 (8)
Erythrocytes (millions)	5.90 ± 1.41 (18)	4.85 ± 0.77 (13)*	4.78 ± 0.76 (8)*	5.24 ± 0.68 (4)
Erythrocytes diameter (μm)	7.07 ± 0.11 (12)	7.13 ± 0.27 (10)	7.02 ± 0.11 (5)	7.03 ± 0.04 (3)
Serum sodium (mEq./l)	154.8 ± 7.1 (24)	158.9 ± 9.1 (18)	158.2 ± 11.3 (10)	153.00 ± 12.3 (6)
Serum potassium (mEq./l)	3.3 ± 0.31 (22)	4.04 ± 0.63 (18)**	3.82 ± 0.47 (10)**	4.71 ± 0.97 (6)**§
Serum calcium (mEq./l)	4.9 ± 0.5 (24)	4.6 ± 0.46 (17)	4.56 ± 0.53 (10)	4.37 ± 0.49 (6)**
Serum chloride (mEq./l)	121.8 ± 13.3 (6)	120.3 ± 10.3 (5)	110.8 ± 11.1 (5)	127.0 ± 39.6 (2)
Clotting time (sec)***	110.0 ± 25.2 (20)	112.6 ± 69.3 (19)	134.6 ± 51.5 (11)	121.9 ± 36.5 (7)
Prothrombin time (sec)	16.0 ± 2.0 (24)	15.7 ± 3.0 (21)	17.1 ± 3.0 (11)	16.8 ± 2.6 (7)
Thrombin time (sec)***	43.9 ± 13.6 (21)	98.3 ± 66.0 (21)**	120.4 ± 65.3 (11)**	71.9 ± 60.3 (7)*
Cortical pH	7.37 ± 0.14 (9)	6.78 ± 0.19 (10)**	7.11 ± 0.02 (5)**	6.77 ± 0.21 (3)**§§

Statistics: different from control group * $P < 0.05$, ** $P < 0.01$; different from animals with recovery § $P < 0.05$, §§ $P < 0.01$.
*** In some animals clotting and thrombin times were infinite during or after ischemia; for statistical analysis a coagulation time of 200 sec was used.

Effects of one hour of complete ischemia on various circulatory and blood parameters in the monkey brain. Measurements were obtained in animals before ischemia (control), after one hour of ischemia, and after thirty to forty-five minutes of blood recirculation. *(Number of animals in parentheses.)*

trolyte concentration on both sides of the cell membrane, it seems to inhibit cell damage from ischemia and permit better blood flow when circulation is re-established.

Jiro Suzuki, Division of Neurosurgery, Tohoku University School of Medicine, Institute of Brain Diseases, 5-13-1, Nagamachi, Sendai, Japan 982

Stephen A. Sacks, Division of Urology, Department of Surgery, UCLA Medical Center, Los Angeles, Ca. 90024

How Humans Are Frozen

There are many versions of what it's like to be frozen. Cartoonists have depicted naked women trapped in transparent blocks of ice. Novelists have described people hanging like slabs of meat in a freezer, or packaged like Sara Lee cupcakes. Others have pictured white, frost-encased hulks of ice on the verge of splintering.

Actually, a frozen person is not all that different from a living person in appearance. The body has the same flesh color and look it had before it was frozen, except that all biologic activity has ceased. Freezing is simply a method of immobilizing a person in time so that he or she can "travel" into the future.

The Freezing Process

In the first stage of the freezing process, physiologic functions are maintained by providing artificial assistance to the vital organs. A heart-lung machine keeps the blood flowing through the body, while ice is applied externally.

Then a chilled chemical solution is substituted for the blood, which is gradually removed from the body. The purpose of the chemical solution is to protect the cells against freezing damage. Such chemicals as glycerol and DMSO (dimethylsulfoxide) act to prevent the breakdown of cell membranes and internal structures.

When the body's temperature approaches $0°$ C ($32°$ F), it

is placed into an insulated container packed with dry ice. During this phase of the operation, the body is transformed into the solid state. A relatively slow freezing rate is desirable to guard against formation of tiny ice crystals within cells.

Long-Term Storage

Finally, the solidly frozen body is wrapped in layers of reflective material, attached to a stretcher, and transferred to a "cryocapsule" for long-term storage. The cryocapsule is an eight-foot-high steel cylinder that operates much like a Thermos bottle.

The body rests within an internal cylinder that is filled with liquid nitrogen (LN_2) to lower its temperature to $-196°$ C ($-320°$ F). At this extremely low temperature, there is essentially no metabolic activity within the body. As the LN_2 evaporates or "boils off," it must be replaced periodically in order to maintain suspension conditions.

A body maintained in this manner can be preserved for thousands of years or longer with virtually no change in its structure or composition. The hope of cryonics is that the appropriation of an open-minded timescale will permit solution of the medical and biological problems that stand in the way of reanimating persons frozen by today's less-than-optimal methods.

Survival of Frozen Dog Kidneys

A method of preserving internal organs for long periods would be a boon for organ transplantation. It would also be a giant step forward in the quest for suspended animation. An organ such as the kidney can be looked upon as a smaller version of the entire organism. It contains several types of tissue, functions in a highly complex manner, and is large enough to make heat transfer difficult—all of which stand in the way of a perfected method of freezing humans.

In the past few years, there have been reports of increas-

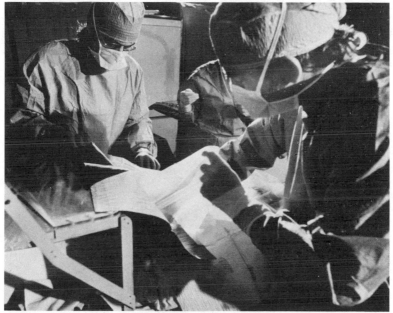

Stage I of the freezing process performed by the Trans Time Cryonic Suspension team.

ing success in freezing dog kidneys. Sunao Kubota has reported that eleven of fourteen excised kidneys cooled at 2-4° C/min to −22° C and then thawed at 70-110° C were able to function adequately, as measured by urine output, after reimplantation into dogs.

Frank M. Guttman has reported an even greater achievement—the successful freezing of dog kidneys to −80° C. In this experiment, sixteen kidneys were frozen for fifteen minutes, thawed by microwave illumination, and reimplanted into dogs from which both kidneys had been removed. Eight of these dogs survived two to fourteen months on a single, previously frozen kidney.

Guttman used a new technique—the circulation of cold helium gas through the blood vessels—in an attempt to achieve a relatively constant and uniform freezing rate.

Sunao Kubota, Department of Surgery, University of Minnesota, Minneapolis, Mn. 55455

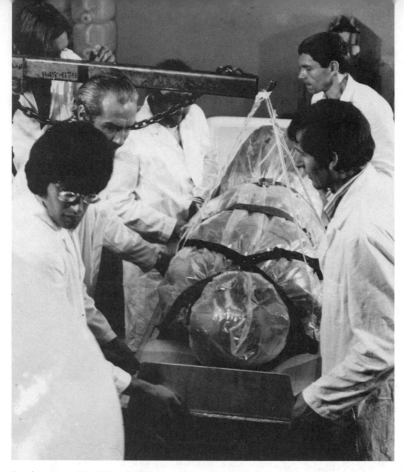

During stage II of the freezing process, the patient is placed into a "cryocapsule" for long-term storage.

Frank M. Guttman, Centre Hospitalier, Jewish General Hospital, 3755 Cote Ste. Catherine, Montreal, P.Q. H3T 1EZ, Canada.

Freeze-Preservation of Rat Hearts

In 1965, Armand M. Karow, Jr., reported reanimation of rat hearts frozen to $-20°$ C for twenty minutes. Since then, attempts to freeze-preserve mammalian hearts at lower temperatures have been generally unsuccessful, though isolated heart cells have survived temperatures as low as $-196°$ C.

However, a recent report from Japan by S. Sumida claims successful preservation of rat hearts frozen to $-196°$ C. The

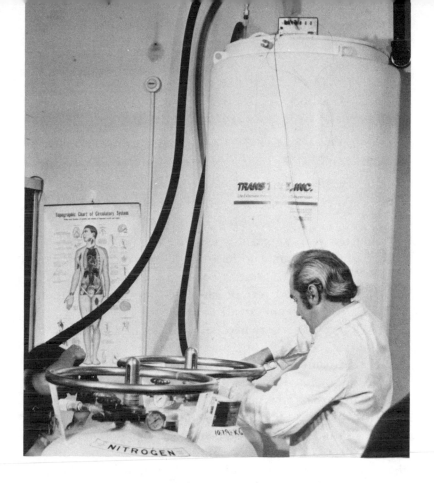

Trans Time president Art Quaife fills cryocapsule with liquid nitrogen to lower body temperature to −320°F.

hearts were perfused with DMSO, ethylene glycol, or glycerol; cooled at 1-2° C/min to −80° C, after which they were plunged into liquid nitrogen; and then maintained for periods ranging from forty-two days to two years. Thawing was done in Ringer's solution at 38° C.

According to Sumida, "the resumption of spontaneous beating and the responses to stimulation by a pacemaker were observed and recorded by a 16 mm movie camera using color film."

If this finding is confirmed, it will represent a major advance in organ preservation.

Armand M. Karow, Jr., Department of Pharmacology, Medical College of Georgia, Augusta, Ga. 30902

S. Sumida, Low Temperature Unit and Fourth Division of Surgery, National Fukuoka Central Hospital, Jonai, Fukuoka 810, Japan

Preserving the Brain

About ten years ago, a TV drama featured the living, isolated brain of a man who had "died" of cancer. The brain could "see," "hear," and "communicate" via electronic hookups, and seemed very much alive by anyone's standards.

Such an idea is not at all far-fetched. Robert White of Case Western Reserve University has kept isolated monkey brains alive (see p. 228), and many researchers have speculated about transplanting the brain into a new body—either biologic or bionic.

It's hard to say how many of us would opt for such an alternative, but it's clear that any attempt to forestall death must give high priority to preserving the brain. A perfected method of brain freezing would almost certainly become the method of choice for whole-body freezing, even if such a method might inflict damage upon other organs.

Furthermore, such a method would encourage cryonic suspension of the isolated brain or head, an option that several persons have already chosen for economic reasons. (See p. 307.) In the future, it should be relatively easy to transplant brains into new bodies, or to graft heads onto such bodies. Those of us who want to hold on to our "own" bodies might request brain transplantation into an identical cloned body. (See p. 346.)

Suda's Experiments

Despite the importance of learning how to preserve the brain, only Isamu Suda of Kobe University in Japan has reported brain-freezing experiments, and most of his work was done in the 1960s. Suda froze and stored isolated cat brains at $-20°$ C for periods ranging from a few days to 7.25 years.

He demonstrated spontaneous electricocortical activity in these brains after slow thawing—even in organs stored for more than five years. However, the quality of the activity declined significantly with increasing time in storage. As Suda put it, there was "extensive reduction of cell density accompanied by evidence of severe hemorrhage" and "many cracks" in cat brains stored for long periods.

In his efforts to preserve cat brains, Suda tried freezing them to $-20°$ C, $-60°$ C, and $-90°$ C, with the aid of the protective chemicals glycerol, dimethylsulfoxide (DMSO), polyvinylpyrrolidone (PVP), and hydrogenated, high-molecular-weight dextran. The best evidence of integrative neuroelectrical activity was obtained with glycerol-perfused brains revived from $-20°$ C. At $-90°$ C, on the other hand, there was no evidence of electrical discharge with any of the cryoprotective agents.

Suggestions for Future Research

Though Suda seems to have assumed that his cat brains were frozen solid throughout the experiment, it's possible that they were not. By perfusing them with glycerol, an agent that depresses the freezing point of biologic fluids, he may have temporarily prevented the brain cells from freezing. Consequently, brains "frozen" for relatively short periods could have been protected from the serious damage that subsequently ensued as the brain cells gradually solidified with increasing time. That there was no apparent electrical activity in brains thawed from $-90°$ C, regardless of the time in storage, suggests that these organs were solidly frozen from the beginning.

It's possible that better protection against freezing damage might be provided by increasing the concentration of glycerol above the 15 percent level used by Suda. Additional protection might be provided by using a better perfusing medium than that used by Suda to prevent the cells from swelling during the cooling process. (See p. 283.) A third change in protocol that might prove beneficial is rapid thawing—a technique that has been used to advantage in other organ preservation experiments.

Suda felt that "individual nerve cell activity . . . may be well preserved" in cat brains frozen to −20° C, even in tissue showing considerable gross damage after long-term storage. Appropriate follow-up of his pioneering work could lead to a perfected method of freezing or supercooling the brain within a decade.

Isamu Suda, Department of Physiology, Faculty of Medicine, Kobe University, Ikuta-ku, Kobe, Japan

Freezing Fetal Rat Pancreases

While no major adult organ has yet been frozen with complete success, this feat has been accomplished with a fetal organ—the rat pancreas. A team of scientists from Oak Ridge National Laboratory and UCLA Medical Center has frozen 16½-17½-day-old fetal rat pancreases to −78° C or −196° C and demonstrated the functional recovery of these organs after thawing.

Maximum survival was obtained at the very slow cooling rate of 0.28° C/min in a high concentration of DMSO. A slow rewarming rate of 4 or 15° C/min, and an unusually slow dilution rate were used to protect against DMSO toxicity. Under these conditions, the experimental pancreases synthesized 80-100 percent as much protein as unfrozen controls, and could be transplanted successfully into adult rats.

An even more impressive demonstration of the viability of these organs was their ability to reverse drug-induced diabetes after transplantation. This ability was comparable to that achieved by transplantation of unfrozen fetal rat pancreases. (See p. 217.)

J. A. Kemp, Department of Biology, UCLA Medical Center, Los Angeles, Ca. 90024

Freezing Rodents, Rabbits, and Monkeys

Legend has it that frozen prehistoric animals have been warmed to life by the sun, but there are no documented cases of animals being revived after solid freezing. Only the hardy insects of the Arctic—protected by their own brand of "antifreeze"—can apparently withstand the rigors of freezing. (See p. 296.)

However, many species are surprisingly resistant to short-term exposure to cold. One example of this resistance is the trick employed at fairs in which an apparently frozen goldfish springs to life when dropped into a bowl of water. What the audience doesn't know is that only the outer layer of the goldfish is actually frozen, not the internal organs or body fluids.

Humans have shown a remarkable ability to recover from short-term exposure to brutal sub-zero weather. In one highly publicized case, a man trapped in an unheated compartment of a jetliner survived the temperature of −40° F during a transcontinental flight.

The limits of animal resistance to freezing were explored in an early series of experiments by Audrey Smith at England's National Institute for Medical Research. Smith was able to resuscitate golden hamsters whose internal body temperature had fallen as low as −5° C (22° F), but who remained in a partly frozen "supercooled" state.

The hamsters were immersed in a chilled propylene glycol bath for forty to sixty minutes. Their ears and paws began to stiffen perceptibly before their deep body temperature had reached zero. Gradually, the entire body surface of the animals became rigid.

A high proportion of hamsters frozen in this way recovered fully after thawing with diathermy and the administration of artificial respiration. It was determined that 40 to 50 percent of their body water had been converted to ice. Most of the hamsters passed blood from their rectum during the first few hours after reanimation. A few animals died several weeks later with perforated gastric ulcers.

Experiments with Rabbits

When Smith cooled rabbits in melting ice for twenty to forty minutes, only one of six animals recovered fully from a body temperature of 9-12° C, and this animal died three days later. None of the rabbits that were partially frozen recovered after thawing.

Although Smith was unable to reanimate frozen rabbits, she found that every animal showed signs of recovery during thawing. In each instance, the heart resumed beating at about 15° C and spontaneous breathing was achieved at 20 to 30° C. At this point, most of the animals regained corneal reflexes and displayed spontaneous movements, but then collapsed and died within an hour.

Autopsies showed massive stomach hemorrhaging. By introducing sodium bicarbonate into the rabbits' stomach prior to freezing, Smith was able to prevent gastric hemorrhaging, but was able to prolong survival for only several hours after resuscitation.

By using a similar technique she was able to resuscitate galagos (small monkeys) after forty minutes at body temperatures below 0° C. Two galagos made an excellent initial recovery, but died within twenty-four hours. Autopsies showed enlarged, blood-stained lungs.

At the time of these experiments (the late 1950s), Smith was optimistic about the prospect of successful freezing of whole organisms. She predicted that improved methods of cooling and resuscitation might soon enable scientists to restore frozen mammals to full health.

Although this prediction has failed to come true, it has

never really been tested. Smith and other cryobiologists soon stopped trying to freeze whole animals and virtually no such experiments have been performed since.

In 1978, Trans Time, Inc. began an animal research program—in conjunction with Cryovita Laboratories (see p. 308)—aimed at improving techniques of whole-body freezing.

Audrey U. Smith, Division of Experimental Biology, National Institute for Medical Research, Mill Hill, London, England

Survival of Frozen Baby Squirrels

In the 1960s, Vojin and Pava Popovic of Emory University studied the effects of cooling on various animal species. They discovered that animals could survive cooling and "supercooling" (below the freezing point of water), but not hard freezing, and that the ability to survive was a function of both temperature and time of exposure. Thus, the survival time of rats at a body temperature of 20-22° C was about twenty-four hours; whereas at 15° C it was only six hours, and at 2-8° C only 1.5 hours.

The Popovics also found that hibernating animals could tolerate cold better than nonhibernating animals. Ground squirrels, for example, could survive a body temperature of 10° C twenty to forty times longer than rats. The differences in survival time between hibernators and nonhibernators tended to disappear at lower temperatures, however, when their hearts stopped beating and their blood circulation ceased.

The best results obtained by the Popovics were with newborn ground squirrels. Six of seven squirrels survived cooling to −3 to −4° C for eleven hours, and ten of twelve squirrels survived cooling to −6° to −8° C for five hours. But when the animals' body temperature was maintained for more than six hours at −6 to −8° C, they froze suddenly and were unable to recover.

Baby squirrels did survive quick-freezing for short periods. Ten of thirteen newborn ground squirrels survived immersion in an alcohol-dry ice bath at −35° C for two minutes. During this time, the animals turned white and rigid as their body temperature was lowered to −15° C. All attempts to bend their limbs or trunk resulted in breakage. Examination of four of these animals revealed that only one was completely frozen, while the others were 80 to 90 percent solid, with the area around the heart and intestines remaining unfrozen.

When seven newborn ground squirrels were immersed in a −35° C bath for fifteen minutes, only one recovered, while none of twelve animals were able to survive exposure to a −70° C bath for periods ranging from one to fifteen minutes. In most of these animals, however, breathing and heartbeat were detected during the rewarming process.

Vojin Popovic and Pava Popovic, Department of Physiology, Emory University Medical School, Atlanta, Ga. 30322

The Frozen Beetle

Every year, millions of animals in the northern reaches of the planet are exposed to brutally cold winters. Many of these animals find relatively warm niches where they go into hibernation. Certain insects go one step further—they enter a state of suspended animation in which they are frozen for months at a time.

L. Keith Miller of the Institute of Arctic Biology has been studying the freezing tolerance of these insects for the past ten years. He has demonstrated that insects such as the adult carabid beetle become solidly frozen in their natural winter habitat (tree stumps), and that they can also withstand freezing in the laboratory.

By using an extremely slow cooling rate (4° per hour), Miller has obtained 67 percent survival in beetles frozen to −87° C (−110° F) for five hours. He has also obtained 90 percent survival in beetles frozen to −70°C at the same cooling rate, and 100 percent survival in beetles frozen to −30° C at a cooling rate of 20° C per hour.

Importance of Cooling Rate

Survival after freezing seemed to depend primarily on the rate of cooling. In general, the slower the cooling rate the higher the survival rate, regardless of the rate of thawing. At relatively high temperatures (−15° C or above), however, there was 100 percent survival even after fast cooling.

Miller has found extreme sensitivity to the rate of cooling in the adult northern tenebrionid beetle. One hundred percent of these insects were able to survive a cooling rate of 0.29° C/min to −49° C without apparent damage, whereas only one of twenty-six beetles could survive a cooling rate of 0.35° C/min to −49 to −53° C. Thus, the percentage of survivors dropped from 100 percent to 4 percent as a result of a change in the cooling rate of only 0.06° C/min. Interestingly, the optimum cooling rate for this species of beetle is similar to that required for the survival of mouse embryos. (See p. 299.)

Although adult beetles have been able to survive freezing only to −87° C, immature Arctic beetles have survived freezing to the temperature of liquid nitrogen (−196° C).

The remarkable ability of these insects to tolerate freezing may be the result of the presence of glycerol or similar compounds in their body fluids. However, some immature insects are resistant to freezing even though they do not contain glycerol, while others cannot survive freezing even though they contain large amounts of glycerol.

The finding that adult insects can tolerate solid-state freezing suggests that the complexity of tissue organization is not the limiting factor in survival. If a complex organism such as the Arctic beetle can survive freezing, it's likely that humans can as well.

L. Keith Miller, Institute of Arctic Biology, University of Alaska, Fairbanks, Alaska 99701

Suspending Animation in Rodents

Scientists at Trans Time, Inc., are trying to determine whether long-term suspended animation is possible without freezing. They have suspended life functions in mice, rats, and hamsters without apparent damage to these animals.

Best results to date have been achieved in hamsters, who are particularly resistant to cold because of their ability to hibernate. Hamsters have survived suspended animation at 0° C for as long as four hours, followed by complete recovery including the ability to produce normal, healthy offspring.

Protocol for Suspension

First, the hamster is placed into a sealed one-quart jar that sits in ice water. After about forty-five minutes, the animal loses consciousness, as its supply of oxygen dwindles. At this time, the hamster does not respond to external stimuli, but is still able to breathe.

Next, the animal is placed upon its back on a bed of crushed ice in an open receptacle to record its temperature and heartbeat. If the time of cardiac arrest is to exceed two hours, 0.5 cc of antacid is administered to the stomach via a feeding tube. The animal is then covered with ice bags, and aluminum foil is stretched across the top of the receptacle.

As the hamster's temperature drops, its breathing becomes shallower and slower. When the temperature reaches 10° C, artificial respiration is administered to provide the animal with additional oxygen. At about 4° C—when natural breathing and heartbeat stop—the hamster is left unattended in a state of suspended animation.

Resuscitation

After several hours, the hamster is removed from the ice-filled receptacle and placed upon its back under a lighted desk lamp, which has been set up to induce a warming rate of approximately 1° C/minute. When the hamster's heartbeat resumes, artificial respiration is reinstituted to help the animal recover. Once natural respiration resumes, the instruments are removed and the animal is turned upright to recuperate on its own.

The Trans Time scientists hope to increase the time of suspended animation by perfusing animals with cryoprotective chemicals to permit induction of body temperatures substantially below 0° C without freezing.

Trans Time, Inc., 1122 Spruce St., Berkeley, Ca. 94707

Suspending the Animation Process

The process by which a tiny fertilized egg grows into a complex, multi-billion-celled organism is remarkable. As the process unfolds, the initial cell multiplies rapidly into highly specialized units that coalesce—as if by magic—to form the tissues and organs of a unique individual.

Biologists have stopped this process "cold" in mice, sheep, goats, and cows by placing embryos into suspended animation at ultra-low temperatures for extended periods. After these embryos were thawed and cultured, they were implanted into receptive females where some of them developed into normal offspring.

Thus far, the procedure has been performed with greatest success in mice by scientists at Oak Ridge National Laboratory. They froze a large number of mouse embryos, which were subsequently thawed and placed into a culture medium to resume growth and development.

The number of embryos recovered after thawing was 90.3 percent of the total frozen, of which 50 to 70 percent reached the blastocyst stage of development. Of more than 2,800

Trans Time scientists perform suspended animation experiment. Hamster is being rewarmed *(under light)* after chilling in ice water.

frozen-thawed embryos, 360 were transferred into receptive female mice immediately after thawing and 600 were transferred after reaching the blastocyst stage.

Sixty-five percent of the foster mothers became pregnant and 43 percent of the transferred embryos developed into full-term fetuses or live-born mice—all of whom appeared normal in every way. Subsequently, thirteen of the second generation mice were allowed to mate and gave birth to litters of normal third-generation mice.

Fetuses and live-born mice developed normally from embryos frozen to −78° C, −196° C, and −269° C, regardless of whether transfer was immediately after thawing or after development to the blastocyst stage. These results compared favorably with those obtained from the transfer of normal unfrozen embryos into mice.

Future Prospects

Animal embryos contain all the essential information for the development of adults. That this information can survive a hard freeze and thaw indicates that human embryos could survive the process as well. Human sperm and eggs have been frozen successfully, and it was reported (but has not yet been confirmed) that the embryo used in a recent test-tube baby procedure in Calcutta, India, had previously been frozen.

It also suggests that only technical problems stand in the way of a perfected method of suspended animation in humans. Though these problems are formidable, there is no reason to believe they cannot be overcome. The field of suspended animation is now at a stage comparable to space travel at the time President Kennedy declared that placing a man on the moon would be a national goal. Just as we knew then that a rocket could take us to the moon if we built one powerful enough to do so, we now know that freezing can preserve us if we design a method sophisticated enough for the human body.

Peter Mazur, Biology Division, Oak Ridge National Laboratory, Oak Ridge, Tn. 37830

High-Pressure Freezing

Imagine stepping into the cocoon of an immense, thick-walled, steel chamber. As the door of the chamber slams shut, you are isolated from all vestiges of the outside world. Bathed in an amniotic-like fluid, you feel as if you've returned to the womb for a journey into the unknown.

Such a chamber may someday be used to induce human suspended animation. In it, a person would be subjected to more than 2,000 atmospheres of pressure, or 32,000 pounds per square inch, while being rapidly frozen to an ultra-low temperature. According to Harold Waitz of the University

of California, Berkeley, high-pressure freezing might eliminate cell damage caused by the formation of ice crystals.

Under normal conditions, ice expands during rapid freezing to form numerous tiny ice crystals that produce lethal,
mechanical, and biochemical changes. But under extremely
high pressures, theorizes Waitz, the water in the cells would
not be transformed into normal ice (ice 1), but would go
into an anomalous, high-density state (ice 3) in which there
is no expansion during crystallization.

After a person was placed into solid-state suspended animation in this manner, the pressure would be released and the
body transferred to a cryocapsule for long-term storage.
Reanimation would require reversal of the procedure within
the same high-pressure chamber.

One advantage of high-pressure freezing over conventional
freezing is the avoidance of cryoprotective chemicals. Such
"anti-freeze" compounds are used to protect against damage
caused by the formation of ice crystals. However, they can be
highly toxic to cells at normal temperatures, and must be
removed from the body during the thawing process.

There are two major problems to be solved before high-
pressure freezing can be used for suspended animation. First
is the matter of going directly into ice 3 from the liquid state
without first going into ice 1. Next is the cell damage caused
by the high pressures produced in the chamber. Previous
attempts to freeze-preserve cells under high pressure have
failed largely because of pressure damage.

Waitz has designed and built a small chamber to test the
high-pressure hypothesis. Thus far, he has had moderate success in freezing yeast cells under high pressure by using a
fluorocarbon liquid as a pressuring medium.

*Harold Waitz, Department of Biophysics, Hilldebrand Hall
—B38, University of California, Berkeley, Berkeley, Ca.
94720*

Can We Learn to Hibernate?

When animals hibernate, their metabolic rate and body temperature are reduced well below normal to enable them to function under low-energy requirements. Induced human hibernation could prove to be a valuable life-extending technique.

While under hibernation, a person's rate of aging might be slowed, possibly as a result of the reduction in body temperature. (See p. 160.) Patients in critical condition might survive for extended periods in a state of hibernation. The condition might even be useful in treating certain diseases.

There is an emerging body of evidence that hibernating animals possess a "trigger" factor in their blood and tissues that causes them to hibernate as well as a countering factor that triggers their arousal from hibernation. This theory was proposed by Dawe and Spurrier after they were able to induce squirrels to hibernate with blood transfusions from hibernating squirrels.

Recently, Rosser and Bruce confirmed this finding by inducing ground squirrels to hibernate during the summer—when they are normally active—by giving them injections of blood or urine from ground squirrels in hibernation during the winter.

The Brain Factor

Further, there is evidence that the factor that triggers hibernation may be secreted by the brain, or that the brain secretes a factor that, in turn, leads to the secretion of the hibernation factor by another organ.

When Swan and Schätte injected extracts of subcortical brains from hibernating ground squirrels intravenously into rats (which do not hibernate), they produced a 35 percent reduction in oxygen consumption and a decline in body temperature of 5° C. The effects lasted from seventy-five minutes to thirty hours. Injections of brain extracts from nonhibernating squirrels caused no significant changes in these parameters.

Henry Swan has coined the word "antabolone" for the brain factor in hibernating animals that suppresses both metabolic rate and the subsequent thermoregulatory response. In earlier experiments, Swan showed that antabolone from the brains of estivating lung fish could induce similar responses in nonhibernating rats.

Albert R. Dawe, Loyola University Stritch School of Medicine, Maywood, Il. 60153

Henry Swan, Department of Clinical Sciences, Colorado State University, Fort Collins, Co. 80523

Trans Time Corporation

The large white backside of an oversized van juts out sharply from a small, slanted driveway in the Berkeley hills. On it, in big black letters, are inscribed the words "Life Extension Through Cryonic Suspension"—a message that no one who drives by is likely to miss. One side of the van is obscured by shrubbery, but the other side shows the stark red-and-black logo of Trans Time. Inc., a California corporation that freezes people.

Trans Time is the largest cryonics company in the world. It operates a multi-purpose facility in nearby Emeryville, which is used to carry out suspensions, maintain cryonic "patients" in long-term storage, conduct suspended animation research, and hold training sessions and meetings. Seven patients are currently stored in "cryocapsules" at the Trans Time facility.

One recent Trans Time project was an attempt to duplicate a suspended animation experiment that had been performed by Gerald Klebanoff of Lackland Air Force Base in the 1960s. A laboratory dog was placed on cardiopulmonary bypass, its blood was washed out and replaced with an arti-

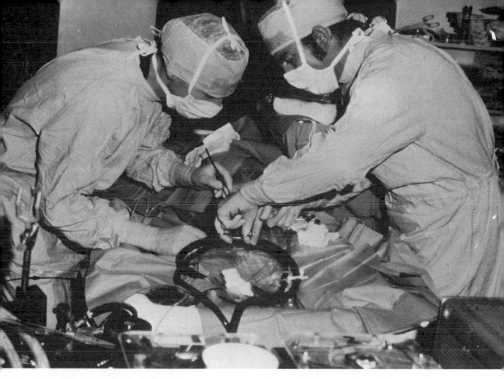

Trans Time scientists perform surgical procedure on dog during suspended animation experiment.

ficial perfusate as its temperature was reduced to 22° C. Then the dog was rewarmed to normal body temperature, as it received new transfused blood. The dog survived seventeen hours.

Trans Time maintains two cryonic suspension teams—one in the San Francisco Bay area, the other in the Los Angeles area—as well as two vans and a smaller emergency rescue vehicle. The Los Angeles suspension team uses sophisticated hospital equipment, which has been set up in a private laboratory in Fullerton, California. (See p. 308.) Trans Time also offers remote standby service to customers throughout the world.

To arrange for cryonics services, individuals must become suspension members of nonprofit organizations that have entered into contractual agreements with Trans Time. As of 1979, two such organizations—the Bay Area Cryonics Society (BACS) in the San Francisco area and the Alcor Life

Extension Foundation in the Los Angeles area—are being serviced by Trans Time.

Suspension members of these groups pay an initial fee, sign legal documents, and provide minimum funding of $50,000 for whole-body freezing or $20,000 for neuropreservation (heads only freezing).

Trans Time, Inc., 1122 Spruce St., Berkeley, Ca. 94707

Bay Area Cryonics Society (BACS)

BACS is a nonprofit, tax-exempt organization in the San Francisco Bay area. It assists its members in preparing for cryonic suspension, promotes and funds life-extension research, and educates the public about cryonics and other aspects of life extension.

Bay Area Cryonics Society, 7710 Huntridge Lane, Cupertino, Ca. 95014

Alcor Life Extension Foundation

Alcor is a nonprofit, tax-exempt organization in the Los Angeles area. It assists its members in preparing for cryonic suspension, promotes and funds life-extension research, and sponsors special events to educate the public.

One such event—the Alcor Life Extension Conference—was held March 11-12, 1978, at the Los Angeles International Hyatt House. Approximately 300 persons attended the conference, which featured prominent scientists, philosophers, and activists discussing the latest research findings and their implications for humanity.

Alcor recently performed an experiment in which a dog was frozen using the techniques currently employed in cryonic suspension, and then portions of its brain were analyzed by light and electron microscopy. They found that most of the macro-structures of the brain cells were "well preserved," but that there was "major damage in the fine cellular organelles."

Alcor Life Extension Foundation, Box 312, Glendale, Ca. 91209

Trans Time Freezes Brain

"We have had the brain of our murdered daughter Patricia Luna Wilson preserved . . . in the hope that future scientific research will allow her to live again through cloning. . . . It is our fervent hope that, whether or not cloning eventually succeeds in this case, scientific research will be aided and this will be one contribution to humanity's conquest of death. More importantly, we support the quest for life extension and scientific immortality because it is a fit memorial to Luna, who so loved life, who was boundless in joy and affection."

In those words, Robert Anton Wilson announced to the world that the brain of his daughter had been frozen by the Trans Time Corporation of Berkeley, California. Since cryonic suspension is generally thought of as a whole-body procedure, this case illustrates some of the less publicized concepts that underlie cryonics.

• First is the fact that bringing a frozen patient back to life will require highly advanced medical techniques that may include reconstruction or regrowing of the entire body or some of its parts via cloning, organ culture, regeneration, or prosthetics. With the currently used freezing methods, it may not be possible to revive a frozen person without extensive reconstructive work.

• Second is the idea that the brain is the only essential organ in the body and that future medical techniques may enable us to improve upon our biological bodies. Even after cryonic suspension has been perfected and it becomes possible to revive a frozen body without substantial repair work, we may choose to dispense with it in favor of a new, improved model. This is particularly likely if we are dealing with a very old or greatly deteriorated body.

• Third is the concept that today's relatively primitive

freezings will lead to future advances, even if it proves impossible to revive some of the early patients. Such progress may occur in three ways:

• from experience gained in carrying out cryonic suspension procedures,

• from funds appropriated for research—either from the estates of those in suspension or from the pockets of those who want to benefit from life-extension advances while they are still alive,

• from a generalized feeling in society-at-large that there is hope for everyone in the struggle against aging and death, and that life extension will benefit society as well as the individual.

The cryonics pioneers can be likened to a cadre of guerrilla fighters who have staked out an extreme position to demonstrate the feasibility of the struggle and to illuminate its value.

Cryovita Laboratories

For anyone who wants to be frozen after death, the "best" place to die is the Los Angeles area. Though cryonic suspension services are available in the San Francisco Bay area; the Detroit, Michigan, area; Indianapolis, Indiana; and South Florida, none can rival the nine-member suspension team assembled by Jerry Leaf of Cryovita Laboratories in Fullerton (a suburb of Los Angeles).

Cryovita Laboratories is the only facility equipped to carry out cryonic suspension according to state-of-the-art surgical procedures. It includes heart-lung machines and membrane oxygenators to replace the patient's cardiopulmonary functions; heat exchangers and perfusion pumps to perform the early phases of the process; a complete physiological monitoring system to measure vital functions while the patient's temperature is being lowered; and all the necessary instrumentation, clothing, and sterilizing equipment to perform surgery under standard operating conditions.

All members of the Cryovita suspension team have undergone extensive training under the direction of Leaf, a biomedical researcher in the Division of Thoracic Surgery at UCLA Medical Center. They are under exclusive contract to the Trans Time Corporation.

The primary objective of Cryovita Laboratories is to conduct cryobiologic research aimed at developing techniques to extend human life. Leaf is currently engaged in preliminary studies to develop a successful method of freezing the heart. He plans to remove hearts from donor dogs supported by total cardiopulmonary bypass, perfuse the hearts with cryoprotective chemicals "never before used in any other laboratory," freeze them to the temperature of liquid nitrogen ($-196°$ C), thaw them by the best available method, and finally reimplant the hearts by the method used by the Stanford University heart transplant team. (See p. 205.)

Leaf also is working with another scientist to develop a protocol to freeze the brain. As in the heart experiments, dogs will be used in this project, which will be aimed at successful reimplantation of the brain after varying periods of storage at ultra-cold temperatures. A major criterion used to determine the viability of the brain after freezing will be the ability of the dog to remember tasks learned prior to the onset of the experiment.

Jerry D. Leaf, Cryovita Laboratories, 4030 N. Palm St., Unit 304, Fullerton, Ca. 92635

Institute for Cryonics Education (ICE)

ICE is a nonprofit, tax-exempt organization whose primary purpose is to support cryonic suspension research. It is affiliated with Cryovita Laboratories.

Institute for Cryonics Education, 4030 N. Palm, Unit 304, Fullerton, Ca. 92635

Cryonics Association

The Cryonics Association (CA) is a nonprofit, tax-exempt, educational corporation dedicated to the "indefinite extension and unlimited improvement" of human life. It focuses primarily on cryonic suspension as a means of extending life.

CA maintains a van, or mobile emergency unit, equipped for the early stages of cryonic suspension. Both the van and CA personnel are made available to the Cryonics Institute for the provision of cryonic suspension services.

CA also publishes *The Immortalist,* a newsletter on cryonics and life extension.

Cryonics Association, 24041 Stratford, Oak Park, Mi. 48237

Cryonics Association: New York Chapter

This newly formed branch of CA is looking for members in the New York City area.

Arthur McCombs, 1326 Madison Ave., New York, N.Y. 10028

Cryonics Institute

The Cryonics Institute (CI) is a nonprofit corporation that provides its members with cryonic suspension services including perfusion and freezing, storage in the CI facility, and long-term maintenance. CI owns a temporary facility in the Detroit area where one patient is currently in storage. The corporation also owns five acres of land in rural Michigan where it plans to build a permanent underground facility for storage and research.

CI has a research program aimed at upgrading cryonic suspension procedures, monitoring the status of patients in storage, and developing improved methods of storage. The institute is currently experimenting with insulation materials and with improvements in construction of storage units.

CI charges a membership fee and a minimum of $29,000 for cryonic suspension and long-term storage.

Cryonics Institute, 24041 Stratford, Oak Park, Mi. 48237

Cryonics Society of South Florida

The Cryonics Society of South Florida is a nonprofit organization that offers cryonic suspension services. It provides its members with "nationwide emergency coverage."

Cryonics Society of South Florida, 2835 Hollywood Blvd., Hollywood, Fl. 33020

Northeast Cryonics Society

This organization is looking for persons interested in cryonics in the New England area.

Lawrence C. Wood III, 27 Blaine Street, Brockton, Ma. 02401

Cryonics Society of Australia

The only functioning cryonics organization outside the United States. Also provides information about anti-aging therapies.

Cryonics Society of Australia, P.O. Box 18, O'Connor, A.C.T., 1601, Australia

Institute for Advanced Biological Studies

The primary purpose of the nonprofit, tax-exempt Institute for Advanced Biological Studies (IABS) is to conduct research on the freeze-preservation of tissues, organs, and organisms. IABS also is a membership organization that promotes life extension and cryonics.

The first IABS research project was to perfuse and freeze a very old dog, using techniques approximating those used in humans. Projected IABS research projects include the freeze-preservation of the kidneys and brains of several species, including rabbits and salamanders; a study of the comparative effectiveness of glycerol and DMSO as cryoprotective agents; and the determination of the best temperature and concentrations of protective chemicals for long-term cryopreservation.

At some point in the near future, IABS expects to offer cryonic suspension services, either directly or through other cryonics organizations.

Institute for Advanced Biological Studies, Inc., 2901 N. Pennsylvania St., Indianapolis, In. 46205

The Prometheus Society

The Prometheus Society is a nonprofit organization that promotes such future-oriented goals as life extension and space exploration. The society is currently striving to establish a National Institute on Low Temperature Biology to pursue research in organ preservation and suspended animation.

Prometheus Society, 102 Morris Drive, Laurel, Md. 20810

Are the Russians Freezing People?

There have long been rumors that key Soviet leaders have secretly been placed into cryonic suspension over the past decade. Efforts to trace these rumors down have thus far been unsuccessful.

Cryobiologic research is currently being conducted by M. S. Puskar and others at the Institute for Cryobiology and Cryomedicine in Kharkov, and there is an Institute for the Study of Resuscitation, headed by V. A. Negovskii, in Moscow. There is no evidence that either of these institutes has been involved in the freezing of humans. There was once a story in the *National Inquirer* that Negovskii had been freezing people, but no details were given and the claim was denied by Negovskii.

There is one intriguing report in a Soviet text on tissue therapy (see p. 238) about lung-freezing experiments performed by S. I. Yutanov in 1961. "It was shown," states the text, "that auto-transplanted lung, preserved by freezing at a temperature of −30° C up to 30 days, differed but little by its functional properties from the transplanted unpreserved own lung." No further information was supplied.

M. S. Puskar, Institute for Cryobiology and Cryomedicine, Kharkov, U.S.S.R.

V. A. Negovskii, Laboratory for Resuscitation of the Organism, AMN CCCP, St. of the 25th of October 9, Moscow, U.S.S.R.

Is Walt Disney Frozen?

A most persistent rumor is that Walt Disney is frozen. Every time Disney's name comes up, it seems, someone asks about his alleged freezing. As a result, many people have come to believe that the famed cartoonist lies preserved in ice in some secret hideaway.

Even the recent story that Disney was cremated and that his ashes are stored in Forest Lawn Memorial Park in Glendale, California, has failed to still the rumors about his freezing. Since it's impossible to prove that a box of ashes sitting in a cemetery is actually the remains of Disney, the rumors will probably continue.

The best bet, however, may be a story that was circulated at the time of Disney's death—that he made a death-bed request to be frozen, but was instead cremated by his relatives. The moral of the story is that people who wish to be frozen after death should make plans to do so while they're still in good health—even if they are exceedingly wealthy.

Chapter 10

Extended Parenthood and Aphrodisiacs

Preserving Embryos for Future Parenthood

When we're able to add years of youthful vigor to our lives, we may also be able to extend our years of childbearing. But even today, it's possible to postpone parenthood by placing our sperm cells into cold storage. Normal children have already been born as a result of artificial insemination with sperm frozen up to fifteen years. And egg cells have been preserved in a similar manner.

If we'd like our future child to be the genetic product of two persons living today, we need merely fuse an appropriate embryo in the laboratory (see p. 390) and then freeze-preserve it for future use. (See p. 299.) Or if we want to produce a future clone of ourself, or someone else we know, it may already be possible to create such an embryo (see p. 352) and then freeze it.

When we have our sperm cells or embryos thawed in the future—in fifty years, 500 years, or 5,000 years—we should have several options for parenthood. If we are still capable of bearing children, we might decide to have the child by "natural" means. If the technology for laboratory gestation has been perfected (see p. 391), we might choose to have it test-tube baby. Otherwise, we will probably just hire a surrogate mother, in whose uterus the embryo would be placed for the nine-month gestation period.

In any case, the child would be created as the result of a

decision made in the distant past—a decision we're capable of making right now.

Combating the Aging Effects of the "Milk Hormone"

When a woman's breasts produce milk after childbirth, it's largely the result of the action of the pituitary hormone prolactin. This hormone also plays a key role in the reproductive process by stimulating the corpus luteum—a yellow brown body at the site of the released egg—to secrete progesterone, the hormone that prepares the uterus for pregnancy.

However, when the woman grows older, prolactin becomes an agent of destruction rather than creation. Joseph Meites of Michigan State University has demonstrated a "remarkable" increase in blood prolactin levels in rats with advancing age that parallels their declining reproductive capacity.

Excessive prolactin secretion in old rats may be a cause of the increased incidence of pituitary cancer in these animals. Virtually all old rats are afflicted with pituitary tumors that secrete little LH and FSH (the hormones that stimulate the ovaries), but huge amounts of prolactin.

High prolactin secretion is also believed to be responsible for the increased incidence of spontaneous mammary tumors in aging rats. Treatments that increase prolactin secretion in female rats hasten the development of mammary tumors, whereas treatments that decrease prolactin secretion inhibit the appearance of these tumors. High fat consumption has been linked to increased prolactin activity as well as a high incidence of breast cancer in humans (see p. 66)—a finding that has been confirmed in rats at Meites' laboratory.

Although prolactin levels do not appear to rise substantially in aging humans, there is a complicating factor—the activity of growth hormone. According to Meites, about 15 percent of the growth hormone produced in humans can do anything that prolactin can do, and competes with it for the same receptor sites in cells. As a result, it's difficult to evaluate changes in prolactin activity with age in humans.

Recent studies have shown that ergot drugs such as bromoergocryptine, that inhibit the activity of prolactin, can reduce the size of human pituitary tumors that secrete prolactin. However, the use of ergot drugs has been less successful in treating breast cancer—perhaps because of the prolactin-like activity of growth hormone. An appropriate combination of drugs that inhibits both prolactin and growth hormone might prove effective in treating breast cancer.

Another ergot drug—lergotrile—which has been used to extend the life span of mice (see p. 252) has also been shown to promote resumption of estrus cycling in old rats.

Joseph Meites, Department of Physiology, Michigan State University, East Lansing, Mi. 48824

Rejuvenating the Female Reproductive System

Young, postpubertal female rats undergo periodic estrus cycles characterized by changes in their reproductive organs that jibe closely with their pattern of mating. Thus, the female goes into heat only when she is ovulating and capable of becoming pregnant.

When female rats grow old, they experience a decline in their capacity to ovulate and in the size of the litters they bear. They move from regular to irregular estrus cycles to constant estrus to irregular pseudo pregnancies and finally to anestrus (total lack of cycling). This pattern is similar to, but somewhat different from, the menopausal changes that occur in women.

During the past decade, scientists at Michigan State University under the direction of Joseph Meites have identified the neuroendocrine pattern that characterizes reproductive function in female rats, described the changes that take place as the animals age, and developed various methods of reversing these changes in old animals.

They've found that aging female rats exhibit a decline in estrogen and progesterone secreted by the ovaries, which reflects the diminished capacity of the pituitary gland to secrete LH (luteinizing hormone) and FSH (follicle stimulating hormone), as well as reduced production of LHRH (luteinizing hormone releasing hormone)—the hypothalamic hormone that regulates the reproductive activity of the pituitary gland and, at the highest level, a reduction in the catecholamines dopamine and norepinephrine—the brain neurotransmitters that may trigger the entire reproductive process.

At the same time, there is a marked elevation of the pituitary hormone prolactin, which plays a critical role in maintaining pregnancy and in stimulating the production of milk after birth, and in the indolamine serotonin, the brain neurotransmitter that seems to inhibit the reproductive process.

Restoring Estrus Cycling

The Michigan State scientists have had remarkable success in reversing many of the changes of reproductive aging. They have been able to restore ovulation and regular or irregular estrus cycling in old rats (twenty to twenty-three months of age) by electrical stimulation of the preoptic area of the hypothalamus, by subjecting the animals to ether stress; or by giving them daily injections of epinephrine (a catecholamine), L-Dopa (a catecholamine precursor), ACTH (the pituitary hormone that stimulates the adrenal glands), or progesterone (the ovarian hormone that supports pregnancy).

Scientists at New Mexico University have shown that estrus cycling can be restored in old rats by giving them the drug lergotrile, which suppresses prolactin levels.

The fact that all these treatments can rejuvenate the female reproductive system in rats suggests that reproductive function in these animals is suppressed but not eliminated by the aging process. Meites believes that loss of reproductive function in old age probably originates in the hypothalamus, which is believed to be the seat of neuroendocrine control.

Ovary Transplants

As evidence for this point of view, Meites refers to an experiment he conducted with H. H. Huang, in which the ovaries of very old rats (thirty months of age) were transplanted into young rats whose ovaries had been removed. Despite the fact that the old ovaries were small and "miserable-looking," they became functional after receiving appropriate hormonal stimulation from the young animals' neuroendocrine system. .

The relative ease with which the rat reproductive system can be rejuvenated does not appear to be readily applicable to humans. Postmenopausal human ovaries degenerate more with age than rat ovaries, and are unresponsive to stimulation by pituitary hormones. On the other hand, no clinical efforts have been made to reverse reproductive aging in women, and there have been reports of restored menstrual bleeding in postmenopausal patients receiving estrogen, progesterone, or L-Dopa.

H. H. Huang, Department of Physiology, Michigan State University, East Lansing, Mi. 48824

Caroline O. Wiggins, University of New Mexico School of Medicine, Albuquerque, N.M. 87131

Inducing Pregnancy in Old Rats

The acid test for any reproductive system is its ability to conceive, nurture, and deliver healthy offspring. After years of efforts at rejuvenating the reproductive system of old female rats, Joseph Meites sought to find out if experimentally rejuvenated rats could become pregnant and produce viable litters.

He studied three groups of constant-estrus rats, sixteen to eighteen months of age. One group of twelve rats, which served as controls, was injected daily with corn oil. Two experimental groups of ten and twelve rats were given daily injections of 1 mg of progesterone in corn oil. As soon as the experimental rats underwent two consecutive estrus cycles, young fertile males (five to six months of age) were placed into the breeding cages of both the progesterone-treated and control females. After mating, the animals in one of the experimental groups were maintained on 2 mg of progesterone daily for an additional twenty-one days.

Every rat tested became either pseudopregnant or pregnant. Of the twelve control rats, five became pregnant; of the ten rats receiving 1 mg of progesterone, four became pregnant; and of the twelve rats receiving 2 mg of progesterone after mating, six became pregnant.

However, none of the pregnancies produced viable offspring. In most cases, the fetuses were dead in utero by mid-gestation. Several of the animals maintained their pregnancies beyond the normal twenty-one-day period, but failed to give birth. When examined after thirty days, the fetuses were dead and the mothers tended to have infected oviducts.

It was apparent that restoration of estrus-cycling did not significantly improve the pregnancy rate of old rats or help them to produce viable offspring. Meites feels that pregnancy failure in old rats may occur because of age-related deficiencies in the uterine environment or in the capacity of the ovaries and placenta to secrete hormones. He believes that further hormonal manipulation could lead to restoration of full reproductive competence in old female rats.

Joseph Meites, Department of Physiology, Michigan State University, East Lansing, Mi. 48824

The Seventy-Year-Old Mother

Imagine the excitement caused by the birth of a healthy baby to a seventy-year-old woman. Such an event would not only enthrall us as a human interest story, it would astound us with its implications for humanity. It would suddenly raise the prospect of extended youth for women, increased options for parents, enhanced career opportunities for women, and additional population pressure for society.

Most important would be its impact as a symbol of our increasing ability to control our own destinies. It would be a sign that we are demolishing the biologic barriers to freedom, just as our migration to outer space is demolishing environmental barriers.

Segall and Timiras of the University of California, Berkeley, have been able to arrest aging in young rats by feeding them a diet deficient in the essential amino acid tryptophan. (See p. 68.) They've linked this effect to biochemical alterations in the central nervous system and are seeking pharmacologic means of duplicating it in old animals.

One of their most remarkable findings is that female rats deprived of tryptophan are able to reproduce at advanced ages. The longevity record for motherhood is held by a Berkeley rat who gave birth to a litter of normal offspring

Rat mother tends to offspring after giving birth at the advanced age of twenty-eight months.

at twenty-eight months of age—which is roughly equivalent to a woman of seventy.

Considerable research will be necessary to develop safe and effective therapies to extend reproductive age in humans, but it appears to be a feasible goal. There seems to be no immutable chronologic limit to motherhood. It's probably only a matter of time before women in their fifties, sixties, and older can have children.

Hypersexual Behavior During L-Dopa Therapy

When a seventy-six-year-old man who had been sexually inactive for years suddenly begins to chase nurses around the hospital with an amorous glint in his eye, it's time to take notice. Sidney K. Shapiro of the University of Minnesota encountered just such a case among Parkinson's Disease patients receiving L-Dopa therapy. As the dosage of L-Dopa was increased, the man's sex drive accelerated until he became extremely nervous, restless, and unable to sleep.

Hypersexual behavior in patients taking L-Dopa has been reported by many other investigators. Markku T. Hyyppä of the University of Turku in Finland found that ten of forty-one patients (24 percent) told of "increased libido" after receiving L-Dopa and five of these patients (12 percent) had "strongly increased sexual activity." In similar studies, the incidence of hypersexuality has been as low as 1 percent, but it may be that some patients are too embarrassed to report their heightened sexual feelings.

The feeding of L-Dopa to laboratory rats has produced variable results. Some investigators, including Hyyppä, have reported that L-Dopa plus the enzyme inhibitor RO 4-4602 (which enhances the action of L-Dopa) decreases the sexual activity of male rats. Others, including Gessa and Tagliamonte of the University of Cagliari in Italy, have found that L-Dopa and RO 4-4602 "markedly increase" the sexual activity of male rats.

One explanation for the inconsistency of these findings

may be that the aphrodisiac effect of L-Dopa has occurred in sexually sluggish animals, while the inhibitory effect has occurred in sexually vigorous animals. Certainly, the hypersexual behavior noted in Parkinson's patients receiving L-Dopa occurred in a sexually depressed population. These findings suggest that L-Dopa has potential in reawakening the sexual appetite of sexually depressed individuals, but has little stimulatory effect in sexually vigorous individuals.

Since L-Dopa has been shown to increase the mean life span of mice (see p. 155), its apparent aphrodisiac effect in humans and in rats may be a consequence of a more generalized rejuvenation effect. Another finding that suggests this possibility is the occurrence of vaginal bleeding in three postmenopausal women, whose average age was sixty-three, after treatment with L-Dopa, as reported by Hyyppä. Similar findings in aging rats suggest a possible return of reproductive capacity.

Sidney K. Shapiro, 1218 Medical Arts Building, Minneapolis, Mn. 55402

Markku T. Hyyppä, Department of Neurology, University of Turku, SF-20520, Turku, 52, Finland

G. L. Gessa, Department of Pharmacology, Cagliari University School of Medicine, Cagliari, Sardinia, Italy

Studying the Effects of L-Dopa on Human Sexuality
The stories of hypersexual behavior in patients taking L-Dopa for Parkinson's Disease led Angrist and Gershon of New York University to study the effects of the drug on human sexuality. They administered high doses of L-Dopa to two groups of psychiatric patients: ten suffering from schizophrenia, and six from other disorders.

Sexual effects were reported in four of the ten schizophrenics. Two male patients had sexual delusions that were expressed more intensely and graphically after they received L-Dopa. One claimed he had been made impotent when a physician had performed a rectal examination during his adolescence. The other complained of disturbances of the head and spine, which he felt had been caused by attempts at autofellatio (oral stimulation of his own penis) in the past.

One female patient displayed a dose-related increase in agitation caused by delusions of sexual advances by male patients on the ward. Another female patient, who had been preoccupied with sex in the past, became "spectacularly" seductive and hypersexual on L-Dopa. On a dose of 5 grams a day, she stripped, ripped her pajamas bizarrely, and attempted to seduce any male she came close to.

Among the six males in the nonschizophrenic group, sexual effects were reported in three patients. One had unexpected erections at unusual times, such as while playing Ping-Pong with a nurse. Another reported the return of erections for the first time in several years. The third, a twenty-six-year-old homosexual, who had been somewhat hypersexual before receiving L-Dopa, began masturbating compulsively at the rate of four to five times daily instead of his usual four to five times a week.

Samuel Gershon, Department of Psychiatry, Neuropsychopharmacology Research Unit, New York University School of Medicine, New York, N.Y. 10016

Amphetamine Alters Sexual Behavior

While studying the effects of amphetamine—a central nervous system stimulant—on psychotic behavior, Angrist and Gershon of New York University noted unusual sexual behavior in three of nine chronic abusers of the drug.

One male patient felt increased sexual tension, which

led to compulsive masturbation whenever he received amphetamine. Another male patient became preoccupied and expressed guilt about his past homosexual experiences. On another occasion, he accused a male patient of making sexual advances toward him (which the other patient denied) and said he felt "like killing him."

The one female patient in the group began to display seductive behavior and "propositioned" the investigator.

Burton Angrist, Department of Psychiatry, Neuropsychopharmacology Research Unit, New York University School of Medicine, New York, N.Y. 10016

Drug-Induced Hypersexuality in Rats

If humans had been involved, it would have been a front-page story. As it was, the scientists watched in awe as male rats exposed to receptive females turned into perpetual sex machines. Hour after hour, the frenzied animals engaged in a spectacular orgy. When a female wasn't available, the supercharged males would feverishly mount each other, or anything that resembled another rat. The orgy finally climaxed with all the animals trying to mount each other at the same time.

This extraordinary event took place in the late 1960s at the National Heart Institute where Alessandro and Paola Tagliamonte and Gian L. Gessa were exploring the origins of sexual behavior. They found that a combination of the drugs PCPA (parachlorophenylalanine), which depletes the concentration of serotonin in the brain, and pargylene, which inhibits the enzyme monoamine oxidase (MAO), induced compulsive sexual behavior in male rats.

Other groups have produced similar findings in male mice, male and female cats, and female monkeys. Sexual stimulation also has been generated in animals by a combination of PCPA and the male sex hormone testosterone, which plays a key role in producing sex drive in both males and females.

After returning to Italy, Gessa and Tagliamonte proposed that male sexual behavior "is reciprocally controlled by a central serotinergic inhibitory and dopaminergic stimulatory mechanism." According to this theory, sexual behavior in the male is inhibited by brain serotonin and stimulated by brain dopamine. Thus, any treatment that either decreases scrotonin (as PCPA does) or increases dopamine (as L-Dopa does) should be a potential aphrodisiac.

Alessandro Tagliamonte, Department of Pharmacology, Cagliari University School of Medicine, Cagliari, Sardinia, Italy

Reproductive Hormone Boosts Sexuality in Rats

Sexuality in both male and female rats depends upon the activity of the reproductive hormones. Removal of the testes or ovaries stops all sexual behavior in these animals. In order to study the mechanism responsible for sexual activity in the rat, Robert L. Moss of Southwestern Medical School in Dallas examined the sexual effects of all known hormones involved in the reproductive cycle on castrated and intact rats of both sexes.

He found that LHRH (luteinizing hormone releasing hormone)—the hypothalamic factor that triggers the reproductive cycle—increased and intensified sexual activity in all groups tested. The effect was inconsistent in response to LHRH alone, but was quite potent when LHRH was administered after a priming dose of estrone in females or testosterone in males. The best and most consistent sexual response occurred three to four hours after treatment and lasted for about eight hours.

Robert L. Moss, Department of Physiology, University of Texas Health Science Center at Dallas, Southwestern Medical School, Dallas, Tx. 75235

Drug Treatment of Impotence

Impotence occurs with increasing frequency in men as they grow older. In most cases, it is triggered by a fear reaction to normal physiologic changes of aging. A man may become apprehensive because his ability to achieve and maintain an erection has declined. Before long, he finds that he cannot get an erection at all. The more he worries about his lack of potency, the less likely he is to regain it.

There are also men whose sex life is prematurely curtailed because of physical reasons. For example, diabetics become increasingly prone to impotence as they grow older.

Recent discoveries that sexual behavior may be controlled by alterations in neurotransmitter levels in the brain have opened new vistas in the treatment of impotence. As a result, clinical trials have been instituted with several neurohormones.

Of particular interest is the effect of PCPA—which has proved to be a potent sex stimulant in animals—on humans suffering from impotence. O. Benkert of Munich, Germany, has found that PCPA, at a dosage of 1 gram per day, has little or no therapeutic effect compared to placebo. Benkert feels that a higher dosage of PCPA might be more effective in recharging flagging sexual appetites, but has yet to test this hypothesis because of the side effects of the drug, which include mental dullness, headache, and vertigo.

PCPA and Testosterone Therapy

Headache sufferers invariably experience depressed sexual function. In an effort to improve the sexual functioning of headache sufferers, Federigo Sicuteri of Florence, Italy, gave sixteen male patients, age forty to sixty-five, a daily dose of 15 mg/kg of PCPA (orally) and 350 μg/kg of testosterone propionate (injected intramuscularly). He found a "highly significant increase in the number of erections . . . with a lively accompaniment of sexual fantasy" when compared to patients receiving PCPA and placebo or placebo alone. He also found a "striking improvement in psychologic condition" among patients receiving PCPA and testosterone, who appeared "more lively, sociable, and younger" than controls.

Sicuteri speculates that the action of PCPA in lowering the concentration of serotonin in the brain "sensitizes central structures involved in sexual stimulation," which allows testosterone (which is usually ineffective when given alone) to trigger dormant sexual nerve pathways. Acknowledging the problem of the side effects of PCPA, he suggests that new, less toxic serotonin inhibitors might provide better therapy for sexually inadequate patients.

TRH and LHRH

Benkert has been experimenting with two hormones from the hypothalamus region of the brain—TRH (thyrotropin-releasing hormone), which is involved in thyroid function, and LHRH, which is involved in reproductive function. He has found no beneficial effect of TRH over placebo, but some benefit from LHRH, particularly during the period following its use.

Benkert studied six sexually impotent patients in a double-blind trial of LHRH given as a nasal spray. All six patients received placebo spray for two weeks; then three patients received LHRH spray (1 mg/day) for four weeks, and the other three received placebo spray for the same period. Finally, the entire group was given placebo spray for two weeks. Afterwards, the patients filled out questionnaires for two months.

The results showed that one patient who received LHRH experienced a significant increase in penile erections that continued after the treatment period. The second patient in the LHRH group experienced a strong increase in penile erections after changing from LHRH to placebo spray. The third LHRH patient reported an unpleasant sensation in his

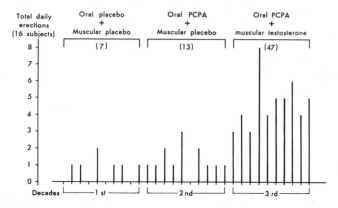

Aphrodisiac effect of oral parachlorophenylalanine (PCPA) and muscular testosterone as indicated by the number of erections during the third decade (ten-day period) of testing.

genitals and emission of semen during urination while on LHRH, but experienced an increase in penile erections after discontinuing the drug.

O. Benkert, Psychiatrische Klinik der Universität München, Munich, Germany

Federigo Sicuteri, Department of Clinical Pharmacology, University of Florence, Florence, Italy

An Aphrodisiac for Women?

As the male orderly entered the hospital room, he saw two female patients making love on a bed. They were kissing and petting frantically, as if in the grip of some mysterious force. After a few voyeuristic moments, he turned to leave, only to feel the hot breath of one of the women, who had left her partner and lunged at him. She pinned him to the wall and began to grind her half-naked body against him. He wrenched free and ran down the hall screaming.

This scene reportedly occurred at the Clarke Institute of Psychiatry in Toronto, where seven schizophrenic women were receiving a new therapeutic regimen including the amino acid tryptophan, an enzyme (monoamine oxidase) inhibitor, and selected psychotropic drugs. Five of the seven women showed a significant increase in sexual activity and three displayed highly exaggerated behavior, such as gro-tesque sexual posturing, sexual assaults on male attendants and female nurses, and overt homosexual acts among them-selves.

The results of the study, conducted by Doust and Huszka, contradict most other studies on neurotropic sex stimulation. Tryptophan is a direct precursor of serotonin and its use leads to an accumulation of serotonin in the brain. A reduc-tion in brain serotonin is believed to be a key factor in trig-gering sexual response. That tryptophan therapy should lead to an aphrodisiac effect suggests that the control of human sexual behavior involves complex mechanisms that respond differently to varying conditions.

John W. Lovett Doust, Clarke Institute of Psychiatry, 250 College St., Toronto, 2B, Ontario, Canada

. . . And Men Too?

It looks as if women are not alone in their susceptibility to the aphrodisiac effects of tryptophan. A recent report from England by Egan and Hammad describes exaggerated sexual behavior in five male patients, aged nineteen to thirty-two, who were given L-tryptophan. All five patients were suffering from depression when put on the tryptophan regimen.

One of them, aged twenty-two, became so agitated on tryptophan that he was taken off the drug after a week. The other three young men showed considerable improvement after one to two weeks of treatment, but with remarkable "sexual disinhibition."

At first, they talked about sex incessantly and made un-characteristically overt sexual overtures to women patients. Soon they were frequently reaching out to touch various parts of the female patients' bodies, as if compelled to do so. When the dosage of tryptophan was reduced, they were able to control their sexual behavior.

The fifth subject, a seventy-one-year-old man, behaved in a similar fashion after receiving tryptophan, except that he wasn't hospitalized at the time. His sudden preoccupation with sex startled everyone around him and he was soon admitted to a psychiatric hospital after "indecently" assaulting a woman.

The vast majority of reports concerning patients given tryptophan make no mention of sexual side effects of any kind. One report from England mentions more than 500 patients treated with L-tryptophan, without a single apparent case of hypersexuality.

Two things stand out when analyzing the instances of hypersexuality among patients receiving tryptophan. First is the fact that most of them were being treated for schizophrenia complicated by depression at the time of their sexual seizures. Since disturbances in neuroendocrine activity have been implicated in the genesis of schizophrenia, it's possible that such individuals are uniquely primed to react sexually to tryptophan.

Second is the fact that ten of the eleven patients who exhibited hypersexual behavior after receiving tryptophan were also on psychotropic drugs—a finding that suggests some type of drug interaction effect as being responsible for their subsequent behavior. At least one of these drugs, chlorpromazine, has been shown to have potential as an anti-aging agent. (See p. 276.)

One investigator, Ian Oswald of Royal Edinburgh Hospital in Scotland, reports "lewd and libidinous" behavior in individuals under psychiatric care, after taking either oral tryptophan or intravenous 5-hydroxytryptophan (a by-product of tryptophan metabolism). He even mentions the case of a dog who got spontaneous orgasms after receiving tryptophan.

George P. Egan, Liverpool Psychiatric Day Hospital, Liverpool, England

Alan D. Broadhurst, West Suffolk Hospital, Bury St. Edmunds, England

Ian Oswald, University Department of Psychiatry, Royal Edinburgh Hospital, Edinburgh, Scotland

Electrical Sex Stimulation

The brain is our primary sex organ. Sex drive originates in the brain and sexual pleasure is expressed through circuits that feed directly into it. One approach to the problem of sexual dysfunction is direct stimulation of the areas of the brain that control sexual function.

For the past two decades, scientists have demonstrated that electrical stimulation of the brain (ESB) through implanted electrodes can provoke specific sexual responses in laboratory animals. Through trial and error, they've traced the primary locus of sexual control to the medial preoptic area of the anterior hypothalamus.

In a recent experiment, Merari and Ginton of Tel Aviv University in Israel implanted twenty-two electrodes throughout this section of the brain in twenty-two male rats. They found that electrical stimulation through five of these electrodes induced "highly exaggerated" sexual behavior including a "great increase" in the frequency of intercourse and ejaculation.

In some animals, they noted that the number of ejaculations "markedly exceeded the normal figure which can be obtained by a rat before being exhausted." In order to accommodate the sexual needs of these animals, the Israeli scientists had to provide four or five females for each male.

Such an exaggerated sexual response could only be provoked by electrodes placed in "a small preoptic region [of the brain] less than 1 millimeter lateral to the midline." Interestingly, they also found that highly aggressive behavior could be induced by stimulation of electrodes adjacent to and sometimes overlapping those inducing sexual stimulation.

Ariel Merari, Department of Physiology, Tel Aviv University, Tel Aviv, Israel

Do Women Possess a Sex Scent?

In most of the animal kingdom, the female of the species releases a scent called a pheromone that lures the male into a sexual rendezvous. Until recently, there was little indication that primates possess such a scent, but now there is evidence that female rhesus monkeys secrete a pheromone-like substance.

The isolation of pheromones from rhesus monkeys was achieved by Richard P. Michael in England from a pool of vaginal washings obtained from three donor females. When this substance was applied to the sexual skin of four other females, each paired with a different male, there was an immediate, marked increase of sexual activity in all the males.

Before application of the sex scent, the four males made ten mounting attempts during 22 tests, with no ejaculations. After treatment, there were 213 mounting attempts during twenty-six tests, with fourteen ejaculations. In three of the pairs, the aphrodisiac effect wore off as soon as the scent was removed; whereas in the fourth pair, the effect continued for a considerable period afterwards.

The dramatic increase in sexual activity occurred despite the fact that the females were unreceptive to intercourse and frequently refused the mounting attempts of the males. Even when the males were able to overcome this resistance, intromission was often difficult because of the atrophic state of the females' genital tracts. In one case, where the female could not be "persuaded" to engage in sexual activity, the male masturbated to ejaculation several times.

The sex scent isolated from the female monkeys was identified as a series of simple, short-chain aliphatic acids. Waltman and Tricomi of Cumberland Medical Center in Brooklyn have examined vaginal secretions from five women, aged twenty-six to sixty-nine, and found a combination of acids similar to those found in the rhesus monkey. They noted a striking decrease of one of these acids—butyric acid—in the vaginal secretions of two postmenopausal women.

It's possible that vaginal secretions can be used to produce an aphrodisiac scent that might induce the male of the human species to become as sexually active as his simian counterpart.

Richard P. Michael, Primate Behaviour Research Laboratories, Institute of Psychiatry, Bethem Royal Hospital, Beckenham, Kent, England

Richard Waltman, Department of Obstetrics and Gynecology, Brooklyn-Cumberland Medical Center, Brooklyn, N.Y. 11201

Chapter 11

Regeneration, Cloning, and Identity Reconstruction

Can We Regenerate Our Bodies?

If you slice a starfish into several pieces, each one will grow into an entire new starfish. Cut an earthworm in half and each part will develop into a new earthworm. Chop off the tail or limbs of a newt salamander and these appendages will grow back as good as new.

But go one step higher in the evolutionary chain—to the frog—and there is considerable loss of regenerative ability. And when it comes to humans, we find severe restraints on the ability to regenerate lost or damaged tissue.

When we cut ourselves, the skin grows back but not nearly as well as before. The scar tissue we form to bind our wounds is never as good as the original tissue. Though we can replace red and white blood cells, skin cells and, to some degree, liver cells, we're at a loss when it comes to growing back severed limbs or replacing lost brain cells.

Or are we? Recent evidence suggests that the capacity for regeneration lies dormant within each of our cells, and that we may soon be able to unleash the remarkable regenerative powers within us. Before examining this evidence, let's take a look at how regeneration occurs in the newt.

When the limb of a newt is cut off, the cells surrounding the amputation site are "driven back in time" to an earlier stage of development. They form a mound of undifferentiated cells called the blastema, which then grows into a functional duplicate of the original limb. This process, which is called epimorphosis, requires reversal and then acceleration of cellular events that occur in all organisms when they develop from embryos into adults.

The evidence that we can induce regeneration in our own bodies is as follows:

• All mammals, including humans, are believed to possess the capacity to regenerate appendages while they are still embryos. Regeneration of amputated limb buds has been demonstrated in rat embryos.

• Every cell in the human body is believed to retain the genetic information to develop into a duplicate organism, or clone. Cloning has been demonstrated in carrots and frogs, and has been claimed in humans.

• Partial limb regeneration has been induced in "non-regenerating" species through the use of transplanted nerve tissue, hormone therapy, and electrical stimulation.

These findings suggest that we have the innate ability to regenerate body parts and to repair damaged tissue caused by injury, disease, and aging.

Facts about Limb Regeneration

When a new limb is growing at the amputation site of a newt, nerve fibers pervade the wound and regenerating tissue. If these fibers are removed prior to amputation or during the regeneration process, the new limb will not develop. These facts were discovered in the 1940s by Marcus Singer of Case Western Reserve University. Since then, Singer has continued to explore the regeneration process with emphasis on the nerve or neurotrophic factor that triggers the process, and the nature of the response to the neurotrophic factor. His findings include the following:

• All nerve cells, including those in the brain, central nervous system (CNS), and sense organs, can supply the neurotrophic factor.

• The neurotrophic phenomenon is always centrifugal

in direction. It moves outward from the cell body toward the end of the nerve.

• There must be a minimum or threshold number of nerve fibers at the amputation surface for limb regeneration to occur. Below this threshold regeneration does not occur; above the threshold it always occurs, but the extent and speed of the process is not related to the number of fibers.

• Vertebrates who do not regenerate their limbs—such as the frog, lizard, and mouse—have many fewer nerve fibers per unit of amputation wound than does the newt. Consequently, their nerve supply is presumably inadequate to trigger the regeneration process.

• The effectiveness of an individual nerve cell in promoting regeneration is directly related to how much of its axon (transmitting end) is available at the amputation surface.

• The neurotrophic factor is believed to be chemical in nature, and is probably discharged directly from the axon into the wound and regenerating tissue.

• The neurotrophic factor may be composed largely of protein macromolecules—with its transmission possibly accelerated by cyclic AMP (adenosine 3'-5' monophosphate)—an important agent in energy metabolism.

• Extracts from newt brain tissue can be used to recharge a denervated amputation site, as measured by the rate of newly synthesized protein.

• Brain extracts from the frog (a nonregenerating species) are just as effective in recharging amputation sites in the newt as are extracts from the newt brain.

• Limb regeneration can be induced in the frog and lizard (both nonregenerating species) by surgically augmenting the nerve supply at the amputation site.

• The neurotrophic factor is probably not produced by nerve cells alone, but by all living cells in all species. Apparently, nerve cells produce much more of it than other cells.

These findings suggest that regeneration may be a universal biologic phenomenon, occurring to varying degrees in all species, including humans, and that its expression is controlled by forces amenable to manipulation.

Marcus Singer, Department of Anatomy, School of Medicine and Developmental Biology Center, Case Western Reserve University, Cleveland, Oh. 44106

Does Regeneration Prevent Cancer?

Cancer cells are immortal. If unchecked, they will continue to divide forever. When they seize control of the human body, normal cells become helpless in the face of their onslaught.

Regenerating cells also display rapid growth in the process of replacing lost tissue. Within hours, they go through a remarkable series of evolutionary steps.

The power that drives the regeneration process has been linked to three forces: a chemical factor within nerve cells, a bioelectric field of energy, and a hormonal control system.

Some scientists believe that the powerful life force of regeneration is capable of controlling the powerful death force of cancer.

One line of evidence that suggests this possibility is the fact that malignant tumors appear to be relatively rare in regenerating species.

A more provocative line of evidence involves attempts to produce cancer in regenerating species by the introduction of known chemical carcinogens. In one experiment, the injection of carcinogens produced malignant tumors in only two of 500 animals. Similar results were obtained when the carcinogen N-methyl-N-nitro-N-nitrosoguanidene (NG) was implanted within newt eyes from which the lens had been removed surgically. Not only was there no sign of cancer in any of the animals tested, but in ten of ninety-nine eyes, the lens regenerated from both the dorsal and ventral part of the iris, which is normally incapable of forming a lens.

When carcinogens were injected into the tail (which can regenerate) and the trunk (which cannot) of another amphibian, *Triturus cristatus*, the results varied considerably. Tumors appeared in 16 percent of the trunk-injected animals, but in only nine percent of those injected in the tail. Moreover, most of the trunk tumors proved to be lethal, whereas most of the tail tumors healed spontaneously.

Similarities Between Cancer Cells and Regenerating Cells

Similarities have been noted with regard to some of the changes that take place within the membranes of both cancer cells and regenerating cells. For example, new proteins (antigens) found on the surface of cancer cells are very much like those found on regenerating cells. Interestingly, similar proteins are found on fetal cells.

Another striking similarity between cancer cells and regenerating cells is the fact that negatively charged bioelectricity is associated with both these conditions. Cancerous tissue is generally negative in polarity compared to normal tissue and the regeneration process is characterized by a sudden changeover from positive to negative polarity. It's possible that disruption of bioelectric fields around cells may be a basic cause of cancer.

In their review of the cancer-related aspects of regeneration, Donaldson and Mason suggest that intensive study of the changes that take place within the membranes of both cancer cells and regenerating cells—as well as the bioelectric currents that surround them—could lead to a better understanding of both processes. If the regeneration process proves to be a potent cancer antagonist, then we may be able to develop therapies to keep us youthful, unscarred, and free from one of our most deadly diseases.

Donald J. Donaldson, Department of Anatomy, University

of Tennessee Center for the Health Sciences, Memphis, Tn. 38163

Regeneration in Rat Embryos
Before our cells become "fixed" in their lifelong roles as skin cells, bone cells, or muscle cells, they retain sufficient "versatility" for regeneration. The versatility of young mammalian cells has been demonstrated in rat embryos by Elizabeth M. Deuchar in England. Deuchar removed thirty-two embryos from pregnant rats 11.5 days after mating, and then amputated one forelimb bud of each embryo. The amputated embryos were allowed to continue developing in roller bottles for two days—the longest period they could be maintained in good health—and were then examined.

All but three of the embryos formed a new limb bud at the amputation site, eight of which showed completely normal development. There was some indication that the process by which the limb buds developed was similar to that observed in regenerating newts. Unfortunately, the limited survival time of the embryos did not permit her to determine if the new limb buds could grow into normal limbs.

Elizabeth M. Deuchar, Department of Biological Sciences, Hatherly Laboratories, University of Exeter, United Kingdom

Regeneration in Siamese-Twin Cockroaches
The link between regeneration and aging can be seen in the cockroach, an organism that possesses the ability to regenerate severed limbs in youth, but loses this ability in old age.

When Siamese-twin cockroaches were created through parabiosis by Dietrich Bodenstein of the Gerontology Research Center, the old roaches were able to recover their lost regenerative powers.

The recovery was attributed to the transfer of juvenile hormone (see p. 52) from the young roach to its Siamese twin, but could have been the result of replenished neurotrophic factor in the cells of the old insect.

Perhaps the age-related loss of regenerative capacity plays some role in the expression of aging in all organisms including humans. An appropriate experiment would be to explore the effects of parabiosis between old and young rats on wound-healing and nerve cell activity in both partners. The increased longevity of old rat parabionts (see p. 76) may be related to improved regenerative capacity in these animals.

Dietrich Bodenstein, Gerontology Research Center, National Institute on Aging, Baltimore City Hospitals, Baltimore, Md. 21224

Inducing Regeneration in the Newborn Opossum

Mammals cannot regenerate whole body parts. Once their cells become programmed for specific tasks, they lose the ability to repair major structural damage. No fully developed mammal can regrow an amputated limb, for example.

It may be that the lack of regenerative ability in mammals is due to the relative lack of nerve tissue at the amputation site. Marcus Singer and others have induced partial limb regeneration in such nonregenerating species as the frog and lizard by transplanting nerve tissue to the amputated area.

Accordingly, Merle Mizell of Tulane University sought to discover if limb regeneration could be induced in a mammalian species. He chose the opossum as his experimental model for two reasons: The opossum (and other marsupials) is born at an early stage of development, before its cells are fully programmed; during the first week of life, the opossum's immune system is inoperative, permitting transplants without rejection problems.

Mizell first cut off the forelimbs of newborn opossums and

noted a minimal regenerative response. He observed a somewhat better response when he cut off the opossums' hindlimbs, which are less developed than the forelimbs. In one animal, a reasonable facsimile of a limb developed, with rudimentary digit-like protuberances.

Mizell then cut off the hindlimbs of newborn opossums still clinging to their mother's pouch, after implanting cerebral brain tissue from young animals into their limbs. When tissue from the forebrain of tadpoles was used, there was a positive regenerative response in three of fourteen cases, which surpassed the response from simple amputation, but was still incomplete.

But when he used opossum brain tissue, there was a positive response in eight of thirty cases that approached full-fledged regeneration. After eighteen days of regrowth, a recognizable foot-like structure emerged from the amputation site and, during the next twenty days, it acquired many of the characteristics of a fully developed foot including three toes.

Mizell's manipulation of the regenerative response in the opossum suggests that mammalian cells may possess the innate ability to regenerate entire limbs.

Merle Mizell, Department of Biology, Tulane University, New Orleans, La. 70118

Electrically Stimulated Limb Regeneration

Imagine a small computerized device that regulates the bioelectric healing system in your body. Anytime you suffer serious physical damage—by cutting yourself, in an automobile accident, or from the bullet of a gun—the device is applied to the wound to induce perfect healing. No scar tissue. No plastic surgery. No dismemberment. No death from trauma.

Sound incredible? Not if you accept the ideas of Robert O. Becker of the Veterans Administration Hospital in Syracuse, New York, who believes that electronic regeneration therapy has virtually unlimited potential. Nor if you consider the limb-regeneration experiments of Becker and others.

These scientists have discovered a "current of injury" that stimulates cells to regrow and heal the injury. In a regenerating species such as the newt, an injury generates a positive charge of about 20 millivolts (thousandths of a volt), which soon switches to a negative polarity and gradually declines to zero when regeneration is complete. In a nonregenerating species such as the frog, there also is an initial positive charge of 20 millivolts that declines to zero, but without ever changing to negative polarity.

In 1967, Stephen Smith induced partial limb regeneration in the frog by implanting a piece of silver wire soldered to a piece of platinum wire, which served as a crude battery in the frog's tissue fluid. In this fashion, he was able to generate a low negative current that triggered a regenerative response.

In a later study, Becker implanted a modified version of Smith's device with an electrical resistor into the amputated stumps of twenty-one-day-old rats. He achieved varying degrees of regeneration with a medium current, but his best result occurred in an animal that received a current of 8 nanoamperes at 100 millivolts with a 10 megohm (million ohms) resistor. The animal regenerated its missing upper limb down to the elbow joint, including regrowth of muscle, nerve, bone, and blood vessels.

In 1973, Smith implanted battery-operated devices into amputated frog stumps. His best results were obtained when the device was implanted in the area (dorsal-postaxial) from which the original limb had grown. Of twenty-one surviving animals, all demonstrated some degree of regeneration. One animal achieved perfect regeneration of its severed limb, which soon became indistinguishable from a normal limb.

Robert O. Becker, Department of Orthopedic Surgery, Veterans Administration Hospital, Irving Avenue and University Place, Syracuse, N.Y. 13210

Stephen D. Smith, Department of Anatomy, University of Kentucky College of Medicine, Lexington, Ky. 40506

Boosting Our Healing Ability

In 1973, a forty-five-year-old man came to the Veterans Administration Hospital in Syracuse, New York, with an ankle fracture that had failed to heal, despite two years of therapy and two operations. Instead of having the leg amputated, the man became the first patient to receive a wound-healing therapy developed after sixteen years of animal research by Robert O. Becker.

First Becker implanted a silver wire electrode into the patient's ankle. A battery-powered device was used to deliver a constant, very low electrical current into the ankle of from 300 to 400 nanoamperes (billionths of an ampere) at 0.2 to 0.8 volts. After two months, X-rays showed that the bone had begun to heal. The electrode was removed and, after another month, the patient was able to walk without pain. X-rays showed that the fracture had healed completely. Four months after the start of the treatment, Becker removed a piece of anklebone and found it to be entirely normal.

Becker believes bioelectric forces trigger the regenerative process and that these forces can be augmented to improve wound-healing in humans and, eventually, to induce the regeneration of whole body parts.

Electrotherapy to improve bone-healing in humans is now being evaluated in the Syracuse V.A. Hospital, as well as in several other institutions in the U.S. and Europe. Becker believes that organisms lose regenerative ability as they increase in complexity because more and more of their nerve tissue becomes concentrated in the brain, leaving less available for the rest of the body. As a result, the body is unable to generate the voltage needed for regeneration.

Robert O. Becker, Department of Orthopedic Surgery, Veterans Administration Hospital, Irving Avenue and University Place, Syracuse, N.Y. 13210

Regeneration and Aging

Recent findings suggest that manipulation of factors involved in regeneration could help to restore youthful strength and vigor. Of major interest is the fact that various hormones involved in aging have been implicated in the regeneration process.

Removal of the pituitary gland in newts prevents these animals from regenerating. A similar effect can be achieved by giving them somatostatin, a hypothalamic factor that blocks the release of growth hormone, prolactin, and insulin. Regeneration can be restored in newts without a pituitary by giving them prolactin. Interestingly, prolactin has also been linked to the occurrence of cancer in several species.

It's been demonstrated that several types of cells, including human lymphocytes (immune system cells), can be returned to an earlier stage in development by exposure to prolactin, electric current, or PHA (a plant lectin used to test immune response). It appears, therefore, that all mammalian cells may possess the ability to "go back in time" if they are provided with appropriate stimulation.

Another finding with clinical implications is the discovery by Robert O. Becker that adult salamanders can survive surgical removal of up to 50 percent of their ventricular myocardium (heart muscle). These animals were able to resume normal blood circulation within five hours of the operation and, within twenty-four hours, there was apparently total restoration of the missing heart muscle. According to Becker, the tissue repair observed in this experiment was "more rapid and competent than any previously reported."

Becker theorizes that a perineural cell network that surrounds active neurons in the brain may be the source of the transmission system that regulates the regeneration process. Control of such a system might make it possible to regenerate brain cells as well as body cells.

Robert O. Becker, Veterans Administration Hospital, Irving Avenue and University Place, Syracuse, N.Y. 13210

Regenerating Brain Cells

Swedish scientists have demonstrated that rat brain neurons display partial axonal regeneration after induced mechanical or chemical damage.

The axon is the long, fluid-filled cylindrical end of the neuron that transmits messages to other neurons, and transports nutrients and other essential substances to and from the cell body.

Regrowth of amputated axons was particularly extensive in neurons containing serotonin, in contrast to a "very feeble" regenerative response in catecholamine-containing neurons. Both types of neurons have been implicated in normal and pathologic aging.

Anders Björklund, Department of Histology, University of Lund, 5-223 62, Lund, Sweden

Nerve Growth Factor Spurs Brain Regeneration

Injections of nerve growth factor (NGF) into the adult rat brain "markedly stimulate" the growth of new axonal sprouts from damaged brain cells. Scientists at the University of Lund in Sweden have found that NGF accelerates or potentiates the regeneration of central catecholamine and indolamine neurons, and that these cells may depend upon NGF for growth and maintenance as well as for regrowth.

NGF is a highly potent peptide (protein) that bears a

resemblance to insulin. It has been found in mouse tumors and snake venom, but is most commonly derived from mouse salivary glands.

NGF may be (or may be related to) the neurotrophic factor postulated by Marcus Singer as the key to regeneration in all species. (See p. 335.) It has yet to be identified in the human nervous system, although there is circumstantial evidence that it exists in human neurons.

NGF has been given to children suffering from neuroblastoma—the most common extracranial solid malignancy of childhood—in an attempt to retard the spread of the disease, but there was no evidence of clinical improvement in these patients.

It's possible that NGF or a similar compound derived from humans might be helpful in treating age-related neurologic disorders such as Parkinson's Disease (see p. 250), or in reversing the neurologic decline of normal aging.

Anders Björklund, Department of Histology, University of Lund, 5-223 62, Lund, Sweden

William C. Mobley, Department of Neurobiology, Stanford University Medical School, Stanford, Ca. 94305

Cloning: A Substitute for Immortality

Reproduction is Nature's way of striving for immortality. The creation of each new generation ensures the continuation of the species, even if each individual is condemned to die.

One reason we have children is to get aboard the evolutionary bandwagon. By creating a child that carries a portion of our genetic heritage, we seek to perpetuate some part of our self, and in so doing contribute to the survival of the race. We become parents as a substitute for personal immortality.

The closest we can come to perpetuating our self—short

of actual immortality—is through cloning, the creation of a genetic duplicate.

The idea of cloning fascinates us so because it symbolizes the value of the individual. When we fantasize about duplicating Rembrandt, Einstein, or Marilyn Monroe, we do so in the knowledge that these figures were unique and irreplaceable. And if we cherish our own uniqueness, we may be interested in a "carbon copy" of *our* self.

Actually, the idea of replacing the self is still very much in the realm of science fiction, even if human cloning is right around the corner. A clone would be very different from the individual whose genetic material was used to create it, primarily because of their different backgrounds.

Cloning is just the first step in the reconstruction of individual identity. To create anything approaching a true duplicate of an individual, we'd have to fabricate the person's mind and personality, as well as his or her body.

How Cloning Is Accomplished

Cloning was first accomplished by F. C. Steward of Cornell University, who grew entire carrots from individual cells cultured in a coconut-milk mixture. Other plants were subsequently cloned by similar methods. Animal cloning was first accomplished in England by John B. Gurdon building upon the work of Thomas King and Robert Briggs in the United States.

Gurdon first destroyed the nucleus of an unfertilized frog egg cell with ultraviolet radiation. Next, he obtained intestinal epithelial cells from a tadpole and removed the nucleus from one of these cells by drawing it into a micropipette (thin tube). Then he transplanted the intestine-cell nucleus into the egg. Finally, he induced the transformed egg to develop into a genetic "twin" of the tadpole from which the nucleus had been obtained. Normal, fertile adult frog clones of both sexes were developed in this manner.

In his early experiments, Gurdon could produce cloned frogs only from young, relatively undifferentiated cells. Later on, he and others showed that the potential of intestinal or skin cell nuclei to grow into clones becomes restricted as the cells differentiate (become more specialized), but that the restrictions are reversible in a small number of cases. The cloning capacity of differentiated cells has been improved by adding spermine to the transplantation medium, and by altering the temperature at which the nuclear transplant is performed.

Cloning mammals has proved more difficult than cloning frogs because of the relatively small size of mammalian eggs compared to amphibian eggs. J. D. Bromhall of Oxford University has reported early cell division in unfertilized rabbit eggs into which he transplanted nuclei from embryonic female cells, but has not yet been able to develop a full-fledged rabbit clone.

Cell Fusion

One method that Bromhall used to perform nuclear transplants is cell fusion. With this technique, the cells are induced to give up their nuclei by spinning them in a centrifuge while they are in a solution containing the chemical cytochalasin B. The separated donor cell nuclei are then fused with enucleated egg cells by incubating them in a medium containing Sendai virus, which triggers the fusion process. Bromhall's best results were achieved when the donor nuclei and egg cells were "synchronized" (at the same stage of cell division).

Cell fusion has also been used to "reconstruct" mouse and human cells. In one experiment, Harris and Hayflick fused the nuclei and cytoplasms of human cells at various stages of cell division in tissue culture. They were able to demonstrate that the biologic "clock" that controls cellular "aging" —the number of divisions that cells will undergo in culture —is apparently located in the cell nucleus. (See p. 30.)

Several laboratories are currently trying to perfect cloning in mice. Procedures similar to cloning have already been achieved, and it's likely that mouse clones will be produced in the foreseeable future—an accomplishment that will pave the way for human cloning.

John B. Gurdon, MRC Laboratory of Molecular Biology, University Medical School, Hills Road, Cambridge, CB2 2QH, England

J. D. Bromhall, Department of Zoology, Oxford University, South Parks Road, Oxford OX1 3PS, England

Audrey L. Muggleton-Harris, Department of Biology, University of Massachusetts, Amherst, Ma. 01003

Variations on Cloning

When an egg is fertilized, its nucleus, which contains half the mother's chromosomes, gets together with the sperm nucleus, which contains half the father's chromosomes. They then proceed to form two pronuclei, one carrying the maternal chromosomes, the other the paternal chromosomes. Finally, they fuse together to form a new nucleus, the unique product of both sets of chromosomes.

Hoppe and Illmensee have produced mice with only one parent by removing either the male or female pronucleus from the fertilized egg and then inducing the remaining pronucleus to double its complement of chromosomes. After the egg developed into an early-stage embryo, they implanted it into the uterus of a surrogate mother, where it continued to develop.

In this fashion, seven live female mice were born—five of maternal origin and two of paternal origin, depending upon whether the female or male pronucleus was retained in the egg. Even the mice of paternal origin developed into females because the male embryos (with a Y/Y chromosome profile)

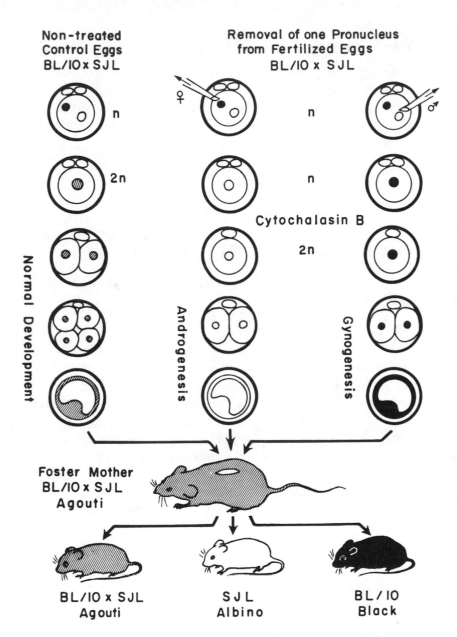

Experimental scheme for the production of homozygous-diploid mice derived from either the paternal or maternal genome. Removal of either the male or female pronucleus leads to the development of uniparental embryos which are implanted into a foster mother. The resulting "half-cloned" female mice can be of either maternal (SJL albino) or paternal (BL/10) origin. The development of nontreated control mice is shown in left column.

Foster mother *(top)* with her unusual "offspring" including *(from left to right)* a maternally derived black female, a paternally derived white female, and a normally derived littermate.

all died early in the developmental process. (Normal males have an X/Y chromosome profile.)

The mice produced by Hoppe and Illmensee differ from true clones because they carry only half their parent's chromosomes. They are called homozygous diploid uniparental mice, but a simpler term for them might be "half-clones."

In another variation on cloning, Jacek A. Modlinski used micromanipulation to transplant nuclei from embryonic cells into fertilized eggs whose own nucleus was retained. In a few cases, he was able to develop embryos with four parents to the blastocyst stage. Though Modlinski made no attempt to implant these embryos into surrogate mothers, Beatrice Mintz has created hundreds of healthy multi-parented mice by fusing entire embryos together.

Mintz has also produced identical mice by dissembling early-stage embryos into single cells and implanting each cell into surrogate mothers. The mice that were produced as a result of this procedure were clones of the original embryo, which had been fertilized in the normal manner.

Peter C. Hoppe, The Jackson Laboratory, Bar Harbor, Me. 04609

Jacek A. Modlinski, Department of Embryology, Institute of Zoology, University of Warsaw, Warsaw, Krokowskie Przed-micscie, 26/28, Poland

Beatrice Mintz, Institute for Cancer Research, Philadelphia, Pa. 19111

Is Human Cloning Possible?

In 1978, science writer David Rorvik announced he had taken part in the first human cloning. The event was chronicled in a book (*In His Image*) that describes a wealthy old businessman (Max) who bankrolled the project, and a scientist (Darwin) who created a clone of Max that was grown in the body of a young surrogate mother. The cloning was supposedly performed in a distant country under strict secrecy.

At this writing, very few people believe Rorvik's story because of his failure to provide evidence of the alleged cloning. All the participants in his "nonfiction" book are fictional characters, and no scientific details are presented. While Rorvik does provide information about cloning techniques, there is nothing in the book that couldn't have been obtained from existing scientific literature.

A Likely Possibility

However, there are few scientists who deny that human cloning is possible, and some who think it can be achieved in the near future. Certainly there's no mystery about *how* to clone a human being. Most of the technical problems have already been solved, including the successful implantation of a test-tube embryo into the uterus of a woman. (See p. 389.)

The one major problem that apparently remains is the delicate matter of transplanting the nucleus of the cell of the individual to be cloned into the enucleated egg cell. And even this feat may have been achieved by Landrum B. Shettles, a reproductive biologist who was dismissed in 1973 from Columbia University for attempting to perform test-tube fertilization for a Florida woman, Doris Del Zio.

Shettles' superior at Columbia, Raymond Vande Wiele, destroyed the embryonic tissue and was subsequently sued by Mrs. Del Zio and her husband John for thwarting their chance to bear a child. In a highly publicized trial, the Del Zios won a $50,000 judgment.

Now working in Randolph, Vermont, Shettles claims to have extracted the nucleus from a human egg and replaced it with the nucleus from a spermatogonium (an early sperm cell). According to Shettles, the transformed egg was then induced to undergo eight cell divisions to form the pre-embryonic cluster of cells that normally moves into the uterus to develop into an embryo.

Shettles says he terminated the experiment before he could determine if the embryo would actually develop into a clone of the individual who provided the donor cell. Such a determination could only be made by implanting it into a woman's uterus—an experiment that might be condemned as unethical in the absence of prior experiments in lower mammals.

Interestingly, Shettles is an old friend of Rorvik, with whom he once collaborated on a book about how to predetermine the sex of a child. Shettles is the only reproductive biologist who has given 100 percent backing to Rorvik's cloning story. "I'd bet my life on it," he said, when asked to comment on Rorvik's claim.

David Rorvik, c/o Future Presentations, 1000 Westmount, Los Angeles, Ca. 90060

Landrum B. Shettles, Department of Ob-Gyn, Gifford Memorial Hospital, Randolph, Vt. 05060

The Latest Advance in Cloning

In July, 1979, Karl Illmensee reported the first cloning of a mouse at the Fiftieth Anniversary Symposium of the Jackson Laboratory in Bar Harbor, Maine.

Illmensee removed the nucleus from the differentiated donor cell of a mouse embryo and implanted it into a recently fertilized egg cell. He then removed the male and female pronuclei from the egg cell, induced the egg (with its new donor nucleus) to develop into a new embryo, and then transplanted the embryo into a mouse foster mother. He used an enzyme test to indicate whether the embryo was the sole genetic product of the donor cell.

According to Illmensee, three genetically identical, healthy adult mice have been produced via this procedure. His next step will be to determine if nuclei from adult mouse cells have the capacity to develop into clones.

Karl Illmensee, University of Geneva, Geneva, Switzerland

Research Benefits of Cloning

Public reaction to cloning has generally reflected personal fears and fantasies. People have raised the spectre of totalitarian governments creating multiple "Hitlers" or armies of brainwashed "robots." Others have shown interest in cloning only celebrities such as Robert Redford or Linda Ronstadt. Still others have suggested that it might be "fun" to have a little clone around the house.

One reason for the public's failure to deal with anything beyond the melodramatic implications of cloning is the curious downplaying of the idea by the scientific community. Most scientists seem to regard cloning as a trivial achievement that has little value for science or for humanity. Yet, there are important reasons to favor the development of cloning, with profound implications for us all.

First is the fact that cloning is a highly effective method of genetic inbreeding. Producing large numbers of duplicate animals will enable us to learn a great deal about how genetics contributes to growth and maturation, the expression of various diseases, and the aging process.

Cloning provides an excellent model for the study of aging. At various ages, animals of the same genotype could be used to analyze changes of aging, as well as to evaluate therapies aimed at controlling the aging process. One issue that might be resolved through the use of cloning is whether lethal, time-dependent damage occurs in DNA, RNA, or cellular proteins with advancing age.

Spare-Part Clones

The creation of "decerebrated" spare-part clones has been suggested by Paul Segall of the University of California at Berkeley. Segall believes it may be possible to develop clones with normal, healthy bodies, but no consciousness and hence no identity of any kind, who could be placed into cryonic suspension as insurance against loss or degeneration of body parts.

The replacement of an ailing heart with the heart of a clone, for example, would present no rejection problems and would provide us with an organ ideally suited to our body—another young, healthy heart of "our own." If necessary, a spare-part clone could provide us with an entire new body, within which our brain could be transplanted.

The possibility of spare-part clones raises questions about the "rights" of clones and the advisability of creating such a "life" form in the first place. For one thing, it's possible that we will eventually develop spare parts that are comparable, or even better, than our own by artificial means. However, it may be a very long time before such alternatives can rival the performance of organs developed within the human body.

Paul Segall, Department of Physiology/Anatomy, University of California, Berkeley, Berkeley, Ca. 94720

Identity Reconstruction: The Ultimate Strategy for Survival

Suppose you had been placed into cryonic suspension under unfavorable conditions . . . your body damaged severely by primitive freezing methods and hours without oxygen . . . your brain a mere shell of its former self.

It is now late in the twenty-first century. There are highly advanced methods of repairing brain damage, but your case still appears hopeless. Not even the most optimistic scientist dares estimate how much longer it will take before you can be revived, or whether it will be possible to revive you at all.

But then a radical new approach is suggested. Instead of leaving you to an "infinity" of frozen solitude, an attempt will be made to reconstruct your identity—to replace your mind and personality as well as your body.

The first step is easy. A clone is produced from one of the cells you had preserved before your "death." As the clone develops into an embryo, a laser scanning device "reads" the structural patterns in the relatively undamaged portions of your brain. This information is relayed to a super computer that uses it to "deduce" the information that once existed in the more-damaged portions of your brain. The computer then creates a compositive picture of the original structure of your entire brain.

As soon as the embryonic clone becomes sufficiently mature, the information from your brain, as re-created by the computer, is slowly "fed" into the clone's brain by appropriate electronic stimulation of the afferent nerves leading to the brain. The clone continues to receive information about your past throughout its period of physical development, without ever becoming conscious.

Eventually, the clone develops into an adult human being that looks exactly like you and, if the computer has done its job well, has the identical memories, thinking ability, and emotional makeup that you had before you lost consciousness. Then the clone is awakened and you're alive again.

As you regain consciousness, you recall the last few days of your previous life . . . how you became progressively sicker and weaker . . . how the entire world seemed to be irretrievably slipping from your grasp . . . how the final plans were made to place you into cryonic suspension.

When your doctor explains how you were brought back to life, you say: "Great! My old body was no good to me anymore. Who needs it?" And you think about how wonderful it is to be alive again.

But are you *really* you? Or are you an imposter? A very good copy, but still not the real thing? What if the original you was still conscious? What if more than one copy of you had been made? Who are you? Who have you become? Are you still alive? Or are you dead?

Such questions are fascinating even if we never develop the ability to reconstruct an individual's mind and personality. As we learn more about consciousness and come closer to achieving physical immortality, the issue of personal identity will assume increasing importance in our lives.

Chapter 12

Can We Become Physically Immortal?

What Is the Maximum Human Life Span?

A common myth is that the maximum human life span—which appears to be slightly more than 100 years of age—is actually 150 or more. It began with biblical figures like Methuselah, who allegedly lived 969 years, and has been fostered by promoters pushing "anti-aging" diets or lifestyles.

The myth gained respectability in the early 1970s, when scientists, such as Alexander Leaf of Harvard University, reported that members of certain civilizations had lived far beyond the age of 100. The groups singled out for their "longevity" were the inhabitants of Abkhasia in Soviet Georgia, Kashmir's Hunza Land, and the village of Vilca-bamba in Ecuador.

All three civilizations consist of simple peasant types who live off the land in remote mountainous regions. They embody the concept of utopia as an ancient civilization isolated from the "corrupting" forces of modern life—a concept vividly depicted in James Hilton's novel *Lost Horizon*, which glorified the residents of the Himalayan community of Shangri-La.

The notion of the inhabitants of such remote civilizations attaining ages of 120 to 170, with little or no disease or disability, has become generally accepted. Everywhere, it seems, we see photographs of wrinkled "centenarians" climbing mountains, performing exotic folk dances, or celebrating the "joys" of old age. One company even sent a camera crew to Soviet Georgia to create a series of TV commercials showing the old folks consuming cups of yogurt in order to sell the "health benefits" of their product.

Avoiding Military Service

The only thing wrong with all this fuss is that it's all apparently untrue. No one has ever produced documentation that any one in Russia, Kashmir, Ecuador, or anyplace else has lived to the ripe old ages claimed in these stories. In most cases, there are no birth certificates or other written documents to authenticate the claims, while in other cases, there is clear evidence of fraud on the part of the oldsters.

According to Soviet gerontologist Zhores Medvedev, who now works at the National Institute for Medical Research in London, many men in the U.S.S.R. took the names of their fathers to avoid military service during World Wars I and II—a practice that was particularly popular in the Caucasus mountain region of Georgia. These claims were officially endorsed by the government when Joseph Stalin, himself a Georgian, took a personal interest in the centenarian reports as he grew older.

As local government officials promoted sensational claims of extreme old age to please Stalin, the local oldsters began to enjoy the attention they were getting. Years later, when investigators from the U.S. and other countries arrived, they were easy prey for the Georgians, who had been lying about their ages for decades.

A Pattern of Exaggeration

Recently, Mazess and Forman presented evidence debunking the myth of exceptional longevity in Vilcabamba. In cooperation with Ecuadorian scientists, they conducted a census of the village of Vilcabamba, including 850 of its 1,000 residents, and constructed family genealogies, that were matched against church and civil records.

Shirali-babe Muslimou of Barzava Village, Leriksky Region, Azerbaijan, Soviet Socialist Republic—who was alleged to be 168 years of age when he died.

The investigation showed that the average Vilcabamba "centenarian" was about eighty-six years of age, and that the oldest inhabitant in the village was only ninety-six. A pattern of exaggeration was uncovered, which usually began at age seventy and amounted to as much as twenty to forty years in some cases. Though they found more persons over age sixty (10.6 percent) in Vilcabamba than in the general population (7 percent), this was largely the result of the fact that younger persons had been leaving the village, rather than any apparent longevity factor.

According to the *Guinness Book of World Records*, the oldest person in history—for whom there is authentication—was Pierre Joubert, a Canadian who died at the age of 113 years, 124 days on November 16, 1814. Another Canadian, Mrs. Ellen Carroll, who died in 1943, was alleged to be 115 years of age, but this figure was never authenticated. Only sixteen persons, nine of whom have been authenticated, are listed as having lived to the age of 110.

A great deal of time, money, and effort has gone into the study of allegedly long-lived peoples in the hope of finding the "secrets" to good health and long life. The widespread belief in the extreme longevity of these people and the gullibility of scientists in accepting assertions to that effect indicate a strong, but misguided, desire for an extended life span. It's time we stopped searching for the "fountain of youth" and put our full weight behind biomedical life-extension research.

Zhores Medvedev, National Institute for Medical Research, Mill Hill, London, England

Richard B. Mazess, Department of Radiology (Medical Physics), University of Wisconsin Hospitals, Madison, Wi. 53706

Getting on the Longevity Express

According to recent studies, the maximum life span of our hominid ancestors increased rapidly over the last million years—reaching a peak rate of increase of fourteen years per 100,000 years about 100,000 years ago. (See p. 19.) At that point, the evolutionary drive for longevity seems to have been stalled, probably because of changes in our patterns of reproduction.

Now that we're getting the ball rolling again, it's important to point out that we're just carrying on a long and natural tradition. For the past 65 million years, there has been a progressive lengthening of maximum life span. What's remarkable is not that we're resuming the pattern, but that we're likely to compress millions of years of evolution into less than a century.

By deciphering the secrets of Nature, we are developing shorthand methods for evolutionary change. Within the next fifty to 100 years, we may be able to double the human life span—a feat that took about 3 million years the last time around, and far longer the time before that.

By getting on the longevity express, we're merely carrying out an evolutionary mandate that has been implicit in our genes since the dawn of biologic time.

Why Do We Live Twice as Long as Chimpanzees?

Human beings live about twice as long as chimpanzees. Yet there is remarkable similarity in the genetic structure of the two species. Why the great difference in life span between us and our simian relatives? How did longevity evolve in such related species?

George Sacher has calculated that longevity in mammals can be accounted for, in large part, by four variables:

• Brain size—which has a strong positive correlation with life span

• Body size—which is moderately correlated with life span

• Energy metabolism—which has a strong inverse correlation with life span (life span increases as metabolic rate decreases)

• Body temperature—which is positively correlated with life span

The finding that long-lived mammals tend to have a higher temperature than short-lived mammals appears to contradict the theory that lowering body temperature in mammals may extend life span. (See p. 160.) It may be that only "cold-blooded" animals can benefit from reduced body temperature, or that increased body temperature conveys a species advantage that does not hold for all individuals.

Two Similar Rodents of Varying Life Span

Sacher has been collaborating with Hart and Brash in a study of two similar rodents with significantly different maximum life spans—*Mus musculus*, the wild-type house mouse that lives about 1,200 days, and *Peromyscus leucopus*, the wild field mouse that lives about 3,000 days.

Sacher has found that the weight of liver, kidney, heart, and spleen in *Mus* is equal to or greater than in *Peromyscus*, despite the lower body weight of *Mus*. This finding may be related to the fact that the young *Mus* has a 33 percent higher metabolic rate than the young *Peromyscus*. On the other hand, the brain weight of *Peromyscus* is 1.6 times that of *Mus*.

Brash and Hart have found that the DNA excision repair rate in response to ultraviolet injury is 2.5 times greater in long-lived *Peromyscus* than in short-lived *Mus*. Recently, they found a slight age-dependent decrease in DNA damage in the livers of *Peromyscus* and *Mus*, with slightly less of a decrease in *Peromyscus* than in *Mus*. These data support the idea that DNA repair capability is a factor in determining the rate of aging in mammals.

An earlier study by Hart and Setlow showed that the DNA repair rate is almost twice as great in humans as in chimpanzees, which may be one of the reasons we live so much longer than chimps do.

George A. Sacher, Division of Biological and Medical Research, Argonne National Laboratory, Argonne, Il. 60439

Ronald W. Hart, Department of Radiology, Ohio State University, Columbus, Oh. 43210

The Future Evolution of Longevity

According to Richard Cutler of the Gerontology Research Center, the "rapid" increase in maximum life span over the past several million years was probably generated by relatively few genetic changes, with most occurring in critical

Variable	Unit	Mus musculus		Peromyscus leucopus	
		Male	Female	Male	Female
Expectation of life	day	563	647	1,451	1,388
Standard deviation	day	329	292	626	612
Maximum life span	day	1,200	1,250	3,000	2,850
Initial death rate, q_0	$(day)^{-1} \times 10^4$	1.26 (34%)	2.48 (43%)	1.08 (20%)	1.24 (14%)
Gompertz slope, α	$(day)^{-1} \times 10^3$	4.26 ± 0.37	3.45 ± 0.48	1.66 ± 0.14	1.64 ± 0.10
Doubling time, $0.693\alpha^{-1}$	day	163	201	418	426
Number of complete lives	–	192	160	166	159

In addition to the complete lives, survival information was obtained from fractional lives of animals removed from the populations for experimental uses. Expectation of life is calculated from birth, but excludes animals that died before weaning. The parameters q_0 and α were estimated from least square linear regression of logarithm of age-specific death rate log q_x on age x (Eq. 3). The factor in parentheses after the q_0 value is the percentage error variation. The slope coefficient α is given with its standard error. Life table programs were written by S. A. Tyler, Argonne National Laboratory.

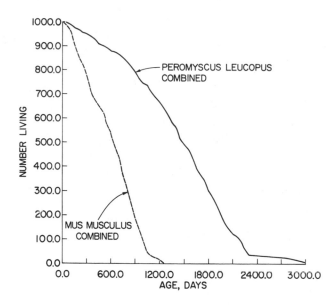

Differences in life span and other parameters for captive populations of *Mus musculus* (the house mouse) and *Peromyscus leucopus* (the white-footed mouse).

regulatory systems. These changes, he believes, served to counteract a few primary aging processes.

Cutler's current research strategy is aimed at identifying the primary aging processes, and developing treatments to control their expression. His first target area is chromatin, the complex of nucleic acids and proteins that comprises the genetic apparatus of the cell.

As possible antidotes to aging chromatin, Cutler suggests increasing the concentration of chromatin repair enzymes, free radical scavengers, antioxidants, and proteolytic enzymes that selectively remove abnormal proteins.

Another means of increasing life span, suggests Cutler, might be to slow down our rate of development. Such changes apparently occurred during the evolution of longevity, as evidenced by the fact that the rate of developmental change in animals tends to be proportional to their characteristic rates of aging. Developmental changes also appear to be responsible for the increase in maximum life span achieved in rodents by dietary manipulation. (See p. 60.)

The 200-Year-Old Human

Cutler envisions the future evolution of longevity in terms of a proportional increase in every stage of life. Thus, a human being with a maximum life span of 200 years might take forty years to develop into a fully grown adult, would enjoy about 110 years of good health and vigor, and experience about a fifty-year period of senescence.

Cutler's version of the 200-year-old human includes a doubling of brain size without a concomitant increase in body weight. Such an individual might look much like a six-year-old looks today in terms of body/brain proportion, but would be sexually mature and fully grown.

Richard G. Cutler, Gerontology Research Center, National Institute on Aging, Baltimore City Hospitals, Baltimore, Md. 21224

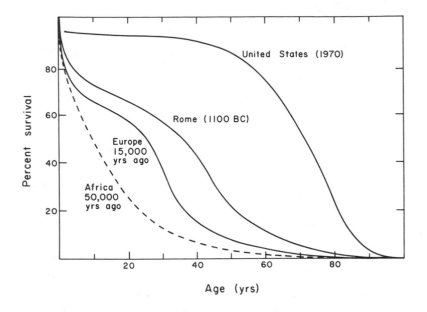

Changes in human survival in the past 50,000 years. During this period there has been little or no change in maximum life span, although there have been major increases in mean life span.

The Value of Longitudinal Aging Studies

The best way to study aging is by following individuals—at frequent intervals—throughout their lives. The resulting biologic, medical, and psychologic profiles of these individuals can provide a wealth of accurate information about the aging process, and differences in the rate of aging among individuals. This type of study is called a longitudinal study.

A one-time investigation of persons of different ages—or cross-sectional study—is fraught with methodologic pitfalls. The findings of such studies are inevitably "contaminated" by hereditary and environmental differences among the various generations studied. Some of the factors that distort cross-sectional data are selective mortality and morbidity caused by differences in genetic makeup, medical care, economic conditions, and lifestyle.

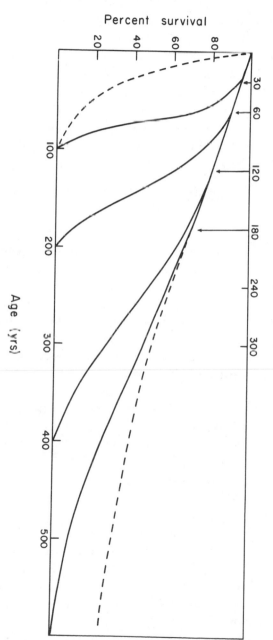

Survival curves in the past, present, and possible future. Dotted lines represent exponential decline curves with the smallest fraction of senescent individuals. The first dotted curve, with a maximum life span potential of 100 years, occurred about 10,000 years ago; the second curve represents an infinite life span potential.

Longitudinal-study populations are also needed to assess the effects of drug, nutritional, and exercise therapies on aging and resistance to disease. If we have extensive documentation on the changes of aging within a population, we can better evaluate the effects of new therapies.

At present, there are only a handful of ongoing longitudinal aging studies. These studies should be expanded and exploited to their full potential. But even more to the point is the desirability of measuring aging changes in *all* individuals from the time of birth. Such data would be invaluable in developing anti-aging regimens tailored to each individual.

The Baltimore Longitudinal Aging Study

When subjects in the Baltimore Longitudinal Aging Study come to the Gerontology Research Center for one of their regular visits, they stay there for 2½ days and 2 nights. During this period, they undergo an extensive battery of physiologic, biochemical, and psychologic tests, and are interviewed in depth about diet, physical activity, sexual habits, and other aspects of their behavior.

Such visits take place at two-year intervals if subjects are under sixty, at eighteen-month intervals if they are between sixty and sixty-nine, and annually if they are seventy or older. All subjects must be in essentially good health when entering the study, which began in 1958 with 650 active, community-dwelling male volunteers, ranging in age from their early twenties to their mid-nineties. The size of the study population has remained relatively constant over the years, as replacements have been recruited for those dropping out because of poor health or change of residence.

In 1978, a program to recruit women subjects was started, with initial efforts aimed at the wives, children, and other relatives of the male subjects. Inclusion of women in the study population will produce data that should provide insight into the differences between aging in males and fe-

Further retardation of development and fetalization of characteristics as a model for the future evolution of man

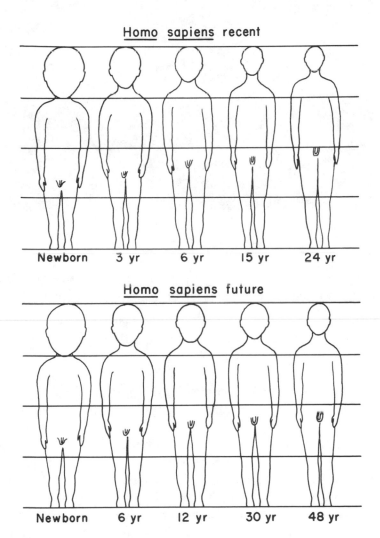

Homo sapiens recent

| Newborn | 3 yr | 6 yr | 15 yr | 24 yr |

Homo sapiens future

| Newborn | 6 yr | 12 yr | 30 yr | 48 yr |

The proportional changes in body and brain size in man during postnatal development, and how these changes might appear in a man whose maximum life span potential had evolved to 200 years.

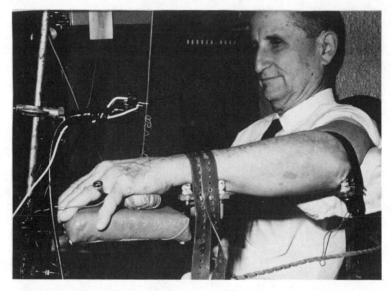
A volunteer in the Baltimore Longitudinal Aging Study is tested to measure sensory and motor nerve conduction velocities.

males, particularly with regard to the eight- to nine-year life span advantage that women currently enjoy over men.

Baltimore Longitudinal Aging Study, Gerontology Research Center, National Institute on Aging, Baltimore City Hospitals, Baltimore, Md. 21224

The Duke Longitudinal Aging Study
The first multidisciplinary longitudinal aging study in the U.S. was started in 1955 at the Duke Center for the Study of Aging and Human Development. The first part of the study included 256 healthy, noninstitutionalized men and women volunteers, sixty to ninety years of age, from the Durham, North Carolina, area. In the second part of the study, which was started in 1968, 502 men and women, aged forty-six to seventy, were chosen at random from the ranks of the local health insurance association.

The Duke-study subjects return every two years or so for a two-day series of intensive tests and examinations. Each subject is coded for approximately 788 pieces of information, of which 336 are medical; 109, psychiatric or neurologic; 109, psychologic; and 234, sociologic. The study is primarily concerned with medical, behavioral, and social factors, and places little emphasis upon physiologic and biologic aging. Its design is particularly suited for the evaluation of mental function in the aged.

Duke Longitudinal Aging Study, Duke University Medical Center, Durham, N.C. 27710

The Boston Normative Aging Study

Since 1963, more than 2,000 male veterans have been examined every five years at the Veterans Administration Outpatient Clinic in Boston, as part of a longitudinal study of aging. The subjects were recruited on a volunteer basis and screened for an initial state of good health. All socioeconomic and ethnic groups in the Boston area were included, but blue collar workers and blacks were underrepresented, despite special efforts to attract members of these groups.

A major objective of the Boston Normative Aging Study is to develop methods of determining functional age—the actual physical and mental condition a person is in, or perceived to be in, regardless of chronologic age.

In a related project, Rose and Bell of the Boston Normative study team have been trying to devise methods of predicting longevity. By studying death certificates and interviewing survivors of the deceased, they have compiled a list of 222 variables, which they believe to be predictive of life expectancy.

Boston Normative Aging Study, Veterans Administration Outpatient Clinic, Boston, Ma. 02130

The U.S.S.R. Institute of Gerontology

The U.S.S.R. Institute of Gerontology—located in the Ukrainian capital city of Kiev—includes a geriatric hospital

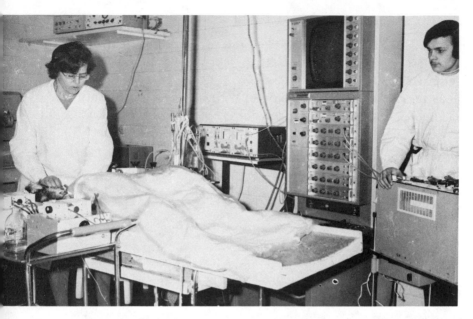

One of the rooms of the Laboratory of Physiology at the U.S.S.R. Institute of Gerontology in Kiev.

where old persons with medical problems are treated, with facilities for the study of normal aging in healthy subjects, and a separate complex of laboratories for animal research.

The institute was set up in 1958 by the Presidium of the Academy of Medical Sciences of the U.S.S.R. It includes the Department of Clinical Gerontology and Geriatrics, which is concerned with the study of aging and treatment of the diseases of aging. One of the primary responsibilities of this department is the evaluation of new therapies for the treatment of premature aging. (See p. 238.)

Basic aging research is conducted at the institute's Department of Experimental Gerontology and Geriatrics, which is primarily concerned with the study of the mechanisms of aging.

The Department of Gerohygiene deals with the social, hygienic, and geographic factors that influence the health, activities, and life span of older persons.

Institute of Gerontology, AMS U.S.S.R., Academy of Medical Sciences, Vyshgorodskaya 67, 252655, Kiev-114, U.S.S.R.

The American Aging Association (AGE)

AGE is a national lay-scientific health organization patterned after the American Heart Association. It was started by Denham Harman of the University of Nebraska to support biomedical aging research, and to find practical means of increasing our span of healthy productive life.

Members receive *AGE News* four times a year. AGE also publishes a quarterly journal devoted to biomedical aging research. Every year, AGE sponsors a scientific meeting that features a full-day symposium on some problem of concern to older individuals. Raven Press has published each of these symposiums to date.

American Aging Association, University of Nebraska Medical Center, 42 and Dewey Ave., Omaha, Ne. 68105

The Orentreich Foundation for the Advancement of Science

When Truman Capote was asked by Johnny Carson to select a small group of people with whom he might want to live on a desert island, the first name that came from his lips was Norman Orentreich, the New York physician who originated the hair transplant operation.

Orentreich has maintained a significant, long-term aging research program financed entirely from private sources for the past seventeen years. His foundation is supported by more than 200 benefactors including prominent socialites, MDs, pharmaceutical firms, and other foundations. (See p. 254.)

Orentreich Foundation for the Advancement of Science, 910 Fifth Ave., New York, N.Y. 10021

The Linus Pauling Institute of Science and Medicine

Linus Pauling is the most prominent advocate of the "health benefits" of high vitamin C intake (see p. 142) which is the subject of much of the research conducted at his non-profit institute in California. One of the concepts emphasized at the Pauling Institute is "orthomolecular" medicine —the effect on human health of alterations in the balance of natural compounds within the body.

Three projects at the institute involve the aging process. These include the possible role of deamidation—a biochemical reaction that changes the properties of proteins—as a control mechanism for aging; the usefulness of urine analysis as a means of measuring physiologic age (see p. 380), and the extent to which diet affects the rate of physiologic aging.

Linus Pauling Institute of Science and Medicine, 2700 Sand Hill Road, Menlo Park, Ca. 94025

The Committee for Elimination of Death

A nonprofit, tax-exempt organization that promotes physical immortality. The committee publishes *Chairman's Chat*, a bulletin that deals with the philosophy of immortalism. It also offers a three-minute recorded "Voice of Life" message by phone.

A. Stuart Otto, P.O. Box 696, San Marcos, Ca. 92069

The Committee for an Extended Life Span

A nonprofit, tax-exempt organization that promotes the extension of human life. The committee publishes *Life Lines*, a bulletin that contains prolongevity information.

A. Stuart Otto, P.O. Box 696, San Marcos, Ca. 92069

The Foundation for Infinite Survival

The Foundation for Infinite Survival is a nonprofit, tax-exempt scientific organization dedicated to "life-extension and control of aging." The foundation operates a Health Testing Center where individuals can obtain "complete multiphasic medical examinations."

The foundation also offers a long-term program involving "disease prevention, health maintenance, and 'Phase I' life extension modalities."

Funds from these programs are directed toward a basic research effort that focuses on the development of "experimental 'Phase II' therapies designed to slow and eventually reverse the aging process."

Foundation for Infinite Survival, P.O. Box 4000-C, Berkeley, Ca. 94704

Long Life Magazine

Long Life Magazine covers the full spectrum of life-extension activities and research. It features reports on cryonics and suspended animation, biomedical aging research, rejuvenation therapies, and the implications of life extension. The magazine is published six times a year.

Long Life Magazine, Box 490, Chicago, Il. 60690

Rejuvenation

Rejuvenation is the official journal of the International Association on the Artificial Prolongation of the Human Specific Lifespan. It features articles on aging and rejuvenation research and therapies in English and in French.

Rejuvenation, Fabiolalaan, 12 Knokke-Zoute, B-8300, Belgium

Why Measure the Human Aging Rate?

Unless we learn how to measure the rate of human aging, it will be extremely difficult to evaluate anti-aging therapies. The reason for this difficulty is that the only measure of aging accepted today—maximum life span—is indirect, imprecise, and impracticable in long-lived species.

Thus, gerontologists work with relatively short-lived species, such as rats or mice, whose maximum life span is only about three years. Even so, aging experiments are costly and time-consuming, particularly if one is studying the effects of a regimen on the animals' entire life span. And any regimen that succeeds in prolonging maximum life span requires experiments that take four or five years or longer.

Moreover, the maximum life span approach is virtually impossible in humans—not only because of the prohibitive length and expense of such an experiment, but also because of the questionable ethics of putting humans on experimental regimens for long periods of time.

An alternative approach might be to put large numbers of old persons—who would be expected to die off at a certain rate within five to ten years—on a particular regimen, and then compare their subsequent mortality with that of a control group. However, such an approach would also be extremely expensive, would be complicated by the many diseases that old persons are commonly afflicted with, and would be worthless if the regimen being tested were effective only if started at an earlier stage in the life span.

Hence, it is imperative that we develop reliable methods to measure the rate of aging—both in animals and in humans.

"Assays for Aging" in Rodents

One approach to measuring the rate of aging in rodents has been to compare the physical properties of tendon fibers from the tails of mice or rats of different ages. These fibers are made of collagen, the most abundant extracellular protein in the body.

The results of these experiments have been inconclusive. In some studies, it appears that collagen aging is an accurate reflection of biologic age. For example, underfeeding has been found to retard the aging of collagen fibers in rats only when started at a young age, which corresponds to its ability to extend life span in rats. (See p. 60.)

On the other hand, collagen fibers from the tails of cats and rats of the same age have been found to age at about the same rate. Since cats live considerably longer than rats, this finding suggests that collagen aging is a function of time rather than of biologic aging.

The Latest Study

The most recent study of collagen aging, by David Harrison of Jackson Laboratory, failed to resolve the issue. Harrison showed that collagen aging, as assessed by the breaking times of tail tendon fibers in urea, occurs about twice as rapidly in a species of wild mice (*Mus musculus*) than in a similar species (*Peromyscus leucopus*). Since *Peromyscus* lives about 2.5 times as long as *Mus* (see p. 363), thus finding supports the idea that collagen aging reflects biologic aging.

But when Harrison examined the breaking times of tendon tail fibers from thirteen different strains of mice of the same genotype, he found no correlation between collagen aging and the variations in life span among these strains. Nor did he find accelerated collagen aging in mice subjected to autoimmune disease and irradiation, which both shorten life span.

Harrison further suggests that retarded collagen aging in underfed rats may be the result of lower-than-normal tail temperatures in these animals rather than food restriction. Several studies have demonstrated that collagen aging is retarded at reduced temperatures—a finding that supports the idea that lowered body temperature may slow the aging process in mammals. (See p. 160.)

A Battery of Tests

Harrison's study of tail collagen aging was the first in a series of studies, in which he hopes to develop a battery of tests to measure biologic aging in rodents. Among the potential "assays for aging" that he is investigating are minimum and maximum oxygen consumption, responses of spleen and circulating lymphocytes to antigenic challenge, urine-concentrating ability, rate of hair regrowth, bone thickness and structure, blood pressure, and rate of metabolic removal of certain drugs.

He is evaluating the sensitivity of these assays by using them to measure the effects of various life-span-extending and rejuvenation procedures. These include food restriction, transplantation of the intact thymus gland and bone marrow cells from young animals into old ones (see p. 196), parabiosis between young and old animals (see p. 253), and long-term removal of the pituitary gland. (See p. 50.)

David E. Harrison, The Jackson Laboratory, Bar Harbor, Me. 04609

Attempts to Measure Human Aging

One way of measuring human aging can be used only in dead persons. The test involves treatment of collagen from diaphragm tendon with the digestive enzyme bacterial collagenase. Since this type of collagen becomes progressively resistant to enzymatic digestion with advancing age, the test can be used to estimate chronologic age. Hamlin and Kohn were able to predict the age of seven cadavers with considerable accuracy after obtaining specimens of diaphragm collagen at autopsy.

Other scientists have sought to develop test batteries to measure the rate of human aging in living persons. J. W. Hollingsworth attempted to define physiologic age in 450 survivors of the atomic bomb explosion at Hiroshima. Of seventeen functions tested, good correlations with age were found for hair-graying, skin elasticity, systolic blood pressure, and hearing ability.

In a later effort, Alex Comfort expanded upon this series by adding tests from numerous other sources. He tried to cover the entire spectrum of human physiology by including tests of blood biochemistry, cell function, immune capacity, central nervous system activity, and cognitive abilities. Comfort envisioned his battery of tests as a tool to evaluate the

Assessing picture recognition ability as part of a battery of tests developed by Richard Hochschild to measure biologic aging.

anti-aging effects of compounds such as antioxidants, but it has yet to be used for this purpose.

Richard Hochschild has developed ten tests to measure biologic aging, which he intends to use in assessing the anti-aging potential of compounds now being used clinically. Most of Hochschild's tests are computerized versions of standard tests of functions that decline significantly with age. They measure short-term memory, picture recognition, reaction time, decision time, movement speed, vital capacity (of the lungs), forced expiratory volume, accommodation (of vision), vibratory sense (through the fingertips), and pitch ceiling (ability to hear high tones).

Hochschild has proposed that these tests be used to evaluate lecithin, which has been implicated in the expression of cognitive function (see p. 265), and deanol, which has been used (by Hochschild) to extend the life span of mice. (See p. 274.)

James W. Hollingsworth, Department of Medicine, University of Kentucky College of Medicine, Lexington, Ky. 40506

Alex Comfort, Institute for Higher Studies, 2311 Garden St., Santa Barbara, Ca. 93105

Richard Hochschild, Department of Medicine, University of California, Irvine, Irvine, Ca. 92715

Analyzing Urine to Measure Aging

Scientists at the Linus Pauling Institute are trying to measure human aging by assessing biochemical changes in urine obtained from subjects of various ages. The technique involves identifying 185 substances in each urine sample followed by computerized pattern recognition procedures. About 30 percent of these substances apparently undergo age-related changes that permit calculation of a subject's age.

Thus far, biochemical profiles have been developed through analysis of the urine of 235 individuals at the V.A. Hospital in Sepulveda, California. The Pauling Institute is seeking funds to create a bank of urine samples from healthy persons, which could be calibrated with their subsequent health records in an attempt to define the value of urine analysis as a measure of aging. They hope to use this method of measurement to evaluate the effects of high doses of vitamins C, E, and other agents on the aging process.

Linus Pauling Institute of Science and Medicine, 2700 Sand Hill Road, Menlo Park, Ca. 94025

The New Science of "Health Building"

"Everybody wants to live forever," goes the theme song of the film *Pumping Iron*, which celebrates the toil and glory of body building. But even body builders grow old and wrinkled, as their powerful muscles become ravaged by the sands of time.

If we want to conquer aging, we'll have to build up far

more than our muscles. What we need is a scientific approach to health building . . . to the creation of a "physiologic fortress" against the destructive forces of Nature.

We need a potent, well-balanced neuroendocrine system; a vigorous and vigilant immune system; an efficient, multipurpose cellular repair system; and an enhanced ability to regenerate dying cells, tissues, and organs.

In order to develop the science of health building, we need an accurate, sensitive, and easily administered battery of tests to measure health in the absence of disease. An instrument that will enable us to determine our rate of biologic aging, probability of getting specific diseases, and life expectancy.

The test results should be expressed in simple terms that anyone can understand—perhaps by a graduated scale of 1 to 10. An overall "health number" might be issued, as a measure of our general health status, and a more detailed "health index," as a measure of the status of various systems. Thus, our health number could be 8, with our cardiovascular and immune systems rated at 9 and 7, respectively.

Once we have a viable scoring system, we will be in a position to evaluate potential health-building therapies, such as vitamin C, nucleic acids, exercise, Gerovital-H_3, anti-crosslinking enzymes, or anything at all. The effects of the therapy, whether beneficial or detrimental, would be reflected in our health score.

Any therapy that protects us against aging or reverses the aging process would be expected to upgrade our entire health index; whereas a therapy that does not affect aging directly, such as exercise, might boost our cardiovascular score, without significantly affecting any other score. As time goes by, the test battery could be adjusted to better fit the data it generates.

Clearly, the new science of health building would be a passport to better health, longer life, and physical immortality.

The Drug Delivery Revolution

Everyone assumes that the anti-aging therapies of the future will be delivered into the body with today's conventional dosage forms—that we will take a pill to retard the aging process, or receive injections to rejuvenate our aged bodies. Yet, there is strong evidence that conventional dosage forms, such as pills and injections, are a major obstacle to the development of anti-aging therapies, and that medicine is on the verge of a drug delivery revolution that will play an important role in the control of human aging.

Today's conventional dosage forms represent an indirect, inexact, "sledgehammer" approach to the administration of drugs. By exposing the body to widely fluctuating levels of potentially toxic agents, they subject us to serious risks of drug-induced illness. Although we all know about the harmful side effects of drug therapy, it's time we realized that it is our dosage forms that are primarily at fault, rather than the drugs themselves.

Oral Therapy

Take orally administered drugs, for example. Before the drug contained in a pill reaches its intended target within the body, it must first pass through the digestive system, and then be absorbed into the bloodstream for transport. This roundabout routing system exposes every organ and tissue to unwanted pharmacologic action, necessitates the ingestion of excessive amounts of drug, and prevents the use of natural compounds as therapeutic agents.

After a pill is swallowed, it produces higher than necessary blood and tissue levels of drug, which then proceed to fall below desired levels before the next pill is taken. By repeating this erratic, sawtooth pattern of drug levels three or four times a day (every time we take a pill), we expose ourselves to potentially severe side effects, often without providing satisfactory therapeutic action.

Such primitive dosage forms may be tolerable for short time periods, as in antibiotic therapy for infections, but they are inadequate for long-term treatment of chronic conditions such as cancer,·diabetes, atherosclerosis, hypertension, arthritis, and aging. If we want to treat such conditions effectively, we need sophisticated therapeutic systems that can recharge failing nerve and muscle cells, replenish declining hormones and enzymes, and restore homeostatic balance to an organism in the process of disintegration.

Therapeutic Systems

The first generation of therapeutic systems has been developed by the Alza Corporation of Palo Alto, California. Alza's systems are self-powered devices that continuously release small amounts of drug into the body at precisely controlled rates.

One disease of aging that is now being treated with a therapeutic system is glaucoma, in which there is a buildup of pressure within the eye that can lead to blindness. Conventional treatment of glaucoma involves the application of eyedrops containing pressure-reducing drugs at least twice a day. In contrast, Alza's ocular delivery system—a thin, flexible disc worn beneath the eyelid—delivers drug at a constant rate for a week. The system maintains normal eye pressure on a twenty-four-hour basis with a substantially smaller amount of drug than eyedrop therapy.

Other Alza therapeutic systems include a twenty-four-hour, time-release pill; a small, futuristic wafer that delivers drugs directly through intact skin; an IUD that provides natural hormonal contraception without systemic side effects; a portable infusion pump for intravenous (IV) drug therapy outside the hospital; and biodegradable substances that release drugs within the body while disappearing from the site of application.

Jacqueline Horvath, Alza Corporation, Box J, 950 Page Mill Road, Palo Alto, Ca. 94304

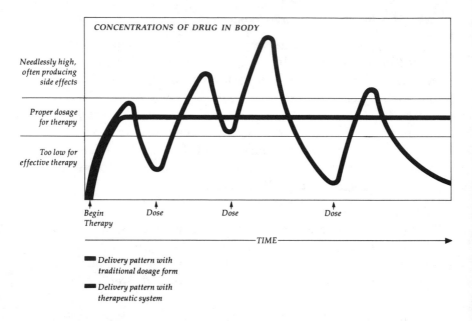

CONCENTRATIONS OF DRUG IN BODY

Needlessly high, often producing side effects

Proper dosage for therapy

Too low for effective therapy

Begin Therapy · Dose · Dose · Dose

TIME

▬ Delivery pattern with traditional dosage form

▬ Delivery pattern with therapeutic system

Comparison of constant drug delivery pattern produced by therapeutic systems and fluctuating drug delivery pattern produced by conventional dosage forms.

The First "Space Age" Dosage Form

Do you gag at taking pills? Are you traumatized by the long needles used to give injections? Have you been victimized by unpleasant side effects from both these dosage forms? If so, you're in for a treat because a new and exciting way of taking drugs has arrived.

It's called the Transdermal Therapeutic System (TTS) and it represents a medical breakthrough—the controlled delivery of drugs through the skin into the bloodstream. (See p. 219.) In appearance, the TTS seems nothing more than a small, circular piece of tape that you slap onto your skin like a Band-Aid. But the TTS does far more than simply protect you; it provides sophisticated medical treatment without injuring or irritating the skin.

The TTS was developed by Alza Corporation. It comprises four distinct layers, each with its own function. The outside layer, the shiny, silvery surface that everyone sees, is an impermeable backing membrane. Beneath it is an ultra-thin reservoir that contains about 1 mg of drug. Next is a microporous membrane through which the drug diffuses at a constant rate. The inside layer, which touches the skin, is an adhesive that contains an initial priming dose of drug.

The TTS is a generic system capable of delivering a great many drugs for many different purposes—at the infusion rate appropriate for each drug. It is technically capable of administering most bioactive compounds with molecular weights under 800 that are soluble in both oil and water. High-molecular-weight compounds such as insulin are unsuitable for use in the TTS.

The First Transdermal System

Alza's first transdermal system is for delivery of scopolamine to prevent the nausea and vomiting associated with motion sickness. Scopolamine is highly effective in preventing this condition, but cannot be taken in conventional dosage forms because of undesirable side effects. However, the TTS permits safe, continuous delivery of the drug for up to three days.

Alza is collaborating with two major pharmaceutical companies—Boehringer-Ingelheim and CIBA-GEIGY—to develop other transdermal systems. Among the applications anticipated for the TTS are the treatment of hypertension, angina (heart pain), peripheral vascular disease, stroke, respiratory disease, post-menopausal hormone deficiency, and mental impairment caused by aging or senility.

Jacqueline Horvath, Alza Corporation, Box J, 950 Page Mill Road, Palo Alto, Ca. 94304

A Unique Research Tool

Alza Corporation has developed a unique research tool— an osmotic minipump that continuously delivers solutions of

Alza's first transdermal therapeutic system prevents motion
sickness by delivering the drug
scopolamine at a controlled rate
through intact skin behind the
ear.

experimental agents into laboratory animals at controlled
rates for up to two weeks.

When implanted beneath the skin of a mouse, rat, or
other laboratory animal, the minipump's osmotic agent draws
in water from the surrounding tissues, which generates hy-
drostatic pressure on its collapsible reservoir, which contains the experimental agent. What results is a controlled
flow of the agent through a delivery portal at the end of the
device. The minipump can be used to deliver bioactive agents
directly into the brain or other tissues by means of an attached catheter.

Among the many potential uses of the minipump in biomedical aging research would be the evaluation of the effects
on life span of such drugs as thymosin (see p. 203), L-Dopa
(see p. 155), and deanol. (See p. 274.) It could also be used to
determine the effects of combinations of such drugs administered from two or more minipumps implanted in the same
animal.

Jacqueline Horvath, Alza Corporation, Box J, 950 Page Mill Road, Palo Alto, Ca. 94304

How Computers Will Help to Achieve Immortality

Computers already play a major role in medicine. They are useful in diagnosis, record-keeping, treatment, and research. At present, they serve primarily as information processors, but in the future—as "artificial intelligence" evolves—they can be expected to design experiments, analyze data, prescribe and administer therapies, induce suspended animation, and help to redesign our genetic makeup. The result of these developments will be rapidly accelerating progress toward the conquest of aging, disease, and death. Here are some hints of things to come.

Three-Dimensional Diagnosis

In the last few years, computerized axial tomography (CAT) scanners have enabled physicians to look into the bodies of their patients with a degree of accuracy never before achieved. The computers in these machines process thousands of cross-sectional "slices" of the inside of the body to construct realistic images of organs and tissues.

On the horizon is a truly amazing sequel: enlarged, three-dimensional, full color, holographic visualizations of internal organs and tissues in natural physiologic motion. For the past seven years, Thomas Huang of Purdue University has been investigating the implications of computer holography for medical diagnosis. Though currently produced holographic images are not yet clear enough for clinical application, Huang is confident the technique can be substantially improved in the near future. Computer holography will help us to evaluate the effects of exercise, nutrients, and drugs on the body in addition to its value as a diagnostic aid.

Computer Modeling

Scientists at Duke University are developing a computer model to assess the degree of sickness in individual patients.

Thus far, the model has been used to study patients suffering from a form of congenital heart disease. In the future, this type of model will be used to measure the degree of sickness in all patients, and to assess the degree of health in individuals not suffering from any disease.

At Michael Reese Medical Center, a computer program for hypertension has been able to prescribe treatment for the disease about as well as human physicians. In this study, the computer made treatment "recommendations" which physicians were free to follow or reject, and this approach was compared to treatment prescribed by physicians alone. The computer's recommendations were accepted in 275 of 296 instances, and the computer proved to be as effective and safe as physicians in lowering blood pressure.

Tomorrow's computer models could eliminate physicians entirely by communicating directly with patients. Each of us could have a home computer plugged into an electronic medical system, and portable electronic devices to measure blood pressure, blood chemistry, and other parameters of health, which would also be connected to the system. Under these circumstances, it might be necessary to visit the doctor's office only for complex testing or surgery.

Accelerating Medical Progress

A fully computerized system would improve the quality of medical care while accelerating the pace of medical progress. With such a system, every diagnosis, prescription, and treatment result could instantaneously be transmitted to all interested physicians and scientists as well as to a central coordinating facility.

At this facility, there could be continuous clinical and epidemiologic studies of all therapeutic regimens, with input from every country on the planet. A perpetual onslaught of findings, generalizations, hypotheses, and suggestions for future study could be generated by a combination of computer and human analysis. There could be ongoing evaluation of drugs, nutrients, lifestyle parameters, and environmental agents—with firm conclusions relayed simultaneously to everyone plugged into the system. A similar, interrelated computer system for animal research could provide us with a lightning-quick network for progress in life extension.

Computerized Therapy

Computers will also play a critical role in delivering life-extension therapies. They will provide the "brain power" to regulate the flow of life-extending agents according to the needs of the body. Drugs and nutrients will be administered by small, computerized therapeutic systems—either implanted or applied externally—which will act like artificial organs to restore and maintain youthful homeostatic patterns within the body.

In the future, all medical treatment, including surgery and suspended animation, will be under computer control. This will enable us to perform extraordinarily sophisticated and delicate operations to regenerate damaged tissue or to replace it with artificial tissue. The ultimate use of such techniques will be genetic engineering, whereby deleterious genes or gene systems will be altered by insertion of synthesized genes or gene fragments, or by reconstruction of natural genes.

Thomas S. Huang, Department of Electrical Engineering, Purdue University, West Lafayette, Ind. 47907

Max A. Woodbury, Division of Biomathematics, Duke University Medical Center, Durham, N.C. 27710

Fredric L. Coe, Department of Medicine, Michael Reese Medical Center, Chicago, Il. 60616

Starting Life in a Test Tube
The biggest medical story of 1978 was the first confirmed birth of a baby conceived outside the mother's body. The

event was the culmination of more than a decade of test-tube fertilization research by Steptoe and Edwards, as well as extensive testing of the procedure in animals by a host of other researchers.

As the "baby of the century," Louise Brown began her life in the following manner. First, her mother was given hormone therapy to promote the ovulation of more than one egg (superovulation). Then the eggs were harvested via a surgical technique called laparoscopy. Next, they were placed with her father's sperm into a Petri dish containing a special fertilization medium.

After fertilization, the eggs were moved to another medium where they began to divide. Several days later, an early-stage embryo showing regular cleavage (cell division) was transplanted into her mother's uterus through a catheter. At the time of the embryo transplant, the drug indomethacin was given to inhibit uterine contractions, and during the early stages of pregnancy, additional hormones were administered to support the growth of the embryo.

Steptoe and Edwards had to perform more than sixty embryo transplants before their initial success with Louise.

Robert G. Edwards, Physiological Laboratory, Downing Street, Cambridge, CB2 3EG, England

Test-Tube Babies and Longevity

In the public mind, the concept of test-tube babies tends to conjure up images of a depersonalized society governed by totalitarian force. Such a reaction is in part the result of the popularity of Aldous Huxley's book *Brave New World*, which depicts such a society. It also reflects deep-seated fears about the effects of such a radical change in so basic an institution as motherhood—fears that have long been fueled by religious beliefs about the dangers of "playing God."

However, the truth of the matter is that the potential benefits of test-tube baby technology are so great and extensive that they far outweigh the potential risks of its abuse. They range from the possibility of eliminating "birth" defects to the creation of immortal superbeings with extraordinary physical and mental powers.

Once we are able to scrutinize the entire reproductive process directly, we will be in a position to accelerate our knowledge of how life develops. We will learn a great deal more about how cells differentiate; which factors are involved in cell regulation; how the nervous, endocrine, and immune systems develop; and how chemicals, nutrients, viruses, and other agents affect fetal development.

With therapeutic access to a rapidly evolving embryo-fetus during gestation—the most critical period in human life—we will learn how to prevent or cure virtually all developmental disorders, whether of congenital or acquired origin. Even the most lethal inherited defects should eventually be preventable.

The ability to control the reproductive process is likely to play a major role in correcting our most universal inherited defect—limited life span. It will help us to uncover the genetic basis for aging and age-related diseases, and to discover the means by which the factors that limit life span are expressed in developing organs and systems.

With such knowledge at our fingertips, we should soon be able to inhibit some of these life-limiting factors with nutritional and drug therapies and, in the long run, to prevent them with genetic engineering.

Under such conditions, every new child could be programmed to remain youthful and vigorous forever, rather than to grow old and die. And perhaps those of us already into middle or old age could be reprogrammed to go into reverse—to grow young instead of old.

Genetic Engineering of Immortality

In our vast and incredible universe, there may be many races living in distant star systems who have evolved into immortal beings. Just as each of us is programmed to grow old and die, the individuals of these races may be programmed to remain young, strong, and vigorous forever.

At this time in the evolution of the human race, we have just begun to explore methods of modifying the biologic constraints on longevity. We are developing dietary and drug therapies to increase both the quality and the length of our lives—either by boosting our resistance to aging and disease, or by retarding their expression.

Anti-aging and rejuvenation therapies aim to alter the consequences of the genetic control systems that determine the rate of human aging and our susceptibility to disease. Such an approach can work in two ways: by bolstering the action of beneficial genes or by hampering the action of deleterious genes.

Such therapies will, hopefully, enable us to prolong health, vigor, and life span well beyond our current limitations. However, true immortality will probably require reprogramming of the genetic basis for longevity—a development that will necessitate major advances in genetics and gerontology.

First, we will have to identify the genes or gene systems involved in human aging. Recent studies suggest that relatively few genes may be critical to the aging process, and that they may be regulatory rather than structural genes. (See p. 20.) Two candidates that have been proposed as possible mediators of the aging process are the genes that control immune function and DNA repair. (See p. 193.)

After we learn what genes are involved in aging, we'll have to determine the mechanisms by which they act. There are currently many theories of how genes control aging, but little evidence to back any of them, and insufficient data upon which to base any remedial action.

Finally, we'll need genetic engineering techniques capable of changing the genetic patterns or structures responsible for the aging process. Though genetic engineering is still in its infancy, the initial steps toward the development of such techniques have already been taken.

Recombinant DNA

It was only twenty-five years ago that the structure of the DNA molecule was elucidated, and only ten years ago that the first gene was synthesized. The recent discovery of restriction enzymes (endonucleases) that can cleave and splice DNA indicates that we are on the verge of extraordinary advances in the next few decades.

Scientists can now take apart DNA molecules and put them back together again in different sequences. They can also transfer genetic information from one organism to another. In a recent tour de force, a joint research team from the City of Hope and Genentech, Inc., used recombinant DNA technology to create a microbe that manufactures human insulin.

First they synthesized the two genes that control the production of insulin in the pancreas. Then they joined the two synthetic insulin genes to a gene from the bacterium *E. Coli.* When they inserted this new genetic combination into fresh *E. Coli,* the organism's DNA-reading apparatus could not differentiate the foreign genes from its own. As a result, it began to produce insulin—an ability that became a permanent part of each new generation of bacteria.

If we can transform bacteria into miniature insulin factories with the primitive genetic engineering techniques available today, there's every reason to expect that future advances will enable us to transform ourselves into physically immortal beings with superhuman powers.

Keiichi Itakura, Division of Biology, City of Hope National Medical Center, Duarte, Ca. 91010

David V. Goeddel, Division of Molecular Biology, Genentech, Inc., 460 Point San Bruno Blvd., South San Francisco, Ca. 94080

A Look at the Future

The most pertinent issue for readers of *The Life-Extension Revolution* is the question of whether they will be able to benefit from advances in the life-extension sciences. Is life span extension likely to occur in the near future? What can readers do to increase their chances of living a longer, healthier life?

The answer, aside from personal health care, lies in the support of life-extension research. The key to our survival as individuals is the creation of a large-scale, multi-disciplinary program to develop effective methods of aging control, rejuvenation, and suspended animation. Widespread public support for such a program could lead to an extended life span for many of us alive today.

In my opinion, we can achieve at least partial success in extending the human life span by the year 2000. Among the goals I believe to be eminently attainable by the turn of the twenty-first century are prevention of the age-related decline of the immune and neuroendocrine systems, liquid-state suspended animation in humans, and the ability to restore some degree of youthful vigor in the elderly.

By the year 2025, it could be possible for us to gain complete control over the aging process, and to develop highly advanced methods of rejuvenation and repair of aging, disease, and accident victims. And, by the middle of the twenty-first century, we could well become true immortals—genetically reprogrammed to live on indefinitely, instead of growing old and dying.

The Life-Extension Revolution represents the first step in a campaign to stimulate public support for a large-scale program to extend the human life span. Future efforts will include a philanthropic foundation for the funding of life-extension research, a clinic for the evaluation of life-extension therapies, and a clearinghouse for information and ideas about life extension. Anyone who wishes to know more about these projects should get in touch with me:

—SAUL KENT
R.D. 1, Box 418B
Woodstock, N.Y. 12498

References

PAGE

Chapter 1 Why Do We Grow Old and Die?

19. Cutler, R. G. "Evolution of Human Longevity and the Genetic Complexity Governing Aging Rate," *Proceedings of the National Academy of Sciences, USA,* November, 1975, Vol. 72, 4664–4668.

19. Cutler, R.G. "Nature of Aging and Life Maintenance Processes," *Interdisciplinary Topics in Gerontology,* 1976, Vol. 9, 83–133.

19. Cutler, R.G. "Evolution of Longevity in Primates," *Journal of Human Evolution,* 1976, Vol. 5, 169–202.

19. Cutler, R.G. "Evolution of Longevity in Ungulates and Carnivores," *Gerontology,* 1979, Vol. 25, 69–86.

19. Sacher, G.A. "Longevity, Aging, and Death: An Evolutionary Perspective," The Kleemeier Award Lecture, presented at the meeting of The Gerontological Society, San Francisco, Nov. 21, 1977.

19. Hart, R.W., and Setlow, R.B. "Correlation Between Deoxyribonucleic Acid Excision-Repair and Life-Span in a Number of Mammalian Species," *Proceedings of the National Academy of Sciences, USA,* June, 1974, Vol. 71, 2169–2173.

20. Kohn, R.R. "Human Aging and Disease," *Journal of Chronic Diseases,* 1963, Vol. 16, 5–21.

20. Kohn, R.R. "Diseases and Aging," in Kohn, R.R., *Principles of Mammalian Aging.* Englewood Cliffs, N.J.: Prentice-Hall, 1971.

23. Dilman, V.M. "Ageing, Metabolic Immunodepression and Carcinogenesis," *Mechanisms of Ageing and Development,* 1978, Vol. 8, 153–173.

PAGE
23. Kent, S. "Longer Life Span Hinges on Control of Aging as well as Degenerative Diseases," *Geriatrics*, August, 1976, Vol. 31, 128–131.
23. Kent, S. "What's Behind the Dramatic Increase in Cardiovascular Mortality with Aging?," *Geriatrics*, September, 1976, Vol. 31, 132–139.
23. Kent, S. "Is Diabetes a Form of Accelerated Aging?," *Geriatrics*, November, 1976, Vol. 31, 140–151.
25. Terry, R.D., and Gershon, S. (eds). *Aging*, Vol. 3, *Neurobiology of Aging*. New York: Raven Press, 1976.
25. Kent, S. "Classifying and Treating Organic Brain Syndromes," *Geriatrics*, September, 1977, Vol. 32, 87–96.
26. Brizzee, K.R. "Gross Morphometric Analyses and Quantitative Histology of the Aging Brain," in Ordy, J.M., and Brizzee, K.R. (eds). *Neurobiology of Aging: An Interdisciplinary Life-Span Approach*. New York: Plenum Press, 1975.
26. Brody, H. "Organization of the Cerebral Cortex," *Journal of Comprehensive Neurology*, 1955, Vol. 102, 511–556.
26. Konigsmark, B.W., and Murphy, E.A. "Neuronal Population in the Human Brain," *Nature*, 1970, Vol. 228, 1335–1336.
26. Kent, S. "Scientists Count Brain Cells to Figure Theory of Aging," *Geriatrics*, April, 1976, Vol. 31, 114–123.
27. Scheibel, M.F., and Scheibel, A.B. "Structural Changes in the Aging Brain," in Brody, H., Harman, D., and Ordy, J.M. (eds). *Aging*, Vol. 1, *Clinical, Morphologic, and Neurochemical Aspects in the Aging Central Nervous System*. New York: Raven Press, 1975.
27. Feldman, M. "Degenerative Changes in Aging Dendrites," *The Gerontologist* (Abstract), 1976, Vol. 14, 36.
27. Kent, S. "Structural Changes in the Brain May Short-Circuit Transfer of Information," *Geriatrics*, June, 1976, Vol. 31, 128–131.
29. Strehler, B.L. "On the Histochemistry and Ultrastructure of Age Pigment," in Strehler, B.L. (ed). *Advances in Gerontological Research*, Vol. 1. New York: Academic Press, 1964.
29. Brizzee, K.R., Kaack, B., and Klara, P. "Lipofuscin: Intra- and extra-neuronal Accumulation and Regional Distribu-

PAGE

tion," in Ordy, J.M., and Brizzee, K.R. (eds). *Neurobiology of Aging: An Interdisciplinary Life-Span Approach.* New York: Plenum Press, 1975.

29. Zeman, W. "The Neuronal Ceroid-Lipofuscinoses—Batten-Vogt Syndrome: A Model for Human Aging?," *Advances in Gerontological Research,* 1971, Vol. 3, 147.

29. Siakotos, A.N., and Armstrong, D. "Age Pigment: A Biochemical Indicator of Intracellular Aging," in Ordy, J.M., and Brizzee, K.R. (eds). *Neurobiology of Aging: An Interdisciplinary Life-Span Approach.* New York: Plenum Press, 1975.

29. Kent, S. "Solving the Riddle of Lipofuscin's Origin May Uncover Clues to the Aging Process," *Geriatrics,* May, 1976, Vol. 31, 128–137.

30. Hayflick, L. "The Limited In Vitro Lifetime of Human Diploid Strains," *Experimental Cell Research,* 1965, Vol. 37, 614.

30. Kohn, R.R. "Aging and Cell Division," *Science,* 1975, Vol. 188, 203–204.

30. Schneider, E.L., and Mitsui, Y. "The Relationship Between In Vitro Cellular Aging and In Vivo Human Age," *Proceedings of the National Academy of Sciences, USA,* October, 1976, Vol. 73, 3584–3588.

30. Kent, S. "Cell Division and Aging," *Geriatrics,* August, 1978, Vol. 33, 81–85.

33. Harrison, D.E. "Normal Function of Transplanted Marrow Cell Lines from Aged Mice," *Journal of Gerontology,* March, 1975, Vol. 30, 286–288.

33. Harrison, D.E. "Genetically Defined Animals Valuable in Testing Aging of Erythroid and Lymphoid Stem Cells and Microenvironments," in Bergsma, D. and Harrison D.E. (eds). *Genetic Effects on Aging.* New York: Alan R. Liss, 1978.

36. Comfort, A. "The Position of Aging Studies," *Mechanisms of Ageing and Development,* 1974, Vol. 3, 1–31.

36. Hayflick, L. "Current Theories of Biological Aging," in Thorbeck, G.J. (ed). *Biology of Aging and Development.* New York: Plenum Press, 1975.

PAGE
37. Hochschild, R. "A Drug Against Time," private communication.
38. Bjorksten, J. "Why Grow Old?," *Chemistry*, June, 1974, Vol. 37, 6–11.
38. Bjorksten, J. "The Crosslinkage Theory of Aging: Clinical Implications," *Comprehensive Therapy*, February, 1976, Vol. 2, 65–74.
38. Cutler, R.G. "Crosslinkage Theory of Aging: DNA Adducts in Chromatin as a Primary Aging Process," in *International Symposium on Protein and Other Adducts to DNA: Their Significance to Aging, Carcinogenesis and Radiation Biology*, Williamsburg, Va., May 2–6, 1975.
39. Harman, D. "Free Radical Theory of Aging: Dietary Implications," *American Journal of Clinical Nutrition*, 1972, Vol. 25, 839.
39. Harman, D., Eddy, D.E., and Noffsinger, J. "Free Radical Theory of Aging: Inhibition of Amyloidosis in Mice by Antioxidants; Possible Mechanism," *Journal of the American Geriatrics Society*, May, 1976, Vol. 24, 203–209.
39. Eddy, D.E., and Harman, D. "Free Radical Theory of Aging: Effect of Age, Sex and Dietary Precursors on Rat-Brain Docosahexanoic Acid," *Journal of the American Geriatrics Society*, May, 1977, Vol. 25, 220–228.
39. Harman, D., Heidrick, M.L., and Eddy, D.E. "Free Radical Theory of Aging: Effect of Free-Radical-Reaction Inhibitors on the Immune Response, *Journal of the American Geriatrics Society*, September, 1977, Vol. 25, 400–407.
40. Walford, R.L. *The Immunologic Theory of Aging*. Copenhagen: Munksgaard, 1969.
40. Walford, R.L. "Immunologic Theory of Aging: Current Status," *Federation Proceedings*, 1974, Vol. 33, 2020.
40. Burnet, F. M. "An Immunological Approach to Ageing," *Lancet*, 1970, Vol. 2, 358.
40. Kent, S. "Can Normal Aging Be Explained by the Immunologic Theory?," *Geriatrics*, May, 1977, Vol. 32, 111–121.
41. Spiegel, P.M. "Theories of Aging," in Timiras, P.S. (ed).

PAGE
Developmental Physiology and Aging. New York: Macmillan Company, 1972.
41. Rosenfeld, A. *Prolongevity.* New York: Alfred A. Knopf, 1976.
43. Frolkis, V.V. "Regulation and Adaptation Processes in Aging (Regulatory-Adaptive Theory)," *The Main Problems of Soviet Gerontology.* Kiev, 1972.
43. Chebotarev, M.F., Frolkis, V.V. "Research in Experimental Gerontology in the USSR," *Journal of Gerontology,* April, 1975, Vol. 30, 441–447.
43. Dilman, V.M. "Age-Associated Elevation of Hypothalamic Threshold to Feedback Control and its Role in Development, Ageing and Disease," *Lancet,* 1971, Vol. 1, 1211–1219.
45. Finch, C.E. "Catecholamine Metabolism in the Brains of Aging Male Mice," *Brain Research,* 1973, Vol. 52, 261–276.
45. Finch, C.E. "Physiological Changes of Aging in Mammals," *Quarterly Review of Biology,* 1976, Vol. 51, 49–83.
45. Finch, C.E. "Neuroendocrine and Autonomic Aspects of Aging," in Finch, C.E., and Hayflick, L. (eds). *Handbook of the Biology of Aging.* New York: Van Nostrand Reinhold Company, 1977.
46. Reichel, W., Garcia-Bunuel, R. "Pathologic Findings in Progeria: Myocardial Fibrosis and Lipofuscin Pigment," *American Journal of Clinical Pathology,* 1970, Vol. 53, 243–253.
46. Reichel, W., Garcia-Bunuel, R., and Dilallo, J. "Progeria and Werner's Syndrome as Models for the Study of Normal Human Aging," *Journal of the American Geriatrics Society,* May, 1971, Vol. 19, 369–375.
46. Martin, G.M. "Genetic Syndromes in Man With Potential Relevance to the Pathobiology of Aging," in Bergsma, D., and Harrison, D.E. (eds). *Genetic Effects on Aging.* New York: Alan R. Liss, 1978.
46. Brown, W.T., Little, J.B., Epstein, J., et al. "DNA Repair Defect in Progeric Cells," in Bergsma, D., and Harrison, D.E. (eds). *Genetic Effects on Aging.* New York: Alan R. Liss, 1978.

PAGE
47. Adelman, R.C. "Age-Dependent Effects in Enzyme Induction—A Biochemical Expression of Aging," *Experimental Gerontology*, 1971, Vol. 6, 75–87.
47. Adelman, R.C., and Britton, G.W. "The Impaired Capability for Biochemical Adaptation During Aging," *Bioscience*, October, 1975, Vol. 25, 639–643.
47. Adelman, R.C. "Disruptions in Enzyme Regulation," in Parke, D.V. (ed). *Enzyme Induction*. Oxford: Plenum Press, 1975.
47. Adelman, R.C., Britton, G.W., Rotenberg, S., et al. "Endocrine Regulation of Enzyme Activity in Aging Animals of Different Genotypes," in Bergsma, D., and Harrison, D.E. (eds). *Genetic Effects on Aging*. New York: Alan R. Liss, 1978.
48. Roth, G.S. "Changes in Hormone Binding and Responsiveness in Target Cells and Tissues During Aging," in Cristofalo, V.J., Roberts, J., and Adelman, R.C. (eds). *Explorations in Aging*. New York: Plenum Press, 1974.
48. Roth, G.S. "Reduced Glucocorticoid Binding Site Concentration in Cortical Neuronal Perikarya from Senescent Rats," *Brain Research*, 1976, Vol. 107, 345–354.
48. Roth, G.S. "Hormonal Receptor and Responsiveness Changes During Aging: Genetic Modulation," in Bergsma, D., and Harrison, D.E. (eds). *Genetic Effects on Aging*. New York: Alan R. Liss, 1978.
49. Wodinsky, J. "Hormonal Inhibition of Feeding and Death in Octopus: Control by Optic Gland Secretion," *Science*, December, 1977, Vol. 198, 948–951.
50. Everitt, A.V. "The Hypothalamic-Pituitary Control of Aging and Age-Related Pathology" (Abstract), 10th International Congress of Gerontology, 1975, Jerusalem, Israel, June 22–27.
50. Everitt, A.V., and Ficarra, M.A. "Effects of Hypophysectomy on the Aging of Skeletal Muscle in Rat Hind Leg" (Abstract), 11th International Congress of Gerontology, 1978, Tokyo, Japan, August 20–25.
51. Segall, P.E., Ooka, H., Rose, K., et al. "Neural and Endocrine Development After Chronic Tryptophan Deficiency

PAGE

in Rats: I. Brain Monoamine and Pituitary Responses," *Mechanisms of Ageing and Development,* 1978, Vol. 7, 1–17.
51. Segall, P.E. "Interrelations of Dietary and Hormonal Effects in Aging," *Mechanisms of Ageing and Development,* in press.
52. Williams, C.M. "The Juvenile Hormone," *Scientific American,* February, 1958, Vol. 198, 67–75.
53. Denckla, W.D. "Role of the Pituitary and Thyroid Glands in the Decline of Minimal 0$_2$ Consumption with Age," *Journal of Clinical Investigation,* February, 1974, Vol. 53, 572–581.
53. Denckla, W.D. "A Time to Die," *Life Sciences,* 1975, Vol. 16, 31–44.
53. Denckla, W.D. "Systems Analysis of Possible Mechanisms of Mammalian Aging," *Mechanisms of Ageing and Development,* 1977, Vol. 6, 143.
55. Kanungo, M.S. "A Model for Aging," *Journal of Theoretical Biology,* 1975, Vol. 53, 253–261.
55. Kanungo, M.S., Thakur, M.K., and Das, R. "Alterations in Chromosomal Proteins as a Function of Age of Rats" (Abstract), 11th International Congress of Gerontology, 1978, Tokyo, Japan, August 20–25.
57. Strehler, B.L. *Time, Cells, and Aging.* New York: Academic Press, 1977.

Chapter 2   Diet and Longevity

58. Ross, M. H., and Bras, G. "Dietary Preference and Diseases of Aging," *Nature,* July 19, 1974, Vol. 250, 263–265.
58. Ross, M.H., and Bras, G. "Food Preference and Length of Life," *Science,* October 10, 1975, Vol. 190, 165–167.
58. Ross, M.H., Lustbader, E., and Bras, G. "Dietary Practices and Growth Responses as Predictors of Longevity," *Nature,* August 12, 1976, Vol. 262, 548–553.
58. Ross, M.H. "Dietary Behavior and Longevity," *Nutrition Reviews,* October, 1977, Vol. 35, 257–265.
60. McCay, C.M., Dilley, W.E., and Crowell, M.F. "Growth Rates of Brook Trout Reared upon Purified Rations, upon Dry Skim Milk Diets and upon Feed Combinations of

PAGE

Cereal Grains," *Journal of Nutrition,* 1929, Vol. 1, 233.

60. McCay, C.M., Maynard, L.A., Sperling, G., et al. "Retarded Growth, Life Span, Ultimate Body Size and Age Changes in the Albino Rat After Feeding Diets Restricted in Calories," *Journal of Nutrition,* 1939, Vol. 18, 1.

60. McCay, C.M., Sperling, G., and Barnes, L.L. "Growth, Ageing, Chronic Diseases, and Life-Span in Rats," *Archives of Biochemistry,* 1943, Vol. 2, 469.

60. McCay, C.M. "Chemical Aspects of Ageing and the Effect of Diet upon Ageing," in Lansing, A.I. (ed). *Cowdrey's Problems of Ageing.* Baltimore: The Williams & Wilkins Co., 1952.

62. Berg, B.N. "Nutrition and Longevity in the Rat. I. Food Intake in Relation to Size, Health, and Fertility," *Journal of Nutrition,* 1960, Vol. 71, 242.

62. Berg, B.N., and Simms, H.S. "Nutrition and Longevity in the Rat. II. Longevity and Onset of Disease with Different Levels of Food Intake," *Journal of Nutrition,* 1960, Vol. 71, 255.

62. Ross, M.H. "Nutrition and Longevity in Experimental Animals," in Winick, M. (ed). *Nutrition & Aging.* New York: John Wiley & Sons, 1976.

62. Kent, S. "What Nutritional Deprivation Experiments Reveal about Aging," *Geriatrics,* October, 1976, Vol. 31, 141–144.

63. Roe, F.J.C., and Tucker, M.J. "Recent Developments in the Design of Carcinogenicity Tests on Laboratory Animals," *Proceedings of the European Society for the Study of Drug Toxicity,* 1973, Vol. 15, 171–177.

63. Tucker, M.J. "The Effect of Calorie Intake and Diet on Cancer Incidence," private communication.

63. Ross, M.H., and Bras, G. "Lasting Influence of Early Caloric Restriction on Prevalence of Neoplasms in the Rat," *Journal of the National Cancer Institute,* 1971, Vol. 47, 1095–1113.

64. Masoro, E.J. "Aging and Fat Metabolism" (Abstract), the 145th Annual Meeting of the American Association for the Advancement of Science, 1979, Houston, Texas, January 3–8.

PAGE
65. Weisburger, J.H. "Environmental Cancer," *Journal of Occupational Medicine,* April, 1976, Vol. 18, 245–252.
65. Marquardt, H., Rufino, F., and Weisburger, J.H. "On the Aetiology of Gastric Cancer: Mutagenicity of Food Extracts After Incubation with Nitrite," *Food Cosmetics Toxicology,* 1977, Vol. 15, 97–100.
65. Weisburger, J.H., Reddy, B.S., and Wynder, E.L. "Colon Cancer: Its Epidemiology and Experimental Production," *Cancer,* May, 1977, Vol. 40, 2414–2420.
65. Alcantara, E.N., and Speckmann, E.W. "Diet, Nutrition, and Cancer," *American Journal of Clinical Nutrition,* 1976, Vol. 29, 1035–1047.
66. Rudzinska, M.A. "The Use of a Protozoan for Studies on Aging. III. Similarities Between Young Overfed and Old Normally Fed Tokophyra Infusionium," *Gerontologia,* 1962, Vol. 6, 206.
67. Andres, R. "Lack of Effect of Mild and Moderate Obesity on Longevity in Middle-Aged and Elderly People" (Abstract), 11th International Congress of Gerontology, 1978, Tokyo, Japan, August 20–25.
67. Danowski, T.S., Nolan, S., and Stephen, T. "Obesity," *World Review of Nutrition and Dietetics,* 1975, Vol. 22, 270–279.
67. Goodrick, C.L. "Body Weight Change over the Life Span and Longevity for C57BL/6J Mice and Mutations Which Differ in Maximal Body Weight," *Gerontology,* 1977, Vol. 23, 405–413.
68. Ross, M.H. "Life Expectancy Modification by Change in Dietary Regimen of the Mature Rat," *Proceedings of the Seventh International Congress of Nutrition,* 1966, Vol. 5, 35–38.
68. Segall, P.E., and Timiras, P.S. "Patho-Physiologic Findings After Chronic Tryptophan Deficiency in Rats: A Model for Delayed Growth and Aging," *Mechanisms of Ageing and Development,* 1976, Vol. 5, 109–124.
71. Dayton, S., and Pearce, M.L. "Prevention of Coronary Heart Disease and Other Complications of Atherosclerosis

PAGE

by Modified Diet," *American Journal of Medicine,* 1964, Vol. 46, 751–762.

72. Kannel, W.B., and Gordon, T. "The Framingham Diet Study: Diet and the Regulation of Serum Cholesterol," Section 24, Washington, D.C., Dept. of Health, Education & Welfare, 1970.

72. Kannel, W.B., Castelli, W.P., Gordon, T., et al. "Serum Cholesterol, Lipoproteins and the Risk of Coronary Heart Disease," *Annals of Internal Medicine,* 1971, Vol. 74, 1.

72. Miettinen, M., Turpeinen, O., Karvonen, M.J., et al. "Effect of Cholesterol-Lowering Diet on Mortality from Coronary Heart Disease and Other Causes: A Twelve-Year Clinical Trial in Men and Women," *Lancet,* 1972, Vol. 2, 835–838.

73. Coronary Drug Project Research Group. "Clofibrate and Niacin in Coronary Heart Disease," *Journal of the American Medical Association,* 1975, Vol. 231, 360–381.

73. Eisenberg, S., and Levy, R.I. "Lipoprotein Metabolism," *Advances in Lipid Research,* 1975, Vol. 13, 1–89.

73. Jackson, R.L., Morrisett, J.D., and Gotto, A.M., "Lipoproteins and Lipid Transport: Structural and Functional Concepts," in Rifkind, B.M., and Levy, R.I. (eds). *Hyperlipidemia: Diagnosis and Therapy.* New York: Grune & Stratton, Inc., 1977.

73. Mao, S.J.T., Sparrow, J.T., Gilliam, E.B., et al. "Mechanism of Lipid-Protein Interaction in the Plasma Lipoproteins: Lipid-Binding Properties of Synthetic Fragments of Apolipoprotein A–II," *Biochemistry,* 1977, Vol. 16, 1150–1156.

74. Goldstein, J.L., and Brown, M.S. "Lipoprotein Receptors, Cholesterol Metabolism, and Atherosclerosis," *Archives of Pathology,* 1975, Vol. 99, 181–184.

74. Brown, M.S., and Goldstein, J.L. "Familial Hypercholesterolemia: A Genetic Defect in the Low-Density Lipoprotein Receptor," *New England Journal of Medicine,* 1976, Vol. 294, 1386–1390.

76. Hruza, Z. "Increase of Cholesterol Turnover of Old Rats

PAGE

Connected by Parabiosis with Young Rats," *Experimental Gerontology,* 1971, Vol. 6, 103–107.

76. Hruza, Z. "Effect of Endocrine Factors on Cholesterol Turnover in Young and Old Rats," *Experimental Gerontology,* 1971, Vol. 6, 199–204.

76. Hruza, Z., and Zbuzkova, V. "Decrease of Excretion of Cholesterol During Aging," *Experimental Gerontology,* 1973, Vol. 8, 29–37.

76. Crouse, J.R., Grundy, S.M., and Ahrens, E.H. Jr. "Cholesterol Distribution in the Bulk Tissues of Man: Variation with Age," *Journal of Clinical Investigation,* 1972, Vol. 51, 1292.

78. Miller, G.J., and Miller, N.E. "Plasma-High-Density-Lipoprotein Concentration and Development of Ischaemic Heart-Disease," *Lancet,* 1975, Vol. 1, 16–19.

78. Castelli, W.P., Doyle, J.T., Gordon, T., et al. "HDL Cholesterol Levels (HDLC) in Coronary Heart Disease (CHD): A Cooperative Lipoprotein Phenotyping Study," *Circulation* (Abstracts), October, 1975, Vol. 51, 97.

78. Rhoads, G.G., Gulbrandsen, C.L., and Kagan, A. "Serum Lipoproteins and Coronary Heart Disease in a Population Study of Hawaii Japanese Men," *New England Journal of Medicine,* 1976, Vol. 294, 293–298.

78. Carew, T.E., Hayes, S.B., Koschinsky, T., et al. "A Mechanism by Which High-Density Lipoproteins May Slow the Atherogenic Process," *Lancet,* 1976, Vol. 1, 1315–1317.

79. Buchwald, H.R., Moore, B., and Varco, R.L. "Surgical Treatment of Hyperlipidemia," *Circulation* (Supplement 1), 1974, Vol. 49, 1–37.

79. Blankenhorn, D. "Evidence for Regression/Progression of Atherosclerosis in Man," in *Proceedings of the International Workshop Conference on Atherosclerosis,* 1975, London, Ontario, Canada.

79. Wissler, R.W. "Problems and Progress in Understanding Progressive Atherogenesis," *Cardiovascular Research Center Bulletin,* January–March, 1977, 69–86.

81. "Evaluation of Longevity Center 26–30 Day Inpatient Pro-

PAGE

gram—An Analysis of 893 Patients," Longevity Research Institute, 1978.

81. *Aviation Medical Bulletin,* March, 1978, Atlanta, Ga., Aviation Insurance Agency, Inc.

81. Leonard, J.N., Hofer, J.L., and Pritikin, N. *Live Longer Now—The First One Hundred Years of Your Life.* New York: Grosset & Dunlap, 1974.

81. Pritikin, N., and McGrady, P.M. Jr. *The Pritikin Program for Diet and Exercise.* New York: Grosset & Dunlap, 1979.

83. Mann, G.V. "A Factor in Yogurt Which Lowers Cholesteremia in Man," *Atherosclerosis,* 1977, Vol. 26, 335–340.

83. Nair, C.R., and Mann, G.V. "A Factor in Milk Which Influences Cholesteremia in Rats," *Atherosclerosis,* 1977, Vol. 26, 363–367.

84. Spritz, N., and Mehkel, M.A. "Effects of Dietary Fats on Plasma Lipids and Lipoproteins: An Hypothesis for the Lipid Lowering Effect of Unsaturated Fatty Acids," *Journal of Clinical Investigation,* 1969, Vol. 48, 78.

84. Grundy, S.M. "Effects of Polyunsaturated Fats on Lipid Metabolism in Patients with Hypertriglyceridemia," *Journal of Clinical Investigation,* 1975, Vol. 55, 269.

84. Simons, L.A., Hickie, J.B., and Ruys, J. "Treatment of Hypercholesterolaemia with Oral Lecithin," *Australian and New Zealand Journal of Medicine,* 1977, Vol. 7, 262–266.

85. Ederer, F., Leren, P., Turpeinen, O., et al. "Cancer Among Men on Cholesterol-Lowering Diets—Experience from Five Clinical Trials," *Lancet,* July 24, 1971.

85. Carroll, K.K. "Experimental Evidence of Dietary Factors and Hormone-Dependent Cancers," *Cancer Research,* November, 1975, Vol. 35, 3374–3383.

85. Hopkins, G.J., and West, C.E. "Possible Roles of Dietary Fats in Carcinogenesis," *Life Sciences,* 1976, Vol. 19, 1103–1116.

85. Wynder, E.L., MacCornack, F., Hill, P., et al. "Nutrition and the Etiology and Prevention of Breast Cancer," *Cancer Detection and Prevention,* 1976, Vol. 1, 293–310.

PAGE
86. Castelli, W.P., Gordon, T., Hjortland, M.C., et al. "Alcohol and Blood Lipids: The Cooperative Lipoprotein Phenotyping Study," *Lancet*, July 23, 1977.
87. Corrigan, G.E. "Autopsy Pathology of Alcoholism," *Annals of the New York Academy of Sciences*, 1976, Vol. 273, 385–387.
88. Yudkin, J. *Sweet and Dangerous*. New York: Bantam Books, 1972.
88. Grande, F. "Sugar and Cardiovascular Disease," *World Review of Nutrition and Dietetics*, 1975, Vol. 22, 248–269.
88. Grande, F., Anderson, J.T., and Keys, A. "Sucrose and Various Carbohydrate-Containing Foods and Serum Lipids in Man," *American Journal of Clinical Nutrition*, 1974, Vol. 27, 1043–1051.
91. Freis, E.D., "Salt, Volume and the Prevention of Hypertension," *Circulation*, April, 1976, Vol. 53, 589–595.
92. Burkitt, D.P., Walker, A.R.P., and Painter, N.S. "Dietary Fiber and Disease," *Journal of the American Medical Association*, August 19, 1974, Vol. 229, 1068–1074.
92. Burkitt, D.P. "Epidemiology of Cancer of the Colon and Rectum," *Cancer*, March, 1971, Vol. 28, 13.
92. Kay, R.M., and Truswell, A.S. "Effect of Citrus Pectin on Blood Lipids and Fecal Steroid Excretion in Man," *American Journal of Clinical Nutrition*, February, 1977, Vol. 30, 171–175.

Chapter 3 Environmental Stress and Longevity

95. Selye, H. *The Stress of Life* (revised edition). New York: McGraw-Hill Company, 1978.
95. Selye, H. *Stress Without Distress*. Philadelphia: J.B. Lippincott Company, 1974.
95. Selye, H. *Hormones and Resistance*, 2 volumes. New York, Heidelberg, Berlin: Springer-Verlag, 1971.
96. Oniani, T.N., Molnar, P.P., and Naneishvili, T.L. "On Two Phases of the Paradoxical State of Sleep," *Soobshch Akad Gruz SSR*, March, 1969, Vol. 56, 685–688.
96. Oniani, T.N., Koridze, M.G., Kavkasidze, M.G., et al. "Effect of Electrical Stimulation of Reticular Formation and

PAGE

Hypothalamus on the Structure and Ratio of Different Phases of Sleep," in Oniani, T.N. (ed). *Mekhanizmi Deyatelnosti Golovnogo Mozga.* Tbilisi: Metsniereba Publications, 1975.

96. Oniani, T.N. "On the Functional Significance of Sleep," *Acta Neurobiologiae Experimentalis,* 1977, Vol. 37, 223–246.

97. Rogot, E., Fabsitz, R., and Feinleib, M. "Daily Variation in USA Mortality," *American Journal of Epidemiology,* 1976, Vol. 103, 198–211.

98. Friedman, M., and Rosenman, R.II. *Type A Behavior and Your Heart.* New York: Fawcett Crest Books, 1974.

99. Barnes, B.O., and Barnes, C.W. *Solved: The Riddle of Heart Attacks.* Ft. Collins, Colorado: Robinson Press, 1976.

100. Phillips, G.B. "Relationship Between Serum Sex Hormones and Glucose, Insulin, and Lipid Abnormalities in Men With Myocardial Infarction," *Proceedings of the National Academy of Sciences, USA,* April, 1977, Vol. 74, 1729–1733.

100. Kannel, W.B., Hjortland, M.C., McNamara, P.M., et al. "Menopause and Risk of Cardiovascular Disease—The Framingham Study," *Annals of Internal Medicine,* 1976, Vol. 85, 447–452.

101. Anderson, T.W., LeRiche, W.H., and MacKay, J.S. "Sudden Death and Ischemic Heart Disease—Correlation with Hardness of Local Water Supply," *New England Journal of Medicine,* 1969, Vol. 280, 805–807.

101. Anderson, T.W., Neri, L.C., Schreiber, G.B., et al. "Ischemic Heart Disease, Water Hardness and Myocardial Magnesium," *Canadian Medical Association Journal,* August 9, 1975, Vol. 113, 199–203.

101. Neri, L.C., Hewitt, D., Schreiber, G.B., et al. "Health Aspects of Hard and Soft Waters," *Journal of the American Water Works Association,* August, 1975, 403–409.

102. Klevay, L.M. "Coronary Heart Disease: The Zinc/Copper Hypothesis," *American Journal of Clinical Nutrition,* July, 1975, Vol. 28, 764–774.

102. Allen, K.G.D., Klevay, L.M., and Springer, H.L. "The Zinc and Copper Content of Seeds and Nuts," *Nutrition Reports International,* September, 1977, Vol. 16, 227–230.

PAGE
102. Klevay, L.M. "The Role of Copper and Zinc in Cholesterol Metabolism," in Draper, H.H. (ed). *Advances in Nutritional Research*, Vol. 1. New York: Plenum Press, 1977.

102. Allen, K.G.D., and Klevay, L.M. "Cholesterolemia and Cardiovascular Abnormalities in Rats Caused by Copper Deficiency," *Atherosclerosis*, 1978, Vol. 29, 81–93.

103. Harker, L., Ross, R., Slichter, S., et al. "Homocysteine-Induced Arteriosclerosis: The Role of Endothelial Cell Injury and Platelet Response in its Genesis," *Journal of Clinical Investigation*, 1976, Vol. 58, 731–741.

103. Ross, R., Glomset, J., and Harker, L. "Response to Injury and Atherogenesis," *American Journal of Pathology*, March, 1977, Vol. 86, 675–684.

103. Wissler, R.W., Fischer-Dzoga, K., and Chen, R. "Lipids in the Arterial Wall," in Schetler, G., and Weizel, A. (eds). *Atherosclerosis III*. Berlin: Springer-Verlag, 1971.

103. Moore, S. "Thromboatherosclerosis in Normolipemic Rabbits. A Result of Continued Endothelial Damage," *Laboratory Investigation*, 1973, Vol. 29, 478–487.

103. Minick, C.R., and Murphy, G.E. "Experimental Induction of Atheroarteriosclerosis by the Synergy of Allergic Injury to Arteries and Lipid Rich Diet. II. Effect of Repeatedly Injected Foreign Protein in Rabbits Fed a Lipid-Rich Cholesterol-Poor Diet," *American Journal of Pathology*, 1973, Vol. 73, 265–300.

104. Benditt, E.P., and Benditt, J.M. "Evidence for a Monoclonal Origin of Human Atherosclerotic Plaques," *Proceedings of the National Academy of Sciences, USA*, June, 1973, Vol. 70, 1753–1756.

104. Pearson, T.A., Wang, A., Solez, K., et al. "Clonal Characteristics of Fibrous Plaques and Fatty Streaks from Human Aortas," *American Journal of Pathology*, November, 1975, Vol. 81, 379–387.

106. Anderson, T.W. "Mortality from Ischemic Heart Disease—Changes in Middle-Aged Men since 1900," *Journal of the American Medical Association*, April 16, 1973, Vol. 224, 336–338.

PAGE

106. Anderson, T.W. "A New View of Heart Disease," *New Scientist*, February 9, 1978, 374–376.

111. Doll, R., and Peto, R. "Mortality in Relation to Smoking: 20 Years' Observations on Male British Doctors," *British Medical Journal*, December 25, 1976, Vol. 2, 1525–1536.

111. Gentleman, J.F., and Forbes, W.F. "Cancer Mortality for Males and Females and Its Relation to Cigarette Smoking," *Journal of Gerontology*, May, 1974, Vol. 29, 518–533.

111. Rickert, W.S., and Forbes, W.F. "Changes in Collagen with Age—VI. Age and Smoking Related Changes in Human Lung Connective Tissue," *Experimental Gerontology*, 1976, Vol. 11, 89–101.

115. Cole, P. "Cancer and Occupation: Status and Needs of Epidemiologic Research," *Cancer*, 1977, Vol. 39, 1788–1793.

115. Nicholson, W.J. "Cancer Following Occupational Exposure to Asbestos and Vinyl Chloride," *Cancer*, 1977, Vol. 39, 1794–1801.

115. Anderson, H.A., Lilis, R., Daum, S.M., et al. "Household Contact Asbestos Neoplastic Risk," *Annals of the New York Academy of Sciences*, 1976, Vol. 271, 311–323.

115. McMichael, A.J., Andjelkovic, D.A., and Tyroler, H.A. "Cancer Mortality among Rubber Workers: An Epidemiologic Study," *Annals of the New York Academy of Sciences*, 1977, Vol. 271, 125–137.

115. Radford, E.P. "Cancer Mortality in the Steel Industry," *Annals of the New York Academy of Sciences*, 1977, Vol. 271, 228–237.

116. Clayson, D.B., and Shubik, P. "The Carcinogenic Action of Drugs," *Cancer Detection and Prevention*, January, 1976, Vol. 1, 43–77.

118. Heyden, S., Tyroler, H.A., Cassel, J.C., et al. "Coffee Consumption and Mortality in a Community Study—Evans County, Georgia," *Zeitschrift für Ernährungswissenschaft*, 1976, Vol. 15, 143–150.

118. Greden, J.F. "Coffee, Tea and You," *The Sciences*, January, 1979, Vol. 19, 6–11.

119. Shubik, P. "Food Additives (Natural and Synthetic)," pre-

sented at the American Cancer Society—National Cancer Institute National Conference on Nutrition in Cancer, Seattle, Wash., June 29–July 1, 1978.

120. Goldby, S. *Food.* New York: McGraw-Hill Yearbook of Science and Technology, 1975.

120. Seltzer, R.J. "Work on New Synthetic Sweeteners Advances," *Chemical and Engineering News,* August 25, 1975, Vol. 53, 27–28.

121. Curtis, H.J., and Crowley, C. "Chromosome Aberrations in Liver Cells in Relation to the Somatic Mutation Theory of Aging," *Radiation Research,* 1963, Vol. 19, 337–344.

121. Curtis, H.J., Leith, J., and Tilley, J. "Chromosome Aberrations in Liver Cells of Dogs of Different Ages," *Journal of Gerontology,* 1966, Vol. 21, 268–270.

121. Storer, J.B. "Effect of Aging and Radiation in Mice of Different Genotypes," in Bergsma, D., and Harrison, D.E. (eds). *Genetic Effects on Aging.* New York: Alan R. Liss, 1978.

121. Archer, V.E. "Occupational Exposure to Radiation as a Cancer Hazard," *Cancer,* 1977, Vol. 39, 1802–1806.

121. Baskin, Y. "U Scientists Study UV Light and Cancer," Public Relations Release from University of Utah Medical School, July 18, 1978.

123. Ott, J.N. *Health and Light.* New York: Pocket Books, 1976.

124. *Quality of Life in the US Metropolitan Areas, 1970* (Summary), Midwest Research Institute, 1975.

125. Glasser, M., Greenburg, L., and Field, F. "Mortality and Morbidity During a Period of High Levels of Air Pollution," *Archives of Environmental Health,* December 15, 1967, Vol. 15, 684–694.

125. Lave, L.B., and Seskin, E.P. "Air Pollution, Climate, and Home Heating: Their Effects on U.S. Mortality Rates," *American Journal of Public Health,* July, 1972, Vol. 62, 909–916.

125. Lave, L.B., and Seskin, E.P. "Air Pollution and Human Health," *Science,* August 21, 1970, Vol. 169, 723–733.

126. Fridovich, I. "Oxygen Is Toxic!," *BioScience,* July, 1977, Vol. 27, 462–466.

PAGE
126. Halliwell, B. "Superoxide Dismutase, Catalase and Gluta-thione Peroxidase: Solutions to the Problems of Living with Oxygen," *New Phytology,* 1974, Vol. 73, 1075–1086.
128. Windle-Taylor, E. "The Relationship Between Water Quality and Human Health: Medical Aspects," *Journal of the Royal Society of Health,* 1978, Vol. 98, 121–129.
128. States, S.J. "Weather and Death in Birmingham, Alabama," *Environmental Research,* 1976, Vol. 12, 340–354.
128. Rogot, E., and Padgett, S.J. "Associations of Coronary and Stroke Mortality with Temperature and Snowfall in Selected Areas of the United States, 1962–1966," *American Journal of Epidemiology,* 1976, Vol. 103, 565–575.
128. Anderson, T.W., and LeRiche, W.H. "Cold Weather and Myocardial Infarction," *Lancet,* February 7, 1970, Vol. 1, 291–296.

Chapter 4 Anti-Aging Therapies
131. Harman, D. "Prolongation of the Normal Life Span by Radiation Protection Chemicals," *Journal of Gerontology,* 1957, Vol. 12, 257.
131. Harman, D. "Prolongation of the Normal Life Span and Inhibition of Spontaneous Cancer by Antioxidants," *Journal of Gerontology,* 1961, Vol. 16, 247.
131. Harman, D. "Free Radical Theory of Aging: Effect of Free Radical Inhibitors on the Life Span of Male LAF$_1$ Mice—Second Experiment," *The Gerontologist,* 1968, Vol. 8, 13.
131. Comfort, A., Youhotsky-Gore, I., and Pathmanathan, K. "The Effects of Ethoxyquin on the Longevity of C$_3$H Strain Mice," *Nature,* 1971, Vol. 229, 254.
131. Huu-Hoi, N.P., and Ratsimamanga, A.R. "Retarding Action of Nordihydroguaiaretic Acid on Aging in the Rat," *CR Society of Biology* (Paris), 1959, Vol. 153, 1180.
131. Oeriu, S., and Vochitu, E. "The Effect of the Administration of Compounds Which Contain Sulfhydril Groups on the Survival Rates of Mice, Rats, and Guinea Pigs," *Journal of Gerontology,* 1965, Vol. 20, 417.
131. Passwater, R.A., and Welker, P.A. "Human Aging Research, Part 2," *American Laboratory,* May, 1971.

PAGE
131. Dormandy, T.L., "Free-Radical Oxidation and Antioxidants," *Lancet,* March 25, 1978, 647–650.
136. Tappel, A.L., Fletcher, B., and Deamer, D. "Effect of Antioxidants and Nutrients on Lipid Peroxidation Fluorescent Products and Aging Parameters in the Mouse," *Journal of Gerontology,* 1973, Vol. 28, 415.
136. Johnson, J.E., Mehler, W.R., and Miquel, J. "A Fine Structural Study of Degenerative Changes in the Dorsal Column Nuclei of Aging Mice. Lack of Protection by Vitamin E," *Journal of Gerontology,* April, 1975, Vol. 30, 395–411.
137. Kent, S. "Do Free Radicals and Dietary Antioxidants Wage Intracellular War?," *Geriatrics,* January, 1977, Vol. 32, 127–136.
137. Kohn, R.R. "Effect of Antioxidants on Life-Span of C57BL Mice," *Journal of Gerontology,* 1971, Vol. 26, 378.
137. Green, J. "Vitamin E and the Biological Antioxidant Theory," *Annals of the New York Academy of Sciences,* 1972, Vol. 203, 29.
138. Aslan, A. "Theoretical and Practical Aspects of Chemotherapeutic Techniques in the Retardation of the Aging Process," presented at the Symposium on Theoretical Aspects of Aging, 1974, Miami, Florida, February 7–8.
138. Packer, L., and Smith, J.R. "Extension of the In Vitro Lifespan of Human WI-38 Cells in Culture by Vitamin E," in Cristofalo, V.J., Roberts, J., Adelman, R.C. (eds). *Advances in Experimental Medicine and Biology,* Vol. 61, *Explorations in Aging.* New York: Plenum Press, 1975.
138. Packer, L., and Smith, J.R. "Extension of the Lifespan of Cultured Normal Diploid Cells by Vitamin E: A Reevaluation," *Proceedings of the National Academy of Sciences, USA,* April, 1977, Vol. 74, 1640–1641.
140. Anderson, T.W., and Reid, D.B.W. "A Double-Blind Trial of Vitamin E in Angina Pectoris," *American Journal of Clinical Nutrition,* October, 1974, Vol. 27, 1174–1178.
141. Haeger, K. "Long-Time Treatment of Intermittent Claudication with Vitamin E," *American Journal of Clinical Nutrition,* 1974, Vol. 27, 1179.
142. Massie, H.R., Baird, M.B., and Piekielniak, M.J. "Ascorbic

PAGE

Acid and Longevity in Drosophila," *Experimental Geron-tology*, 1976, Vol. 11, 37–41.

142. Davies, J.E.W., Ellery, P.M., and Hughes, R.E. "Dietary Ascorbic Acid and Life Span of Guinea Pigs," *Experimental Gerontology*, 1977, Vol. 12, 215–216.

144. Cameron, E., and Campbell, A. "The Orthomolecular Treatment of Cancer. II. Clinical Trial of High-Dose Ascorbic Acid Supplements in Advanced Human Cancer," *Chemical-Biological Interactions*, 1974, Vol. 9, 285–315.

144. Cameron, E., Campbell, A., and Jack, T. "The Orthomolecular Treatment of Cancer. III. Reticulum Cell Sarcoma: Double Complete Regression Induced by High-Dose Ascorbic Acid Therapy," *Chemical-Biological Interactions*, 1975, Vol. 11, 387–393.

144. Cameron, E., and Pauling, L. "Supplemental Ascorbate in the Supportive Treatment of Cancer: Prolongation of Survival Times in Terminal Human Cancer," *Proceedings of the National Academy of Sciences, USA*, October, 1976, Vol. 73, 3685–3689.

144. Cameron, E., and Pauling, L. "Supplemental Ascorbate in the Supportive Treatment of Cancer: Reevaluation of Prolongation of Survival Times in Terminal Human Cancer," *Proceedings of the National Academy of Sciences, USA*, September, 1978, Vol. 75, 4538–4542.

146. Marquardt, H., Rufino, F., and Weisburger, J.H. "Mutagenic Activity of Nitrite-Treated Foods: Human Stomach Cancer May Be Related to Dietary Factors," *Science*, May 27, 1977, Vol. 196, 1000–1001.

148. DeCosse, J.J., Adams, M.B., Kuzma, J.F., et al. "Effects of Ascorbic Acid on Rectal Polyps of Patients with Familial Polyposis," *Surgery*, November, 1975, Vol. 78, 608–612.

148. DeCosse, J.J., Condon, R.E., and Adams, M.B. "Surgical and Medical Measures in Prevention of Large Bowel Cancer," *Cancer*, May, 1977, Vol. 40, 2549–2552.

148. Ginter, E. "Cholesterol: Vitamin C Controls Its Transformation to Bile Acids," *Science*, February 16, 1973, Vol. 179, 702–704.

148. Turley, S.D., West, C.E., and Horton, B.J. "The Role of

PAGE

Ascorbic Acid in the Regulation of Cholesterol Metabolism and in the Pathogenesis of Atherosclerosis," *Atherosclerosis,* 1976, Vol. 24, 1–18.

148. Spittle, C.R. "Atherosclerosis and Vitamin C," *Lancet,* December 11, 1971.

150. Luberoff, B.J. "Symptomectomy with Vitamin C—A Chat with Robert Cathcart, M.D.," *Chemtech,* February, 1978, 75–86.

150. Yew, M.S. " 'Recommended Daily Allowances' for Vitamin C," *Proceedings of the National Academy of Sciences, USA,* April, 1973, Vol. 70, 969–972.

150. "Vitamin C Toxicity," *Nutrition Reviews,* August, 1976, 236–237.

150. Herbert, V., Jacob, E., Wong, K.T.J., et al. "Low Serum Vitamin B_{12} Levels in Patients Receiving Ascorbic Acid in Megadoses: Studies Concerning the Effect of Ascorbate on Radioisotope Vitamin B_{12} Assay[1-4]," *American Journal of Clinical Nutrition,* February, 1978, Vol. 31, 253–258.

151. Frost, D.V. "The Two Faces of Selenium: Can Selenophobia be Cured?," *CRC Critical Reviews in Toxicology,* October, 1972, 489–501.

152. Stacpoole, P.W. "Pangamic Acid (Vitamin B_{15})," *World Review of Nutrition and Dietetics,* 1977, Vol. 27, 145–163.

153. Pelton, R.B., and Williams, R.J. "Effects of Pantothenic Acid on the Longevity of Mice," *Society for Experimental Biology and Medicine,* 1958, Vol. 99, 632–633.

155. Cotzias, G.C., Miller, S.T., Nicholson, A.R. Jr., et al. "Prolongation of the Life-Span in Mice Adapted to Large Amounts of L-Dopa," *Proceedings of the National Academy of Sciences, USA,* June, 1974, Vol. 71, 2466–2469.

155. Cotzias, G.C., Miller, S.T., Tang, L.C., et al. "Levodopa, Fertility, and Longevity," *Science,* April 29, 1977, Vol. 196, 549–550.

156. Massie, H.R., Baird, M.B., and Williams, T.R. "Increased Longevity of Drosophila Melanogaster with Diiodomethane," *Gerontology,* 1978, Vol. 24, 104–110.

157. Sperling, G.A., Loosli, J.K., Lupien, P., et al. "Effects of

PAGE

Sulfamerazine and Exercise on Life Span of Rats and Hamsters," *Gerontology*, 1978, Vol. 24, 220–224.

158. Cristofalo, V.J. "Hydrocortisone as a Modulator of Cell Division and Population Life Span," in Cristofalo, V.J., Roberts, J., and Adelman, R.C. (eds). *Advances in Experimental Medicine and Biology*, Vol. 61, *Explorations in Aging*. New York: Plenum Press, 1975.

158. "Aspirin in Coronary Heart Disease—The Coronary Drug Project Research Group," *Journal of Chronic Diseases*, 1976, Vol. 29, 625–642.

159. Pilgeram, L.O. "Abnormalities in Clotting and Thrombolysis as a Risk Factor for Stroke," *Thrombosis Et Diathesis Haemorrhagica*, 1974, Vol. 31, 245–264.

160. Liu, R.K., and Walford, R.L. "The Effect of Lowered Body Temperature on Lifespan and Immune and Non-Immune Processes," *Gerontologia*, 1972, Vol. 18, 363–388.

160. Liu, R.K., and Walford, R.L. "Mid-Life Temperature-Transfer Effects on Life-Span of Annual Fish," *Journal of Gerontology*, February, 1975, Vol. 30, 129–131.

162. Myers, R.D., and Taksh, T.L. "Thermoregulation Around a New Set-Point Established in the Monkey by Altering the Ratio of Sodium to Calcium Ions Within the Hypothalamus," *Journal of Physiology* (London), 1971, Vol. 218, 609–633.

162. Myers, R. D. "Species Continuity in the Thermoregulatory Responses of the Pigtailed Macaque to Monoamines Injected into the Hypothalamus," *Comprehensive Biochemistry and Physiology* (A), 1975, Vol. 51, 639–645.

162. Myers, R.D., Gisolf, C.V., and Mora, F. "Role of Brain Ca^{2+} in Central Control of Body Temperature During Exercise in the Monkey," *Journal of Applied Physiology*, April, 1977, Vol. 43, 689–694.

164. Rosenberg, B., Kemeny, G., Smith, L.G., et al. "The Kinetics and Thermodynamics of Death in Multicellular Organisms," *Mechanisms of Ageing and Development*, 1973, Vol. 2, 275–293.

PAGE
164. Janoff, A.S., and Rosenberg, B. "Chemically Evoked Hypothermia in the Mouse: Toward a Method for Investigating Thermodynamic Parameters of Aging and Death in Mammals," *Mechanisms of Ageing and Development,* 1978, Vol. 3, 335–349.

164. Sharkawi, M., and Cianflone, D. "Disulfiram-Induced Hypothermia in the Normal Rat; Its Attenuation by Pimozide," *Neuropharmacology,* 1978, Vol. 17, 401–404.

164. Loosen, P.T., Nemeroff, C.B., Bissette, G., et al. "Neurotensin-Induced Hypothermia in the Rat: Structure-Activity Studies," *Neuropharmacology,* 1978, Vol. 17, 109–113.

164. Brown, M., Rivier, J., and Vale, W. "Bombesin: Potent Effects on Thermoregulation in the Rat," *Science,* May 27, 1977, Vol. 196, 998–1000.

Chapter 5   How Exercise Extends Life Span

167. Morris, J.N., Adam, C., Chave, S.P.W., et al. "Vigorous Exercise in Leisure-Time and the Incidence of Coronary Heart-Disease," *Lancet,* February 17, 1973, 333–339.

168. Epstein, L., Miller, G.J., Stitt, F.W., et al. "Vigorous Exercise in Leisure Time, Coronary Risk-Factors, and Resting Electrocardiogram in Middle-Aged Male Civil Servants," *British Heart Journal,* 1976, Vol. 38, 403–409.

169. Cooper, K.H., Pollock, M.L., Martin, R.P., et al. "Physical Fitness Levels vs. Selected Coronary Risk Factors: A Cross-Sectional Study," *Journal of the American Medical Association,* 1976, Vol. 236, 165–169.

170. Paffenbarger, R.S., Jr., Laughlin, M.E., Gima, A.S., et al. "Work Activity of Longshoremen as Related to Death from Coronary Heart Disease and Stroke," *New England Journal of Medicine,* 1970, Vol. 282, 1109–1114.

170. Paffenbarger, R.S., Jr., Gima, A.S., Laughlin, M.E., et al. "Characteristics of Longshoremen Related to Fatal Coronary Heart Disease and Stroke," *American Journal of Public Health,* 1971, Vol. 61, 1362–1370.

170. Paffenbarger, R.S., Jr., and Hale, W.E. "Work Activity and Coronary Heart Mortality," *New England Journal of Medicine,* 1975, Vol. 292, 545–550.

PAGE

170. Paffenbarger, R.S., Jr., Hale, W.E., Brand, R.J., et al. "Work-Energy Level, Personal Characteristics, and Fatal Heart Attacks: A Birth-Cohort Effect," *American Journal of Epidemiology*, 1977, Vol. 105, 200–213.

173. Paffenbarger, R.S., Jr., Wing, A.L., and Hyde, R.T. "Physical Activity as an Index of Heart Attack Risk in College Alumni," *American Journal of Epidemiology*, 1978, Vol. 108, 161–175.

174. Wood, P.D., Haskell, W., Klein, H., et al. "The Distribution of Plasma Lipoproteins in Middle-Aged Male Runners," *Metabolism*, November, 1976, Vol. 25, 1249–1257.

174. Martin, R.P., Haskell, W.L., and Wood, P.D. "Blood Chemistry and Lipid Profile of Elite Distance Runners," *Annals of the New York Academy of Sciences*, 1977, Vol. 301, 346–360.

174. Wood, P.D., Haskell, W.L., Stern, M.P., et al. "Plasma Lipoprotein Distributions in Male and Female Runners," *Annals of the New York Academy of Sciences*, 1977, Vol. 301, 748–763.

175. Lopez-S, A. "Effects of Exercise on Serum Lipids and Lipoproteins," in Day, C.E., and Levy, R.S. (eds). *Low Density Lipoproteins*. New York: Plenum Press, 1976.

175. Kent, S. "Does Exercise Prevent Heart Attacks?," *Geriatrics*, November, 1978, Vol. 33, 95–104.

176. Leon, A.S., and Blackburn, H. "The Relationship of Physical Activity to Coronary Heart Disease and Life Expectancy," *Annals of the New York Academy of Sciences*, 1977, Vol. 301, 561–578.

176. Leon, A.S., Conrad, J., Hunninghake, D., et al. "Exercise Effects on Body Composition, Work Capacity and Carbohydrate and Lipid Metabolism of Young Obese Men" (Abstract), *Medicine & Science in Sports*, Spring, 1977, Vol. 9, 60.

177. Hartung, G.H., Foreyt, J.P., Mitchell, R.E., et al. "Relationship of Diet and HDL Cholesterol in Sedentary and Active Middle-Aged Men" (Abstract), *Circulation*, part II, October, 1978, Vol. 58, 204.

178. Selvester, R., Camp, J., and Sanmarco, M. "Effects of Exer-

PAGE

cise Training on Progression of Documented Coronary Arteriosclerosis in Men," *Annals of the New York Academy of Sciences,* 1977, Vol. 301, 495–508.

181. Bassler, T.J. "Marathon Running and Immunity to Atherosclerosis," *Annals of the New York Academy of Sciences,* 1977, Vol. 301, 579–592.

181. Noakes, T., Opic, L., Beck, W., et al. "Coronary Heart Disease in Marathon Runners," *Annals of the New York Academy of Sciences,* 1977, Vol. 301, 593–619.

181. Milvy, P. "Statistical Analysis of Deaths from Coronary Heart Disease Anticipated in a Cohort of Marathon Runners," *Annals of the New York Academy of Sciences,* 1977, Vol. 301, 620–626.

182. Mertens, D.J., Shephard, R.J., and Kavanagh, T. "Long-Term Exercise Therapy for Chronic Obstructive Lung Disease," *Respiration,* 1978, Vol. 35, 96–107.

184. Goodrick, C.L. "The Effects of Exercise on Longevity and Behavior of Hybrid Mice Which Differ in Coat Color," *Journal of Gerontology,* February, 1974, Vol. 29, 129–133.

184. Retzlaff, E., Fontaine, J., and Furuta, W. "Effects of Daily Exercise on Life-Span of Albino Rats," *Geriatrics,* March, 1966, Vol. 21, 171–177.

185. Edington, D.W., Cosmas, A.C., and McCafferty, W.B. "Exercise and Longevity: Evidence for a Threshold Age," *Journal of Gerontology,* March, 1972, Vol. 27, 341–343.

186. De Vries, H.A., and Adams, G.M. "Comparison of Exercise Responses in Old and Young Men: I. The Cardiac Effort/Total Body Effort Relationship," *Journal of Gerontology,* March, 1972, Vol. 27, 344–348.

186. Karvonen, M.J., Klemola, H., Virkajarvi, J., et al. "Longevity of Endurance Skiers," *Medicine & Science in Sports,* January, 1974, Vol. 1, 49–51.

186. Karvonen, M.J. "Endurance Sports, Longevity, and Health," *Annals of the New York Academy of Sciences,* 1977, Vol. 301, 653–655.

187. Suominen, H., Heikkinen, E., Parkatti, T., et al. "Lifelong Physical Training and Biological Aging" (Abstract), pre-

PAGE

sented at the 11th International Congress of Gerontology, 1978, Tokyo, Japan, August 20-25.

Chapter 6 Can We Become Immune to Aging?

189. Walford, R.S., Meredith, P.J., and Cheney, K.E. "Immunoengineering: Prospects for Correction of Age-Related Immunodeficiency States," in Makinodan, T., Yunis, E. (eds). *Comprehensive Immunology,* Vol. 1, *Immunology and Aging.* New York: Plenum Press, 1976.

189. Gerbase-Delima, M., Liu, R.K., Cheney, K.E., et al. "Immune Function and Survival in a Long-Lived Mouse Strain Subjected to Undernutrition," *Gerontologia,* 1975, Vol. 21, 184.

190. Jose, D.G., Stutman, O., Good, R.A. "Long-Term Effects on Immune Function of Early Nutritional Deprivation," *Nature,* 1973, Vol. 241, 57.

190. Kent, S. "Immunoengineering May Increase Longevity," *Geriatrics,* June, 1977, Vol. 32, 107–110.

191. Smith, G.S., and Walford, R.L. "Influence of the Main Histocompatibility Complex on Ageing in Mice," *Nature,* December 22/29, 1977, Vol. 270, 727–729.

191. Meredith, P.J., and Walford, R.L. "Effect of Age on Response to T- and B-Cell Mitogens in Mice Congenic at the H-2 Locus," *Immunogenetics,* 1977, Vol. 5, 109–128.

191. Walford, R.L., Smith, G.S., Meredith, P.J., et al. "Immunogenetics of Aging," in Schneider, E.L. (ed). *The Genetics of Aging.* New York: Plenum Press, 1978.

192. Smith, G.S., and Walford, R.L. "Influence of the H-2 and H-1 Histocompatibility Systems upon Lifespan and Spontaneous Cancer Incidences in Congenic Mice," in Bergsma, D., and Harrison, D.E. (eds). *Genetic Effects on Aging.* New York: Alan R. Liss, 1978.

192. Walford, R.L. "Multigene Families, Histocompatibility Systems, and Aging," *Mechanisms of Ageing and Development,* 1979, Vol. 9, 19–26.

192. Meredith, P.J., and Walford, R.L. "Autoimmunity, Histocompatibility, and Aging," *Mechanisms of Ageing and Development,* in press.

PAGE
193. Walford, R.L., and Bergmann, K. "Influence of Genes Associated with the Main Histocompatibility Complex on Deoxyribonucleic Acid Excision Repair Capacity and Bleomycin Sensitivity in Mouse Lymphocytes," *Tissue Antigens,* in press.
193. Paffenholz, V. "Correlation Between DNA Repair of Embryonic Fibroblasts and Different Lifespan of 3 Inbred Mouse Strains," *Mechanisms of Ageing and Development,* 1978, Vol. 7, 131–150.
193. Beiglie, D.J., and Teplitz, R.L. "Repair of UV Damaged DNA in Systemic Lupus Erythematosus," *Journal of Rheumatology,* 1975, Vol. 2, 149–160.
193. German, J. "DNA Repair Defects and Human Diseases," in Hanawalt, P.C., Friedberg, E.C., and Fox, C.F. (eds). *DNA Repair Mechanisms.* New York: Academic Press, 1978.
193. Klein, J. "H-2 Mutations: Their Genetics and Effect on Immune Functions," *Advances in Immunology,* 1978, Vol. 26, 56–146.
194. Fabris, N., Pierpaoli, W., and Sorkin, E. "Lymphocytes, Hormones and Ageing," *Nature,* 1972, Vol. 240, 557–559.
194. Fabris, N., Pierpaoli, W., and Sorkin, E. "Hormones and the Immunological Capacity. III. The Immunodeficiency Diseases of the Hypopituitary Diseases of the Hypopituitary Snell-Bagg Dwarf Mouse," *Clinical and Experimental Immunology,* 1971, Vol. 9, 209–225.
194. Fabris, N., Pierpaoli, W., and Sorkin, E. "Hormones and the Immunological Capacity. IV. Restorative Effects of Developmental Hormones or of Lymphocytes on the Immunodeficiency Syndrome of the Dwarf Mouse," *Clinical and Experimental Immunology,* 1971, Vol. 9, 227–240.
194. Piantanelli, L., and Fabris, N. "Hypopituitary Dwarf and Athymic Nude Mice and the Study of the Relationships Among Thymus, Hormones, and Aging," in Bergsma, D., and Harrison, D.E. (eds). *Genetic Effects on Aging.* New York: Alan R. Liss, 1978.
196. Makinodan, T., and Alder, W.H. "The Effects of Aging on

PAGE

the Differentiation and Proliferation Potentials of Cells of the Immune System," *Federation Proceedings*, 1975, Vol. 34, 153–158.

196. Hirokawa, K., and Makinodan, T. "Thymic Involution: Effect on T Cell Differentiation," *Journal of Immunology*, 1975, Vol. 114, 1659 1664.

196. Peter, C.P., Perkins, E.H., Peterson, W.J., et al. "The Late Effects of Selected Immune Suppressants, and Immunocompetence, Disease Incidence, and Mean Life Span. III. Disease Incidence and Life Expectancy," *Mechanisms of Ageing and Development*, 1975, Vol. 4, 251–261.

196. Makinodan, T., Deitchman, J.W., Stoltman, G.H., et al. "Restoration of the Declining Normal Immune Functions of Aging Mice" (Abstract), 10th International Congress of Gerontology, 1975, Jerusalem, Israel, June 22-27.

196. Hirokawa, K., Albright, J.W., and Makinodan, T. "Restoration of Impaired Immune Functions in Aging Animals. I. Effect of Syngeneic Thymus and Bone Marrow Cells," *Clinical Immunology and Immunopathology*, 1976, Vol. 5, 371–376.

196. Makinodan, T. "Mechanism, Prevention, and Restoration of Immunologic Aging," in Bergsma, D., and Harrison, D.E. (eds). *Genetic Effects on Aging*. New York: Alan R. Liss, 1978.

196. Kysela, S., and Steinberg, A.D. "Increased Survival of NZB/W Mice Given Multiple Syngeneic Young Thymus Grafts," *Clinical Immunology and Immunopathology*, 1973, Vol. 2, 133–136.

196. Kent, S. "Can Cellular Therapy Rejuvenate the Aged?," *Geriatrics*, August, 1977, Vol. 32, 92–99.

198. Perkins, E.H., Makinodan, T., and Seibert, C. "Model Approach to Immunological Rejuvenation of the Aged," *Infection and Immunity*, 1972, Vol. 6, 518–524.

198. Knight, S.C., Farrant, J., and McGann, L.E. "Storage of Human Lymphocytes by Freezing in Serum Alone," *Cryobiology*, 1977, Vol. 14, 112–115.

PAGE

199. Harrison, D.E., and Doubleday, J.W. "Normal Function of Immunologic Stem Cells from Aged Mice," *Journal of Immunology*, April, 1975, Vol. 114, 1314–1317.

199. Harrison, D.E., Astle, C.M., and Doubleday, J.W. "Stem Cell Lines from Old Immunodeficient Donors Give Normal Responses in Young Recipients," *Journal of Immunology*, April, 1977, Vol. 118, 1223–1227.

201. Halsall, M.H., and Perkins, E.H. "The Restoration of Phytohemagglutinin Responsiveness of Spleen Cells from Aging Mice," *Federation Proceedings*, 1974, Vol. 33, 736.

201. Braun, W., Yajuma, Y., and Ishizuka, M. "Synthetic Polynucleotides as Restorers of Antibody Formation Capacities in Aged Mice," *Journal of the Reticuloendothelial Society*, 1970, Vol. 7, 418.

201. Plescia, O.J., and Braun, W. (eds). *Nucleic Acids in Immunology*. New York: Springer-Verlag, 1968.

201. Rigby, P.F. "The Effect of 'Exogenous' RNA on the Improvement of Syngeneic Tumor Immunity," *Cancer Research*, 1971, Vol. 31, 4.

201. Pilch, Y.H., Ramming, K.P., and Deckers, P.J. "Induction of Anti-Cancer Immunity with RNA," *Annals of the New York Academy of Sciences*, 1973, Vol. 207, 409.

201. Pilch, Y.H., DeKernion, J.B., Skinner, D.G., et al. "Immunotherapy of Cancer with 'Immune' RNA," *American Journal of Surgery*, 1976, Vol. 132, 631–637.

201. Pilch, Y.H., Ramming, K.P., and DeKernion, J.B. "Immunotherapy of Human Malignancies with Immune RNA," *World Journal of Surgery*, 1977, Vol. 1, 625–638.

201. Good, R.A. "Cellular Engineering," *Clinical Bulletin*, January, 1977, Vol. 7, 33–39.

203. Law, L., Goldstein, A.L., and White, A. "Influence of Thymosin in Immunological Competence of Lymphoid Cells from Thymectomized Mice," *Nature*, 1968, Vol. 1, 291.

203. Goldstein, A.L., Asanuma, J.R., Battisto, J., et al. "Influence of Thymosin on Cell-Mediated and Humoral Immune Response in Normal and Immunologically Deficient Mice," *Journal of Immunology*, 1970, Vol. 104, 359.

203. Goldstein, A.L., Guha, A., Howe, M.L., et al. "Ontogenesis

PAGE

of Cell-Mediated Immunity in Murine Thymocytes and Spleen Cells and Its Acceleration by Thymosin, a Thymic Hormone," *Journal of Immunology,* 1971, Vol. 106, 773.

203. Dauphinee, M.J., Talal, N., Goldstein, A.L., et al. "Thymosin Corrects the Abnormal DNA Synthetic Response of NZB Mouse Thymocytes," *Proceedings of the National Academy of Sciences, USA,* 1974, Vol. 71, 2637.

203. Scheinberg, M.A., Goldstein, A.L., and Cathcart, E.S. "Thymosin Restores T Cell Function and Reduces the Incidence of Amyloid Disease in Casein-Treated Mice," *Journal of Immunology,* 1976, Vol. 116, 156.

204. Goldstein, A.L., Cohen, G.H., Rossio, J.L., et al. "Use of Thymosin in the Treatment of Primary Immunodeficiency Diseases and Cancers," *Medical Clinics of North America,* 1976, Vol. 60, 591.

204. Goldstein, A.L., and Rossio, J.L. "Thymosin for Immunodeficiency Diseases and Cancer," *Comprehensive Therapy,* February, 1978, Vol. 4, 49–57.

204. Lipson, S.K., Chretien, P.B., Makuch, R., et al. "Thymosin Immunotherapy in Patients with Small Cell Carcinoma of the Lung: Correlation of In Vitro Studies with Clinical Courses," *Cancer,* in press.

Chapter 7   Transplants and Artificial Organs

205. Rider, A.K., Copeland, J.G., Hunt, S.A., et al. "The Status of Cardiac Transplantation," *Circulation,* October, 1975, Vol. 52, 531–539.

205. Dong, E., Jr., and Shumway, N.E. "Current Results of Human Heart Transplantation," *World Journal of Surgery,* 1977, Vol. 1, 157–164.

205. Baumgartner, W.A., Reitz, B.A., Bieber, C.P., et al. "Current Expectations in Cardiac Transplantation," *Journal of Thoracic and Cardiovascular Surgery,* April, 1978, Vol. 75, 525–530.

207. Christopherson, L.K., Griepp, R.B., and Stinson, E.B. "Rehabilitation After Cardiac Transplantation," *Journal of the American Medical Association,* 1976, Vol. 236, 2082–2084.

PAGE
207. Griepp, R.B., Stinson, E.B., Bieber, C.P., et al. "Control of Graft Arteriosclerosis in Human Heart Transplant Recipients," *Surgery*, March, 1977, Vol. 81, 262–269.
209. Moulopoulos, S.D., Jarvik, R., and Kolff, W.J. "Stage II Problems in the Project of the Artificial Heart," *Journal of Thoracic and Cardiovascular Surgery*, April, 1973, Vol. 66, 662–667.
209. Oster, H., Olsen, D.B., Jarvik, R., et al. "Survival for 18 Days with a Jarvik-Type Artificial Heart," *Surgery*, April, 1975, Vol. 77, 113–117.
209. Lawson, J., Olsen, D.B., Kolff, W.J., et al. "A Three-Month Survival of a Calf with an Artificial Heart," *Journal of Laboratory and Clinical Medicine*, May, 1976, Vol. 87, 848–858.
209. Jarvik, R.K., Lawson, J.H., Olsen, D.B., et al. "The Beat Goes On: Status of the Artificial Heart, 1977," *International Journal of Artificial Organs*, January, 1978, Vol. 1, 21–27.
212. Kincaid-Smith, P. "Modification of the Vascular Lesions of Rejection in Cadaveric Renal Allografts by Dipyridamole and Anticoagulants," *Lancet*, November 1, 1969, Vol. 2, 920–922.
212. Murray, J.E., Tilney, N.L., and Wilson, R.E. "Renal Transplantation: A 25-Year Experience," *Annals of Surgery*, 1976, Vol. 184, 565–573.
212. "The Thirteenth Report of the Human Renal Transplant Society," *Transplantation Proceedings*, 1977, Vol. 9, 9–26.
213. Merrill, J.P. "Dialysis Versus Transplantation in the Treatment of End-Stage Renal Disease," *Annual Review of Medicine*, 1978, Vol. 29, 343–358.
213. Tilney, N.L., Strom, T.B., Vineyard, G.C., et al. "Factors Contributing to the Declining Mortality Rate in Renal Transplantation," *New England Journal of Medicine*, December 14, 1978, Vol. 299, 1321–1325.
213. Jacobsen, S.C., Stephen, R.L., Bulloch, E.C., et al. "A Wearable Artificial Kidney: Functional Description of Hardware and Clinical Results," presented to the Clinical Dialysis and Transplant Forum of the National Kidney Foundation, New York, November 22–23, 1975.

PAGE
213. Kolff, W.J. "Exponential Growth and Future of Artificial Organs," *Artificial Organs*, January, 1977, Vol. 1, 8–18.
213. Klein, E., Autian, J., Bower, J.D., et al. "Evaluation of Hemodialyzers and Dialysis Membranes," *Artificial Organs*, January, 1977, Vol. 1, 21–35.
214. Starzl, T.E., Porter, K.A., Putnam, C.W., et al. "Orthotopic Liver Transplantation in 93 Patients," *Surgical Gynecology and Obstetrics*, 1976, Vol. 142, 487–505.
214. Starzl, T.E., Putnam, C.W., Koep, L.J., et al. "Current Status of Liver Transplantation," *Southern Medical Journal*, April, 1977, Vol. 70, 389–390.
216. Chang, T.M.S. "Semipermeable Aqueous Microcapsules (Artificial Cells) with Emphasis on Experiments in an Extracorporeal Shunt System," *Transactions of the American Society for Artificial Internal Organs*, 1966, Vol. 12, 13.
216. Chang, T.M.S. *Artificial Cells*. Springfield, Illinois: Charles C. Thomas, 1972.
216. Chang, T.M.S., Migchelsen, M., Coffey, J.F., et al. "Serum Middle Molecule Levels in Urea During Long-Term Intermittent Hemoperfusion with the ACAC (Coated Charcoal) Microcapsule Artificial Kidney," *Transactions of the American Society for Artificial Internal Organs*, 1974, Vol. 20, 364.
216. Chirito, E., Reiter, B., Lister, C., et al. "Artificial Liver: The Effect of ACAC Microencapsulated Charcoal Hemoperfusion on Fulminant Hepatic Failure," *Artificial Organs*, January, 1977, Vol. 1, 76–83.
217. Thorsby, E., and Piazza, A. (eds). "Joint Report from the Sixth International Histocompatibility Workshop Conference. II. Typing for HLA-D (LD-1 or MLC) Determinants, Histocompatibility Testing, 1975." Edited by Kissmeyer-Nielsen, F., Munksgaard, Copenhagen, 1975.
217. Terasaki, P.I., Bernoco, D., Park, M.S., et al. "Microdroplet Testing for HLA-A, -B, -C, and -D Antigens," *American Journal of Clinical Pathology*, February, 1978, Vol. 69, 103–119.
217. Terasaki, P.I., Gjertson, D., Bernoco, D., et al. "Twins with Two Different Fathers Identified by HLA," *New England*

PAGE

Journal of Medicine, 1978, Vol. 299, 590–592.

217. Brown, J., Molnar, I.G., Clark, W., et al. "Control of Experimental Diabetes Mellitus in Rats by Transplantation of Fetal Pancreases," *Science,* 1974, Vol. 184, 1377–1379.

217. Brown, J., Clark, W.R., Molnar, I.G., et al. "Fetal Pancreas Transplantation for Reversal of Streptozotocin-Induced Diabetes in Rats," *Diabetes,* January, 1976, Vol. 25, 56–64.

218. Botz, C.K., Leibel, B.S., Zingg, W., et al. "Comparison of Peripheral and Portal Routes of Insulin Infusion by a Computer-Controlled Insulin Infusion System (Artificial Endocrine Pancreas)," *Diabetes,* 1976, Vol. 25, 691–700.

218. Zinman, B., Murray, F.T., Albisser, A.M., et al. "The Metabolic Response to Exercise in Insulin-Treated Diabetics," *Diabetes* (Supplement), 1976, Vol. 25, 333.

218. Albisser, A.M., Leibel, B.S., Zinman, B., et al. "Studies with an Artificial Endocrine Pancreas," *Archives of Internal Medicine,* 1977, Vol. 137, 639–649.

219. Jacobsen, S.C., Stephen, R.L., Luntz, R.D., et al. "Cutaneous Local Anesthesia by Iontophoresis" (Abstract), 23rd Annual Meeting of the American Society for Artificial Internal Organs, Montreal, Canada, April 21–23, 1977.

219. Johnson, R.T., Luntz, R.D., Mandleco, C., et al. "On the Safe Electrical Administration of Ionized Drugs/Iontophoresis," presented at the 30th ACEMB Meeting, Los Angeles, November 5–9, 1977.

220. "The Army's Institute of Surgical Research: Great Institutions of Surgery #3," *Contemporary Surgery,* March, 1973, Vol. 1, 35–36.

221. Clark, L.C., Wesseler, E.P., Kaplan, S., et al. "Emulsions of Perfluorinated Solvents for Intravascular Gas Transport," *Federation Proceedings,* May, 1975, Vol. 34, 1468–1477.

221. Geyer, R.P. " 'Bloodless' Rats Through the Use of Artificial Blood Substitutes," *Federation Proceedings,* May, 1975, Vol. 34, 1499–1505.

221. Geyer, R.P. "Potential Uses of Artificial Blood Substitutes," *Federation Proceedings,* May, 1975, Vol. 34, 1525–1528.

223. Johnson, R.T., and Jacobsen, S.C. "A High Performance and Inexpensive EMG Preamplifier for Artificial Limbs"

PAGE

(Abstract), 11th Annual AAMI Conference, 1976, Atlanta, Georgia, March 21–25.

223. Jacobsen, S.C. "Control Systems for Artificial Arms," Massachusetts Institute of Technology, Ph.D. Thesis, 1973.

223. Jacobsen, S.C., Jerard, R.B., and Knutti, D. "Development and Control of the Utah Arm." Proceedings of the 5th International Symposium on External Control of Human Extremities, Beograd, Yugoslavia, August, 1975.

223. Dobelle, W.H., Mladejovsky, M.G., and Evans, J.R. "Braille Reading by a Blind Volunteer by Visual Cortex Stimulation," *Nature*, 1976, Vol. 259, 111.

224. Mladejovsky, M.G., Eddington, D.K., Evans, J.R., et al. "A Computer-Based Brain Stimulation System to Investigate Sensory Prostheses for the Blind and Deaf," *IEEE Transactions of Biomedical Engineering, BME*, April, 1976, Vol. 23, 289.

224. Mladejovsky, M.G., Eddington, D.K., Dobelle, W.H., et al. "Artificial Hearing for the Deaf by Cochlear Stimulation: Pitch Modulation and Some Parametric Thresholds," *Transactions of the American Society for Artificial Internal Organs*, 1975, Vol. 21, 1.

225. Kolobow, T., Zapol, W.M., et al. "Artificial Placenta: Two Days of Total Extrauterine Support of the Isolated Lamb Fetus," *Science*, October 31, 1969, Vol. 166, 617–618.

226. Björklund, A., Stenevi, U., and Svendgaard, N.-A. "Growth of Transplanted Monaminergic Neurones Into the Adult Hippocampus Along the Perforant Path," *Nature* (London), 1976, Vol. 262, 787–790.

226. Björklund, A., and Stenevi, U. "Reformation of the Severed Septohippocampal Cholinergic Pathway in the Adult Rat by Transplanted Septal Neurons," *Cell Tissue Research*, December 19, 1977, Vol. 185, 289–302.

226. Beebe, B.K., Møllgård, K., Björklund, A., et al. "Ultrastructural Evidence of Synaptogenesis in the Adult Rat Dentate Gyrus from Brain Stem Implants," *Brain Research*, 1979, Vol. 167, 391–395.

227. Perlow, M.J., Freed, W.J., Hoffer, B.J., et al. "Brain Grafts Reduce Motor Abnormalities Produced by Destruction of

PAGE

Nigrostriatal Dopamine System," *Science*, May 11, 1979, Vol. 204, 643–646.

227. White, R.J., Albin, M.S., Locke, G.E., et al. "Brain Transplantation: Prolonged Survival of Brain After Carotid-Jugular Interposition," *Science*, November 5, 1965, Vol. 150, 779–881.

227. White, R.J., Albin, M.S., and Yashon, D., "Neuropathological Investigation of the Transplanted Canine Brain," *Transplantation Proceedings*, 1969, Vol. I, 259–261.

227. White, R.J., Austin, J., Austin, P., et al. "Preparation and Performance of a Non-Central Nervous System Animal," *Surgery*, 1970, Vol. 68, 48–53.

227. White, R.J. "Preparation and Mechanical Perfusion of the Isolated Monkey Brain," *Karolinska Symposia on Research Methods in Reproductive Endocrinology, 4th Symposia-Perfusion Techniques*, October 11–13, 1971, 200–216.

227. White, R.J., Wolin, L.R., Massopust, L.C., Jr., et al. "Primate Cephalic Transplantation: Neurogenic Separation, Vascular Association," *Transplantation Proceedings*, 1971, Vol. III, 602–604.

Chapter 8   Rejuvenation Therapies

229. Aslan, A. "Procaine Therapy in Old Age and Other Disorders (Novocaine Factor H_3)," *Gerontology Clinics*, 1960, Vol. 3, 148.

229. Aslan, A. "The Therapeutics of Old Age—the Action of Procaine," in Blumenthal, H.T. (ed). *Medical and Clinical Aspects of Aging*. New York: Columbia University Press, 1962.

229. Aslan, A. "Gerovital-H_3 Tablets: Metabolic Studies. I. Absorption from Various Segments of the Gastro-Intestinal Tract." Presented at the 26th Annual Meeting of the Gerontological Society, November, 1973, Miami Beach, Florida.

230. Bucci, L., and Saunders, J. "A Psychopharmacological Evaluation of 2-Diethylaminoethyl-paraaminobenzoate (Procaine)," *Journal of Neuropsychiatry*, 1960, Vol. 1, 276.

230. Smigel, J.O., Piller, J., Murphy, C., et al. "H_3 (Procaine

PAGE

Hydrochloride) Therapy in Aging Institutionalized Patients: An Interim Report," *Journal of the American Gerontological Society*, 1960, Vol. 8, 785.
230. Berryman, J.A.W., Forbes, H.A.W., and Simpson-White, R. "Trial of Procaine in Old Age and Chronic Degenerative Disorders," *British Medical Journal*, 1961, Vol. 2, 1683.
230. Fee, S.R., and Clark, A.N.G. "Trial of Procaine in the Aged," *British Medical Journal*, 1961, Vol. 2, 1680.
230. Gericke, O.L., Lobb, L.G., and Pardall, D.H. "An Evaluation of Procaine in Geriatric Patients in a Mental Hospital," *Journal of Clinical and Experimental Psychopathology*, 1961, Vol. 22, 18.
230. Isaacs, B. "Trials of Procaine in Aged Patients," *British Medical Journal*, 1962, Vol. 1, 188.
230. Chebotarev, M.F. "Novocaine in the Treatment of Cardiovascular Affections in Patients of Advanced and Old Age," in Blumenthal, H.T. (ed). *Medical and Clinical Aspects of Aging*. New York: Columbia University Press, 1962.
230. Gordon, P., Fudema, J.J., Snider, G.L., et al. "The Effects of a European Procaine Preparation in an Aged Population. II. Physiological Effects," *Journal of Gerontology*, 1965, Vol. 20, 144.
230. Aslan, A., Parhon, C.I., David, C., et al. "Research on Novocaine Therapy in Old Age." English translation of 7 papers originally published in German in *Die Therapiewoche*, and 4 papers from the Russian *Biull Eksp Biol Med*, Consultants' Bureau, Inc., New York, 1959.
232. Aslan, A., Vrabiescu, A., Domilescu, C., et al. "Long-Term Treatment with Procaine (Gerovital-H$_3$) in Albino Rats," *Journal of Gerontology*, 1965, Vol. 20, 1.
232. Verzar, F. "Note on the Influence of Procaine, PABA, and DEAE on the Aging of Rats," *Gerontologia*, 1959, Vol. 3, 351.
232. Samorajski, T., Sun, A., and Rolstein, C. "Effects of Chronic Dosage with Chlorpromazine and Gerovital-H$_3$ in the Aging Brain," in Nandy, K., Sherwin, I. (eds). *Aging Brain & Senile Dementia*. New York: Plenum Press, 1976.
233. Kurland, M., and Klayman, M. "Gerovital-H$_3$ in the Treat-

PAGE

ment of Depression in a Private Practice Population: A Double-Blind Study." Presented at the Annual Meeting of the Academy of Psychosomatic Medicine, November 20, 1974, Scottsdale, Arizona.

233. Zung, W.W.K., Gianturco, D., Pfeiffer, E., et al. "Pharmacology of Depression in the Aged: Evaluation of Gerovital-H_3 as an Antidepressant Drug," *Psychosomatics*, 1974, Vol. 15, 127–131.

233. Cohen, S., and Ditman, K.S. "Gerovital-H_3 in the Treatment of the Depressed Aging Patient," *Psychosomatics*, 1974, Vol. 14, 15–19.

233. Zwerling, I. "Effects of a Procaine Preparation (Gerovital-H_3) in Hospitalized Geriatric Patients—a Double-Blind Study," *Journal of the American Geriatrics Society*, 1975, Vol. 23, 8.

234. Hrachovec, J.P. "Inhibitory Effect of Gerovital-H_3 on Rat amines, and Monoamine Oxidase Levels," *Lancet*, 1972, Vol. 31, 604.

234. Robinson, D.S., Nies, A., Davis, J.N., et al. "Ageing, Monoamines, and Monoamine Oxidase Levels," *Lancet*, 1972, Vol. 1, 290.

234. MacFarlane, M.D. "Procaine HCl (Gerovital-H_3): A Weak, Reversible, Fully Competitive Inhibitor of Monoamine Oxidase," *Federation Proceedings*, 1975, Vol. 34, 1.

234. Yau, T.M. "Gerovital-H_3, Monoamine Oxidases, and Brain Monoamine Oxidase," in Rockstein, M. (ed). *Theoretical Aspects of Aging*. New York: Academic Press, 1974.

234. Olsen, E.J., Bank, L., Jarvik, L.F. "Gerovital-H_3: A Clinical Trial as an Antidepressant," *Journal of Gerontology*, April, 1978, Vol. 33, 514–520.

234. Jarvik, L.F., and Milne, J.F. "Gerovital-H_3: A Review of the Literature," in Gershon, S., and Raskin, A. (eds). *Aging*, Vol. 2, *Genesis and Treatment of Psychologic Disorders in the Elderly*. New York: Raven Press, 1975.

235. Culbert, M.L. *Freedom from Cancer—the Amazing Story of Laetrile*. New York: Pocket Books, 1977.

235. Ellison, N.M., Byar, D.P., and Newell, G.R. "Special Report on Laetrile: The NCI Laetrile Review—Results of the

PAGE

National Cancer Institute's Retrospective Laetrile Analysis," *New England Journal of Medicine,* September 7, 1978, Vol. 299, 549–552.

235. Dorr, R.T., and Paxinos, J. "The Current Status of Laetrile," *Annals of Internal Medicine,* March, 1978, Vol. 89, 389–397.

235. "Upton OK's Laetrile Test on Humans," *Science,* October 13, 1978, Vol. 202, 196.

238. *Tissue Therapy,* published in Russian by the Institute of Gerontology, Kiev, U.S.S.R., 1975.

241. Gianoli, A.C. "Ten Years of Revitalisation Therapy in General and Clinical Practice," *Zeitschrift für Präklinische Geriatrie,* July, 1975, Vol. 5, 186–192.

241. Revers, W.J., Simon, W.C.M., Popp, F., et al. "Psychological Effects of a Geriatric Preparation in the Aged," *Zeitschrift für Präklinische und Klinische Geriatrie,* September, 1976, Vol. 6, 418–430.

241. Schmidt, J.F., Kalbe, I., Schulz, F.H., et al. "Pharmaco therapy and So-called Basic Therapy in Old Age," paper presented at the 11th International Congress of Gerontology, 1978, Tokyo, Japan, August 20–25.

242. Bittles, A.H., Fulder, S.J., Grant, E.C., et al. "The Effect of Ginseng on Lifespan and Stress Responses in Mice," *Gerontology,* 1979, Vol. 25, 125–131.

242. Golotin, V.G., Berdyshev, G.D., Brekhman, I.I. In, Conference U.S.S.R. Academy of Medical Sciences, Scientific Medical Society of Gerontologists and Geriatricians of the U.S.S.R. and Ukraine, 1968, 94–96.

243. Jussek, E.G., and Roscher, A.A. "Critical Review of Contemporary Cellular Therapy (Celltherapy)," *Journal of Gerontology,* February, 1970, Vol. 25, 119–125.

247. Heaney, R.P. "Estrogens and Postmenopausal Osteoporosis," *Clinical Obstetrics and Gynecology,* April, 1976, Vol. 19, 791–803.

247. Horsman, A., Gallagher, J.C., Simpson, M., et al. "Prospective Trial of Oestrogen and Calcium in Postmenopausal Women," *British Medical Journal,* September 24, 1977, 789–792.

PAGE
248. Horwitz, R.I., and Feinstein, A.R. "Alternative Analytic Methods for Case-Control Studies of Estrogens and Endometrial Cancer," *New England Journal of Medicine,* November 16, 1978, Vol. 299, 1089–1094.
248. Antunes, C.M.F., Stolley, P.D., Rosenshein, N.B., et al. "Endometrial Cancer and Estrogen Use," *New England Journal of Medicine,* January 4, 1979, Vol. 300, 9–13.
249. Boyle, A.J., and McCann, D.S. (eds). "Symposium: Chelation, Amino Acid Metabolism and Disorders of Connective Tissue," *Journal of Chronic Diseases,* 1963, Vol. 16, 267.
249. Sincock, A.M. "Life Extension in the Rotifer Mytilina Brevispina Van Redunca by the Application of Chelating Agents," *Journal of Gerontology,* March, 1975, Vol. 30, 289–293.
249. Peng, C.F., Kane, J.J., Murphy, M.L., et al. "Abnormal Mitochondrial Oxidative Phosphorylation of Ischemic Myocardium Reversed by Ca^{2+}-Chelating Agents," *Journal of Molecular and Cell Cardiology,* 1977, Vol. 9, 897–908.
249. Gordon, G.B., and Vance, R.B. "EDTA Chelation Therapy for Arteriosclerosis: History and Mechanisms of Action," *Osteopathic Annals,* February, 1976.
250. Markham, C.H., Treciokas, L.J., and Diamond, S.G. "Parkinson's Disease and Levodopa—A Five-Year Follow-Up and Review," *Western Journal of Medicine,* September, 1974, Vol. 121, 188–206.
250. Sweet, R.D., and MacDowell, F.H. "Five Years' Treatment of Parkinson's Disease with Levodopa," *Annals of Internal Medicine,* 1975, Vol. 83, 456–463.
252. Fuxe, K. "Dopamine Receptor Agonists in Brain Research and as Therapeutic Agents," *TINS,* January, 1979, 1–4.
253. Ludwig, F.C., and Elashoff, R.M. "Mortality in Syngeneic Rat Parabionts of Different Chronological Age," *Transactions of the New York Academy of Sciences,* 1972, Vol. 134, 582–587.
256. Bjorksten, J. "Approaches and Prospects for the Control of Age-Dependent Deterioration," *Annals of the New York Academy of Sciences,* 1971, Vol. 184, 95–102.
256. Bjorksten, J., Weyer, E.R., and Ashman, S.M. "Study of

PAGE

Low Molecular Weight Proteolytic Enzymes," *Finska Kemists Medd*, April, 1971, Vol. 80, 70–86.

256. Shenk, R.U., and Bjorksten, J. "The Search for Microenzymes: The Enzyme of Bacillus Cereus," *Finska Kemists Medd*, February, 1973, Vol. 82, 26–46.

257. Kohn, R.R., and Leash, A.M. "Longterm Lathyrogen Administration to Rats, with Special Reference to Aging," *Experimental Molecular Pathology*, 1967, Vol. 1, 354–361.

258. Forbes, W.F. "The Effect of Prednisolone Phosphate on the Life-Span of DBA/2J Mice," *Experimental Gerontology*, 1975, Vol. 10, 27–29.

258. La Bella, F.S., and Vivian, S. "Effect of B-Aminopropionitrile or Prednisolone on Survival of Male LAF/J Mice," *Experimental Gerontology*, 1975, Vol. 10, 185–188.

259. Frank, B.S. *A New Approach to Degenerative Disease and Aging.* New York: Patricia Press, 1964.

259. Frank, B.S. *Nucleic Acid Therapy in Aging and Degenerative Disease.* New York: Psychological Library Press, 1968.

259. Frank, B.S. *Dr. Frank's No Aging Diet.* New York: Dial Press, 1976.

259. Frank, B.S. *Nucleic Acid, Nutrition and Therapy.* New York: Rainstone Publications, 1977.

259. Frank, B.S. *Nucleic Acid and Antioxidant Therapy of Aging and Degeneration.* New York: Royal Health Books, Ltd., 1979.

260. Kent, S. "Can Nucleic Acid Therapy Reverse the Degenerative Processes of Aging?," *Geriatrics*, October, 1977, Vol. 32, 130–136.

260. Odens, M. "Prolongation of the Lifespan in Rats," *Journal of the American Geriatrics Society*, 1973, Vol. 21, 450.

261. Goren, C. "Ribonucleic Acid: Influence on the Maze Learning Ability of Rats," *Worm Runner's Digest*, 1965, Vol. 7, 28.

261. Cameron, D.E., Kral, V.A., Solyom, L., et al. "RNA and Memory," in Gaito, J. (ed). *Macromolecules and Behavior.* New York: Appleton-Century-Crofts, 1966.

261. Solyom, L., Enesco, H.E., and Beaulieu, C. "The Effect of

PAGE

RNA on Learning and Activity in Old and Young Rats," *Journal of Gerontology*, 1967, Vol. 22, 1.

262. Deutsch, J.A. "The Cholinergic Synapse and the Site of Memory," *Science*, 1971, Vol. 174, 788–794.

262. Deutsch, J.A., and Rocklin, K. "Anticholinesterase Amnesia as a Function of Massed or Spaced Retest," *Journal of Comprehensive Physiology and Psychology*, 1972, Vol. 81, 64–68.

263. Drachman, D.A., and Leavitt, J. "Human Memory and the Cholinergic System. A Relationship to Aging?," *Archives of Neurology*, 1974, Vol. 30, 113–121.

263. Drachman, D.A. "Memory and Cognition Function in Man: Does the Cholinergic System Have a Specific Role?," *Neurology*, August, 1977a, Vol. 27, 783–790.

263. Bartus, R.T. "CNS Stimulant Effects on Short-Term Memory in Aged Monkeys," *Psychopharmacology*, in press.

263. Bartus, R.T. "Aging in the Rhesus Monkey: Specific Behavioral Impairments and Effects of Pharmacological Intervention," presented at the 11th International Congress of Gerontology, 1978, Tokyo, Japan, August 20–25.

264. Davis, K.L., Mohs, R.C., Tinklenberg, J.R., et al. "Physostigmine: Improvement of Long-Term Memory Processes in Normal Humans," *Science*, July 21, 1978, Vol. 201, 272–274.

264. Sitaram, N., Weingartner, H., and Gillin, J.C. "Human Serial Learning: Enhancement with Arecholine and Choline and Impairment with Scopolamine," *Science*, July 21, 1978, Vol. 201, 274–276.

265. Hirsch, M.J., and Wurtman, R.J. "Lecithin Consumption Increases Acetylcholine Concentrations in Rat Brain and Adrenal Gland," *Science*, October 13, 1978, Vol. 202, 223–224.

265. McGaugh, J.L., and Dawson, R.G. "Modification of Memory Storage Processes," in Honig, W.K., and James, P.H.R. (eds). *Animal Memory*. New York: Academic Press, 1972.

265. McGaugh, J.L., Gold, P.E., Van Buskirk, R., et al. "Modulating Influences of Hormones and Catecholamines on Memory Storage Processes," *Progress in Brain Research*, 1976, Vol. 45, 150–162.

265. Ferris, S.H., Sathananthan, G., Gershon, S., et al. "Neurotransmitter Precursors and Neuropeptides in Senile De-

PAGE

mentia." Presented at the 11th International Congress of Gerontology, 1978, Tokyo, Japan, August 20–25.

266. DeWied, D., Van Wimersma Greidanus, T.J.B., Hohus, B., et al. "Vasopressin and Memory Consolidation," *Progress in Brain Research,* 1976, Vol. 45, 181–194.

267. Legros, J.J., Gilot, P., Seron, X., et al. "Influence of Vasopressin on Learning and Memory," *Lancet,* January 7, 1978, Vol. 1, 41–42.

267. Oliveros, J.C., Jandali, M.K., Timsit-Berthih, M., et al. "Vasopressin in Amnesia," *Lancet,* January 7, 1978, Vol. 1, 42.

268. "Vasopressin to Boost Memory? Clinical Trials Will Tell," *Medical World News,* September 4, 1978, 81.

269. Jacobs, E.A., Winter, P.M., Alvis, H.J., et al. "Hyperoxygenation Effects on Cognitive Functioning in the Aged," *New England Journal of Medicine,* 1969, Vol 281, 753–757.

269. Jacobs, E.A., Alvis, H.J., and Small, S.M. "Hyperoxygenation: A Central Nervous System Activator?," *Journal of Geriatric Psychiatry,* 1972, Vol. 5, 107–121.

269. Ben-Yishay, T., Diller, L., Warga, C., et al. "The Alleviation of Cognitive and Functional Impairments in Senility by Hyperbaric Oxygenation Combined with Systematic Cuing," in Trapp, W.G., Bannister, E.W., Davison, A.J., et al. (eds). *Fifth International Hyperbaric Conference.* Burnaby, Canada: Simon Fraser University Press, 1974, Vol. 1, 424–431.

269. Goldfarb, A.I., Hochstadt, N.J., Jacobson, J.H., et al. "Hyperbaric Oxygen Treatment of Organic Mental Syndrome in Aged Persons," *Journal of Gerontology,* 1972, Vol. 27, 212–217.

269. Fraiberg, P.L. "Oxygen Inhalation in the Control of Psychogeriatric Symptoms in Patients with Long-Term Illness," *Journal of the American Geriatrics Society,* 1973, Vol. 21, 321–324.

269. Edwards, A.E., and Hart, G.M. "Hyperbaric Oxygenation and the Cognitive Functioning of the Aged," *Journal of the American Geriatrics Society,* 1974, Vol. 22, 376–379.

269. Thompson, L.W., Davis, G.C., Obrist, W., et al. "Effects of Hyperbaric Oxygen on Behavioral and Phyisological

PAGE

Measures in Elderly Demented Patients," *Journal of Gerontology*, 1976, Vol. 31, 23–28.

270. Raskin, A., Gershon, S., Crook, T.H., et al. "The Effects of Hyperbaric and Normobaric Oxygen on Cognitive Impairment in the Elderly," *Archives of General Psychology*, 1978, Vol. 35, 50–56.

271. Nandy, K., and Burne, G.H. "Effect of Centrophenoxine on the Lipofuscin Pigment in the Neurons of Senile Guinea Pigs," *Nature*, 1966, Vol. 210, 313.

271. Nandy, K. "Further Study on the Effects of Centrophenoxine on the Lipofuscin Pigment in the Neurons of Senile Guinea Pigs," *Journal of Gerontology*, 1968, Vol. 23, 82.

271. Nandy, K. "Properties of Lipofuscin Pigment in Neurons," *Acta Neuropathology*, 1971, Vol. 19, 25.

271. Hasan, M., Glees, P., and Spoerri, P.E. "Dissolution and Removal of Neuronal Lipofuscin Following Dimethylaminoethyl P-Chlorophenoxyacetate Administration to Guinea Pigs," *Cell Tissue Research*, 1974, Vol. 150, 369.

272. Nandy, K. "Centrophenoxine: Effects on Aging Mammalian Brain," *Journal of the American Geriatrics Society*, February, 1978, Vol. 26, 74–81.

272. Nandy, K., and Lal, H. "Neuronal Lipofuscin and Learning Deficit in Aging Mammals," in *Proceedings of the 10th Collegium Internationale Neuropsychopharmacologicum Congress*. New York: Pergamon Press, in press.

273. Hochschild, R. "Effect of Membrane Stabilizing Drugs on Mortality in Drosophila Melanogaster," *Experimental Gerontology*, 1971, Vol. 6, 133–151.

273. Hochschild, R. "Effects of Various Additives on In Vitro Survival Time of Mouse Macrophages," *Journal of Gerontology*, April, 1973, Vol. 28, 447–449.

273. Hochschild, R. "Effects of Various Drugs on Longevity in Female C57BL/6J Mice," *Gerontologia*, 1973, Vol. 19, 271–280.

274. Hochschild, R. "Effect of Dimethylaminoethanol on the Life Span of Senile Male A/J Mice," *Experimental Gerontology*, 1973, Vol. 8, 185–191.

275. Cherkin, A., and Eckardt, M.J. "Effects of Dimethylaminoethanol upon Life Span and Behavior of Aged Japanese

PAGE

Quail," *Journal of Gerontology*, January, 1977, Vol. 12, 38–45.

275. Haubrich, D.R., Wang, P.F.T., Clody, D.E., et al. "Increase in Rat Brain Acetylcholine Induced by Choline or Deanol," *Life Sciences*, 1975, Vol. 17, 975–980.

276. Ferris, S.H., Sathananthan, G., Gershon, S., et al, "Senile Dementia: Effects of Treatment with Deanol." Presented at the 29th Meeting of the Gerontological Society, New York, October 13–17, 1976.

276. Samorajski, T., and Rolsten, C. "Chlorpromazine and Aging in the Brain," *Experimental Gerontology*, 1976, Vol. 11, 141–147.

Chapter 9   Cryonics and Suspended Animation

281. White, R.J., Massopust, L.A., Jr., Wolin, L.R., et al. "Profound Selective Cooling and Ischemia of Primate Brain Without Pump or Oxygenator," *Surgery*, 1969, Vol. 66, 224–232.

281. White, R.J., Austin, P.E., Austin, J.C., et al. "Recovery of Subhuman Primate After Deep Cerebral Hypothermia and Prolonged Ischaemia," *Resuscitation*, 1973, Vol. 2, 117–122.

282. Hossmann, K-A., and Sato, K. "Effect of Ischemia on the Function of the Sensorimotor Cortex in Cat," *Electroencephalography and Clinical Neurophysiology*, 1971, Vol. 30, 535–545.

282. Hossmann, K-A., and Kleihues, P. "Reversibility of Ischemic Brain Damage," *Archives of Neurology*, 1973, Vol. 29, 375–384.

282. Hossmann, K-A., Lectape-Grüter, H., and Hossmann, V. "The Role of Cerebral Blood Flow for the Recovery of the Brain After Prolonged Ischemia," *Zeitschrift Neurology*, 1973, Vol. 204, 281–299.

282. Hossmann, K-A. "Neuropathological Findings After Prolonged Cerebral Ischemia," in 7th International Congress of Neuropathology (Budapest) Amsterdam, *Excerpta Medica*, 1975, 569–572.

282. Hossmann, K-A., and Zimmerman, V. "Resuscitation of the Monkey Brain After 1H Complete Ischemia. I. Physiologi-

PAGE

cal and Morphological Observations," *Brain Research*, 1974, Vol. 81, 59–74.

282. Hossmann, K-A., and Hossmann, V. "Coagulopathy Following Experimental Cerebral Ischemia," *Stroke*, February, 1977, Vol. 8, 249–254.

282. Takagi, S., Cocito, L., and Hossmann, K-A. "Blood Recirculation and Pharmacological Responsiveness of the Cerebral Vasculature Following Prolonged Ischemia of Cat Brain," *Stroke*, June, 1977, Vol. 8, 707–712.

282. Leninger-Follert, E., and Hossmann, K-A. "Microflow and Cortical Oxygen Pressure During and After Prolonged Cerebral Ischemia," *Brain Research*, 1977, Vol. 124, 158–161.

283. "Mannitol Protects in Aneurysm Repair," *Medical World News*, February 6, 1978, 81–82.

283. Yoshimoto, T., Watanabe, T., Kayama, T., et al. "Experimental Cerebral Infarction—Production and Prevention," Presented at the 6th International Congress of Neurological Surgery, São Paulo, Brazil, June 22, 1977.

284. Sacks, S.A., Petritsch, P.H., and Kaufman, J.J. "Canine Kidney Preservation Using a New Perfusate," *Lancet*, Vol. 2, May 12, 1973, 1024–1028.

286. Kubota, S., Graham, E.F., Crabo, B.G., et al. "The Effect of Freezing Rate, Duration of Phase Transition, and Warming Rate on Survival of Canine Kidneys," *Cryobiology*, 1976, Vol. 13, 455–462.

286. Guttman, F.M., Lizin, J., Robitaille, P., et al. "Survival of Canine Kidneys After Treatment with Dimethylsulfoxide, Freezing at −80° C, and Thawing by Microwave Illumination," *Cryobiology*, 1977, Vol. 14, 559–567.

286. Pegg, D.E., Green, C.J., and Walter, C.A. "Attempted Canine Renal Cryopreservation Using Dimethylsulfoxide Helium Perfusion and Microwave Thawing," *Cryobiology*, 1978, Vol. 15, 618–626.

286. Fahy, G.M. "Analysis of 'Solution Effects' Injury in Biological Systems. III. Rabbit Renal Cortex Frozen in the Presence of Dimethylsulfoxide (DMSO)," private communication.

288. Fahy, G.M., and Karow, A.M., Jr. "Ultrastructure-Function Correlative Studies for Cardiac Cryopreservation. V. Ab-

PAGE

sence of a Correlation Between Electrolyte Toxicity and Cryoinjury in the Slowly Frozen, Cryoprotected Rat Heart," *Cryobiology,* 1977, Vol. 14, 418–427.

288. Karow, A.M., Jr., Abouna, G.J.M., and Humphries, A.L., Jr. (eds). *Organ Preservation for Transplantation.* Boston: Little, Brown & Company, 1974.

288. Alink, G.M., Verheul, C.C., Agterberg, J., et al. "Viability and Morphology of Rat Heart Cells after Freezing and Thawing of the Whole Heart," *Cryobiology,* 1978, Vol. 15, 44–58.

288. Sumida, S. "Freeze Preservation of Rat Hearts" (Abstract). Presented at the 13th Annual Meeting of the Cryobiology Society, Tokyo, Japan, August 6–10, 1978.

290. Suda, I., Adachi, C., and Kito, K. "Studies on the Isolated Cat's Brain In Vitro. I. Isolation Methods and Observation on the Spontaneous Electrical Activity," *Kobe Journal of Medical Science,* 1963, Vol. 9, 41–67.

290. Suda, I., Kito, K., and Adachi, C. "Viability of Long-Term Frozen Cat Brain In Vitro," *Nature* (London), 1966, Vol. 212, 268–270.

290. Suda, I., Kito, K., and Adachi, C. "Cerebral Activity Related to Blood Flow in Cat Brain," in Kao, F.F., Koizumi, K., and Vassalle, M. (eds). *Research in Physiology.* Bologna: Aulo Gaggi, 1971.

290. Suda, I., Kito, K., and Adachi, C. "Bioelectric Discharges of Isolated Cat Brain After Revival from Years of Frozen Storage," *Brain Research,* 1974, Vol. 70, 527–531.

292. Mazur, P., Kemp, J.A., and Miller, R.H. "Survival of Fetal Rat Pancreases Frozen to −78 and −196°," *Proceedings of the National Academy of Sciences, USA,* November, 1976, Vol. 73, 4105–4109.

292. Kemp, J.A., Mazur, P., Mullen, T., et al. "Reversal of Experimental Diabetes by Fetal Rat Pancreas. I. Survival and Function of Fetal Rat Pancreas Frozen to −196° C," *Transplantation Proceedings,* January, 1977, Vol. 9, 325–328.

293. Smith, A.U. "Frostbite in Golden Hamsters Revived from Body Temperatures Below 0° C," *Lancet,* 1954, Vol. 2, 1255.

293. Smith, A.U., Lovelock, J.E., and Parkes, A.S. "Resuscitation

of Hamsters after Supercooling or Partial Crystallization at Body Temperatures Below 0° C," *Nature*, 1954, Vol. 173, 1136.

293. Smith, A.U. "Studies on Golden Hamsters During Cooling to and Rewarming from Body Temperatures Below 0° C. I. Observations During Chilling, Freezing and Supercooling," *Proceedings of the Royal Society of London*, 1956a, B145, 391.

293. Smith, A.U. "Studies on Golden Hamsters During Cooling to and Rewarming from Body Temperatures Below 0° C. II. Observations During and after Resuscitation," *Proceedings of the Royal Society of London*, 1956b, B145, 407.

293. Smith, A.U. "Problems in the Resuscitation of Mammals from Body Temperatures Below 0° C," *Proceedings of the Royal Society of London*, 1957b, B147, 533.

293. Smith, A.U. "Viability of Supercooled and Frozen Mammals," *Annals of the New York Academy of Sciences*, 1959, Vol. 80, 291–300.

293. Smith, A.U. *Biological Effects of Freezing and Supercooling*. Baltimore: Williams & Wilkins Press, 1961.

295. Popovic, P., and Popovic, V. "Survival of Newborn Ground Squirrels after Supercooling or Freezing," *American Journal of Physiology*, May, 1963, Vol. 204, 949–952.

296. Ashina, E. "Frost Resistance in Insects," *Advances in Insect Physiology*, 1969, Vol. 6, 1–49.

296. Miller, L.K. "Freezing Tolerance in an Adult Insect," *Science*, 1969, Vol. 166, 105–106.

296. Miller, L.K. "D-Threitol and Sorbitol as Cryoprotectants in an Adult Insect: Seasonal and Induced Variations," *Physiologist*, 1975, Vol. 18, 320.

296. Miller, L.K., and Smith, J. "Production of Threitol and Sorbitol by an Adult Insect: Association with Freezing Tolerance," *Nature* (London), 1975, Vol. 258, 519–520.

296. Miller, L.K. "Freezing Tolerance in Relation to Cooling Rate in an Adult Insect," *Cryobiology*, 1978, Vol. 15, 345–349.

299. Whittingham, D.G., Leibo, S.P., and Mazur, P. "Survival of Mouse Embryos Frozen to −196° and −269° C," *Science*, October 27, 1972, Vol. 178, 411–414.

PAGE
299. Whittingham, D.G. "Freezing Embryos of Laboratory Species," *Cryobiology*, 1978, Vol. 15, 367–369.

299. Polge, C., and Willadsen, S.M. "Freezing Eggs and Embryos of Farm Animals," *Cryobiology*, 1978, Vol. 15, 370–373.

303. Dawe, A.R., and Spurrier, W.A. "Hibernation Induced in Ground Squirrels by Blood Transfusion," *Science*, 1969, Vol. 163, 298–299.

303. Dawe, A.R., Spurrier, W.A., and Armour, J.A. "Summer Hibernation Induced by Cryogenically Preserved Blood Trigger," *Science*, 1970, Vol. 168, 497–498.

303. Dawe, A.R., and Spurrier, W.A. "Summer Hibernation of Infant (Six-Week-Old) 13-Lined Ground Squirrels, Citellus Tridecemlineatus," *Cryobiology*, 1974, Vol. 11, 33–43.

303. Rosser, S.P., and Bruce, D.S. "Induction of Summer Hibernation in the 13-Lined Ground Squirrel, Citellus Tridecemlineatus," *Cryobiology*, 1978, Vol. 15, 113–116.

303. Swan, H., and Schatte, C. "Antimetabolic Extract from the Brain of the Hibernating Ground Squirrel, Citellus Tridecemlineatus," *Science*, 1977, Vol. 195, 84–85.

304. Klebanoff, G., and Phillips, J. "Temporary Suspension of Animation Using Total Body Perfusion and Hypothermia: A Preliminary Report," *Cryobiology*, February, 1969, Vol. 6, 121.

304. Klebanoff, G., Hollander, D., and Cosimi, A.B. "Asanguinous Hypothermic Total Body Perfusion (TBW) in the Treatment of Stage IV Hepatic Coma," *Journal of Surgical Research*, January, 1972, Vol. 12, 1.

305. Leaf, J.D. "A Pilot Study in Hypothermia, Using Femoral-Jugular-Femoral Bypass and Total Body Washout," *Long Life Magazine*, November/December, 1977, Vol. 1, 135.

306. Gale, L. "Alcor Experiment: Surviving the Cold," *Long Life Magazine*, July/August, 1978, Vol. 2, 59–60.

307. Wilson, R.A. *Cosmic Trigger—Final Secret of the Illuminati.* Berkeley: And/Or Press, 1977.

308. Leaf, J.D. "Cryonic Suspension of Sam Berkowitz: Technical Report," *Long Life Magazine*, March/April, 1979, Vol. 3, 30–35.

312. Negovski, V.A. *Resuscitation and Artificial Hypothermia,*

PAGE

translated by B. Haigh. New York: Consultants Bureau, 1962.

Chapter 10   Extended Parenthood and Aphrodisiacs

315. Meites, J., Lu, K.H., Wuttke, W., et al. "Recent Studies on Functions and Control of Prolactin Secretion in Rats," *Recent Progress in Hormone Research,* 1972, Vol. 28, 471–526.

315. Gregerman, R.J., Bierman, E.L. "Aging and Hormones," in Williams, R.H. (ed). *Textbook of Endocrinology.* Philadelphia: W.B. Saunders Company, 1974.

316. Huang, H.H., Marshall, S., and Meites, J. "Capacity of Old Versus Young Female Rats to Secrete LH, FSH, and Prolactin," *Biology of Reproduction,* 1976, Vol. 14, 538–543.

316. Schneider, E.L. (ed). *Aging,* Vol. 4, *The Aging Reproductive System.* New York: Raven Press, 1978.

316. Quadri, S.K., Kledzik, G.S., and Meites, J. "Reinitiation of Estrous Cycles in Old Constant-Estrous Rats by Central-Acting Drugs," *Neuroendocrinology,* 1973, Vol. 11, 248–255.

316. Huang, H.H., and Meites, J. "Reproductive Capacity of Aging Female Rats," *Neuroendocrinology,* 1975, Vol. 17, 289–295.

316. Huang, H.H., Marshall, S., and Meites, J. "Induction of Estrous Cycles in Old Noncyclic Rats by Progesterone, ACTH, Ether Stress or L-Dopa," *Neuroendocrinology,* 1976, Vol. 20, 21–34.

316. Meites, J., Simpkins, J., Bruni, J., et al. "Role of Biogenic Amines in Control of Anterior Pituitary Hormones," *IRCS Medical Sciences,* 1977, Vol. 5, 1–7.

316. Simpkins, J.W., Mueller, G.P., Huang, H.H., et al. "Serotonin Metabolism in Aging Male Rats: Possible Relation to Gonadotropin Secretion," *Endocrinology,* 1977, Vol. 100, 1672.

317. Lu, K.H., Huang, H.H., Chen, H.T., et al. "Positive Feedback by Estrogen and Progesterone on LH Release in Old and Young Rats," *Proceedings of the Society for Experimental Biology and Medicine,* 1977, Vol. 154, 82–85.

317. Meites, J., Huang, H.H., and Simpkins, J.W. "Recent Studies on Neuroendocrine Control of Reproductive Se-

PAGE

nescence in Rats," in Schneider, E.L. (ed). *Aging,* Vol. 4, *The Aging Reproductive System.* New York: Raven Press, 1978.

317. Wiggins, C.O., and Ratner, A. "Reinitiation of Cyclicity in Aged Anovulatory Rats by Prolactin Suppression," *Federation Proceedings* (Abstract), March 1, 1978, Vol. 37, 3538.

321. Shapiro, S.K. "Hypersexual Behavior Complicating Levodopa (L-Dopa) Therapy," *Minnesota Medicine,* January, 1973, 58–59.

321. Goodwin, F.K. "Psychiatric Side Effects of Levodopa in Man," *Journal of the American Medical Association,* 1971, Vol. 218, 915.

321. Bowers, M.B., Jr. "Sexual Behavior During L-Dopa Treatment of Parkinson's Disease," *Medical Aspects of Human Sexuality,* July, 1972, 94–98.

321. O'Malley, W.E. "Pharmacology of L-Dopa," Symposium at Georgetown University School of Medicine, Washington, D.C., January, 1970.

322. Angrist, B., and Gershon, S. "Clinical Effects of Amphetamine and L-Dopa on Sexuality and Aggression," *Comprehensive Psychiatry,* June, 1976, Vol. 17, 715–722.

322. Sandler, M., and Gessa, G.L. (eds). *Sexual Behavior—Pharmacology and Biochemistry.* New York: Raven Press, 1975.

322. Hyyppä, M.T., Falck, S.C., and Rinne, U.K. "Is L-Dopa an Aphrodisiac in Patients with Parkinson's Disease?," in Sandler, M., Gessa, G.L. (eds). *Sexual Behavior—Pharmacology and Biochemistry.* New York: Raven Press, 1975.

324. Tagliamonte, A., Tagliamonte, P., Gessa, G.L., et al. "Compulsive Sexual Activity Induced by P-Chlorophenylalanine in Normal and Pinealectomized Male Rats," *Science,* 1969, Vol. 166, 1433–1435.

324. Tagliamonte, A., Tagliamonte, P., and Gessa, G.L. "Reversal of Pargyline-Induced Inhibition of Sexual Behaviour in Male Rats by P-Chlorophenylalanine," *Nature,* 1971, Vol. 230, 244–245.

324. Tagliamonte, A., Fratta, W., Del Fiacco, M., et al. "Possible Stimulatory Role of Brain Dopamine in the Copulatory Behavior of Male Rats," *Pharmacology and Biochemistry of Behavior,* 1974, Vol. 2, 257–260.

PAGE
324. Gessa, G.L., and Tagliamonte, A. "Role of Brain Serotonin and Dopamine in Male Sexual Behavior," in Sandler, M., and Gessa, G.L. (eds). *Sexual Behavior—Pharmacology and Biochemistry*. New York: Raven Press, 1975.

326. Benkert, O., Gluba, H., and Matussek, N. "Dopamine, Noradrenaline and 5-Hydroxytryptamine in Relation to Motor Activity, Fighting and Mounting Behavior. I. L-Dopa and DL-Threo-Dihydroxyphenyserine in Combination with Ro 4-4602, Pargyline and Reserpine," *Neuropharmacology*, 1973, Vol. 12, 177–186.

326. Benkert, O., Renz, A., and Matussek, N. "Dopamine, Noradrenaline and 5-Hydroxytryptamine in Relation to Motor Activity, Fighting and Mounting Behavior. II. L-Dopa and DL-Threo-Dihydroxyphenyserine in Combination with Ro 4-4602 and Parachlorophenylalanine," *Neuropharmacology*, 1973, Vol. 12, 187–193.

326. Gessa, G.L., and Tagliamonte, A. "Role of Brain Monoamines in Male Sexual Behavior," *Life Sciences*, 1974, Vol. 14, 425–436.

326. Bond, V.J., Shillito, E.E., and Vogt, M. "Influence of Age and of Testosterone on the Response of Male Rats to Parachlorophenylalanine," *British Journal of Pharmacology*, 1972, Vol. 46, 46–55.

326. Gray, G.D., Davis, H.N., and Dewsbury, D.A. "Effects of L-Dopa on the Heterosexual Copulatory Behavior of Male Rats," *European Journal of Pharmacology*, 1974, Vol. 27, 367–370.

326. Meyerson, B.J., Carrer, H., and Eliasson, M. "5-Hydroxytryptamine and Sexual Behavior in the Female Rat," *Advances in Biochemical Psychopharmacology*, 1974, Vol. 11, 229–242.

326. Gradwell, P.B., Everitt, B.J., and Herbert, J. "5-Hydroxytryptamine in the Central Nervous System and Sexual Receptivity of Female Rhesus Monkeys," *Brain Research*, 1975, Vol. 88, 281–293.

327. Moss, R.L., and McCann, S.M. "Induction of Mating Behavior in Rats by Luteinizing Hormone-Releasing Factor," *Science*, 1973, Vol. 181, 177–179.

327. Moss, R.L., McCann, S.M., and Dudley, C.A. "Releasing

PAGE

Hormones and Sexual Behavior," *Progress in Brain Research,* 1975, Vol. 42, 37–46.

327. Benkert, O. "Studies on Pituitary Hormones and Releasing Hormones in Depression and Sexual Impotence," *Progress in Brain Research,* 1975, Vol. 42, 25–36.

327. Benkert, O. "Clinical Studies on the Effects of Neurohormones on Sexual Behavior," in Sandler, M., and Gessa, G.L. (eds). *Sexual Behavior—Pharmacology and Biochemistry.* New York: Raven Press, 1975.

327. Sicuteri, F., Del Bene, E., and Anselmi, B. "Aphrodisiac Effect of Testosterone in Parachlorophenylalanine-Treated Sexually Deficient Men," in Sandler, M., and Gessa, G.L. (eds). *Sexual Behavior: Pharmacology and Biochemistry.* New York: Raven Press, 1975.

328. Doust, J.W.L., and Huszka, L. "Amines and Aphrodisiacs in Chronic Schizophrenia," *Journal of Nervous and Mental Diseases,* 1972, Vol. 155, 261–264.

329. Egan, G.P., and Hammad, G.E.M. "Sexual Disinhibition with L-Tryptophan," *British Medical Journal,* September 18, 1976, 701.

329. Hullin, R.P., and Jerram, T. "Sexual Disinhibition with L-Tryptophan," *British Medical Journal,* October 23, 1976, 1010.

329. Oswald, I. "Sexual Disinhibition with L-Tryptophan," *British Medical Journal,* December 25, 1976, 1555.

329. Broadhurst, A.D., and Rao, B. "L-Tryptophan and Sexual Behavior," *British Medical Journal,* January 1, 1977, 51–52.

331. Sachs, B.D., and Barfield, R.J. "Copulatory Behavior of Male Rats Given Intermittent Electric Shocks: Theoretical Implications," *Journal of Comprehensive Physiology and Psychology,* April, 1973, Vol. 80, 607–615.

331. Merari, A., and Ginton, A. "Characteristics of Exaggerated Sexual Behavior Induced by Electrical Stimulation of the Medial Preoptic Area in Male Rats," *Brain Research,* 1975, Vol. 86, 97–108.

332. Hendry, L.B., Wichmann, J.K., Hindenlang, D.M., et al. "Evidence for Origin of Insect Sex Pheromones: Presence in Food Plants," *Science,* April 4, 1975, Vol. 188, 59–62.

332. Michael, R.P., Keverne, E.B., and Nonsall, R.W. "Phero-

mones: Isolation of Male Sex Attractants from a Female Primate," *Science*, 1971, Vol. 172, 964–966.

332. Doty, R.L., Ford, M., Preti, G., et al. "Changes in the Intensity and Pleasantness of Human Vaginal Odors During the Menstrual Cycle," *Science*, December 26, 1975, Vol. 190, 1316–1317.

332. Waltman, R., Tricomi, V., and Wilson, G.E., Jr. "Volatile Fatty Acids in Vaginal Secretions: Human Pheromones?," *Lancet*, September 1, 1973, 496.

Chapter 11 Regeneration, Cloning, and Identity Reconstruction

335. Singer, M. "Neurotrophic Control of Limb Regeneration in the Newt," *Annals of the New York Academy of Sciences*, March 22, 1974, Vol. 228, 308–322.

335. Jabaily, J., Rall, T.W., and Singer, M. "Assay of Cyclic 3'-5'-Monophosphate in the Regenerating Forelimb of the Newt, Triturus," *Journal of Morphology*, April, 1975, Vol. 147, 379–384.

335. Singer, M., Maier, C.E., and McNutt, W.S. "Neurotrophic Activity of Brain Extracts in Forelimb Regeneration of the Urodele, Triturus," *Journal of Experimental Zoology*, February, 1976, Vol. 196, 131–150.

335. Jabaily, J.A., and Singer, M. "Neurotrophic Stimulation of DNA Synthesis in the Regenerating Forelimb of the Newt, Triturus," *Journal of Experimental Zoology*, February, 1977, Vol. 199, 251–256.

335. Singer, M., and Ilan, J. "Nerve-Dependent Regulation of Absolute Rates of Protein Synthesis in Newt Limb Regenerates. Measurement of Methionine Specific Activity in Peptidyl-tRNA of the Growing Polypeptide Chain," *Developmental Biology*, 1977, Vol. 57, 174–187.

337. Donaldson, D.J., Minchey, J.W., and Adcock, K. "A Search for Embryonic Antigens in Regenerating Intestine of the Adult Leopard Frog, Rana Pipiens," *Oncology*, 1973, Vol. 28, 523–535.

337. Donaldson, D.J., and Mason, J.M. "Cancer-Related Aspects of Regeneration Research: A Review," *Growth*, 1975, Vol. 39, 475–496.

337. Wertz, R.L., Donaldson, D.J., and Mason, J.M., "X-Ray

PAGE

Induced Inhibition of DNA Synthesis and Mitosis in Internal Tissues During the Initiation of Limb Regeneration in the Adult Newt," *Journal of Experimental Zoology,* February, 1976, Vol. 198, 253–259.

337. Donaldson, D.J., and Mason, J.M. "Inhibition of Epidermal Cell Migration by Concanavalin A in Skin Wounds of the Adult Newt," *Journal of Experimental Zoology,* January, 1977, Vol. 200, 55–64.

339. Deuchar, E.M. "Regeneration of Amputated Limb-Buds in Early Rat Embryos," *Journal of Embryology and Experimental Morphology,* 1976, Vol. 35, 345–354.

339. Rosenfeld, A. *Prolongevity.* New York: Alfred A. Knopf, Inc., 1976, p. 117.

340. Mizell, M. "Limb Regeneration: Induction in the Newborn Opossum," *Science,* July 19, 1968, Vol. 161, 283–286.

340. Mizell, M., and Isaacs, W. "Induced Regeneration of Hindlimbs in the Newborn Opossum," *American Zoology,* 1970, Vol. 10, 141.

341. Becker, R.O. "The Bioelectric Factors in Amphibian Limb Regeneration," *Journal of Bone and Joint Surgery,* 1961, 43A, 643.

341. Becker, R.O., Bassett, C.A.L., and Bachman, C.H. "The Bioelectric Factors Controlling Bone Structure," in *Bone Biodynamics.* Boston: Little, Brown and Company, 1964.

341. Becker, R.O., and Murray, D.G. "A Method for Producing Cellular Dedifferentiation by Means of Very Small Electrical Currents," *Transactions of the New York Academy of Sciences,* 1967, Vol. 29, 606.

341. Becker, R.O. "Stimulation of Partial Limb Regeneration in Rats," *Nature,* 1972, Vol. 235, 109.

342. Becker, R.O. "Augmentation of Regenerative Healing in Man: A Possible Alternative to Prosthetic Implantation," *Clinical Orthopedics,* 1972, Vol. 83, 255.

342. Becker, R.O. "Boosting Our Healing Potential," *Science Year (World Book Encyclopedia),* 1975, 40–55.

342. Smith, S.D. "Induction of Partial Limb Regeneration in Rana Pipiens by Galvanic Stimulation," *Anatomical Record,* 1967, Vol. 158, 89.

342. Smith, S.D. "Effects of Electrode Placement on Stimulation

of Adult Frog Limb Regeneration," *Annals of the New York Academy of Sciences,* 1974, Vol. 238, 500–507.

345. Katzman, R., Björklund, A., Owman, C.H., et al. "Evidence for Regenerative Axon Sprouting of Central Catecholamine Neurons in the Rat Mesencephalon Following Electrolytic Lesions," *Brain Research,* 1971, Vol. 25, 579–596.

345. Wiklund, L., Björklund, A., and Nobin, A. "Regeneration of Serotonin Neurons in the Rat Brain After 5,6-Dihydroxytryptamine-Induced Axotomy," *Annals of the New York Academy of Sciences,* June 12, 1978, Vol. 305, 370–384.

345. Bjerre, B., Björklund, A., and Stenevi, U. "Stimulation of New Axonal Sprouts From Lesioned Monoamine Neurones in Adult Rat Brain by Nerve Growth Factor," *Brain Research,* 1973, Vol. 60, 161–176.

345. Stenevi, U., Bjerre, A., Björklund, A., et al. "Effects of Localized Intracerebral Injections of Nerve Growth Factor on the Regenerative Growth of Lesioned Central Noradrenergic Neurones," *Brain Research,* 1974, Vol. 69, 217–234.

345. Mobley, W.C., Server, A.C., Ishi, D.N., et al, "Nerve Growth Factor," *The New England Journal of Medicine,* 1977, Vol. 297, part I, 1096–1104; part II, 1149–1158; part III, 1211–1218.

347. Briggs, R., and King, T.J. "Factors Affecting the Transplantability of Frog Embryonic Cells," *Journal of Experimental Zoology,* 1953, Vol. 122, 485.

347. Briggs, R., and King, T.J. "Changes in the Nuclei of Differentiating Endoderm Cells as Revealed by Nuclear Transplantation," *Journal of Morphology,* 1957, Vol. 100, 269.

347. Gurdon, J.B. "The Developmental Capacity of Nuclei Taken from Intestinal Epithelium Cells of Feeding Tadpoles," *Journal of Embryology and Experimental Morphology,* 1962, Vol. 10, 622.

347. Gurdon, J.B. "Nuclear Transplantation in Amphibia and the Importance of Stable Nuclear Changes in Promoting Cellular Differentiation," *Quarterly Review of Biology,* 1963, Vol. 38, 54.

347. Gurdon, J.B. *The Control of Gene Expression in Animal Development.* Oxford: Clarendon Press, 1974.

PAGE

347. Gurdon, J.B., Laskey, R.A., and Reeves, O.R. "The Developmental Capacity of Nuclei Transplanted from Keratinized Skin Cells of Adult Frogs," *Journal of Embryology and Experimental Morphology*, 1975, Vol. 34, 93.

347. Marshall, J.A., and Dixon, D.E. "Nuclear Transplantation from Intestinal Epithelial Cells of Early and Late Xenopus Laevis Tadpoles," *Journal of Embryology and Experimental Morphology*, 1977, Vol. 40, 167.

348. Bromhall, J.D. "Nuclear Transplantation in the Rabbit Egg," *Nature*, December 25, 1975, Vol. 258, 719–721.

348. Muggleton-Harris, A.L. "Cellular Events Concerning the Developmental Potentiality of the Transplanted Nucleus with Reference to the Aging Lens Cell," *Experimental Gerontology*, 1971, Vol. 6, 279–285.

348. Markert, C.L., and Ursprung, H. *Developmental Genetics*. Englewood Cliffs, N.J.: Prentice-Hall, 1971.

348. Markert, C.L., and Petters, R.M. "Homozygous Mouse Embryos Produced by Microsurgery," *Journal of Experimental Zoology*, 1977, Vol. 201, 295–302.

349. Tarkowski, A.K. "In Vitro Development of Haploid Mouse Embryos Produced by Bisection of One-Cell Fertilized Eggs," *Journal of Embryology and Experimental Morphology*, 1977, Vol. 38, 187–202.

349. Hoppe, P.C., and Illmensee, K. "Microsurgically Produced Homozygous-Diploid Uniparental Mice," *Proceedings of the National Academy of Sciences, USA*, December, 1977, Vol. 74, 5657–5661.

349. Modlinksi, J.A. "Transfer of Embryonic Nuclei to Fertilised Mouse Eggs and Development of Tetraploid Blastocysts," *Nature*, June 8, 1978, Vol. 273, 466–467.

350. Veomett, G., Prescott, D.M., Shay, J., et al. "Reconstruction of Mammalian Cells from Nuclear and Cytoplasmic Components Separated by Treatment with Cytochalasin B," *Proceedings of the National Academy of Sciences, USA*, May, 1974, Vol. 71, 1999–2002.

350. Mintz, B., and Illmensee, K. "Normal Genetically Mosaic Mice Produced from Malignant Teratocarcinoma Cells,"

PAGE

　Proceedings of the National Academy of Sciences, USA, September, 1975, Vol. 72, 3585–3589.
352. Rorvik, D. *In His Image.* New York: J.B. Lippincott Company, 1978.
352. Shettles, L.B. "Diploid Nuclear Replacement in Mature Human Ova with Cleavage," *American Journal of Obstetrics and Gynecology,* 1979, Vol. 222–225.

Chapter 12　Can We Become Physically Immortal?
358. Leaf, A. "Every Day Is a Gift When You Are over 100," *National Geographic,* 1973, Vol. 143, 93–119.
358. Leaf, A. *Youth in Old Age.* New York: McGraw-Hill, 1975.
359. Medvedev, Z.A. "Caucasus and Altay Longevity: A Biological or Social Problem?," *The Gerontologist,* 1974, Vol. 14, 381–387.
359. Mazess, R.B., and Forman, S.H. "Longevity and Age Exaggeration in Vilcabamba, Ecuador," *Journal of Gerontology,* January, 1979, Vol. 14, 94–98.
362. Sacher, G.A., and Staffeldt, E.F. "Relation of Gestation Time to Brain Weight for Placental Mammals. Implications for the Theory of Vertebrate Growth," *American Naturalist,* 1974, Vol. 108, 593–615.
362. Sacher, G.A. "Maturation and Longevity in Relation to Cranial Capacity in Hominid Evolution," in Tuttle, R. (ed). *Antecedents of Man and After. I. Primates: Functional Morphology and Evolution.* The Hague: Morton Publishers, 1975.
363. Sacher, G.A., and Duffy, P.H. "Age-Dependence of Resting, Average, and Maximum Oxygen Consumption in Mus and Peromyscus" (Abstract), *The Gerontologist* (Part II), May, 1975, Vol. 15, 25.
363. Duffy, P.H., and Sacher, G.A. "Age-Dependence of Body Weight and Linear Dimensions in Adult Mus and Peromyscus," *Growth,* 1976, Vol. 49, 19–31.
363. Hart, R.W., and Trosko, J.E. "DNA Repair Processes in Mammals," in Cutler, R.G. (ed). *Interdisciplinary Topics in Gerontology.* Basel, Switzerland: Karger, Vol. 9, 1976.
363. Sacher, G.A., and Hart, R.W. "Longevity, Aging and Com-

PAGE

parative Cellular and Molecular Biology of the House Mouse, Mus Musculus, and the White-Footed Mouse, Peromyscus Leucopus," in Bergsma, D., and Harrison, D.E. (eds). *Genetic Effects on Aging.* New York: Alan R. Liss, 1978.

363. Sacher, G.A., Brash, D.E., and Hart, R.W. "Physiological and Molecular Factors in Lifespan Differences Within and Between Rodent Species" (Abstract). Presented at the 11th International Congress of Gerontology, 1978, Tokyo, Japan, August 20–25.

364. Cutler, R.G. "Redundancy of Information Content in the Genome of Mammalian Species as a Protective Mechanism Determining Aging Rate," *Mechanisms of Ageing and Development,* 1974, Vol. 2, 381–408.

364. Cutler, R.G. "Evolution of Human Longevity and the Genetic Complexity Governing Aging Rate," *Proceedings of the National Academy of Sciences, USA,* 1975, Vol. 72, 4664–4668.

364. Cutler, R.G. "Alterations with Age in the Informational Storage and Flow Systems of the Mammalian Cell," in Bergsma, D., and Harrison, D.E. (eds). *Genetic Effects on Aging.* New York: Alan R. Liss, 1978.

370. Palmore, E. (ed). *Normal Aging—Reports from the Duke Longitudinal Study, 1955–1969.* Durham, N.C.: Duke University Press, 1970.

370. Palmore, E. (ed). *Normal Aging II—Reports from the Duke Longitudinal Studies, 1970–1973.* Durham, N.C.: Duke University Press, 1974.

371. Rose, C.L., and Bell, B. *Predicting Longevity.* Lexington, Massachusetts: Health Lexington Books, 1971.

376. Harrison, D.E., Archer, J.R., Sacher, G.A., et al. "Tail Collagen Aging in Mice of Thirteen Different Genotypes and Two Species: Relationship to Biological Age," *Experimental Gerontology,* 1978, Vol. 13, 63–73.

376. Harrison, D.E., and Archer, J.R. "Measurement of Changes in Mouse Tail Collagen with Age: Temperature Dependence and Procedural Details," *Experimental Gerontology,* 1978, Vol. 13, 75–82.

378. Hollingsworth, J.W., Hashizume, A., and Hablon, S. "Corre-

PAGE

lations Between Tests of Aging in Hiroshima Subjects: An Attempt to Define 'Physiologic age,' " *Yale Journal of Biology and Medicine*, 1965, Vol. 38, 11–26.

378. Hollingsworth, D.R., Hollingsworth, J.W., Bogitch, S., et al. "Neuromuscular Tests of Aging in Hiroshima Survivors," *Journal of Gerontology*, 1969, Vol. 24, 276–283.

378. Gitman, L. *Multiphasic Health Screening Center Manual*, Brookdale Hospital Center, N.Y., 1969.

378. Comfort, A. "Measuring the Human Ageing Rate," *Mechanisms of Ageing and Development*, 1972, Vol. 1, 101–110.

378. Furukawa, T., Inoue, M., Kajiya, F., et al. "Assessment of Biological Age by Multiple Regression Analysis," *Journal of Gerontology*, April, 1975, Vol. 30, 422–434.

380. Robinson, A.B. "Why Do We Age? Can We Diminish the Rate and Debilitating Effects of Aging?," *Linus Pauling Institute Newsletter*, June, 1978, Vol. 1, 3.

382. Zaffaroni, A. "Therapeutic Systems: The Key to Rational Drug Therapy," *Drug Metabolism Review*, February, 1978, Vol. 8, 191–221.

382. Heilmann, K. *Therapeutic Systems—Pattern Specific Drug Delivery: Concept and Development.* Stuttgart, Germany: Georg Thieme Publications, 1978.

382. Pavan-Langston, D. "New Drug Delivery Systems," in Leopold, I.H., and Burns, R.P. (eds). *Symposium on Ocular Therapy.* New York: John Wiley & Sons, 1976.

382. Brown, H.S., Melzer, G., Merrill, R.C., et al. "Visual Effects of Pilocarpine in Glaucoma—Comparative Study of Administration by Eyedrops or by Ocular Therapeutic Systems," *Archives of Ophthalmology*, 1976, Vol. 94, 1716–1719.

382. Mishell, D.R., and Martinez, J. (eds). *Clinical Experience with the Progesterone Uterine Therapeutic System.* Proceedings of Symposium, Acapulco Workshop, October 15–16, 1976, *Excerpta Medica*, USA, 1978.

382. Ho, D.H.W., Brown, N.S., Benvenuto, J., et al. "Pharmacologic Studies of Continuous Infusion of Arabinosylcytosine by Liquid Infusion System," *Clinical Pharmacology and Therapeutics*, 1977, Vol. 22, 371–374.

382. Theeuwes, F., Bayne, W., and McGuire, J. "Gastrointestinal Therapeutic System for Acetazolamide. Efficacy and

PAGE

Side Effects," *Archives of Ophthalmology,* 1978, Vol. 96, 2219–2221.

382. Kessler, A., and Standly, C.C. "Fertility Regulating Methods," *WHO Chronicle,* May, 1977, Vol. 31, 182–193.

384. Shaw, J.E., and Chandrasekaran, S.K. "Controlled Topical Delivery of Drugs for Systemic Action," *Drug Metabolism Review,* February, 1978, Vol. 8, 223–233.

384. Theeuwes, F., and Yum, S.I. "Principles of the Design and Operation of Generic Osmotic Pumps for the Delivery of Semi-Solid or Liquid Drug Formulations," *Annals of Biomedical Engineering,* April, 1976, 343–353.

385. Siew, C., and Goldstein, D.B. "A Novel Method for Rapid Development of Barbiturate Tolerance and Physical Dependence in Mice," *Federation Proceedings,* 1976, Vol. 35, 269.

385. Amkraut, A.A., Yum, S.I., and Rittenburg, M.B. "Specific Suppression of IgG Plaque Forming Cells (PFC) by Continuous Administration of Antigen from an Implantable Delivery System," *Federation Proceedings,* 1976, Vol. 35, 675.

385. Pinedo, H.M., Zaharko, D.S., Bull, J., et al. "The Relative Contribution of Drug Concentration and Duration of Exposure to Mouse Bone Marrow Toxicity During Continuous Methotrexate Infusion," *Cancer Research,* 1977, Vol. 37, 445–450.

387. "Medical Holography," *Computers and Medicine,* May/June, 1977, Vol. 6, 1–2.

387. Woodbury, M.A., Clive, J., and Garson, A., Jr. "Mathematical Typology: A Grade of Membership Technique for Obtaining Disease Definition," *Computers and Biomedical Research,* 1978, Vol. 11, 277–298.

387. Coe, F.L., Norton, E., Oparil, S., et al. "Treatment of Hypertension by Computer and Physician—a Prospective Controlled Study," *Journal of Chronic Diseases,* 1977, Vol. 30, 81–92.

387. Chan, S.H.H., and Wing, H.J. "A Computer Analysis of Factors Influencing the Cerebello-Thalamo-Cortical Signals," *Computers and Biomedical Research,* 1978, Vol. 11, 481–489.

387. McDonald, C.J. "Use of a Computer to Detect and Respond

PAGE

to Clinical Events: Its Effect on Clinician Behavior," *Annals of Internal Medicine*, 1976, Vol. 84, 162–167.

389. Edwards, R.G., and Fowler, R.E. "Human Embryos in the Laboratory," *Scientific American*, December, 1970.

389. Shettles, L.B. "Human Blastocysts Grown In Vitro in Ovulation Cervical Mucus," *Nature*, 1971, Vol. 229, 343.

389. Petrucci, D. "Producing Transplantable Human Tissue in the Laboratory," *Discovery*, July, 1961.

389. Mukherjee, A.B., and Cohen, M.M. "Development of Normal Mice by In Vitro Fertilization," *Nature*, 1970, Vol. 228, 472–473.

389. "Test-Tube Baby Heralds (Brave) New Medical Era," *Medical World News*, August 7, 1978, 10–12.

390. "Mouse Embryos Grow 8½ Days in Lab Dishes," *Medical World News*, September 4, 1978, 63–64.

391. Cohen, S.N. "The Manipulation of Genes," *Scientific American*, July, 1975, Vol. 233, 24.

393. Cohen, S.N. "Recombinant DNA: Fact and Fiction," *Science*, February 11, 1977, Vol. 195, 654–657.

393. Marx, J.A. "Restriction Enzymes: Prenatal Diagnosis of Genetic Disease," *Science*, December 8, 1978, Vol. 202, 1068–1069.

393. Linn, S. "The 1978 Novel Prize in Physiology or Medicine," *Science*, December 8, 1978, Vol. 202, 1069–1071.

393. Leder, P. "Discontinuous Genes," *New England Journal of Medicine*, May 11, 1978, Vol. 298, 1079–1080.

393. Cleaver, J.E. "Nucleosome Structure Controls Rates of Excision Repair in DNA of Human Cells," *Nature*, December 1, 1977, Vol. 270, 451–453.

393. Itakura, K., Hirose, T., Crea, R., et al. "Expression in Escherichia Coli of a Chemically Synthesized Gene for the Hormone Somatostatin," *Science*, December 9, 1977, Vol. 198, 1056–1063.

393. Goeddel, D.V., Kleid, D.G., Bolivar, F., et al. "Expression of E. Coli of Chemically Synthesized Genes for Human Insulin," *Proceedings of the National Academy of Sciences, USA*, January, 1979.

Index

SOURCES FOR ILLUSTRATIONS

PAGE

22   Kohn, Robert R. "Human Aging and Disease," *Journal of Chronic Diseases*, Vol. 16, p. 6, 1963.

24   *Heart Facts 1979*, p. 8, Copyright ©. Reprinted with permission of the American Heart Association.

28   Scheibel, Madge E., and Scheibel, Arnold B. "Structural Changes in the Aging Brain," in Brody, H., Harman, D., and Ordy, J. M. *Aging*, Vol. 1, *Clinical, Morphologic, and Neurochemical Aspects in the Aging Central Nervous System*, p. 29, Raven Press, New York, 1975.

60   Ross, M. H., and Bras, G. "Food Preference and Length of Life," *Science*, Vol. 190, p. 166, October 10, 1975. Copyright 1975, by the American Association for the Advancement of Science.

63   Ross, M. H. "Nutrition and Longevity in Experimental Animals," in Winick, M. *Nutrition & Aging*, p. 44, John Wiley & Sons, New York, 1976.

69   Segall, P. E., and Timiras, P. S. "Patho-Physiologic Findings After Chronic Tryptophan Deficiency in Rats: A Model for Delayed Growth and Aging," *Mechanisms of Ageing and Development*, Vol. 5, p. 116, 1976.

71   Paul E. Segall, Department of Physiology/Anatomy, University of California, Berkeley, California (unpublished).

80   Antonio M. Gotto, Jr., Chairman, Department of Medicine, Baylor College of Medicine, Houston, Texas. Copyright, Baylor College of Medicine.

114   Doll, R., and Peto, R. "Mortality in Relation to Smoking: 20 Years' Observations on Male British Doctors," *British Medical Journal*, Vol. 2, p. 1529, December 25, 1976.

134   Harman, D. "Free Radical Theory: Effect of Free Radical Reaction Inhibitors on the Mortality Rate of Male LAF$_1$ Mice," *Journal of Gerontology*, Vol. 23, pp. 480, 481, 1968.

144   Massie, H. R., Baird, M. B., and Piekielniak, M. J. "Ascorbic Aid and Longevity in Drosophila," *Experimental Gerontology*, Vol. 11, p. 39, 1976.

145   Davies, J. E. W., Ellery, P. M., and Hughes, R. E. "Dietary Ascorbic Acid and Life Span of Guinea Pigs," *Experimental Gerontology*, Vol. 12, p. 216, 1977.

147   Cameron, E., and Pauling, L. "Supplemental Ascorbate in the Supportive Treatment of Cancer: Prolongation of Survival Times in Terminal Human Cancer," *Proceedings of the National Academy of Sciences, USA*, Vol. 73, p. 3689, 1976.

161   Liu, R. K., and Walford, R. L. "Mid-Life Temperature-Transfer Effects on Life-Span of Annual Fish," *Journal of Gerontology*, Vol. 30, p. 130, 1975.

176   Wood, P. D., Haskell, W. I., Stern, M. P., et al. "Plasma Lipoprotein Distributions in Male and Female Runners," *Annals of the New York Academy of Sciences*, Vol. 301, p. 754, 1977.

176   Wood, P. D., Haskell, W. I., Stern, M. P., et al. "Plasma Lipoprotein Distributions in Male and Female Runners," *Annals of the New York Academy of Sciences*, Vol. 301, p. 754, 1977.

180   Selvester, R., Camp, J., and Sanmarco, M. "Effects of Exercise Training on Progression of Documented Coronary Arteriosclerosis in Men," *Annals of the New York Academy of Sciences*, Vol. 301, p. 502, 1977.

190   Walford, R. L., Meredith, P. J., and Cheney, K. E. "Immunoengineering: Prospects for Correction of Age-Related Immunodeficiency States," in Makinodan, T., and Yunis, E. *Immunology and Aging*, p. 186, Plenum Press, New York, 1976.

195   N. Fabris, Experimental Gerontology Center, I.N.R.C.A., Anconia, Italy.

211   University of Utah Medical Center, Salt Lake City (unpublished).

211   University of Utah Medical Center, Salt Lake City (unpublished).

222   University of Utah Medical Center, Salt Lake City (unpublished).

240   Photo by Saul Kent (unpublished).

245 Clinique La Prairie (unpublished).

247 Clinique La Prairie (unpublished).

251 Markham, C. H., Treciokas, L. J., and Diamond, G. "Parkinson's Disease and Levodopa—A Five-Year Follow-up and Review," *Western Journal of Medicine,* Vol. 121, p. 202, 1974.

257 Bjorksten, J. "Crosslinkage and the Aging Process," in Rockstein, M. *Theoretical Aspects of Aging,* p. 50, Academic Press, New York, 1974.

273 Hochschild, R. "Effect of Dimethylaminoethyl p-Chlorophenoxyacetate on the Life Span of Male Swiss Webster Albino Mice," *Experimental Gerontology,* Vol. 8, p. 181, 1973.

275 Hochschild, R. "Effect of Dimethylaminoethanol on the Life Span of Senile Male A/J Mice," *Experimental Gerontology,* Vol. 8, p. 186, 1973.

284 Hossmann, K-A., and Zimmerman, V. "Resuscitation of the Monkey Brain After 1H Complete Ischemia. I. Physiological and Morphological Observations," *Brain Research,* Vol. 81, p. 63, 1974.

287 Cryovita Laboratories. Photo by Patricia Kelley (unpublished).

288 Trans Time, Inc. (unpublished).

289 Trans Time, Inc. (unpublished).

300 Trans Time, Inc. (unpublished).

305 Trans Time, Inc. (unpublished).

320 Paul E. Segall, Department of Physiology/Anatomy, University of California, Berkeley, California.

328 Sicuteri, F., Del Bene, E., and Anselmi, B. "Aphrodisiac Effect of Testosterone in Parachlorophenylalanine-Treated Sexually Deficient Men," in Sandler, M., and Gessa, G. L. *Sexual Behavior: Pharmacology and Biochemistry,* p. 335, Raven Press, New York, 1975.

350 Hoppe, P. C., and Illmensee, K. "Microsurgically Produced Homozygous-Diploid Uniparental Mice," *Proceedings of the National Academy of Sciences, USA,* Vol. 74, p. 5660, 1977.

351 Hoppe, P. C., and Illmensee, K. "Microsurgically Produced Homozygous-Diploid Uniparental Mice," *Proceedings of the National Academy of Sciences, USA,* Vol. 74, p. 5659, 1977.

360 Institute of Gerontology, Kiev, U.S.S.R.

364 Sacher, G. A., and Hart, R. W. "Longevity, Aging, and Comparative Cellular and Molecular Biology of the House Mouse, Mus musculus, and the White-Footed Mouse, Peromyscus leucopus," in Bergsma, D., and Harrison, D. E. *Genetic Effects on Aging,* Alan R. Liss, New York, pp. 77, 78, 1978.

366 Richard G. Cutler, National Institute on Aging, Gerontology Research Center, Baltimore (unpublished).

367 Richard G. Cutler, National Institute on Aging, Gerontology Research Center, Baltimore (unpublished).

369 Richard G. Cutler, National Institute on Aging, Gerontology Research Center, Baltimore (unpublished).

370 National Institute on Aging, Gerontology Research Center, Baltimore (unpublished).

372 Institute of Gerontology, Kiev, U.S.S.R. (unpublished).

379 Richard Hochschild, Department of Medicine, University of California, Irvine, California (unpublished).

384 Alza Corporation, Palo Alto, California, 1978 Annual Report.

386 Alza Corporation, Palo Alto, California (unpublished).